CATHOLIC QUESTIONS WISE ANSWERS

Edited by MICHAEL J. DALEY

ST. ANTHONY MESSENGER PRESS

Cincinnati, Ohio

Nihil Obstat: Rev. Nicholas Lohkamp, O.F.M.
Rev. Ralph J. Lawrence

Imprimi Potest: Fred Link, O.F.M.
Provincial

Imprimatur: +Most Rev. Carl K. Moeddel, V.G.
Archdiocese of Cincinnati
Januaray 28, 2002

Library of Congress Cataloging-in-Publication Data

Catholic questions, wise answers / edited by Michael J. Daley.
    p. cm.
Includes bibliographical references and index.
 ISBN 0-86716-398-4 (pbk.)
 1. Catholic Church—Doctrines—Miscellanea. I. Daley, Michael J.,
1968–
 BX1754.3 .C38 2001
 282—dc21

                                          2001005999

Cover design by Mary Alfieri
Book design and electronic pagination by Sandy L. Digman

ISBN 0-86716-398-4

Published by St. Anthony Messenger Press

www.AmericanCatholic.org

Printed in the U.S.A.

TABLE OF CONTENTS

INTRODUCTION
1

CHAPTER ONE

ANGELS AND SAINTS

Who is Saint Nicholas?
4

Who is Saint Bernard? What is the story behind
the legendary lactation of Mary?
5

Who is Saint Cloud?
6

Is Genesius an appropriate baptismal name?
How should a baptismal name be chosen?
6

Are archangels saints?
7

Who is Maria Francesca? Is she a patron saint
for the sterile?
8

Are angels male or female?
9

Which saints are called to fight evil spirits?
10

Is there really a devil? If so,
why does God permit him to exist?
10

When were angels created?
11

Do dead children become angels?
11

How are angels ranked?
12

Did Saint Rita murder her sons?
How could a murderer be a saint?
13

Who are Saint Goar and Saint Olaf? Is Saint Olaf the
patron saint of wood-carvers?
14

Are there any married saints? If not, why?
15

Who was Saint Josephine Bakhita? What does she
have to do with Christian-Muslim dialogue?
16

Who is Saint John Neumann? Where are his remains?
17

Are there any patron saints for victims of
rape or sexual abuse?
18

Who is Saint Philomena?
18

Who is Saint Charbel?
20

Does stigmata have anything to do with sainthood?
Why does it manifest itself differently on different persons?
21

What is the true history of Saint Veronica and the veil?
22

How many saints are there?
22

Who is Blessed Imelda?
23

Is there a saint to help find a spouse?
23

What is a seraphic saint?
24

Who are the white martyrs?
25

Is there a saint named Cynthia?
25

Are there any saints for gamblers?
26

Who is Sister Faustina?
26

Is there a patron saint for emergency medical workers?
27

Is Pontius Pilate a saint?
28

Who was Saint Anthony of Egypt?
29

Who is Saint Mungo?
29

Are there any saints from the Old Testament?
30

Does use of the word *legends* discredit
stories about the saints?
30

Who is Saint Christopher?
31

Who is Padre Pio?
32

What is the significance of wine and snakes in
representations of John the Evangelist?
33

Is there a patron saint for lawyers?
33

Why is Saint Bridget often portrayed
with an ox or cow?
34

Is the asceticism of saints penance or masochism?
35

How do people become saints?
37

CHAPTER TWO

MARY AND JOSEPH

Are Marian apparitions real? Why do they occur?
42

Was Mary the real name of Jesus' mother?
43

What is the Black Madonna?
44

Why did Mary need purification?
44

Does the story of the finding in the Temple suggest
that Mary and Joseph were careless parents?
45

Was Saint Joseph an older man? Was he Mary's age?
46

How long did Mary live?
Did she have other children besides Jesus?
47

Are the Garabandal visions approved by the church?
47

Is Mary the Queen of Heaven written about in
the book of Jeremiah? If not, who is?
49

Did Mary attend Mass after the resurrection?
Did she continue going to the Jewish Temple?
49

Where did we get the Litany of the Blessed Virgin?
What do all of those titles mean?
50

Is it more correct to use *thee* rather than *you*
in the Hail Mary?
52

Did Mary and Joseph divorce?
52

Why do we know so little about the life of Mary?
53

Does Mary have a tomb?
54

Why do some statues show Mary stepping on a snake?
55

Does Matthew's Gospel support or
challenge Mary's virginity?
56

Why doesn't Mary appear to Protestants?
57

What is the basis for honoring Mary as Queen of Heaven?
58

Why does the second sorrowful mystery mention a pillar?
58

How could Saint Joseph teach Jesus?
59

When did devotion to Mary begin?
61

How can a person determine what is private
revelation and what is self-delusion?
63

What are the seven sorrows of Mary?
63

Did Mary experience the pangs of childbirth?
64

Can a church have more than one
statue of the Blessed Mother?
64

What is meant when Mary is called Co-Redemptrix?
Is this the teaching of the Church?
65

Why do we know so little about Saint Joseph?
66

What is the significance of the twelve stars on Mary's
crown or around her head in pictures or on statues?
67

How do we know of Mary's parents, Anne and Joachim?
69

Who chose the mysteries of the rosary? Are others possible?
70

What is the hospital rosary?
71

How does the church square the rosary with the
Gospel exhortation not to "multiply words"?
71

What is the third "secret" of Fatima?
72

CHAPTER THREE

CATHOLIC BELIEFS AND PRACTICES

Why is there so much controversy in the church today?
76

What is the church's teaching on indulgences?
78

Can non-Christians go to heaven?
80

How can a person become a Catholic?
81

What is dogma and who determines it?
81

What is meant by Luke 10:16, when Jesus says,
"Whoever listens to you listens to me"?
82

Why doesn't the pope define his own moral and
theological positions as infallible?
83

Is the ordinary magisterium infallible?
85

Where does the belief in original sin come from?
86

What is excommunication?
88

What is the Society of Saint Pius X?
89

What is the church's position on evolution?
90

Can a Catholic believe in karma and reincarnation?
91

How did Jesus exist before the Incarnation?
92

What is the church's teaching about the resurrected body?
92

Why do Catholics believe in immortality?
93

What happened to the good people who
died before Jesus' Resurrection?
95

What do we mean by *sola fide*?
95

Does Pope John Paul II contradict Pius XI in his
views on Catholicism as the one true faith?
97

What is a miracle?
99

Do Catholics still believe in purgatory?
100

What is the Purgatorial Society?
102

Can a Roman Catholic in good standing be a Mason?
103

Is the Knights of Columbus a secret society?
104

What is the canonical status of the religious group Opus Dei?
105

What are theologians?
106

Why must clergy and religious wear certain clothing?
107

Do priests wear skullcaps?
109

What is the significance of the ring that
bishops and cardinals wear?
109

What is an Agnus Dei?
110

What is necessary for a church to become a basilica or shrine?
110

How does a church get its name?
111

How are bishops selected?
113

Why do Catholics eat fish on Friday?
114

What is the church's position concerning penance
and abstinence during Lent and throughout the year?
115

What are the responsibilities of a parish council?
116

Is it mandatory to name children after saints?
117

Why do the holy days of obligation vary from place to place?
117

Do East and West agree on the dates for Christmas and Easter?
119

What determines the date of Easter or when Lent begins?
120

Why do we celebrate Christmas?
120

Is there a hierarchy in lay ministries?
121

How can a priest retire?
122

Who oversees the formation of priests?
123

Why are married ministers from other Christian
denominations allowed to be ordained,
yet priests cannot marry?
124

What is Catholic feminism?
125

What is the history of the Infant of Prague?
127

Does a Communion service on Saturday
fulfill the Sunday obligation?
127

Can a person spread the gospel without preaching?
128

What are the corporal and spiritual works of mercy?
129

What is tithing?
129

Does the church have a policy about filming
movie scenes in churches?
131

CHAPTER FOUR

PASTORAL PUZZLES

What fate awaits those who die outside the church?
134

Why does God allow people to suffer?
135

Can suffering be redemptive?
136

How can a good God allow evil?
138

What was the fate of Judas?
139

Why does God sometimes seem absent to those who pray?
139

What does it mean to be scrupulous?
140

Did Jesus know everything?
142

Does God have a memory?
143

Can God forgive someone who has had an abortion?
145

How does the Father beget the Son?
145

What promises does God make?
146

Did Jesus really think God had abandoned him on the cross?
147

Is this world the best God could make?
148

What is "the dark night of the soul"? Does it cause people to
abandon the sacraments or leave the church?
149

How can we get along with fundamentalists?
150

Should an abused wife forgive and forget her
husband's abuse?
151

What happens to us when we die?
152

Should lapsed Catholics be encouraged to
return to the church?
153

Do those in heaven see what is happening on earth?
154

Is it possible to be married in heaven?
154

Whom should we believe when theologians disagree?
155

Is it appropriate to say a Mass for a pet?
157

How can we get along with Jehovah's Witnesses?
158

Should a Catholic attend the wedding of a Catholic
marrying outside the church with no dispensation?
160

Should people have their children baptized though
the parents no longer attend Mass?
161

How should we treat a wealthy person
who shuns acts of charity?
162

What happens to those who commit suicide?
163

How should we treat children marrying outside the faith?
165

How should we deal with distractions at Mass?
165

What are the signs of the end of the world?
167

Will those living at the end have to die before entering heaven?
168

How should we treat a child's cohabitation
outside of marriage?
169

Was John the Baptist born free from original sin?
170

How can we be happy in heaven without
the things we love here on earth?
171

Who judges us at the end—Jesus or God the Father?
172

Are we made in God's image?
173

Why is it said that when Gregorian Masses have
been celebrated on thirty consecutive days,
the person goes right to heaven?
175

Did God create life on other planets?
178

Why is it forbidden to take Communion to a friend
in a nursing home?
180

CHAPTER FIVE

THE BIBLE

When and where did the word *Bible* originate?
182

What does the church mean when it says
the Bible is without error?
183

How can we be sure what the Bible means?
184

What is the difference between Catholic and Protestant Bibles?
186

Why have some of the names of the books in the Bible changed?
188

Have there been any advances made in scriptural scholarship?
189

Are there "lost" books of the Bible?
191

Does the church define the meaning of biblical texts?
192

When were Adam and Eve created?
193

Where is the Garden of Eden?
194

Why does Adam blame Eve for the sin in the Garden of Eden?
195

Where did Cain find a wife?
196

How could God ask Abraham to sacrifice Isaac?
197

What is God's name?
198

Why does God appear so cruel in the book of Exodus?
200

Why is there so much violence in the Old Testament,
when God forbade killing?
203

Who was Caleb?
205

Is the book of Job fact or fiction?
206

Why does the book of Sirach refer to wisdom as "she"?
206

Who was Jael?
207

Did Samson commit suicide?
208

Why were lepers treated so harshly?
208

Did the Jewish revolt against Rome influence the
writing of the Gospels?
209

What are the symbols of the four evangelists?
210

What does *synoptic* mean?
211

Why do the Gospel accounts differ on some details,
such as the thieves crucified with Jesus?
211

Did Saint Paul write all the letters that bear his name?
212

Does Saint Paul talk about the rapture?
214

What did Saint Paul mean by saying,
"I do that which I do not wish"?
216

What was Saint Paul's "thorn in the flesh"?
216

Can we know we are saved?
217

What does the phrase "asleep in Christ" mean?
217

Why do the Gospels trace Jesus' genealogy
through Joseph rather than Mary?
218

How did Matthew know the temptations of Jesus?
219

Why does John's Gospel say that
John the Baptist did not know Jesus?
220

What exception did Jesus allow for divorce?
222

Why did Jesus curse the fig tree?
223

Why did Jesus say not to call him good?
225

What did Jesus mean when he said he came to bring division?
225

What does "poor in spirit" mean?
227

Did Jesus take the Nazirite vow?
229

Why did Jesus speak harshly to the Canaanite woman?
229

Who was the beloved disciple?
230

Does mention of the beloved disciple mean
that God loves some more than others?
232

Did Jesus see a value in friendship?
233

What does it mean to be born again?
234

How could anyone do works greater than Jesus?
235

Why did Jesus say that Mary has chosen "the better
part" though Martha worked so hard to serve him?
236

What did Jesus mean when he said
we must hate our father and mother?
237

Why must we become like children to inherit the kingdom?
238

What is the meaning of "Son of Man," a title for Jesus?
239

Did Jesus know when the end was coming?
240

What was Jesus referring to when he mentioned
the "stumbling stone"?
241

Is it wrong to call priests "Father?"
243

Was the Last Supper a Passover meal?
244

What do we know about Simon of Cyrene?
245

What does "INRI" mean?
246

Who were the thieves crucified with Jesus?
247

Why did Jesus not want Mary Magdalene
to touch him but urged Thomas to do so?
247

What did Jesus mean when he said sins against
the Holy Spirit will not be forgiven?
248

What is the Gospel of Mark's "awful horror"?
248

What does the Apostles' Creed mean when it says
Jesus descended into hell?
249

Did Jesus rise or was he raised from the dead?
250

What is "the great eschatological test"?
252

Where did Pentecost take place?
253

Who is the Antichrist?
254

Who are the book of Revelation's living creatures?
254

CHAPTER SIX

LITURGICAL PRACTICES

Why should we go to church?
258

How much of the Mass must be attended
to fulfill the Sunday obligation?
260

Is it acceptable to say the rosary during Mass?
261

May a eucharistic minister bless?
262

How were the readings picked for the three-year Mass cycle?
263

Can priests change the words for Mass and the sacraments?
264

What is the difference between Eastern
rite and Roman Catholics?
265

Are lectors permitted to change the wording in the readings?
267

Why does the Nicene Creed lack inclusive language?
268

May the Gospel be recited from memory? Must we
stand during the Gospel reading?
270

Why do we make the Sign of the Cross at the Gospel?
271

Why do we use incense?
272

May deacons preach?
273

What is an acolyte?
274

Why do people no longer bow their heads at
the name of Jesus Christ at Mass and other times?
275

When should we genuflect?
277

Should one kneel to receive Communion?
277

What is the proper way to distribute Communion?
278

Why does the priest and/or deacon
kiss the altar and Gospel book?
279

Must we kneel at Mass?
280

How does one prepare for Communion in the home?
281

What is the proper way to have a home blessed?
282

Is it acceptable to offer a small part of
the host in Communion for the sick?
283

How often can one receive Communion?
284

Are chasubles, gold chalices and sitting in the chair
necessary parts of the Mass?
284

What should one do when the chalice is spilled?
285

Can a eucharistic host be retained for home worship?
285

Where should the tabernacle be?
286

Can a priest say Mass alone?
288

May anyone other than an ordained priest
celebrate Benediction?
288

Why do Catholics recite the creed every Sunday?
288

How long must one fast before receiving Communion?
289

What is the proper fast for Ash Wednesday
and the Fridays of Lent?
290

What should be said when ashes are distributed
on Ash Wednesday?
290

Are parishes supposed to veil both
crosses and statues during Lent?
290

May a Catholic receive Communion at an Orthodox Mass?
291

Is the traditional Latin Mass still valid?
292

What is a Gregorian Mass?
293

Why do we receive palms on Palm Sunday?
294

Who should wash the parishioners' feet on Holy Thursday?
294

Can a baby be baptized during Lent?
295

Why do bishops wear miters?
295

Is "Here Comes the Bride" suitable music
for a church wedding?
296

May a layperson give a eulogy at a funeral Mass?
297

What is the church's teaching regarding cremation?
298

Why are funeral Masses prohibited during Holy Week?
299

Why do modern churches have fewer statues?
300

Are flags allowed in churches?
301

CHAPTER SEVEN

MORALITY

Is it possible never to sin?
304

How can we be free to love God when we are
commanded to do so?
305

How do we fulfill the commandments to love God
and neighbor?
306

What is anact of perfect contrition or an act of perfect love?
308

Where does the saying about "the sins of the fathers"
come from, and is there any truth to it?
308

What is the Heroic Act?
310

Is AIDS God's punishment for sin?
311

What was the sin of Sodom?
312

What is the church's moral position on sex-change operations?
313

Are images of Jesus and the saints idols?
315

How does the church distinguish between
art and pornography?
316

Is it a mortal sin for an adult Catholic to see movies
that are morally offensive?
318

Does the church approve of psychic consultations?
319

What is the origin of the seven capital sins?
320

Is it a sin to miss mass on Sunday?
321

What are we to consider as "servile work" on Sunday?
323

When and to what extent are violations of canon law sinful?
325

How common is mortal sin?
327

Are there serious sins that are not mortal sins?
328

Are diocesan parish priests required
to take the vow of chastity?
330

Does the church permit homosexuals in the clergy?
331

Is it immoral to live with a person of the opposite sex?
332

Is it possible to be unfaithful in marriage
in ways other than adultery?
333

What sexual acts are considered sinful in marriage?
334

Is masturbation sinful?
334

Is it wrong to pray for money?
335

Should parishes promote games of chance
at their fund-raisers?
335

Should alcohol be permitted at church
festivals and social affairs?
337

What is the church's position on capital punishment?
337

Is it sinful to resist extraordinary means of resuscitation?
338

Is it permissible to torture criminals or prisoners of war?
342

Is it a sin to mistreat animals?
344

What is a just war?
345

If taxes are used for an immoral purpose
(such as abortion), should we stop paying?
347

If a baptized Catholic has an abortion, is she
excommunicated from the church?
348

Is organ donation permissible?
349

Are Catholics exempt from jury duty?
352

Are Catholics obligated to support pro-life candidates?
353

What is the sin of contumely?
354

CHAPTER EIGHT

SACRAMENTS

What is required in a baptism?
358

How soon should a baby be baptized?
359

Is baptism a license to sin?
360

How should godparents be chosen?
360

Is confirmation required?
361

At what moment does our Lord become present at Mass?
364

Is the Eucharist a symbol?
365

Does the Mass contradict the Bible?
366

When does Christ cease to be present after consecration?
368

Who consecrates the Eucharist?
369

Who is the minister of the Eucharist?
369

May women lead Communion services?
370

May vegetarians receive the Eucharist?
371

Should water be added to the wine before consecration?
371

Should both bread and wine be taken during Communion?
372

Is it possible to offer Communion to non-Catholics?
372

May the mentally disabled receive the sacraments?
373

Why must we go to confession?
375

Are communal penance services and general
absolution allowed?
377

Has confession become outmoded?
378

What should we confess?
381

How can we go to confession and be forgiven when
we know we will go out and do the same thing again?
382

How can we know the confessor is right?
383

Can a person go to confession too much?
385

Can one confess without any major sins?
385

When did marriage become a sacrament?
386

What is an "internal forum solution"?
389

Does an annulment make children illegitimate?
390

Can a transsexual marry in the church?
391

Is marriage in the church possible for Siamese twins?
392

Is a man forever a priest once ordained?
392

Who can administer and receive the anointing of the sick?
393

When should a priest be called in the event of a death?
395

How many times may a person receive the anointing of the sick?
395

What is the purpose of having the body at the funeral Mass?
397

CHAPTER NINE

PRAYER

How should we pray?
400

Is it unrealistic to believe in physical healings?
402

What does it mean to make reparation
to the hearts of Jesus and Mary?
403

What is the origin of healing Masses?
404

What is the prayer of self-dedication?
406

What is a Pardon Crucifix?
406

Does God hear our prayers?
407

Who wrote the peace prayer of Saint Francis?
409

Who are the dead we pray for at Mass?
409

What is necessary to pray the Way of the Cross?
410

When is Benediction appropriate?
411

What is the Jesus Prayer?
412

What is a charismatic?
413

What is the Morning Offering?
415

Is the Divine Office liturgy?
415

What is *The Cloud of the Unknowing*?
416

What is necessary for a novena?
417

Should Masses be said for the dead?
418

Why do we ask God not to lead us
into temptation in the Our Father?
420

Why are devotions of the scapular, First Friday and First
Saturday not now taught and practiced as they once were?
421

What is mysticism?
423

Are months and days still dedicated?
424

CHAPTER TEN

CHURCH HISTORY

When did the Christian church officially begin to be
called the Catholic church?
428

Who wrote the Apostles' Creed?
429

How old are the requirements for the Easter duty?
430

Who changed the Sabbath observance from
Saturday to Sunday?
431

Is it true Martin Luther gave the world
the question-answer catechism?
432

Why are today's descendants of Abraham, Isaac and
Jacob called Jews rather than Israelites?
433

Why does the priest dress the way he does at Mass?
434

How did we get the names of the wise men?
434

How did the tradition of ashes on Ash Wednesday get started?
435

Who established the liturgical season of Advent and when?
437

How long has the Feast of the Assumption been a holy day?
437

What is the papal tiara?
438

Where did the rosary come from?
438

When were kneelers introduced into worship?
439

Why does Texas have a city named for Saint Anthony?
440

Why did the Jews not accept Jesus?
441

Where did the brown scapular come from?
441

What is the difference between a Jew and a Gentile?
443

Have there been any bad or married popes?
443

How many nails were used at the crucifixion?
445

Where did we get the Sign of Peace?
447

Is the candy cane a religious symbol?
448

When did Latin become the official language of the church?
448

Why has the *filioque* been omitted from the creed?
450

What were the religions of Arabia before Mohammed?
452

Is it wrong to eat blood sausage?
453

Why have the creeds not been revised to include our
belief in the eucharistic real presence?
455

Have there ever been married priests?
456

Have there ever been women deacons or priests?
457

Who presided at the Eucharist in early times?
459

What is necessary for a saint to be
declared doctor of the church?
461

Are there any dogmas about "the church militant"?
462

Was St. Patrick's Cathedral Archbishop Hughes's folly?
464

How did Saint Paul become a Roman citizen?
465

Have there ever been any Franciscan popes?
466

Where did we get the law of the fast?
468

What is the reason for no meat on Fridays during Lent?
470

BIBLIOGRAPHY
473

INDEX
487

It All Begins with a Question

After much thought, in the year 627, the monk Paulinus journeyed to northern England to visit King Edwin, to persuade him to accept Christianity. Edwin, keeper of the ancient traditions, hesitated and decided to summon his advisors. It was decided that Paulinus would remain with them for several days. While in their company, he explained the person and message of Jesus Christ. King Edwin and his advisors were very moved yet troubled. "What to do about the old traditions?" kept echoing in the king's mind. As Paulinus's stay was coming to an end, Edwin gathered his advisors together to come to a final decision as to whether to accept this new faith.

At the meeting one of King Edwin's advisors stood up and said:

> With all due respect, your majesty, when you sit at table with your lords and vassals and break bread, in the winter when the fire burns warm and bright on the hearth and the storm is howling outside, bringing the snow and the rain, it happens that suddenly a little bird flies into the hall. It comes in at one door and flies through the other. For the few minutes that it is inside the hall, it does not feel the cold, but as soon as it leaves your sight, it returns to the dark of winter. It seems to me that the life of humanity is much the same. We do not know what went before and we do not know what follows. If the person of Jesus can speak to us surely of these things, it is well for us to follow it.

Whether it is from the rain of spring or the snow of winter, the human person is anxious, restless. He wants to know why this happens. She wants to know from whence it comes. Much like the bird, we want to make sense of where we have been and where we are going. We want answers. But the faith journey begins not with an answer but with a question. As hard as we try, as much as we attempt to cast them aside, questions arise. Doubts surface. Some are more serious than others. But all remind us that what we know now is not all that we need to know—there is always more. Even when we find "the way, the truth and the life"—Jesus the Christ—we have not an answer but more questions: Who is he? How are we to interpret what Scripture says about him? Does he really hear and respond to our prayers? The list goes on and on.

For nearly one hundred years St. Anthony Messenger has provided a forum for the seeker, the questioner and the restless believer. The "Ask the Wise Man" column has addressed countless faith questions. Their depth is sincere and their range broad. Far from being "canned," these questions have sprung from the lived experience of generations of Catholics. It is my hope and prayer that their questions, and the answers that follow, help you make sense of your own journey of faith.

For Christians the wise teacher is Christ. It can now be revealed, however, that for countless years the "wise man" of St. Anthony Messenger was Father Norman Perry, O.F.M. As I am sure all would admit, it is no easy task to respond pastorally and sensitively to questions of faith and convey the church's beliefs fully and responsibly at the same time. Yet, this was something that Father Norman had a gift for doing— communicating the truth in love. It is to him that this book is dedicated. I would also like to thank the staff of St. Anthony Messenger Press, especially Father Jeremy Harrington, O.F.M., Father Hilarion Kistner, O.F.M., and my editor, Kathleen Carroll for their patience and encouragement and the opportunity to be a part of this project. Finally, to three people who make me wiser and humbler each day, June, Cara and Brendan, I say thank you.

Michael J. Daley

$$\dagger$$

Angels and Saints

The Catholic tradition is a treasury of stories. Our own quest for relationship with God is reflected in the lives of the saints and the legends of angels.

In explaining this journey of relationship, I think it is best to tell a story.

To catch a moment's peace from her busy day, a woman decided to spend a few minutes of reflection and prayer in a church. She had her young son with her. Never having been inside this church before, the boy's eyes were drawn to the church's large stained-glass windows. Overcome with excitement, he pulled on his mother's jacket wanting to know more about them. His mother responded, "They're saints." That seemed to quiet the boy for a few seconds. Soon, though, the boy was pulling at his mother again, "Mommy, Mommy! I know what saints are, Mommy. They let the light in."

In their own ways both angels (divine messengers) and saints (holy men and women of God) "let the light in." Referring to angels, the Catechism of the Catholic Church (329) quotes Saint Augustine, saying:

> *"Angel" is the name of their office, not of their nature. If you seek the name of their nature, it is "spirit"; if you seek the name of their office, it is "angel": from what they are, "spirit," from what they do, "angel."*

The Catechism *adds,*

> With their whole beings the angels are servants and messengers of God. Because they "always behold the face of my Father who is in heaven" they are the "mighty ones who do his word, hearkening to the voice of his word." (Matthew 18:10; Psalm 103:20)

Speaking of the church's holiness, the Catechism *invokes the saints saying, "Since she still includes sinners, she is 'the sinless one made up of sinners.' Her holiness shines in the saints; in Mary she is already all-holy." The call to holiness accepted by the saints is our invitation as well.*

•

Who is Saint Nicholas?

Saint Nicholas of Myra lived and acquired his reputation for sanctity long <u>before</u> the church began its <u>formal process of beatification</u>. He became recognized as a saint by popular acceptance.

Historians and hagiographers generally write that much of what is said about Nicholas is legend. In Nicholas's time there was no investigation and authentication of claimed miracles before canonization. Attributing miracles and wonders to a person was an ancient way of expressing conviction about the holiness of the person.

You will still find Nicholas listed in the various dictionaries of saints, for example *Dictionary of Saints,* by John Delaney. And you will still find Nicholas listed as an <u>optional</u> memorial in the Roman calendar on December 6. An optional memorial means that on that day churches and communities may choose to celebrate either the liturgy in honor of Saint Nicholas or the liturgy for a weekday in Advent.

The December volume of the new twelve-volume set of

Butler's Lives of the Saints has recently been published. Consult it for further information.

Who is Saint Bernard? What is the story behind the legendary lactation of Mary?

According to the concise edition of *Butler's Lives of the Saints*, Saint Bernard of Clairvaux was born near Dijon in France in 1090. He died in 1153 and was canonized in 1174. In 1830 he was declared a doctor of the church. He was called Doctor Mellifluous—the honey-sweet doctor.

As a young man he entered the monastery of Citeaux, which observed the strict, or Cistercian, interpretation of the Benedictine rule. He inspired some thirty-one men to follow him, including four brothers and an uncle.

From Citeaux Bernard was sent to found a new monastery at Clairvaux. He was later joined there by his elderly father and another brother.

Popes, bishops and princes called upon Bernard for advice and to settle differences. Bernard was present at the Second Lateran Council. At the request of the papal legate, Bernard preached against the Albigensian heresy throughout Languedoc. Pope Eugenius commissioned him to preach a crusade after the Seljuk Turks captured Edessa.

Bernard died in 1153 after successfully completing a peace mission in Metz. By the time he died, sixty-eight monasteries had been founded from Clairvaux so that he is counted among the founders of the Cistercian Order.

The Lactation of Saint Bernard is a picture in Madrid's Prado, painted by Bartolome Esteban Murillo, who lived in the seventeenth century. It takes its inspiration from a mystical legend, dating from the fourteenth century, about a prayer experience of Saint Bernard, supposed to have taken place before a statue of the Madonna nursing the infant Jesus. As Bernard prayed, "*Monstra te esse Matrem* (Show yourself a mother)," the statue came to life and the virgin pressed her breast to nourish and wet the lips of Bernard, dry from singing her praises. The picture also illustrates the idea that the Virgin filled him with graces and that his preaching and eloquence were "sweet as milk." At least twenty-seven works of art depict this legend.

Incidentally, Saint Bernard dogs are associated with a different Bernard: Bernard of Montjoux, who did forty years as a missionary in the Alps and founded two hospices to help lost travelers.

Who is Saint Cloud?

The people of Saint Cloud, Minnesota, and Saint Cloud, Florida, will be disappointed that their patron is not better known in this country. According to *Butler's Lives of the Saints*, Saint Cloud (Clodoald) was the grandson of Clovis, King of the Franks.

When Clovis died, his kingdom was divided among four sons. Among those sons were Clodomir, father of Cloud, also called Clodoald, and two other sons. When Clodomir died fighting his cousin Gondomar of Burgundy, Cloud's grandmother and widow of Clovis, Saint Clotilda, took over the raising of the boys. Cloud's uncles, however, conspired to take Clodomir's lands. To secure control they murdered Cloud's brothers, Theodald and Gunther. The eight-year-old Cloud, however, escaped and hid in a hermit's cell. When he became an adult, he made no effort to reclaim the kingdom. Cloud lived a hermit's life near the present town of Saint Cloud (presumably named for him) near Versailles in France. Cloud died at the age of thirty-six. He is invoked for assistance by those who suffer from carbuncles. And, because of a French play on words, he is patron saint of nail makers.

Is Genesius an appropriate baptismal name?
How should a baptismal name be chosen?

Present canon law (855) says simply, "Parents, sponsors and the pastor are to see that a name foreign to a Christian mentality is not given." Certainly, Genesius is not foreign to Christian sentiment.

Actually, there are said to have been four saints who bore the name Genesius: Genesius of Arles, a catechumen martyred after refusing to transcribe an edict ordering the persecution of Christians; Genesius, bishop of Clermont; Genesius, bishop of Lyons; and—legendarily—Genesius the Comedian (actor), traditionally listed as patron of actors.

There is some doubt that Genesius the Comedian really existed. And the same story about an actor who experienced a conversion on stage in the midst of burlesquing the sacrament of baptism and was then martyred by order of the emperor Diocletian (284–305) is told about three other persons besides Genesius.

Since there are certainly at least three saints by the name of Genesius, it is indeed a saint's name. If the connection with the arts is the important thing, Saint Catherine of Bologna is a patron of artists and painters. Saint Cecilia is a patron of poets and musicians. Saint Gabriel and Saint Clare are patrons of television and television workers, and Saint Lucy is a patron of writers.

Are archangels saints?

The best reason for calling the angels Raphael, Gabriel and Michael "saints" is in the definition of the word itself. According to Webster's dictionary, the word *saint* comes from the Latin *sanctus*, meaning "holy." Calling a person "saint" recognizes his or her holiness. Calling an angel "saint" is also a recognition of holiness. Both saints and angels are holy in that they mirror God's goodness and are united to God in love. Likewise, the *Encyclopedic Dictionary of the Bible* has this to say about archangels:

> A very important angel. (I) The word "archangel" occurs only in the NT: in Jude 9 of Michael, and in 1 Thessalonians. Actually, in the Old Testament certain angels are described as in terms equivalent to archangels, such as "the captain of the hosts of the Lord" (Joshua 5:14) and (of Michael) "one of the chief princes" or "the great prince" (Daniel 10:13; 12:1). In Tobit 12:15 Raphael

calls himself "one of the seven who stand before the Lord" (cf. Revelation 8:2).

(II) The traditional number of the archangels varies, Jewish apocalyptic literature reckons either seven, or four or three of them; the rabbis list six or seven of them. They are sometimes identified with the "Four Angels of the Presence" (Jubilees; Testament of the Patriarch Levi [two apocryphal books], etc.). Later Christian tradition counts among the archangels, besides Michael and Raphael, also Gabriel and even Uriel (on the basis of 4 Esdras 4 [apocryphal]).

Finally, note that the Roman rite calendar and sacramentary indicate that the church celebrates on September 29 the feast of Saint Michael, Gabriel and Raphael, Archangels.

Who is Maria Francesca?
Is she a patron saint for the sterile?

In *Butler's Lives of the Saints* and other dictionaries of the saints, you will find this saint under the English listing of Saint Mary Frances of Naples, who died in 1791. Apparently her father, Francis Gallo, was not only hot tempered but also rough and brutal to both Mary Frances and her mother. Baptized Anne Mary Rose Nicolette, Mary had much to suffer when she resisted a marriage her father wished to arrange for her. When she refused, the father locked her in a room and gave her only bread and water.

Eventually he was persuaded to allow her to become a Franciscan tertiary. At first she lived at home and devoted herself to prayer and works of piety. Later she took over the management of a priest's household. She was something of a mystic and mystical phenomena were associated with her. She is said to have received the stigmata—the wounds of Jesus in her own body.

What is her connection with sterile women? It is said that many miracles involving impossible pregnancies were worked through her intercession before her canonization in 1867.

Are angels male or female?

Rob van der Hart begins his book *The Theology of Angels and Devils:*

> Not very long ago theologians could write solid lengthy treatises on angels and devils and grip the attention of their readers to the very end. But in our day, when almost every other theological subject is being discussed with enthusiasm and passion at every level of the Christian community "Angelology"—the theology of spirits—is a subject untouched and almost forgotten.

That may be a slight exaggeration. Yet a half-dozen catechisms and more detailed explanations of the creed did not have "angels" listed in their indexes. In other books they get very brief mention. The new *Catechism of the Catholic Church* does however refer to angels (327–330, 350).

As van der Hart went on to say, angels did get some discussion after the publication of *A New Catechism* (the *Dutch Catechism*). The authors of this book wrote that when Scripture speaks of angels they are often presented under human form, giving concrete form to God's goodness and proclaiming the marvelous truth that God is concerned for us in a thousand ways. But *A New Catechism* left unanswered its own questions: Is their existence a supposition based on Scripture's view of the world? Or is it part of God's message?

Edouard Dhanis, s.j., and Jan Visser, c.ss.r., writing on behalf of the cardinals appointed to examine *A New Catechism*, revised its text. Instead of posing the questions of the original text, they said,

> Exegetes and theologians have not yet fully answered the questions that arise from the steadily growing place the angels occupy in the books of the Old Testament, or from the history and further development of the doctrine of angels. But the existence of angels—as also of devils—is a truth belonging to Catholic doctrine, and of which the Fourth Lateran Council, for example, speaks.

In 1986 Pope John Paul II used his weekly audiences in July

and August to teach about the creed and God the "Creator...of all that is seen and unseen." He voiced what has been common belief about angels for a long time. He reminded his hearers that angels are purely spiritual beings, created by God and given intelligence and free will. They have no bodies, he stated, even if in particular circumstances they reveal themselves under visible forms because of their mission for the good of humans. Referring to certain scriptural passages, the pope spoke of the angels as ambassadors and messengers from God to nations and individual human beings. And he spoke the church's common belief in guardian angels, although it has never been defined that every person has a guardian angel.

Because angels are purely spiritual creatures without bodies, there is no sexual difference between them. There are no male or female angels; they are not distinguished by gender.

Which saints are called to fight evil spirits?

Catholics traditionally ask the intercession of Saint Michael the Archangel in the struggle with evil and the devil. Before the liturgical renewal and the new rite for celebrating the Eucharist, priest and congregation prayed together the following prayer after every low Mass:

> Holy Michael, the Archangel, defend us in the days of battle; be our safeguard against the wickedness and snares of the devil. May God rebuke him, we humbly pray; and do thou, Prince of the heavenly host, by the power of God thrust down to hell Satan and all wicked spirits who wander through the world for the ruin of souls. Amen.

We can also ask the prayers of Saint John the Baptist Vianney, the Cure of Ars, who was assaulted by the devil many times over a period of thirty years.

Is there really a devil? If so, why does God permit him to exist?

In the biblical presentation of events, God created angels before creating our material universe and humankind. The fall of Lucifer and the rebellious angels took place before God created the earth and human beings.

God permits fallen angels or devils to exist for the same reason that fallen human beings are allowed to exist. God's highest praise and glory comes from free, knowing creatures lovingly and willingly serving God and fulfilling the purposes for which God made them. Freedom means the possibility of saying no. What meaning does yes have if a creature cannot say no? And why should any creature be rewarded or merit reward if it cannot say no?

When were angels created?

In a statement about *Christian Faith and Demonology* dated June 26, 1975, the Congregation for Divine Worship refers to writings of Saint Augustine saying he showed Satan at work in the conflict between the two cities (city of man and city of God), "a conflict which began in heaven when God's first creatures, the angels, chose to be faithful or unfaithful to their Lord." This passage reflects a belief that the angels were created before this world and human beings.

In *The Theology of Angels and Devils,* Rob van der Hart says the most common opinion is that the rebellion and punishment of the fallen angels took place long before the beginning of human history.

Do dead children become angels?

There are two kinds of creation. God made a physical, material world with flesh-and-blood creatures, including human beings. God also created entirely spiritual beings called angels. They are superior to us human beings in that they do not experience the limitations of the material body. They are more intelligent than we are. From the Scriptures we know that God has used angels as messengers to human beings and that they exist to give praise and worship to God.

Because it is difficult for us to picture or to imagine what angels are like, artists and writers often "picture" them as humanlike creatures with bodies and wings or in similar ways.

Children are created human beings. They will always be human beings. When they die, they do not become angels—a different kind of creature. Just as Jesus did not become an angel when he died and rose from the dead, neither do the rest of us humans. It is as human children that we know and love our children in this life. It will be as human children that we know and love them in the next life.

When people speak of a child as an angel in heaven, they are really saying that the child was so innocent, so pure, so good that he or she was like "an angel." Even in everyday speech we sometimes talk about our children who have been especially good or loving as "little angels."

It has long been customary to speak of a child's burial Mass as the "Mass of Angels." Mass books simply have a Mass for the burial of a child who died after baptism and a Mass for a child who died without baptism. That is because the prayers reflect the innocence of the child. They do not center on the need for forgiveness and mercy because the infant was incapable of sin.

How are angels ranked?

At the turn of the sixth century Pseudo-Dionysius, drawing on reference to angels in the Scriptures, divided the angels into three hierarchies with three choirs in each hierarchy. That became the common teaching of theologians and the church. But, according to Ludwig Ott in *Fundamentals of Catholic Dogma*, the division of angels into nine orders is not a truth of faith but a free theological opinion.

According to Adolphe Tanquerey in *A Manual of Dogmatic Theology*, Saint Thomas puts the seraphim, cherubim and thrones in the first hierarchy. In the second hierarchy are the dominations, virtues and powers. The third is composed of principalities, archangels and angels. Tanquerey, following Saint Thomas, says the "Seraphim excel in the supreme excellence of all, in being united to God through charity."

Did Saint Rita murder her sons?
How could a murderer be a saint?

Saint Rita did not murder her sons. At least several dictionaries of the saints have no mention at all of Saint Rita in connection with the death of her sons. However, the concise edition of *Butler's Lives of the Saints* sheds some light on the source of this question.

According to Butler's biography Saint Rita's parents married her off at a very young age to a "brutal, dissolute" man with a violent temper. Rita bore him two sons who, unfortunately, took after him rather than her. After eighteen years of marriage her husband experienced a kind of conversion. Shortly afterward he was carried home to Rita, dead. The account says his body was covered with wounds—the implication is that he was murdered.

His sons swore to avenge their father's death. Saint Rita, thinking only of her sons' best interests, prayed that they might die rather than commit the awful sin of murder and lose their souls. Rita's sons fell seriously ill. She nursed them in their sickness and seems to have brought them to forgive their enemy and to their own forgiveness by God.

That is quite a bit different from Saint Rita murdering her sons. It reveals Rita's greater concern for their spiritual salvation than for their continued bodily life.

Practically any collection of the lives of the saints will tell you the rest of Rita's story—how she entered a convent at Cascia after being rejected several times because she had been married, how she practiced severe penances and was devoted to the sufferings of Christ.

But, could a murderer become a saint? A murderer, like any other sinner, can experience a conversion and so completely change his or her life as to earn a reputation for great sanctity.

Whether you want to call Saint Paul a murderer or not, he was an accomplice in the death of Saint Stephen. But Paul (then called Saul) had a conversion and went off to become one of the greatest saints in the church.

It is also very interesting to note that, in his book *Patron Saints*, Michael Freze, S.F.O., lists several men who, while pagan, killed for power, experienced a conversion to Christianity and went off to become saints—for example, Caedwalla, Guntramnus, Solomon (of Brittany) and Vladimir (of Kiev).

God's grace can accomplish great things in those who open their hearts to it!

Who are Saint Goar and Saint Olaf?
Is Saint Olaf the patron saint of wood-carvers?

Saint Goar is one of those persons who reminds us saints are often misunderstood and unappreciated in their own times and places.

Goar was a saint of the sixth century, born in Aquitaine. He became a parish priest, and then turned to a solitary life. It is difficult to separate fact from legend, but he seems to have become known as a miracle worker and attracted a following as a preacher.

According to legend he also drew enemies who accused him of hypocrisy and sorcery. He was pronounced a sorcerer by the less than admirable Bishop Rusticus of Trier. Legend says a three-day-old child then declared Goar innocent and denounced the bishop for his own sinfulness.

The story goes on to say King Sigebert I of Austrasia then deposed Rusticus and offered to make Goar bishop of Trier. Goar, however, died around 575 before deciding whether or not to become bishop. According to *Butler's Lives of the Saints,* names and dates in the legend can hardly be reconciled.

According to *Saints Preserve Us!* by Sean Kelly and Rosemary Rogers, Goar is the patron saint of potters. He is also "invoked against whirlpools," possibly because his home was near a whirlpool on the Rhine at Gewirr.

Michael Freze, S.F.O., in *Patron Saints*, says that King Olaf II of Norway (995–1030) was a talented worker with wood and is the patron saint of wood-carvers. He is described as a pirate before his conversion. In the Middle Ages he was called the perpetual king of Norway and today is still regarded as a national hero and patron saint of Norway.

Are there any married saints? If not, why?

Many married people are and have been saints. But not many of them have been canonized or officially recognized as saints. According to a Catholic News Service report, Pope John Paul II spoke of this situation during his annual meeting with Roman clergy March 5, 1992. At that meeting a pastor appealed to the pope to consider a married couple for canonization. The priest said that today's Catholics need concrete examples of holiness close to their own lives.

The pope answered that this was his own great desire. And he said we should look for lay couples to canonize because married couples "as things stand today...do not generally find support in society, in the Christian community, in dioceses or in parishes."

He pointed out that part of the problem in canonizing married couples is systemic, and in his impromptu remarks suggested the system of canonization needs review. He noted that the Vatican is usually examining the lives of nuns, priests and members of religious orders in reviewing causes for sainthood. That is because their religious orders or other church groups promote their causes. But for laypeople, said the pope, "there's no tradition in this field."

The report concluded by noting that the pope has said the Congregation for Sainthood Causes handles current cases well. But, he added, "The system, the mechanism, should be considered by the People of God, by the Christian community," to see whether some changes are required.

Even with all that in mind, it can be noted that by tradition the church honors the parents of the Blessed Virgin—Joachim and Anne—as saints. In drawing up the present liturgical calendar, the church decided to honor them together in one feast. This better emphasizes that they became holy and worked out their salvation together in their vocation of marriage and parenthood. Saint Isidore the Farmer and his wife, Santa Maria de la Cabeza, are another husband and wife who became holy together.

On October 21, 2001, Pope John Paul II declared as "blessed" Luigi and Maria Beltrame Quattrochi, a lawyer and homemaker who lived in Rome. Luigi died in 1951 and Maria followed in 1965. In declaring them blessed, the pope said that their lives as spouses and parents were models of holiness for all Christians.

Other married people whose holiness has been recognized by the church (without canonizing their spouses) are Saint Peter, Saint Thomas More, Saint Louis of France, Saint Elizabeth of Hungary and Saint Elizabeth Ann Seton.

A book that may be of special interest is *Secular Saints*, by Joan Carroll Cruz.

Who was Saint Josephine Bakhita? What does she have to do with Christian-Muslim dialogue?

Josephine (Giuseppina) Bakhita was beatified by Pope John Paul II on May 17, 1992. The following day in an audience with pilgrims from northern Italy and the Sudan, the pope outlined Josephine's life and virtues in giving her as a special example and inspiration for refugees and victims of plague, famine and any kind of suffering in Africa.

Josephine, as the pope recalled, was born into a family of means in the Sudan near Darfur in 1869. Two slave traders seized her when she was nine. She was so frightened that she could not remember her name when she was asked. They cynically and contemptuously called her *Bakhita*, or "fortunate." In her youth she was sold five times, going from bad situations to worse. Eventually she was brought to Genoa, then Venice in the employ of two Italians. In Italy she entered the Catholic catechumenate and after a year, in 1890, was baptized Josephine.

Three years later, she was received into the novitiate of the Daughters of Charity of Canossa and she made her profession of vows December 8, 1896. As a Daughter of Charity, she did the humble work of cook, sacristan, porter, seamstress and launderer. The pope pointed to her as one who trusted completely in God and abandoned herself to God's will. He noted her charity and readiness to see the providence of God in all that happened to her. He quoted her as saying, "If I were to meet those slave traders who captured me and even those who tortured me, I would kneel down and kiss their hands, because if things had not happened so, I would not now be a Christian and religious."

The pope made her the inspiration for Christian-Muslim dialogue because she came from a Muslim background. Josephine died February 8, 1947, at age seventy-eight.

On October 1, 2000, Sister Josephine was canonized a saint by Pope John Paul II. Her feast day is February 8.

Who is Saint John Neumann? Where are his remains?

Saint John Neumann was born in Bohemia in 1811. He came to America in 1836 and was ordained by Bishop John Dubois of New York. After four years he joined the Redemptorist Order. Some ten years later he was ordained bishop for the Diocese of Philadelphia. He saw to it that the Forty Hours devotion in honor of the Blessed Sacrament was celebrated in every church and established the first American parochial school system. Pope Paul VI canonized him on June 19, 1977, and his feast is January 5. There should be at least a brief biography in almost any dictionary of the saints published after 1977. There is an entry concerning him in the *New Catholic Encyclopedia*.

According to *Catholic Shrines and Places of Pilgrimage in the United States*, published by the Office for the Pastoral Care of Migrants and Refugees, National Conference of Catholic Bishops, the body of Saint John Neumann is buried in the crypt of Saint Peter the Apostle Church, Fifth Street and Girard Avenue, in Philadelphia, Pennsylvania.

This church is also the National Shrine of Saint John Neumann. There are novena devotions in his honor every day of the week, and there is a shrine museum and exhibit.

Are there any patron saints for victims of rape or sexual abuse?

Michael Freze, S.F.O., lists in his book *Patron Saints*, published by Our Sunday Visitor, a number of patrons for victims of rape and child sexual and physical abuse.

He lists Saint Alodia among patrons for those abused as children. She was a ninth-century saint treated cruelly by a Muslim stepfather who hated the Christian faith. In the sixteenth century, Germaine Cousin was hidden away by her father and stepmother because she was born with a deformed hand. She was forced to sleep in a stable and was fed table scraps.

Some victims of their husbands' physical abuse were Fabiola, the wife of a Roman patrician, who died in 399, and Godelieve, starved and beaten by her mother-in-law before being murdered in 1070 at the command of her husband, Bertolf. Victims of incest and the emotionally and mentally disturbed might invoke Saint Dympha, who was beheaded by her unbalanced father who wanted to marry her after her mother's death. In 880, Saint Solangia was murdered by a would-be rapist from whom she tried to escape.

Finally, there is the twelve-year-old Maria Goretti, murdered early in the twentieth century by a crazed neighbor as she fought off his sexual attack. In 1950 Pope Pius XII canonized her and presented her to young people as a model of purity.

Who is Saint Philomena?

The story of Saint Philomena is interesting and unusual. According to *Butler's Lives of the Saints,* a tomb was discovered in the catacomb of Saint Priscilla on May 24, 1802. It was sealed with three tiles inscribed with red paint. The tiles were marked with anchors, arrows, a palm and flower or torch—all indications of sanctity and martyrdom. But the way the tiles were arranged did not make sense. They read, LUMENA PAXTE CUM FI.

Inside the tomb were the bones of a girl believed to be about thirteen to fifteen years old. Her skull had been crushed and with her bones was a vial of what appeared to be dried blood—further indication that she was a martyr.

There were at least two theories to explain the tiles. One was that a careless mason had scratched out the beginning two letters on the first tile and the final two letters on the last tile. Thus the original inscription was (FI) LUMENA PAX TECUM FI (AT)—FILUMENA, PEACE BE WITH YOU!

The other theory was that an illiterate mason had put the tiles in the wrong order. They should have read, PAX TECUM FILUMENA—PEACE BE WITH YOU, FILUMENA.

The bones were gathered and kept with other relics until 1805. Then Pope Pius VII gave the relics to a priest from the Diocese of Nola to be placed in the parish church of Mugnano del Cardinale, near Naples.

The relics were honored as those of Saint Philomena. People asked her intercession, and miracles followed. As word began to spread, miracles and wonders seemed to multiply. A religious sister claimed to have had a vision in which details of Philomena's life were revealed. The visions were dubious, but the pastor wrote a biography of Philomena based on the visions and his own imagination. The church became a place of pilgrimage.

The Venerable Pauline Mary Jaricot, founder of the Society for the Propagation of the Faith, was carried there near the point of death. She was miraculously cured. Philomena also became a favorite saint of Saint John Vianney.

But there arose a problem. Later researchers found evidence that two burials had taken place in the same tomb, one in the second century and another in the eighth or ninth century. They tried to determine whose bones had actually been found and what was the name of the person whose remains were discovered in 1802. They agreed that the miracles that had taken place were proofs of holiness. But, they asked, *whose* holiness?

So there came a third theory of the titles: The tiles had deliberately been placed out of order to indicate Philomena was no longer buried there. Her bones (those of a martyr) had been removed from the tomb in the eighth or ninth century and placed with others in one of the churches of Rome. At a later date, after the bones of Philomena had been removed, a teenager whose name and identity are unknown to us was buried in the same tomb.

In 1961, when the Congregation of Rites revised the calendar of saints, it removed Philomena's name due to lack of historical evidence concerning her life.

Who is Saint Charbel?

Saint Charbel (Sharbel) Makhlouf was canonized in 1977. He was born Joseph Makhlouf in 1828. At age twenty-three he entered a Maronite Monastery called Notre Dame de Mayfouk. After studies at Saint Cyprian de Kfifane Monastery, he was ordained in 1859.

Imitating the life of the desert fathers, he spent the last twenty-three years of his life in complete solitude at SS. Peter and Paul Hermitage near d'Anya. He died there in 1898.

Charbel is known for his very austere life and penances. According to *Lives of the Saints II*, Charbel experienced levitations while at prayer.

A small booklet by Bishop Francis M. Zayek of the Diocese of Maron credits Charbel with the gift of miracles—following his death many miracles have been attributed to his intercession. Charbel has been called the second Saint Anthony of the Desert and the Perfume of Lebanon. Pope Paul VI spoke of him as a heavenly arch or rainbow in the sky uniting East and West.

Does stigmata have anything to do with sainthood? Why does it manifest itself differently on different persons?

When we speak of the stigmata, we refer to those who have been marked by or bear the wounds of Christ in their bodies. Two reference books shed light on your question. *The HarperCollins Encyclopedia of Catholicism*, edited by Richard P. McBrien, states, "On very rare occasions the Catholic Church has accepted an occurrence of the stigmata as authentic, but has never defined their origin or nature, thus allowing physical, psychological and preternatural explanations for these phenomena."

Ian Wilson, in *Stigmata*, declares, "They [stigmata] are one of the most baffling and intriguing of medical and scientific mysteries."

Obviously there are few sure answers we can give or find regarding the stigmata. We are not even certain how the stigmata—wounds of the Passion—looked on Christ's body. We can only speculate. But we do know that the stigmata do not appear the same in all who are believed to have had them.

One stigmatic, for instance, had only the wounds made by the crown of thorns. Two possessed only the wound in the side. Some had the lance wound in the left side (Padre Pio), another in the right side (Saint Francis of Assisi). One had the hand wounds in the wrists, others in the palms of the hands. Since Saint Francis, Wilson reports that there have been over three hundred stigmatics.

Is it significant that more women than men have had the stigmata? What can we conclude from the fact that most stigmatics came from the Dominican and Franciscan Orders? What does it mean that some saints were stigmatics but not all stigmatics were saints?

In his study Wilson notes that some stigmatics seem to have identified with earlier stigmatics—ultimately with Jesus. Wilson notes that,

> A really riveting feature is the extraordinary precision of the mechanism's conformity to the visualization that

triggered it. Stigmata have been precisely positioned to conform with the wounds of a stigmatic's favorite crucifix. Or a wound may have taken on the exact shape, such as a cross.

That seems to imply that the stigmata may occur according to the way the subject pictures or imagines them. Wilson concludes that the presence of the stigmata is not a guarantee of sanctity or the miraculous. He sees the phenomenon as surrounded by mystery but also sees a relationship with the phenomena of multiple personalities and hypnosis and the power of mind over matter.

For another view of stigmatics you can read *They Bore the Wounds of Christ* and *Voices, Visions and Apparitions,* both by Michael Freze, S.F.O.

What is the true history of Saint Veronica and the veil?

Neither Veronica nor her veil is mentioned in the Scriptures. Is Veronica and her story a creation of Christian piety and devotion? Or was her story preserved and handed down in tradition by the early Christians? No one can really answer those questions.

We do know that Veronica's name seems derived from the veil. It seems to come from the Latin words *vera,* "true," and *icon,* "image." We do know from *Our Sunday Visitor's Encyclopedia of Saints* that in the apocrypha *Acts of Pilate* Veronica is identified with the woman suffering from an issue of blood in the Gospel of Matthew.

Legend says Veronica carried the image miraculously imprinted on her veil from the Holy Land to cure the emperor Tiberius of an illness. The veil was seen in Rome in the eighth century. In 1297, by the order of Pope Boniface VIII, the image was brought to St. Peter's.

Fact or legend, Saint Veronica and the veil is an important story that conveys a spiritual lesson and gives Christians much to think about regarding how to serve the Lord with faith and love.

How many saints are there?

The original edition of *Butler's Lives of the Saints*, published between 1756 and 1759, had 1,486 entries. The 1956 revision contained 2,565. *Butler's Lives* is just completing another revision.

But, in the first eight or nine centuries of Christianity, there was no formal process of canonization. People became saints because of popular acclamation. People were believed to be saints because they had been martyred for the faith or they had lived very holy lives. Often their graves became places of pilgrimage and prayer. We have no idea how many people's holiness was not recognized. That is one reason why we have the feast of *All* Saints.

Sometimes the recognition of holiness was particular to an area or community. Sometimes the reputation for sanctity spread beyond national borders.

It was not until 993 that the first official canonization took place. It was then that Pope John XV declared Bishop Ulrich of Augsburg a saint.

In any case there is no complete and exhaustive listing of all the saints or people who are claimed to have been saints.

Who is Blessed Imelda?

Born in 1322, Blessed Imelda Lambertini was the daughter of the Count and Countess Lambertini of Bologna. She appears to have been a very pious child, making and decorating altars in the home. In the days of less frequent Communion when First Communion was at a late age, she longed to receive the Lord. She is quoted as saying, "How can anyone receive Jesus into his heart and not die?"

It is said that when Imelda was eleven the eucharistic host flew from the tabernacle and hovered over her while she prayed. The priest took the host and gave her Communion. She then died in ecstasy.

She is the patron saint of first communicants. Her feast day is May 13.

Is there a saint to help find a spouse?

Several saints suggest themselves as patrons for those looking for spouses and companions in seeking the kingdom of
God. One possible patron is Raphael, the archangel. In the
book of Tobit God sent Raphael to guide Tobias to Sara to claim
her for his wife. The prayer that Tobias and Sara made on their
wedding night is read at many weddings today.

Saint Anthony of Padua is regarded as a kind of holy
matchmaker. In the Basque country of Spain, young women
make pilgrimage to one of his shrines on his feast day to ask
for his help in finding good husbands.

What is a seraphic saint?

The sixth-century writer Dionysius the Aeropagite drew on
different scriptural texts to list nine choirs of angels: seraphim,
cherubim, thrones, dominations, virtues, powers, principalities, archangels and angels.

First in this hierarchy of angels are the seraphim. An individual member of this group is called a seraph.

The seraphim are mentioned in Isaiah 6:1–7. There they
stand before the throne of God praising him and crying out
"Holy, holy, holy is the LORD of hosts." It is a seraph who
touches the lips of Isaiah with a live coal, cleansing him
from sin. Associated with the seraphim is their burning love
for God.

A seraph appears in the story of Francis of Assisi receiving the stigmata (the wounds of Christ's passion) in his body.
Omer Englebert, drawing on Saint Bonaventure, describes the
event. Francis prayed to experience the pains of Christ's passion and to feel the same love that made Christ sacrifice himself for us. Then a seraph with six wings of flame came from
heaven, bearing the likeness of a man nailed to a cross. He imprinted the stigmata upon Francis' body.

Because of this experience and his burning love of God,
Francis is often called the Seraphic Saint and some parishes
and institutions are named Saint Francis Seraph.

Who are the white martyrs?

In the book *How the Irish Saved Civilization*, Thomas Cahill talks about both green and white martyrdom. According to Cahill, Ireland was unique in that Christianity was introduced there without bloodshed (red martyrdom). No Irish martyrs emerged until the time of Elizabeth I. Cahill states that this lack of martyrdom disturbed the Irish, so they conceived at first of a green martyrdom.

Green martyrs left behind the comforts and pleasures of ordinary human society to live hermits' lives on mountain-tops or lonely islands. As Cahill puts it, they went "to one of the green no-man's islands outside tribal jurisdiction." There they studied Scripture and communed with God after the example of the anchorites in the Egyptian desert. Ireland could not duplicate the barren terrain of the Egyptian desert, thus this green martyrdom gave way to the more social life of monasticism.

Against this background, Cahill introduces Columcille ("Dove of God")—also called Columba or Crimthaann. Born in 521, a prince with a title to kingship, he chose to become a monk, and by age forty-one he had founded forty-one monasteries. Because Columba was held responsible for the Battle of Cuil Dremmen in which three thousand men died, he became an exile. As penance he set out to save as many people as had died in the battle.

Columba, with twelve relatives, founded a monastery on Iona off the coast of Scotland that became famous throughout Europe. Monks from Iona in turn set out for what they called a white martyrdom. "[H]enceforth all who followed Columcille's lead were called to the white martyrdom, they who sailed into the white sky of morning, into the unknown, never to return."

Is there a saint named Cynthia?

In *A Saint for Your Name*, Cynthia is the feminine form of *Synesius*, Greek for "understanding."

The very short biography says that Synesius was a Roman martyr beheaded in 279 under the emperor Aurelian. December 12 is Synesius's feast day.

Saint Diana is also known as Cynthia. A worldly young woman, she was converted by hearing a sermon. She became a Dominican sister after overcoming strong opposition from her family. She died in 1236. Her feast day is June 9.

Are there any saints for gamblers?

Sean Kelly and Rosemary Rodgers, in *Saints Preserve Us!* list two saints whose intercession might be asked for those struggling with a gambling habit or addiction.

One of those saints is Camillus de Lellis, who was a compulsive gambler. While a soldier, he literally lost the shirt off his back. He became a penitent at the age of twenty-five and dedicated his life to the service of the sick. He became the founder of the Servants of the Sick and a pioneer in hospital hygiene and diet.

The second saint is Bernardine of Siena, the great preacher and promoter of devotion to the Holy Name of Jesus. His preaching against gambling bankrupted a playing-cards printer. The printer, however, turned things around and made a fortune selling a Holy Name line of holy cards.

There is no patron listed for those who want to bet the horses or play the lottery or bingo. But they might ask Saint Patrick for the luck of the Irish. And perhaps it would not be irreverent or sacrilegious to pray to Saint Matthias, chosen by lot at the inspiration of the Holy Spirit to take the place of Judas among the apostles after Pentecost.

Who is Sister Faustina?

According to an article in the *National Catholic Register*, February 7, 1993, by Father George Kosicki, C.S.B., Sister Faustina Kowalska of the Most Blessed Sacrament was born in Poland in 1905. At the age of twenty she entered the convent, where she became the doorkeeper, gardener and cook.

She was a woman of much prayer and contemplation, gifted by God with great insights about his mercy.

At the command of God and her spiritual director, she began to record these insights and revelations in a spiritual diary. Though Faustina had just two years of schooling, says Father Kosicki, her diary has astounded theologians and is considered by some equal to the writings of Saint Catherine of Siena and Saint Teresa of Avila. Her message is to trust completely in God's mercy and that to receive mercy we must give it to others.

Part of the significance for our times of what she has recorded are the words of Jesus, "Mankind will have no peace until it turns with trust to my mercy." And no one, no sin, no situation can keep us from receiving God's mercy if we turn to God in trust.

The day chosen for her beatification is of some significance, states Kosicki, because our Lord told Faustina he wanted this day to be celebrated as the "Feast of Mercy—a day of unimaginable graces, a day on which the very floodgates of mercy will be opened for all who turn to him with trust." The beatification is an invitation to join Faustina's constant prayer: "Jesus, I trust in you."

She was canonized a saint by Pope John Paul II on April 30, 2000.

Is there a patron saint for emergency medical workers?

Saint Catherine of Siena, Elizabeth of Hungary or Albert the Great might be sources of inspiration for ambulance drivers and medical technicians.

There are also other saints who might serve as role models for those in the medical and health-care professions. Camillus de Lellis and John of God are accepted as patrons of nurses. The archangel Raphael and Saint Agatha are regarded as patrons of hospitals. Luke, Cosmas and Damian are patrons of doctors and Cosmas and Damian double as patrons of pharmacists. Januarius is the patron of blood banks. Saint Michael is the patron of radiologists.

Emergency workers might also want to take Saint Bernard of Montjoux, the patron of mountaineers, or Saint Blaise, who saved the boy with a fish bone stuck in his throat, as their patron.

The church has in some instances declared certain saints as patron saints for countries or certain groups of people. But in many cases saints have become the patrons of different groups because of popular traditions and devotions originating with the people.

Is Pontius Pilate a saint?

There is no historical certainty about what finally happened to Pontius Pilate. What we have are different legends that have woven many purely imaginary details about Pilate.

We do know that after the death of Christ and ten years of rule in Judea, Pilate was recalled to Rome by Emperor Tiberius on a charge of committing atrocities against the Samaritans. It seems clear that Tiberius died before Pilate reached Rome.

According to Eusebius, Pilate was exiled to Gaul and committed suicide there. But Louis Hartman, in the *Encyclopedic Dictionary of the Bible*, calls the historical value of this statement doubtful. Taking up on Eusebius's version of events, some Christian legends have it that Pilate's body was thrown first into the River Tiber, then into the Rhone and finally into Lake Lucerne. These tales say that every Good Friday Pilate rises from the waters and washes his hands in the lake.

Hartman also reports another legend that Pilate and his wife, Procla (sometimes referred to as Claudia Procula), were put to death as Christian martyrs. On the basis of this legend, Pilate and Procla are venerated as saints in the Abyssinian church on June 25. The Greek church honors Procla alone on October 27.

Neither Pilate nor his wife were ever canonized by the pope. The canonization procedure began only in the early

Middle Ages. Before that time, people became known as saints by public acclaim. Pilate and Procla have never been venerated as saints by the universal church.

Who was Saint Anthony of Egypt?

Saint Anthony of Egypt is not always listed or spoken of by that name. His name is also sometimes spelled without an *h*—*Antony*.

He is listed in most dictionaries of the saints under "Anthony," "Anthony, Abbot" or "Anthony of Egypt," with January 17 as his feast day.

In brief he lived A.D. 251–356. He was born at Koman in upper Egypt. He spent most of his life as a hermit and finally founded a community of hermits. He is regarded as the founder of Christian monasticism and was famous for his wisdom and holiness as well as his asceticism. Many came to him for advice, including the Roman emperor Constantine.

Who is Saint Mungo?

The story of Saint Mungo as told in the various collections of lives of the saints could provide the story line for a soap opera. As these books tell it, a British princess by the name of Thenaw became pregnant by an unknown man. She was thrown from a cliff but survived unharmed.

She was then put in a boat and set adrift on the Firth of Forth. The boat landed at Culross where the princess was given help and shelter by Saint Serf. Apparently, when her child was born, Thenaw named him Kentigern. But Serf, who helped raise the child, called him *Mungo*, meaning "darling." Kentigern or Mungo (the collections will usually have references under both names) grew up to become a hermit living in the area of Glasgow, Scotland.

In about 540, because of his holiness, he was ordained a bishop. Later, he was driven from the area by feuding tribal chiefs. Mungo is said to have founded a monastery at Llanelwy in Wales. Near the end of his life, he returned to

Glasgow. With Saint Thenaw, Kentigern or Mungo is copatron of Glasgow.

Are there any saints from the Old Testament?

Some Old Testament names are in *The Book of Saints*, compiled by the Benedictine Monks of Saint Augustine's, Ramsgate. Some may also be found in lists of Christian names—without any notation of sanctity or a cult. In other dictionaries of the saints, there simply are no listings for these biblical figures.

In *The Book of Saints* the Ramsgate Monks use three different designations: (1) R.M., listed in the *Roman Martyrology;* (2) A.C., Approved Cult—there is positive evidence the person was venerated as a saint; and (3) P.C., Popular Cult—the person was referred to as a saint by ancient writers.

At the same time remember there was no formal process of canonization until 993. Earlier than that, people were accepted as saints by common opinion.

Abraham (October 9), David (December 29), Moses (September 9) and Samuel (August 20) are listed in the *Roman Martyrology*. The Greeks celebrate a feast of David and all the ancestors of Jesus on December 19. Adam and Eve (December 24) are listed as having an approved cult.

Remember, however, *The Book of Saints* was published before the 1969 revision of the calendar and the revision of the *Roman Martyrology* is still underway. Some changes may occur.

Does use of the word *legends* discredit stories about the saints?

Stories do grow up around historical events and persons—including saints and religious figures. Some stories are almost pure invention. In other cases details are changed, added or magnified. That is simple fact. It is recognized by hagiographers and was recognized by the church itself in the revision of the liturgical calendar and the celebration of feasts following Vatican II.

Austin Flannery, O.P., in *The Saints in Season*, gives the principles stated by the Congregation of Rites for eliminating feasts, noting, "Present-day Christians rightly want their devotion to the saints to have a sound historical basis."

Apocryphal texts, rejected from the Bible by the church, are testimony that even concerning Jesus, the Blessed Virgin and Saint Joseph, people created stories to convey certain lessons or to fill in details people would like to know. How many wise men (magi) came from the East to the stable at Bethlehem? Scriptures do not tell us that. We have come to speak of three. But one tradition (legend) is that there were eight, another twelve. Because the number of gifts were three, we seem to have settled on the number three! Some versions have names for these wise men, and most of us think of them as kings, although that is nowhere in Scripture.

Did Saint Patrick really drive all the snakes out of Ireland? Did Saint George really slay a dragon? Legends say they did.

Legends do not grow up around ordinary people or events. Legends are a way of saying something of great importance took place. Legends are ways of saying this man or woman was someone out of the ordinary, a great, wonderful, powerful or holy person.

We have legends about George Washington chopping down the cherry tree to convey the truth that George Washington was a great man, known for his honesty.

So, too, legends can be ways of saying God does wonderful things in and through saints, people of extraordinary holiness. In addressing the literal truth of the Bible, someone once said, "All of it is true, and some of it really happened." We can say the same about legends of the saints.

Who is Saint Christopher?

Was there a Saint Christopher? The *Roman Martyrology* lists Christopher as a martyr in Lycea under King Decius. Early on in church history, he was venerated in both the East and the West. As early as 452, a church was dedicated to him in Bithynia.

We know very little more about him for sure. But stories and legends about him were formed, embroidered and added to over the centuries.

According to these he was a man of great strength and stature—a giant twenty-four feet tall. The *New Catholic Encyclopedia* tells us the famous legend about him carrying the Christ child on his shoulders across a river, but that story did not appear until the Middle Ages.

Butler's Lives of the Saints says the legends about Christopher led to the belief that if a person looked on an image of the saint he or she would suffer no harm that day. Consequently, a statue or image of Saint Christopher was often found at the church door.

That and the Christ child story may explain why Saint Christopher became the patron of travelers and why his statue was placed on many dashboards.

The *Golden Legend*, put into English by William Caxton, says Saint Christopher carried Christ four ways: on his shoulders, in his body, in his mind by devotion and in his mouth by preaching and confessing.

The implication, of course, is that we are all to bear Christ in our hearts and minds and carry him to others by our words and example.

The 1969 revision of the Roman calendar eliminated the liturgical celebration of Christopher's feast. At that time the number of saints' feasts was significantly reduced to accentuate the celebration of ordinary days. Prime targets in the reduction were saints whose origins are clouded with dubious legends and facts.

Who Is Padre Pio?

Padre Pio was baptized Francesco and his family name was Forgione. He was born in 1887 of poor peasant parents in the village Pietralcina in the province of Foggia in southern Italy. At age fifteen he entered the Capuchin Franciscans and took the religious name of Pio.

Pio was ordained to the priesthood in 1910. He was

drafted for military service in World War I but was immediately released from service when it was discovered he had tuberculosis.

In 1917 he was assigned to the Friary of San Giovanni Rotondo. On September 20, 1918, he had a vision of Jesus. At the end of the vision, he had the wounds of Jesus in his hands and feet—like Saint Francis of Assisi before him.

While he very rarely left the friary after he received the stigmata, busloads of people came to see him over the following years. Many claimed miraculous cures, even at a distance, and spoke of seeing or being visited by Padre Pio in their difficulties.

Padre Pio spent ten hours a day in the confessional, and penitents said he told them things or referred to things about them that he could not know by ordinary means or in the course of ordinary events.

He was beatified by Pope John Paul II on May 2, 1999.

What is the significance of wine and snakes in representations of John the Evangelist?

In at least some religious houses on December 27, the feast of Saint John, the religious superior blesses wine, which is then drunk at the meal. The old Roman ritual contained a blessing of wine for this feast. This commemorates the legend that once, while at Ephesus, John was given a cup of poisoned wine to drink. Before drinking he blessed the cup and the poison departed the cup in the form of a serpent.

According to Francis X. Weiser, in the *Handbook of Christian Feasts and Customs,* as late as 1952 Catholics in central Europe brought wine and cider to church for blessing on the feast of Saint John. They then took it home, and some of them poured a bit of the blessed wine or cider into every barrel in the cellar.

The blessed wine is called by some the "love of Saint John." In some places the bride and groom at a wedding are given a sip to drink. In other cases a sip of the wine is given to a dying person as a sacramental.

Is there a patron saint for lawyers?

At least four saints are listed as patrons for lawyers: Saint Catherine of Alexandria, Saint Genesius, Saint Ives (Ivo) and Saint Thomas More.

Saint Thomas More became chancellor of England under King Henry VIII, who eventually had Thomas beheaded for his refusal to accept the Act of Supremacy.

In many dioceses there is a Catholic guild of lawyers and an annual Red Mass (Lawyer's Mass). It takes the name *Red* from the votive Mass of the Holy Spirit, which was celebrated during the Middle Ages at the opening of the courts. The priest wore red vestments for this Mass.

Why is Saint Bridget often portrayed with an ox or cow?

Saint Bridget of Ireland, according to the *Book of Saints,* is called "the Mary of the Gael." She founded the first nunnery on Irish soil and became the "spiritual mother" of all Irish nuns. She is especially known for her mercy and pity for the poor.

Sometimes she appears with a cow because she is the patron of dairy workers. According to one legend, when she had no milk to give a leprous woman, Bridget gave her water that changed to milk. The woman was healed. A second story says that Bridget once gave all the butter from her family's cows to the poor. She then prayed for more butter, and her prayers were answered.

Bridget is also sometimes pictured holding a cross and with a flame over her head, or with a pen and book. John Delaney, in his *Dictionary of Saints,* writes that Bridget founded a school of art at Kildare famous for its illuminated manuscripts and especially for the *Book of Kildare,* praised as one of the finest.

Is the asceticism of saints penance or masochism?

How do we reconcile the severe penances of some saints with the obligation we have to take care of our bodily health? It is very difficult to judge the saints and their actions by our own mind-set. How do we know the motives upon which they acted? What is heroic holiness, and what is reckless unconcern for the consequences of their actions?

In his book *What Is a Saint?* Jacques Douillet writes about the severe penance and mortification of certain saints, among them Saint Francis of Assisi and the Desert Fathers. He suggests, among other things, that it is "hardly possible to judge the inmost motives of these giants of fasting and watching. We are poor judges in this matter: The bent of our contemporaries cannot be said to incline them to admire austere saints."

This is a good observation in this age of television commercials that urge, "Be good to yourself!" and "You can have it all!" and suggest that responsible, safe sex simply means using condoms. Public opinion is not tilted toward self-denial, mortification and a penitential life.

Motivation is the most important element in evaluating the actions of the saints. They are not practicing penance for penance's sake or for public attention. Their bodily mortification is part of their quest for God.

In the words of Douillet,

> Saints do not look for suffering. Like all the rest of us, they have at first to inflict privations on themselves lest they give in to temptations of the senses.... In this way Thomas More's hair shirt was a sort of training for the martyrdom which he did not know would one day be offered him: He wanted to make sure that, amid the world's business and the delights of humanism, he would always love and serve God first. As saints increase in love for God it seems that mortification is not so much chosen as imposed on them by necessity. Their ever-growing consciousness of God's holiness calls for an ever-growing perfection of personal integrity; it is like a process of cleansing, through which their love for God

takes them so that their progress towards him may not be slowed down in any way.

So, indeed, there is a place for penance and mortification. Human and religious experience indicates they are necessary for anyone who seriously seeks to overcome sin and grow in holiness. But can a person err in judgment concerning acts of penance and self-denial that can seriously undermine bodily health and therefore be avoided? It is certainly possible. And sometimes, it seems, saints have better perspective and judgment concerning the actions of other people than their own.

Bernard Häring, in *The Law of Christ*, after speaking of the necessity and even obligation of practicing bodily mortification, says that obligation differs very much in individual cases. He says much depends on the temperament, the profession, the condition and state of life and the vocation of individuals. Häring says,

> If they exceed the bounds of moderation, penitential exercise and discipline cease to be virtue, for the acts of penance must always be acts of the virtue of temperance. Saint Jerome, himself given to austere practice of penance, says: "We do not enjoin immoderate and violent fasting. Through such acts weak bodies are ruined and illness sets in before the foundation of holiness is laid down." Thomas Aquinas repeats the words of warning also attributed to Saint Jerome: "...He offers rapine to God in the guise of sacrifice who tortures himself excessively through vile food and insufficient nourishment or through lack of sleep."

To the point, Francis of Assisi, who was given to severe acts of mortification and penance, urged moderation on his followers. When he discovered at a general chapter that many of his friars were wearing iron breastplates and rings against their flesh, he commanded that they be removed. On another occasion when a companion trying to imitate him in his fasting cried out in the night that he was dying of hunger, Francis made everyone rise and eat with the friar who was overdoing it. His biographer, Thomas of Celano, says Francis carefully admonished each one to consider his own strength in the service of God. He said that to deprive the body indiscreetly of what it needs was a sin just the same as it is a sin to give it superfluous things at the prompting of gluttony.

Yet, it is interesting that Francis had little mercy concerning his own body, which he sometimes called "brother ass." Toward the end of his life, worried about indulging "brother ass," he asked the advice of one of his brothers about yielding to his body's desire for respite and care. That friar asked him what he could have done in the service of Christ without the help of his body and told him that his body deserved better from him. Francis thanked the friar for his wisdom in helping him resolve his uncertainties. He then went on to make a kind of apology to his body, saying, "Rejoice, brother body, and forgive me, for behold, I now gladly fulfill your desires, I hasten to give heed to your complaints."

The important thing to notice is that in the case of these saints their actions do not stem from a kind of masochism. They did not take perverse pleasure in torturing themselves. They perceived these acts of penance as necessary for controlling the desire for pleasure that is sinful or will lead to sin. These acts appear to us as extreme, but saints are people given to extremes, totally dedicating themselves to eliminating sin in their lives and bringing about the kingdom of God in this world and in their own lives. It is as though they are responding to Jesus' words, "the good news of the kingdom of God is proclaimed, and everyone tries to enter it by force" (Luke 16:16).

We might judge their actions unwise, excessive and even unreasonable. But in the end they must be judged by their own lights and motives, by the love of God and the desire to enter the kingdom even at the great cost of amazing acts of mortification and self-denial.

How do people become saints?

Before speaking about the process of canonization, it is important to stress that the church does not make or "create" saints. Rather, in declaring someone a saint, the church makes aware to the faithful, in a formal and official way, that a person has led a virtuous and holy life and is worthy of emulation by all.

The word *canon* comes from the Greek and means "measuring rod" or "standard." The process of canonization was not always as organized and formal as it is today. Before it was regulated by Pope John XV in A.D. 993, saint making was a very local affair. The title of saint was bestowed by acclamation in the local church community. The consensus was that certain people had lived such holy lives or given their lives for Christ (martyrs) so fully that they were among the saints in heaven. The evidence that people believed them to be saints is found in their prayers and devotions. Over time, however, abuses arose and the process was eventually taken over by the church and new rules and standards were instituted.

In 1983 Pope John Paul II issued new guidelines, which led to the overhauling of the saint-making process. In 1988 he renamed the Vatican congregation charged with the task of investigating these petitions the Congregation for the Causes of Saints.

The process of canonization takes place in three major stages. The first stage examines the life of the candidate in an attempt to determine whether he or she lived a life of faith and morals. This is done at the local, or diocesan, level. If the bishop feels the nomination merits it, he appoints someone to examine the candidate's life. The results are then given to the Vatican where the candidate is evaluated. In the course of the investigation, if the person is proven to have lived a life of holiness, he or she is recommended to the next level of the process and given the title "servant of God," or *venerable.*

Beatification is the next level. At this stage an extraordinary event, or miracle, is required to indicate the candidate is in heaven and interceding on behalf of the faithful. (Martyrs of the faith, however, do not need to be connected with miracles.) If an event happens that cannot be scientifically explained and it is attributed to the intercession and mediation of the candidate invoked by the faithful, the venerable candidate is declared *blessed*. At this point the church allows the blessed to be venerated by a particular group or geographic region where the person holds a special relationship and importance.

The final stage is canonization. Not all those who have been beatified are necessarily declared saints. Another extraordinary event is needed for this next step. If and when it occurs, the pope issues a bull of canonization and declares in a public and elaborate ceremony the person a saint and worthy of veneration by the whole church.

If you're interested in learning more about this, read the book, *Making Saints: How the Catholic Church Determines Who Becomes a Saint, Who Doesn't, and Why*, by Kenneth L. Woodward.

$$\dagger$$

MARY AND JOSEPH

There is a familiar saying that goes something like, "If you want to know what the children are like, look at the parents."

Fortunately, for the Holy Family, this is very true—child reflects parents, parents reflect child. You meet one, you meet the other. A story from England brings this out well.

On his weekly visits to the orphanage, a Protestant minister desired to see where the children were with their prayers. He asked each child to come and recite the Our Father and Apostles' Creed. Upon finishing the Our Father, one boy, who had previously been to a Catholic school, instinctively started praying the Hail Mary, to which the minister retorted, "We'll have none of that. On to the Creed!" The boy proceeded until he came to "born of the..." where he stopped and said, "Here she comes again—what would you like me to do now, Reverend?"

Our Catholic tradition proudly proclaims that in meeting Jesus, one meets his parents, Mary and Joseph. The parents are not obstacles to the son but beloved blessings of relationship that mediate the love of Jesus to us.

Though a silent figure in the Gospels, Saint Joseph looms large in the Catholic tradition, serving as a model for all fathers.

*Declared Patron of the Universal Church by Pope Pius IX in
1870, Saint Joseph has his feast day celebrated on March 19. He
also has an additional feast of Saint Joseph the Worker, which is
celebrated on May 1.*

*Of Mary the tradition is full of titles, prayers, stories and
feasts. The* Catechism *speaks of her in these words:*

> By her complete adherence to the Father's will, to his Son's re-
> demptive work, and to every prompting of the Holy Spirit, the
> Virgin Mary is the church's model of faith and charity. Thus
> she is a "preeminent and...wholly unique member of the
> Church"; indeed, she is the "exemplary realization" (typus) of
> the Church. (967, quoting Lumen gentium 53, 63)

•

Are Marian apparitions real? Why do they occur?

To understand from a human perspective what Mary contributes to the spiritual life and devotion of many people,
you might read what the sociologist Andrew Greeley has
written on this subject in any number of his nonfiction published works.

And if you read the U.S. bishops' pastoral letter *Behold
Your Mother: Woman of Faith* (November 21, 1973) and Pope
John Paul II's encyclical letter (March 25, 1987), you will find
an excellent statement of the reasons for and theology of devotion to Mary.

Of course, none of these visions (such as at Fatima or
Lourdes) is necessary for salvation. The deposit of faith was
complete with the death of the last apostle. There are no new
truths about God or our way to salvation that emerge from
various apparitions and visionaries.

All claims that God is acting personally or through Mary
(or an angel or saint) are not to be accepted at face value. In
fact, the church subjects those who claim visions and the
theology of their "revelations" to rigorous scrutiny before
stating that the visionaries are worthy of belief or that the
church finds no reason to disbelieve. In no case does the
church demand belief or proclaim that belief is necessary.

Always, the church looks first for a natural explanation where apparitions or miracles are claimed.

Any bishop, pope or church commission examining claims of miracles and apparitions starts with healthy skepticism. There is always the realization on their part of the great spiritual harm that can be caused by charlatans or mentally disturbed people.

The Scriptures and tradition of the church give us all that is necessary for salvation. Human beings have emotions and feelings, however, as well as an intellect. We are, as we say, body and soul. We can acknowledge many things as true on an intellectual level and not be moved to action.

A person can accept as true that smoking is dangerous to his or her health and go on smoking. Another knows what drug addiction can do yet continues taking cocaine. That same person may be moved when confronted with pictures of the lungs of a smoker or a friend who dies from an overdose of drugs to quit the addiction.

What means more: to read a letter from your friend telling you your wife loves you or for your wife to take you in her arms, kiss you with much feeling and murmur in your ear, "I love you!"?

God takes us where and as we are. As Jesus worked miracles to call people to faith, God may act in our times through signs and wonders to call us to faith and to *act* on our faith. Every apparition calls us to what we already know we should do from the gospel—to pray, to do penance, to live in the love of God and each other.

Perhaps we should look upon the instances of apparitions that have been judged to be genuine not as necessary but as gifts from God, useful and helpful to salvation.

Was Mary the real name of Jesus' mother?

According to *The Compact Bible Dictionary, Mary* is the Greek form of the Hebrew *Miriam*. It does not seem unreasonable to presume Mary, the mother of Jesus, and other Marys of her time were named for Miriam, the sister of Moses. To know for sure, somehow their parents would have had to tell us.

Mary was certainly not an uncommon name at the time of Jesus. The New Testament names at least five Marys besides the mother of Jesus. Mary Magdalene, Mary of Bethany, Mary the wife of Clopas, Mary the mother of John Mark and Mary of the Church of Rome.

Unless a name has the same spelling and pronunciation, in a language employing the same kind of script and alphabet, that name is going to be changed somehow when translated into another language. For example, Webster's dictionary gives *Matthaios* as the Greek form or origin of *Matthew* and *Mattityah* as Hebrew for Matthew.

People who wrote and spoke Aramaic, Hebrew or Greek did not use English names and spellings.

What is the Black Madonna?

The Black Madonna is a painting, or icon, that depicts the Blessed Virgin holding the child Jesus on her arm. The painting is held in tremendous reverence by the people of Poland.

The shrine at Czestochowa, Poland, where the icon is kept, draws pilgrims from all over Poland and other countries. Mary is honored under the title of Our Lady of Czestochowa. She has been hailed as the savior of Poland since it survived an invasion by Swedish forces in the seventeenth century. Mary is said to have appeared then above the shrine, shielding it and the monastery there with her cloak. This inspired Polish resistance.

The origins of the painting are lost in time, but it seems to have been brought to Poland late in the fourteenth century. It is called the Black Madonna because the colors of the painting have been darkened by age and smoke from a fire in 1690.

Why did Mary need purification?

Uncleanness in the Old Testament was associated with four things: (1) food, (2) leprosy, (3) contact with a corpse and (4) childbirth and sexual functions causing any discharge of blood from a man's or woman's sexual organs.

According to John McKenzie's *Dictionary of the Bible*, the concepts and meaning of *clean* and *unclean* cannot be defined exactly. Cleanness was associated with fitness for participation in cult. Morality was not a factor; uncleanness was somehow a physical quality. McKenzie suggests that by the time of Jesus the Hebrews themselves no longer fully understood the basis for uncleanness. The purification of Mary in Luke's Gospel is connected with the requirements of Leviticus 12:1–8.

The morally spotless, sinless, grace-filled Mary was obedient to the demands of Jewish ritual law and went through the prescribed ceremony of purification.

Does the story of the finding in the Temple suggest that Mary and Joseph were careless parents?

Let's give Mary and Joseph the benefit of the doubt. Any member of a modern family that has taken a vacation trip to Disney World or gone to the business section of a city such as Chicago or New York for shopping or entertainment events knows how easy it is for people to get separated in the confusion of large crowds and the distractions of new and exciting sights.

More to the point, though, to make any kind of judgment like that, you would have to know the customs of the time, what Mary and Joseph knew and could expect of a youth of Jesus' age, the maturity of Jesus at twelve and their past experiences with this young boy. In view of all Mary and Joseph had done and suffered in the past to protect this son, could they really be careless and negligent where his welfare was concerned? Doesn't that seem out of character?

William Harrington, O.P., in *A New Catholic Commentary on Holy Scripture*, states, "As a Jewish boy of twelve Jesus was well able to look after himself and his parents would naturally have taken it for granted that he was with one of the scattered groups of the returning Nazareth caravan."

Other commentaries make it clear the evangelist tells this story to make a much more important point than that Jesus got lost or separated from his parents. The trip to Jerusalem here is meant to prefigure the later journey to Jerusalem for his passion and death. He will be separated from his mother and disciples and lost to them, once again, for three days. The telling of this earlier event becomes the occasion for revealing who Jesus is—the son of the Father in heaven—and what his mission is. The claims of the Father on him will override all other demands. His mission will break the natural ties of family.

When Mary and Joseph find Jesus in the Temple, Mary's words are, "Son, why have you done this to us?" They hardly sound like the words of a mother full of self-reproach or guilty feelings. Nor are Jesus' words apologetic. He takes it for granted Mary and Joseph should have known where to find him. No wonder all that happened was something of mystery to Mary!

Was Saint Joseph an older man? Was he Mary's age?

No one knows for sure how old Saint Joseph was when he was espoused to Mary. Nor does anyone really know if he was a bachelor or widower with children by a first wife. There have been all kinds of opinions and efforts to fill in what the Gospels do not tell us. Some writers theorize that indeed Joseph was an older man, that he had been married and had children by a first wife and that he was a widower espoused to Mary. Those who speculate in this fashion see their idea protecting the doctrine of Mary's virginity and perhaps explaining the text that speaks of the "brothers and sisters of the Lord."

Contemporary Scripture scholars would not be likely to favor either the theory that Joseph was old or the theory that he was a widower when he married Mary. They maintain that Mary needed a young husband to provide for the child she was to bear and that a man of some strength and vigor was needed to take his family into exile and act as protector and provider for Jesus and Mary.

As a matter of fact, in their pastoral letter on the Blessed Virgin, *Behold Your Mother*, the United States bishops stated, "According to the customs of her time and people, Mary was probably no more than fourteen when her parents arranged her marriage, and Joseph probably about eighteen. God asked great things of them both and they responded to his call with dedicated love."

How long did Mary live? Did she have other children besides Jesus?

No one really knows the age of the Blessed Virgin when she died. In fact, theologians argue *whether* Mary actually died. Most say yes, others that she just fell asleep (referred to as the "dormition" of Mary). The church has never defined this.

Those who pray the Franciscan Crown always add two Hail Marys to the seven decades of the crown because of a tradition that Mary died at age seventy-two.

It is Catholic dogma—faith—that Mary was a virgin when Jesus was born and remained even afterward a virgin. Luke and Matthew make it quite clear that before Jesus was born Saint Joseph had taken Mary into his home as his wife.

Because of references in the Gospels to the brothers and sisters of Jesus, some Protestants maintain Mary had other children. Catholics say such references are either ways of speaking of kinsmen (cousins, etc.) or that the brothers are Joseph's children by an earlier marriage.

Are the Garabandal visions approved by the church?

Encountering Mary: Visions from La Salette to Medjugorje, by Sandra L. Zimdars-Swartz, gives an objective, straightforward account of the events at Garabandal and the controversy surrounding them. In brief, between 1961 and 1963 four young girls claimed to have apparitions of angels and the Blessed Virgin. At times paranormal phenomena were associated with the alleged apparitions. The claims of apparitions were clouded by retractions and then reassertions of what occurred.

After reciting what was claimed to have happened, Zimdars-Swartz details the reactions of church authorities. Bishop Doroteo Fernandez of Santander established a commission to investigate the events and issued two statements in 1961. According to Zimdars-Swartz, "He called for prudence and asked that judgment on the nature of the phenomena be suspended pending further developments. He also asked religious and laity to refrain from visiting Garabandal."

In 1962 Fernandez's successor, Bishop Beita Aldazabal, received a note from the commission reasserting its previous position: The events at Garabandal lacked a supernatural character.

Bishop Aldazabal, on July 8, 1965, made yet another statement that nothing had caused the commission to change its judgment. It was not self-evident that the character of the events was supernatural. But he also said no grounds had been found in doctrine or in the claimed spiritual recommendations for an ecclesiastical condemnation.

A new bishop, Puchol Monti, on March 17, 1967, "Bluntly declared that there had been no apparition and no message and deplored the impudent conduct of at least some of the Garabandal supporters."

Yet another bishop, Jose Cirarda Lachiondo, supported the position of the first three bishops in a statement made on October 9, 1968. He noted that his predecessor, Monti, had consulted with the Holy See and had affirmed that all the events in Garabandal had a natural explanation.

After advocates continued to promote the alleged apparitions and challenged his authority to judge their authenticity, Lachiondo issued a lengthy report to his fellow bishops in 1970. He reported that Bishop Monti had sent the entire file on the apparitions to the Sacred Congregation for the Doctrine of the Faith accompanied by the text of his March 17, 1967, statement.

After examining the file and other documentation, Cardinal Ottaviani, then head of the congregation, had concluded the question had been meticulously examined and settled by the bishop himself. There was no reason for the congregation to intervene. Cirarda Lachiondo said that he himself had twice visited Rome to discuss the matter with the congregation, the Chancery of State and the pope.

Rome, he said, had no desire to intervene and made no declaration. The bishop prohibited all special manifestations of piety at Garabandal and forbade priests to go to the village without special authorization. He said the decree should be motivation enough for all bishops to discourage pilgrimages and exercises in respect to the alleged apparitions.

Obviously there are people who insist the studies were flawed. They continue to maintain the apparitions were genuine. But the position of the church on the matter is clear.

Is Mary the Queen of Heaven written about in the book of Jeremiah? If not, who is?

Depending on the commentary you read, in this context the queen of heaven is the Greek goddess Astarte or the Babylonian goddess Ishtar. Both were names for a fertility goddess. Statues or amulets depicted her as a nude woman. Prostitution was part of her worship. All the members of the family played a part in her cult.

According to one commentary the cakes offered the goddess were star-shaped. According to another the cakes were in the shape of a nude woman. She is called the queen of heaven because she was identified with the planet Venus as the goddess of love.

Did Mary attend Mass after the Resurrection? Did she continue going to the Jewish Temple?

Early in the Acts of the Apostles (2:42) we read: "They [the Jerusalem community] devoted themselves to the apostles' teaching and fellowship to the breaking of the bread and the prayers."

Further, in 1 Corinthians 11:20–33, Paul speaks not only of the institution of the Eucharist but also the faults of those at Corinth in celebrating the Eucharist. It is thus clear that the church of the apostles celebrated the Eucharist. Scripture does not tell us whether Mary participated and received Communion. But it is reasonable to think that she was among

49

those present for the breaking of the bread (what we now call Mass).

It also seems evident from Acts that the early Jewish-Christians continued to go to the Temple for prayer (Acts 3:1; 5:20). It would seem that Mary, too, would have continued to go to the Temple.

Where did we get the Litany of the Blessed Virgin? What do all of those titles mean?

According to the *Dictionary of Mary*, the Litany of the Blessed Virgin has a long history. Many of the praises in the litany came from prayers of the Greek church, in particular the Akathist Hymn, which was to be sung standing out of reverence for the Incarnation. Each of twenty-four strophes (parts of stanzas) began with a succeeding letter of the Greek alphabet and concluded alternately with "Rejoice, O Virgin Spouse" and "Alleluia."

The form of the litany was modeled on the earlier Litany of the Saints. The *Dictionary* speculates that the Litany of the Blessed Virgin originated in Paris. It probably dates from between 1150 and 1200.

The Litany of the Blessed Virgin is sometimes called the Litany of Loreto, because we know it was used at the Shrine of Our Lady of Loreto, as early as 1558. Pope Sixtus V gave approval to the prayer in 1587. Over the years the church added the invocations "Queen conceived without sin" and "Queen assumed into heaven," "Queen of the most holy rosary" and "Queen of peace." In 1980, the Congregation for Sacraments and Divine Worship directed that the invocation "Mother of the Church" be inserted at the proper place.

According to *Our Lady in Catholic Life*, by Lawrence G. Lovasik, in biblical language justice is the perfect observance of God's commandments. Mary was perfectly responsive to the will of God; thus, she is the reflection of God's own holiness. She mirrors the holiness of God. She is the "mirror of justice."

Mary can be called the Seat of Wisdom because wisdom

became incarnate in her son, Jesus, whom she carried in her womb. And she herself possessed and practiced true wisdom in the highest degree.

The rose is regarded as the queen of flowers. Goodness and holiness flower in the saints. Mary, the queen of saints, can be called the Mystical Rose and in her are found the mystical mysteries.

According to Lovasik the "Tower of David" was the strongest tower in the wall of Jerusalem. It was so strong it survived Rome's destruction of the city of Jerusalem. Lovasik sees the church as the new Jerusalem and Mary as the strong point in the church's fight against evil.

"Ivory" is suggestive of peace, wealth and joyous feasting. Wealthy people among the ancients lined their palaces with ivory. Lovasik, then, calls Mary a Tower of Ivory reaching to the heavens as a sign of peace. In her is the wealth of grace that comes from union with God.

Chapters 6 and 7 in 1 Kings described the Temple that Solomon built. The author writes that the entire Temple was overlaid with gold! So, too, the altar and many of the furnishings were of gold (7:48-50). Mary was the temple of God; her womb "housed" the Lord. She is the House of Gold.

The planet Venus is called the morning star because it appears in the eastern sky just before or at sunrise. Mary is the Morning Star that heralds the coming of Jesus, the sun of justice and the dawning of the day of redemption.

In chapters 25 and 40 of Exodus, there is a description of the Ark of the Covenant. It was a symbol of God's presence to Israel. In the ark were placed the commandments of the Law— God's covenant with Israel. Mary was the Ark of the Covenant in the sense that her womb contained the maker of the Law; she made God present to humankind in the incarnation of the Son.

Is it more correct to use *thee* rather than *you* in the Hail Mary?

There really is no theological point involved. There is no *official* translation anywhere. There is no text in the *Enchiridion of Indulgences*. Some prayerbooks use *you* and *your* while others use *thee, thy* and *thou*. It is a matter of personal preference and generational differences, what sounds best to a person's ear and what he or she memorized as a child.

When it comes to the Lord's Prayer, the sacramentary uses *thy* in the first part of the prayer. Our bishops thought that was the way people learned the prayer and they would be most familiar and comfortable with it. Yet in the priest's part and in the doxology following the prayer the sacramentary uses *you* and *your* to address the Father.

The biggest reason for using one over the other *(thee* or *you)* is for unity in public and common prayer.

Did Mary and Joseph divorce?

Verses describing the events before Jesus' birth are read in the Gospels for the Fourth Sunday of Advent (A cycle), the Vigil of Christmas and the feast of Saint Joseph, Husband of Mary (March 19). Saint Matthew tells us in chapter one of his Gospel that while they were betrothed but before they lived together, Mary was "found to be with child from the Holy Spirit. Her husband Joseph, being a righteous man and unwilling to expose her to public disgrace, planned to dismiss her quietly."

A person needs some awareness of the Old Testament law to understand the situation of Joseph in discovering the pregnancy of Mary. By law he was considered the husband of Mary as the result of their betrothal even though he had yet to take her into his home. Deuteronomy directs what is to be done if a betrothed woman has relations with another man. Unless she was raped, she is to be stoned.

The book of Numbers allows a trial by ordeal if a husband suspects adultery but cannot prove it. If, after drinking a mixture of holy water and dust from the floor of the dwelling, the woman miscarried or became sterile, she was guilty. If she remained able to bear children, she was innocent. Whatever happened, the ordeal would be tremendously embarrassing for the woman.

In *The Gospel According to St. Matthew*, Alexander Jones says that at the time of Joseph and Mary it cannot be proved there was a legal duty of denunciation or that Joseph was sacrificing legal scruples in making the choice he did. Joseph was a just, righteous man. He was concerned with doing the right thing. Mary was obviously with child. Knowing Mary, he cannot believe her blameworthy. He can think, says Jones, only of some unknown, perhaps supernatural cause.

He would not subject Mary to some procedure before a village court. He will divorce her quietly—perhaps without offering any specific reason as far as the public is concerned.

Henry Wansbrough, O.S.B., in the *Nelson Commentary on Matthew*, proposes that the word *righteous* means Joseph knew Mary to be guiltless. The motive for divorce was his own sense of unworthiness and wondering how he could fit into God's plan for Mary.

Why do we know so little about the life of Mary?

Most Catholics would like to hear much more about the life of Jesus' mother. The problem is that we really know only what little the Gospel writers have told us. Historians, Scripture scholars and archaeologists try to help us know more about Mary by writing about what the customs of people and nations were like at her time.

Writers of meditations and homilies try to imagine what Mary felt about the things taking place in her life and how she responded to particular graces. But only Scripture provides anything close to what we would consider a firsthand account of Mary's life.

There have been mystics who said they received revelations about the life of Mary, details about her childhood, what she felt and experienced. But they do not always tell the same stories. Their accounts differ and may even conflict. Of course there is always the problem in such accounts that we do not know what came from God and what came from the imagination of the mystic.

A book called *The Life of Mary as Seen by the Mystics* was compiled by Raphael Brown. The mystics referred to are Venerable Mary of Agreda, Venerable Catherine Emmerich, Saint Bridget of Sweden and Saint Elizabeth of Schonau. Their accounts are in harmony with the Gospel stories.

Does Mary have a tomb?

Our Lord has a tomb in the old city of Jerusalem. Of course, the tomb is empty. Christians venerate the tomb as the resting place of Jesus for three days before his glorious Resurrection. Since our Lady may have died before she was assumed "body and soul" into heaven, she, too, may have had a temporary resting place. The faith of the church is that this miracle took place "when the course of her earthly life was completed." The dogmatic definition of Pope Pius XII in 1950 did not resolve the question of whether or not Mary actually died and was buried. Most theologians believe that Mary, like Jesus, did in fact die. Hence, she could have been buried. Tradition says that when Christians came to venerate her remains, the tomb was empty.

Saint Germanus of Constantinople (who died around 743) considered that "it was in keeping not only with her divine motherhood but also with the unique sanctity of her virginal body that it was incorrupt and carried up to heaven."

We do not know for sure where Mary was buried (if she was indeed buried before the Assumption). There are even other locations given for the original burial place of Jesus in Jerusalem. Some Christians may have presumed that Mary's remains were extant somewhere since awareness of her assumption was not *universally* accepted until the early Middle Ages. From then on, the belief that Mary was assumed into heaven "body and soul" was universally believed by both the Eastern and Western church up until the sixteenth century and the Protestant Reformation. Today, most Protestant Christians do not believe that she was assumed. Eastern Orthodox Christians share our Catholic belief but do not accept it as defined dogma.

Why do some statues show Mary stepping on a snake?

Around 1830 Saint Catherine Laboure received a vision of the Blessed Virgin and was told to have a medal struck. On the front of the medal was to be the figure of Mary standing atop a globe representing the earth; she was to be shown crushing the head of a serpent with her feet.

From Mary's hands were to appear rays of light representing grace. Around the rim of the medal were to be the words, "O Mary conceived without sin, pray for us who have recourse to thee." On the reverse side of the medal would be a cross surmounting the letter *M* and the sacred hearts of Jesus and Mary. The medal was made and because of the miracles associated with it has come to be known as the Miraculous Medal.

In catalogs of religious articles there are statues called Our Lady of Grace. They picture Mary standing on a globe with a serpent beneath her feet, similar to her representation on the Miraculous Medal.

These statues (and the Miraculous Medal) associate Mary with the woman in chapter 3 of Genesis and the woman clothed with the sun in chapter 12 of Revelation. Genesis 3:14–16 contains the words of God condemning the serpent for leading Adam and Eve into sin. There God pronounces he will "put enmity between you and the woman and your offspring and hers. He will strike at your head while you strike at his heel."

Chapter 12 of Revelation speaks of the woman clothed with the sun whose son the dragon seeks to devour. In both instances the serpent or snake represents the devil and evil. Both passages are applied to Mary as the woman whose offspring will conquer Satan.

Does Matthew's Gospel support or challenge Mary's virginity?

Any number of commentaries will throw light on the verses 18–25 of the first chapter of Matthew, particularly the meaning of the word until in Matthew 1:25: "but had no marital relations with her until she had borne a son; and he named him Jesus."

Perhaps the most important thing to keep in mind is that the original text of Matthew was written in Greek and the author came from a Semitic background. Any English translation merely attempts to convey what the author meant in the original language.

Analyzing Matthew 1:25, in *The Gospel According to Matthew*, Alexander Jones writes,

> Matthew makes this statement of the period which directly concerns him, his purpose being to safeguard the virginal nature of the conception and birth of Jesus. Of the period following the birth he says nothing. His sentence would best be paraphrased: She brought forth a son without having relations with Joseph. The Semitic turn of phrase, "not...until," while denying the action for the period preceding the verb borne, implies nothing for the period which follows it: c.f. Genesis 8:7, 1 Timothy 4:13, etc.

Raymond Brown, S.S., says much the same thing in *The Birth of the Messiah*. Brown notes that to understand this passage we must look at the verse in its immediate context and the context of the whole Gospel. Matthew's immediate concern is to stress Mary's virginity before the child's birth and the fulfillment of the Isaian prophecy.

And, he says, in English when something is negated until a particular time, occurrence after that time is usually assumed. But in Greek and Semitic, "such a negation often has no indication at all about what happened after the limit of the 'until' was reached."

Why doesn't Mary appear to Protestants?

God can reveal or manifest himself to anyone he chooses in any way he chooses. He can call anyone he wishes to be his instrument. God spoke to Moses in the burning bush. God called and directed Abraham through heavenly messengers. Isaiah was given a vision of an angel touching his lips with a fiery coal and a message from heaven.

To Saint Margaret Mary Alacoque, God revealed himself and his messages in a vision of the Sacred Heart of Jesus. To Francis of Assisi, Jesus spoke from the cross. Later, in a vision of a seraph (angel), Francis received the stigmata—the wounds of Jesus. In later days we believe that God has used his Blessed Mother to call people to conversion and penance through appearances to Saint Bernadette, the children of Fatima and Blessed Juan Diego.

God can reveal himself to believer or unbeliever as suits his purpose. But it does seem more likely that God would choose a person predisposed to accept and act on such a revelation.

Father Adolphe Tanquerey, in his book *The Spiritual Life*, says that invariably God makes revelations only to those who are already fervent and have already been raised to the mystic state. God usually seems to choose simple, humble and childlike people for his revelations. Perhaps that is because they are more ready to believe and act on what God asks of them. Any vision or apparition is a demand of faith.

Finally, it would be reasonable to suppose that in making a revelation, God would do it in a way that fits the subject's religious background and mind-set. God would make use of the culture in which the person has been spiritually formed and nourished and would use images and symbols that already have meaning for the subject of the revelation. A Catholic, then, would be more likely than others to accept the Blessed Mother as God's agent of revelation.

What is the basis for honoring Mary as Queen of Heaven?

The queenship of Mary is associated or linked with the king-ship of Christ her son. She is the "Queen Mother."

In 1954 Pope Pius XII established the feast of the Queenship of Mary. But as one of the mysteries of the rosary, the coronation (queenship) of Mary goes back at least to the fifteenth century and perhaps to Saint Bonaventure's Marian Psalter in the thirteenth century.

Before that the *Salve Regina* (Hail, Holy Queen) was com-posed by Herman Contractus in the eleventh century. Often recited with the rosary, it is one of the four breviary anthems of Mary.

In establishing the feast of the Queenship of Mary in the encyclical *Ad Caeli Reginam*, Pius XII found its roots in the words of the angel Gabriel predicting that the son of Mary would reign forever (Luke 1:32–33) and the words of Elizabeth who saluted Mary as "the mother of my Lord" (Luke 1:43). He also drew on the fathers of the church such as Saint Ephrem and argued for Mary's queenship theologically from her di-vine parenthood.

Why does the second sorrowful mystery mention a pillar?

Though it is true that no pillar is mentioned in the scriptural accounts of Jesus' scourging, there is one attached to the sec-ond sorrowful mystery in the *Enchiridion of Indulgences*. The mystery is listed this way on the presumption that Jesus was scourged at a pillar, which is not unreasonable given the prac-tice of the time.

Ferdinand Prat, S.J., in *Jesus Christ: His Life, His Teaching, and His Work*, describes the Roman punishment of scourging:

> The sufferer, despoiled of his clothes, was bound by the hands to a low column, and was kept from moving out of the bending position, so that all the strokes might reach their mark, and that the executioner might wield them with greater force.

One source says such a column was a little higher than two feet. *Jesus and His Times*, edited by Kaari Ward, quotes Cicero as having said scourging was the most cruel and hideous of punishments. In Palestine it was reserved for criminals without Roman citizenship—usually revolutionaries, delinquent slaves or the most barbarous offenders.

After telling us that scourging was perhaps invented by the Persians and spread in the Middle East by Alexander the Great, the entry on scourging says it was refined by the Romans to produce a very slow and extremely painful death. It was administered with a short leather whip tipped with lead balls and bits of sharp sheep bone, after the condemned was stripped and bound to a post.

Jesus and His Times notes that the object of scourging was to produce so much loss of blood, pain and circulatory shock that the victim would be near death. The historian Josephus is cited as writing that some Jews had been torn to pieces by the scourge before they were crucified.

How could Saint Joseph teach Jesus?

How much did Jesus know about what was to happen to him, and how much and what kind of knowledge did he have in general? Jesus was both divine and human. In him were united the divine and human natures. How much of the divine knowledge was in his human awareness? How conscious was he of his divinity at different points in his life?

Theologians have come up with different answers to that last question.

All would agree, however, that Jesus had to acquire what is called experiential knowledge. An infant may learn from his mother that a burning match is hot. But the child acquires a different kind of knowledge of that match burning if he sticks his finger in the flame. Now that child has experiential knowledge, knowledge that comes from the senses. Similarly, we may read how to build a birdhouse. But we learn how to build a birdhouse by doing it.

We can certainly speak of Saint Joseph and the Blessed

Mother *teaching* Jesus to do things, helping him acquire, in the very least, experiential knowledge. Being truly *human* as well as divine, he did acquire human knowledge in a human way. The first teachers for all of us are our parents and guardians.

In his human nature Jesus could and did experience parental love in Joseph and Mary. He could learn from them and the rabbis (as appears to be the case when he was discovered in the Temple as an adolescent) about the sacred Hebrew writings and the law of his people. He could certainly learn in an experiential way what it means to be just, to love and care for the poor, from Joseph and Mary. It hardly seems reasonable to believe that as an infant lying in the crib he had complete human awareness (the awareness of a full-grown person) or the human knowledge that he could have as a thirty-three-year-old man at the time of his death.

Part of human development is becoming able to think and reason for ourselves; we develop mentally as well as physically. We become able to learn by ourselves. We learn to plan and imagine new things.

Inventive and imaginative people, such as Edison and Ford, gave us the electric lightbulb and the gasoline-powered automobile. Who taught Edison to invent the lightbulb? Who taught Ford to give us the automobile?

In a *sense* we could say that all those who taught them and helped them develop their mental abilities taught them to give us these things. But their actual discoveries or inventions were their own. No one showed Edison how to make an electric bulb that worked.

Similarly, no one "taught" Jesus to do the things only he could do, such as giving us the Eucharist. Though surely aware of the symbolic potential of bread (manna in the desert, etc.) from Hebrew Scriptures, Jesus himself conceived the "idea" of the Eucharist. Jesus himself established this marvelous and wonderful way of showing his love for us.

When did devotion to Mary begin?

There is a wealth of information on devotion to the Blessed Virgin in the *Dictionary of Mary* and in the *New Catholic Encyclopedia*. Both locate the roots of devotion to Mary in the Scriptures themselves and the accounts of the Nativity, the wedding at Cana and the Passion narratives.

According to the *Dictionary of Mary*, excavations at the site of the Basilica of the Annunciation in Nazareth brought to the surface some thirty inscriptions and graffiti in Greek, Hebrew, Aramaic, Syriac and Armenian that give "sure proof" that the Jewish Christians of Palestine believed in the divinity of Christ before the Council of Nicaea and practiced devotion to the martyrs and to Mary as early as the third century.

The same source speaks of inscriptions and graffiti under Saint Peter's Basilica going back to the second or third century and portraying Mary as a protector for the faithful departed and their mediatrix with Christ. In the catacombs of Saint Priscilla, there are frescoes with that same theme.

Second-century baptismal creeds mention Mary as the mother of Jesus; he was "born of the Holy Spirit and the Virgin Mary." A eucharistic prayer from the same century mentions her as well.

Saint Athanasius, who died in 373, proposed Mary as an example to dedicated virgins. At about the same time Saint Ambrose devoted a series of writings to Mary as a model of virgins.

The bishops of the United States in their pastoral letter of 1973, *Behold Your Mother,* say that devotion to Mary began to grow wondrously with the Council of Ephesus. At this council in 431 the church affirmed its belief and doctrine that Mary is the mother of God. In the years after, Pope Sixtus III rebuilt the Basilica of Saint Mary Major in Rome to commemorate this declaration. The earliest or original form of the prayer "We fly to thy patronage, O Holy Mother of God" may come from the Ephesus period.

Certainly from the fifth century, liturgical feasts of Mary were celebrated. The first seems to have been a "remembrance of Mary" as part of the Christmas season. Later came feasts of the Annunciation, Assumption and others.

In the seventh century the Marian antiphon *"Ave Maris Stella"* was written, followed by a stream of hymns and antiphons through the centuries.

During the tenth century the Little Office of the Blessed Virgin Mary appeared, Saturdays were devoted to Mary and the title Mother of Mercy spread through the West.

The eleventh century witnessed the beginning of the Cathedral of Notre Dame de Chartres, the composition of the Hail, Holy Queen and the *Alma Redemptoris Mater*. Just before the time of Saint Francis and Saint Dominic, the Litany of the Blessed Virgin was shaped and the first half of the Hail Mary was used in prayer. Saint Bernard of Clairvaux preached a spirituality centered around Mary. In 1163 the Cathedral of Notre Dame of Paris was begun.

In the thirteenth century the scapular was presented to Saint Simon Stock, Duns Scotus defended the doctrine of the Immaculate Conception and the month of May was first dedicated to Mary.

The fifteenth century saw the writing of the *Memorare*, Thomas á Kempis urged recourse to Mary in the spiritual life, a feast of the Sorrows of Mary was established, the rosary was approved by Pope Alexander VI, Michelangelo carved the Pieta, and the *Salve Regina* was the first prayer recited in the New World by Columbus and his crew.

The Blessed Virgin appeared to Juan Diego at Guadalupe in 1531, and in 1543 Martin Luther affirmed the Immaculate Conception.

With the next centuries came more Marian feasts and writings. In 1830 the Miraculous Medal was struck in response to a vision given Saint Catherine Laboure. In 1858 Our Lady appeared to Saint Bernadette, and in 1917, to the children at Fatima. In 1921 the Legion of Mary was founded. The dogma of Mary's assumption was proclaimed and a Marian Year observed in 1950.

Why did devotion to Mary begin? The first followers of Jesus, and those who came after them, reflecting on her role in the life of Jesus and the Scriptures, probably at least intuitively saw Mary as an intercessor with her son and the Father, the first disciple and the model for all who would follow Christ—the same reasons we honor Mary.

How can a person determine what is private revelation and what is self-delusion?

Prayer is all about talking to God and asking God to "talk" to us. It is not unusual, in the quiet of this experience, to sense or feel God encouraging us like a friend, speaking to us in moments of discouragement, talking to us of the things that are important to us. This experience is comforting and brings us peace, and should be accepted as a kind of grace from God. This is a time when we are receptive to what God asks of us. It is a time when we discover God calling us to greater holiness and fidelity to our roles and responsibilities in life.

However, if someone hears loud voices, sees startling things and is given messages demanding unusual things, questions should be asked about that person's emotional state. It is important to examine the *kinds* of things that are being heard, particularly whether they are in keeping with the Scriptures and what the church teaches. Sound counsel should be sought from a spiritual director in such a case, and often other professional help is warranted and recommended.

Remember, though, we cannot make our Christian lives depend on extraordinary signs. Many of our greatest saints have experienced "arid" times in their prayer lives, and many holy people have been very close to our Lord without claiming any special sort of "private revelation." God has publicly revealed all that is necessary for our salvation; we must be content with (and grateful for) that.

What are the seven sorrows of Mary?

The seven sorrows are (1) the prophecy of Simeon, (2) the flight into Egypt, (3) the loss of the child Jesus in the Temple, (4) Mary meets Jesus on the Way of the Cross, (5) the crucifixion of Jesus, (6) Mary receives the body of Jesus taken down from the cross and (7) the burial of Jesus.

There is a rosary of the seven sorrows of Mary—three beads and a crucifix with seven groups of seven beads. You pray this rosary by beginning with three Hail Marys in memory of the tears Mary shed because of Jesus' suffering, praying to obtain the true sorrow for your sins. Then you say the Hail Mary on each of the groups of beads while recalling the sorrows of Mary.

The rosary concludes with the versicle, "Pray for us, O most sorrowful Virgin," and the response, "That we may be made worthy of the promises of Christ."

Did Mary experience the pangs of childbirth?

Because the church teaches as a matter of faith that Mary was conceived without sin and Genesis depicts the pain of childbirth as a consequence of original sin, some people conclude that Mary did not experience pain in giving birth to Jesus. Some will also argue that Mary did not die before her assumption into heaven because death is seen as the result of original sin.

The church makes no doctrinal pronouncement on these matters. Pope Pius XII carefully avoided any statement about whether Mary died or not when he proclaimed the doctrine of Mary's assumption into heaven.

At the same time many argue that if Jesus was not exempt from death and pain and suffering, it was appropriate that Mary also be subject to pain and death. That would also be appropriate if we human beings are to identify with Mary as the first and model disciple of Jesus. Dr. Ludwig Ott, in *Fundamentals of Catholic Dogma*, gives it as the more common opinion that Mary did indeed die.

Can a church have more than one statue of the Blessed Mother?

The recently released document on art, architecture and worship, *Built of Living Stones*, states in 136:

The placement of images can be a challenge, especially when a number of cultural traditions are part of a single parish community and each has its own devotional life and practices. Restraint in the number and prominence of sacred images [cf. Vatican II's Document on the Liturgy #125] is encouraged to help people focus on the liturgical action that is celebrated in the church.

Volumes could be written about how many statues are too many, what kind of art is in good taste and how the devotions and traditions in a particular parish should be respected.

The feelings and devotion of all should be considered in a case where parishioners disagree on a choice of statues, or where a second has been donated. Perhaps the original statue could be put in a church or school hall. Or it might be placed in an outdoor shrine if it is especially dear to many parishioners.

What is meant when Mary is called Co-Redemptrix? Is this the teaching of the church?

According to the *Dictionary of Mary*, the title for Mary, Co-Redemptrix, has been used by some within the church since the fourteenth century.

However, as the U.S. Catholic bishops pointed out in the pastoral letter *Behold Your Mother: Woman of Faith*, Co-Redemptrix, like Dispensatrix of Graces, was a title altogether avoided by the Second Vatican Council.

Properly understood, Marian titles such as Mediatrix or Dispensatrix of Graces and Co-Redemptrix find their justification in Mary's cooperation in the saving and redeeming work of Jesus—on her act of faith and *fiat* ("let it be done to me according to your word").

She is the mediatrix in that the incarnate, redeeming Son of God is born of and comes to us through Mary. She may be spoken of as co-redemptrix because of her role in the Incarnation and her participation in the sufferings of Christ at the foot of the cross.

Yet, as the German bishops in their *The Church's Confession* of Faith: A Catholic Catechism for Adults and others point out, the use of such titles should not obscure the fact that our salvation and grace are completely and entirely dependent on Christ. The use of such titles for Mary should not be taken to suggest that Christ's act of redemption was not completely and entirely sufficient in itself for our salvation. Mary's role in our redemption is completely secondary to and dependent on Jesus' act.

Why do we know so little about Saint Joseph?

It is a fact that our knowledge about Saint Joseph is limited. But that is true of many other holy people in the New Testament—including the Blessed Virgin. Even our knowledge of Jesus' life—especially the years before his baptism by John—is "limited."

The reason for this is that no evangelist sat down to write a life of Jesus. The Gospel writers did not intend to write biographies of Jesus.

Matthew and Luke do speak of the events concerning the birth of Jesus and the finding of the child Jesus in the Temple. But then they leap forward to the preaching of John the Baptist in the desert and the baptism of Jesus at the Jordan. Mark says nothing of Jesus' childhood but begins with John the Baptist preaching. John, after his theological prologue, also begins with the Baptist's appearance and preaching.

This is not because the evangelists wished to trivialize the early years of Jesus or counted Mary and Joseph as of no real importance. The Gospel writers were concerned with the *meaning* of Jesus—especially his meaning for the churches for which they were writing many years after his death and Resurrection: What did Jesus say and teach? How did that apply now? They wanted to show that Jesus fulfilled the prophecies, that he was the Savior, the Messiah, the awaited one. They wanted to show that Christians are redeemed by Jesus, that they are called to share in his death and Resurrection. They wanted to recall what Jesus said and taught about prayer and living in the love of God.

Few details are given about any of the apostles or disciples of Jesus. Our knowledge of any of those who were near and close to Jesus is only fragmentary. These Gospels are, after all, rather brief accounts of what Jesus said and did.

Joseph's role in the life of Jesus and God's plan is finished before the public life of Jesus begins. He vanishes from the accounts of Matthew and Luke rather quickly. He is barely mentioned in Mark and John. That does not mean that the evangelists wished to trivialize or count Joseph as of no importance. Neither does the church. Nor should Christians.

Joseph has been declared patron of the universal church, a model for fathers of families, protector of workers, patron of social justice. Pope Leo XIII declared that Joseph's preeminent sanctity places him next to the Blessed Virgin among the saints. The church recognizes and grants indulgences for a litany in honor of Saint Joseph. We celebrate the feasts of the Holy Family, Joseph the Husband of Mary and Joseph the Worker. Pope Paul VI added the name of Joseph to the Eucharistic Prayer.

As recently as August 15, 1989, Pope John Paul II issued an *Apostolic Exhortation on the Person and Mission of Saint Joseph in the Life of Christ and of the Church* in which he reflects for us on (1) the Gospel portrait of Joseph, (2) Joseph as the guardian of the mystery of God, (3) the just man and husband, (4) work as an expression of love, (5) the primacy of the interior life and (6) Joseph as the patron of the church in our day.

Some other references you might be interested in include *Joseph the Just Man*, by Rosalie Marie Levy; *Joseph: The Man Closest to Jesus*, by Francis Filas, S.J.; and *Discovering Saint Joseph*, by Andrew Doze.

What is the significance of the twelve stars on Mary's crown or around her head in pictures or on statues?

The stars find their source in the vision of John in the book of Revelation. There John tells us,

A great portent appeared in heaven: a woman clothed with the sun, with the moon under her feet, and on her head a crown of twelve stars. She was pregnant and was crying out in birth pangs, in the agony of giving birth. (Revelation 12:1–2)

Later in that chapter John relates that this woman gives birth to a son destined to rule all the nations and the son is caught up to God and his throne. The woman is at enmity with and pursued by a huge red dragon who, we are told, is Satan or the devil. While the woman flees to a safe place in the desert prepared for her by God, the dragon and its angels wage war against Michael and his angels in heaven. Cast down to earth, the dragon, called the ancient serpent, pursues the woman, who escapes him. So he wages war against her offspring.

As you can see, this vision is filled with symbols. It appears that John intended his readers to see in the woman clothed with the sun the people of Israel or the new people of God. The twelve stars are one indication of that. They can be taken as representing the twelve constellations of the zodiac. But they can also be seen as symbols of the twelve tribes of Israel and the twelve apostles.

At least on a second level, or in an applied sense, Christians have also seen our Blessed Lady in the woman of Revelation. The reason should be evident. The woman finds herself in a struggle with Satan. Satan is defeated by the blood of the Lamb—the son to whom she gives birth. The woman in Revelation certainly recalls the words of God speaking to the serpent in Genesis:

I will put enmity between you and the woman,
and between your offspring and hers;
he will strike your head,
and you will strike his heel. (3:15)

Christians have also long seen Mary in this woman in Genesis.

As a result Mary is often spoken of as the "woman clothed with the sun." Artists or sculptors depict her crushing the head of a serpent and standing on the moon with her head surrounded by or crowned by stars.

How do we know of Mary's parents, Anne and Joachim?

The Bible does not tell us much about the life of Mary or her ancestry. Since Matthew and Luke trace the genealogy of Jesus through Joseph, his foster father, they do not mention the parents and forebears of Mary. Nor does any other biblical source. Father Leonard Foley's *Saint of the Day* informs us:

> In the Scriptures, Matthew and Luke furnish a legal family history of Jesus, tracing ancestry to show that Jesus is the culmination of great promises. Not only is his mother's side neglected, we also know nothing factual about them except that they existed. Even the names Joachim and Anne come from a legendary source [the *Protoevangelium of Saint James*] written more than a century after Jesus died.
>
> ...Whether we rely on the legends about Mary's childhood or make guesses from the information in the Bible, we see in her a fulfillment of many generations of prayerful persons, herself steeped in the religious traditions of her people....
>
> Joachim and Anne—whether these are their real names or not—represent that entire quiet series of generations who faithfully perform their duties, practice their faith and establish an atmosphere for the coming of the Messiah, but remain obscure.

The parents of Mary were like so many good, loving and heroic parents today who go faithfully about their work and life task of raising families in the Lord. They received little attention or fame—not even an Old Testament mention. Yet they were great in virtue and grace, holy and loved by God.

Who chose the mysteries of the rosary? Are others possible?

In their November 21, 1973, pastoral letter on the Blessed Virgin Mary, *Behold Your Mother: Woman of Faith,* the U.S. National Conference of Catholic Bishops commented on the rosary. They reminded us that the rosary is more than a matter of racing through a string of familiar prayers, and they spoke of the importance of reflecting on the mysteries. They also wrote:

> Besides the precise rosary pattern long known to Catholics, we can freely experiment. New sets of mysteries are possible. We have customarily gone from the childhood of Jesus to his passion, bypassing the whole public life. There is rich matter here for rosary meditation, such as the wedding feast at Cana, and incidents from the public life where Mary's presence and Mary's name serve as occasions for her son to give us a lesson in discipleship.... Rosary vigils have already been introduced in some places with an instructive use of readings from Old Testament as well as New, and with a recitation of a decade or two, if not all five, in a public celebration of the rosary, hymns can be introduced as well, and time periods of silent prayer.

Why have more people not taken the liberty of experimenting with different mysteries and styles of rosary recitation? People do not easily change their habits of prayer. The familiar and accustomed bring comfort and ease us into prayer. Most prayer books or leaflets, moreover, and the *Enchiridion of Indulgences* itself, continue to simply list the traditional fifteen joyful, sorrowful and glorious mysteries of the rosary.

But some people took up the bishops' encouragement to experiment with the rosary. Walter Kern in his 1979 *New Liturgy and Old Devotions*, suggests mysteries for each day of the week. Besides the traditional joyful, sorrowful and glorious mysteries, expressed in Scripture quotes, he offers doctrinal, Genesis, preparation for the redeemer and final mysteries (such as "Jesus will judge the living and the dead"). Joanne Turpin wrote *The Healing Mysteries: A Rosary for the Sick*, which lists mysteries such as the healing of the crippled man at the pool of Bethesda, the healing of the woman with an infirmity of the spirit, the healing of the paralytic at Capernaum, the healing of the woman suffering from hemorrhage and the healing of the blind man at Jericho.

Certainly, any prayerful meditation on the many mysteries of the lives of Jesus and Mary is possible and positive.

What is the hospital rosary?

There is no mention of it in the *Enchiridion of Indulgences*. However, in the past special provisions were made for those who were sick and obliged to pray the Divine Office or Liturgy of the Hours. For the whole office they could substitute a certain number of psalms—in other words, say a kind of abbreviated office because they did not have much strength or were unable to concentrate very long. Franciscan priests have long had the privilege of substituting the lay brothers' office (now fifty-five Our Fathers) for the Liturgy of the Hours for a just reason.

The hospital rosary might be a way of praying in the spirit of the rosary when you are ill or otherwise unable to pray the whole rosary or even five decades of the rosary.

In order to obtain the indulgences attached to praying the rosary in church or in a family group or as a religious community or pious association, or any of the other indulgences, you must pray continuously at least five decades of the rosary. Further, to obtain the indulgences for group recitation, vocal prayer must be accompanied by meditation of the mysteries, which must be announced in the manner customary in the place.

How does the church square the rosary with the Gospel exhortation not to "multiply words"?

In their 1973 pastoral letter *Behold Your Mother*, the bishops of the United States wrote that it is unwise to reject the rosary without first trying to pray it "simply because of the accusation that it comes from the past, that it is repetitive and ill-suited to sophisticated moderns." They pointed to the scriptural riches of the rosary and the fact that its prayers are part of the mainstream going back to the early centuries of Christian devotion.

Speaking to the particular point of "multiplying words," the bishops stated:

The recommended saying of the rosary does not consist merely in "telling the beads" by racing through a string of familiar prayers. Interwoven with the prayers are the "mysteries." Almost all of these are related to saving events in the life of Jesus, episodes in which the mother of Jesus shared. Nor is rhythmic prayer alien to modern man, as is shown by the attraction of Eastern religions for many young people today.

The bishops concluded by suggesting ways of combining scriptural reading from both Old and New Testaments, hymns and periods of silent prayer with the saying of the beads.

The point in all of this is, of course, that the rosary should never be a simple parroting of words and phrases or mindless verbal rattling, nor should any prayer be. As the king in *Hamlet* says of his own distracted prayer, "Words without thoughts never to heaven go." But the very rhythm and gentle flow of the rosary can help us relax and fasten our minds on the Lord.

What is the third "secret" of Fatima?

There is an excellent book on Fatima, though now somewhat dated, titled *The Sun Danced at Fatima*, by Joseph Pelletier, A.A. While it was published without an imprimatur, it contains a laudatory preface by Bishop John Wright.

According to Father Pelletier, it was on July 13, 1917, that the most startling revelations took place. The contents of that apparition he divides into three parts: Part I—a vision of hell; Part II—a prediction of World War II and that the world would be punished with famine and persecution of the church and pope, a request for the consecration of Russia to the Immaculate Heart of Mary and for communions of reparation, and promises about Russia's conversion and world peace; Part III—unknown.

Father Pelletier goes on to say that the first two parts of the apparition were put into writing by Sister Lucia in her memoirs (1937 and 1941) and given to the bishop of Leira, Jose Alves Correia da Silva. Only in 1942 were these first two parts revealed by Cardinal Schuster.

Late in 1943 or early in 1944, Sister Lucia put the third part into writing. What she wrote was given in a sealed envelope to the bishop of Leira on June 17, 1944. The bishop took this envelope and put it unopened into another larger envelope, which he sealed. Sister Lucia and the bishop agreed that the secret would be opened either upon her death or in 1960—whichever came earlier—and communicated to the world.

Before Bishop Correia died on December 4, 1957, the Sacred Congregation for the Doctrine of the Faith asked for photocopies of all the Fatima writings of Sister Lucia. The bishop decided not to open and photocopy the letter in the sealed envelope. Instead he sent it to the congregation through the papal nuncio.

Drawing on the research of Father Joaquin Maria Alonso, Pelletier says that Pope Pius XII did not open and read the secret. However, in 1960 Pope John XXIII did open and read the letter in the presence of Cardinal Ottaviani, who also was allowed to read it. The letter was again sealed and sent to the secret archives of the Vatican. Pelletier says it is not certain that Pope Paul VI read the secret, but Alonso says he probably did.

As Pelletier observes, "the wildest rumors" have circulated about what Sister Lucia wrote. But he says that Cardinal Ottaviani stated all the things that circulate are fantasy.

Why did Pope John XXIII decide not to publish what was in the letter? Only Pope John could answer that question, and it does not seem that he gave his reasons to anyone. He evidently thought it would not be beneficial or wise to comment on or to reveal what Sister Lucia wrote.

On May 13, 2000, at the beatification Mass of Francisco and Jacinta Marto, the other two Fatima visionaries, Pope John Paul II ordered the publication of the so-called third secret of Fatima. Cardinal Angelo Sodano, Vatican Secretary of State, said that the third part concerned "the war waged by atheist systems against the Church and Christians" and also made reference to the ministry and suffering of a "bishop clothed in white" going so far as to say this person "falls to the ground, apparently dead under a burst of gunfire."

The Vatican has interpreted this message in light of the assassination attempt on Pope John Paul II's life in St. Peter's Square May 13, 1981. In conversations with the Vatican and pope, Sister Lucia, the surviving visionary, has confirmed this interpretation.

It is important to remember, though, that we are talking here of *private* revelation. As the *Catechism of the Catholic Church* explains:

> Throughout the ages, there have been so-called private revelations, some of which have been recognized by the authority of the church. They do not belong, however, to the deposit of faith. It is not their role to improve or complete Christ's definitive revelation, but to help live more fully by it in a certain period in history. (67)

$\dagger$

CATHOLIC BELIEFS AND PRACTICES

In the beginning of the fourth century, a violent persecution came to the church in Africa. Civil authorities there did not want Christians just to denounce their faith, but to turn in their sacred texts, the Scriptures, as well. Without them, it was reasoned, they would lose a key resource for practicing their faith. In the face of torture and imprisonment, though, many remained firm and were given the name "confessors." Others, however, were not so strong. Some, including bishops and priests, wanting to avoid further bloodshed and loss of life, gave the Scriptures over to authorities. They were given the name of traditors "one who handed over." From that word we get "traitor." The Latin word traditio gives us another word. It means the same thing but strikes the ears much more positively—tradition. It is our lifeblood. It is what we breathe. Through the special prerogative of the magisterium, it is the vocation of all Christians. But just what is tradition?

Tradition has two principal parts: content and process. Content refers to the teachings and practices that have been handed over or passed down through successive generations of believers. The content of tradition can be seen either as essential (tradition with a capital T, which can't be changed) or

nonessential (lowercase t—it can be changed for good reason).
Process refers to the way in which tradition has been handed over.
The process of tradition takes two forms: oral *and* written. *Oral is*
the most ancient form and consists of teachings passed on through
the spoken word. Eventually the spoken word is collected and, for
preservation, is written down, becoming written tradition, or
Scripture.

Speaking of tradition, the Catechism of the Catholic
Church *quotes Saint Irenaeus (circa* A.D. *130–200), a man who*
saw it as his duty to defend the tradition of the faith as an
apologist and bishop. He writes:

> *Indeed, the Church, though scattered throughout the whole*
> *world, even to the ends of the earth, having received the faith*
> *from the apostles and their disciples...guards [this preaching*
> *and faith] with care, as dwelling in but a single house, and*
> *similarly believes as if having one soul and a single heart, and*
> *preaches, teaches, and hands on this faith with a unanimous*
> *voice, as if possessing only one mouth. (173)*

It is our responsibility, it is our privilege.

•

Why is there so much controversy in the church today?

Obviously, there is controversy and dissent in the church, particularly in the wake of Vatican II. Some confusion might have
been avoided by better planning and instruction to prepare
people for the liturgical changes of the Second Vatican
Council. And more adult education would have made for a
better understanding of the teaching that emerged from the
council.

But confusion and controversy have been part of the life
of the church since its founding by Christ. The church has
never lived in a historical vacuum. It has always been affected
by the time and state of history.

There was disagreement between Peter and Paul. Strain
existed in the early Christian community because of the influx
of Gentiles that resulted from the missionary efforts of Paul.

The "Council" of Jerusalem gathered to resolve the issues of whether Gentiles had to be circumcised and observe Jewish dietary laws.

The Gospels and Epistles of John were written, in part, to deal with theological disagreements within the church.

With the political division of the Roman Empire in the East and West came struggles over authority in the church and questions about the primacy of the bishop of Rome. Violent disagreements over whether Christ was truly man or truly God, how the Holy Spirit proceeds from the Father and Son, and whether Mary can be called the Mother of God occasioned many church councils to define the belief of the church.

When the migration of nations took place and uncultured, half-civilized tribes cut a bloody and violent way through Europe, church institutions and lives faced destruction.

Well-intentioned reformers threw the church into inner chaos by electing new popes while the chair of Peter was already occupied. Good Christians agonized over which of three claimants to the papacy was the legitimate successor to Peter and which were antipopes.

Inner corruption gave rise to the Protestant Reformation and the demand for spiritual change with further political division and conflicts between Christians.

Just as any country is affected by political movements, war, modern inventions, scientific discoveries, technical advances and natural catastrophes, so are the people of God, the church. Often it takes time to adapt to the needs and circumstances of the moment, to recognize what the problems are and organize effectively to cope with them.

The church now finds itself in the midst of tremendous change in the world. There are ideological clashes between East and West (sound familiar?), Christians and Muslims, and a struggle between political and economic systems. Developing nations demand a greater share of the wealth and the goods of the world. Within nations the poor and those lacking power are seeking greater control of their own lives and more of their nations' material benefits.

In our country values are changing. Attitudes about sex

and marriage are in flux. Economic and social shifts have altered family and married life, relations between men and women, between bosses and workers, unions and employers in society and the workplace. Technology has transformed the media of communication and entertainment. Events are reported instantly. New theories, discoveries, ideas and opinions gain instant attention everywhere.

Medicine, with its new discoveries and methods of treatment, has opened up all kinds of possibilities—and given rise to questions of morality never before contemplated.

If we experience confusion in other areas of life, should it surprise us if we find even considerable confusion and disagreement within the church concerning religious issues affected by the same climate and changes?

The important thing is to believe and trust that Christ is with his people, that the Spirit of God is present and acts in us to help us find our way through the confusion. We have the Gospel and a large body of truth handed down to us to apply to life as we find it today. The church, with the help and grace of God, has come through periods of terrible stress and upheaval before. Despite such periods, it has been a source of strength and comfort to its people.

These are not the worst of times; the church of God is not about to collapse. These are days that test us as Christians and Catholics. We need to act together as a community of believers where love unites us in a common, respectful search for truth, to meet the challenges of our times.

What is the church's teaching on indulgences?

Pope Paul VI, in 1968, in the wake of Vatican II, did authorize new norms and a handbook, the *Enchiridion of Indulgences*.

All general grants and ordinances concerning indulgences that were not included in the new *Enchiridion* were revoked by Paul VI's action. Echoing the words of Paul VI and canon law, the *Catechism of the Catholic Church* defines indulgences as follows:

"An indulgence is a remission before God of the temporal punishment due to sins whose guilt has already been forgiven, which the faithful Christian who is duly disposed gains under certain prescribed conditions through the action of the church which, as the minister of redemption, dispenses and applies with authority the treasury of the satisfactions of Christ and the saints."

"An indulgence is partial or plenary according as it removes either part or all of the temporal punishment due to sin." Indulgences may be applied to the living or the dead. (1471, quoting *Indulgentiarum doctrina*, Norm 1; Norm 2; cf. Norm 3)

The power of the pope to grant indulgences rests on the power of the keys—the power given him by Jesus to bind and loose.

In granting indulgences the pope draws on the treasury of the church—the superabundant merits of Jesus and the merits of the communion of saints.

The *Enchiridion* established three *general* grants followed by other grants attached to particular pious works or prayers. General grants of partial indulgences are made (1) for those who raise their minds to God with humble confidence in the performance of their duties and in bearing the trials of life and add some pious invocation; (2) to the faithful who give of themselves or their goods in the spirit of faith and mercy to serve their brothers and sisters in need; and (3) to the faithful who, in the spirit of penance, voluntarily deprive themselves of what is licit and pleasing to them.

These general grants are followed by others attached to particular prayers and acts, such as reading the Scriptures, adoration of the Blessed Sacrament and prayer before a crucifix.

Indulgences obtained under the norms before Pope Paul VI's new norms remain valid. But now you can obtain indulgences only under the new norms.

Can non-Christians go to heaven?

In the *Dogmatic Constitution on the Church* (#16), the Vatican II Council fathers wrote:

> Those who have not yet received the gospel are related to the People of God in various ways. There is, first, that people to which the covenants and promises were made, and from which Christ was born according to the flesh (cf. Romans 9:4–5): In view of the divine choice, they are a people most dear for the sake of the fathers, for the gifts of God are without repentance (cf. Romans 11:28–29).
>
> But the plan of salvation also includes those who acknowledge the Creator, in the first place amongst whom are the Muslims: They profess to hold the faith of Abraham, and together with us they adore the one, merciful God, mankind's judge on the last day.
>
> Nor is God remote from those who in shadows and images seek the unknown God, since he gives to all men life and breath and all things (cf. Acts 17:25–28), and since the Savior wills all men to be saved (cf. 1 Timothy 2:4). Those who, through no fault of their own, do not know the gospel of Christ or his church, but who nevertheless seek God with a sincere heart, and moved by grace, try in their actions to do his will as they know it through dictates of their conscience—those too, may achieve eternal salvation.
>
> Nor shall divine providence deny the assistance necessary for salvation to those who, without any fault of theirs, have not yet arrived at an explicit knowledge of God, and who, not without grace, strive to lead a good life.

So the fathers of the council do not exclude anyone acting in good faith from the possibility of salvation. They do go on, however, to speak of the church's mission from Christ to bring the gospel to all people, baptizing them and doing its part to achieve the full realization of God's plan in which he has constituted Christ as the source of salvation for the whole world. The *Catechism of the Catholic Church* repeats these teachings (839–856) where it discusses the church and its relationship to non-Christians and its missionary mandate. Recently released by the Congregation for the Doctrine of the Faith is another pertinent document: *Dominus Iesus* (On the Unicity and Salvific Universality of Jesus Christ and the Church), which follows the lead and teachings of both Vatican II and the *Catechism*.

How can a person become a Catholic?

It is not difficult to become a Catholic. That is not to deny or dismiss, however, the long and searching faith journey of many people. The usual way is through the Rite of Christian Initiation of Adults (RCIA). It is the liturgical and formational process of Christian initiation.

It is often helpful to accompany a Catholic friend or relative to the nearest (or most inviting) Catholic parish or mission to express your interest in learning more about the life and faith of Catholics and possibly joining the church.

The priest or pastor will help direct the inquirer to the RCIA program. The program directors should help you find a sponsor or companion to mentor you as you learn about the faith.

What is dogma and who determines it?

As Louis Bouyer's *Dictionary of Theology* indicates, the word *dogma* usually refers to truth defined by the *extraordinary magisterium* of the church—the pope or an ecumenical council pronouncing a truth to be revealed divinely and part of the church's infallible belief and teaching (cf. *Catechism of the Catholic Church* 88–90).

Bouyer goes on to say, however, the term *dogma* is sometimes extended to "include the truths contained in the Word of God as expounded by the *ordinary magisterium* of the church, even though these truths have never been the object of a conciliar or papal definition."

Early in church history, various councils defined as dogma truths about the Holy Trinity, the relationships of the persons in the Trinity, and the person and natures of

Christ as different heresies arose.

In our Catholic belief it is the infallible teaching of the popes and councils that is "protected." While the ordinary magisterium in instances can be in error, it certainly enjoys the presumption of truth over individual theologians. Among theologians each person's teaching or reliability is as good as his or her insights and theological arguments.

It is possible, in the case of nondefined truths, that theologians disagree whether particular propositions or beliefs are divinely revealed in Scripture or have been continuously taught or believed by the church as a whole to be divinely revealed and part of the content of revelation.

What is meant by Luke 10:16, when Jesus says, "Whoever listens to you listens to me"?

In his commentary on Luke, Father Eugene LaVerdiere says that Luke definitely wants the reader to see beyond the seventy disciples immediately sent forth by Jesus. They are the link with the future. They are to continue the teaching task of Jesus and so are those who will come after the seventy—the elders and leaders of the churches Luke will write about in the Acts of the Apostles.

In a sense the teaching of Jesus and the mission of proclaiming the Good News is given over to the whole church, to everyone who is a disciple of Jesus. It is the task and office of the pope and bishops, when the belief of the church and teaching of Jesus is in question, to formulate, express and proclaim authoritatively the teaching of Jesus' church. They do not do that in a vacuum. They consult the tradition of the church, consider how all the people of God seem to understand Jesus' teaching, as well as investigate what the theologians have to say.

In some cases those in authority and leadership may first have to sift out what has been accepted as a matter of *discipline* in the tradition of the church (for example, the practice of women wearing hats) from what has been accepted as *dogma* or the *institution of Jesus* in the church.

Jesus can use individuals to act in a prophetic way. He can, even today, make specific individuals his instruments to convey "messages." This seems to be the case, for instance, with the three children of Fatima, Saint Margaret Mary Alacoque and Bernadette Soubirous. In these cases there really is not new teaching being given. In pronouncing that the revelations given these people are "worthy" of belief, the church authority first looks carefully at the holiness and emotional character of those claiming to be bearers of divine messages. The church authority considers whether or not what the person claiming a revelation says is in harmony with the public revelation given to God's people by Jesus and his disciples. In the end the faithful are free to give belief to the claimed private revelation to the extent we believe that God has been active in giving the revelation.

Vatican II recognized that other churches, though not possessing the complete message of Jesus or all the means of salvation, can be instruments of God's grace and can communicate the word of God given to Jesus' followers. The individual person or minister will be speaking for Jesus to the extent that what is preached conforms to what Jesus taught and handed over to the apostles and disciples to the tradition of the church.

Why doesn't the pope define his own moral and theological positions as infallible?

The questions of infallibility, the authority of papal and episcopal ordinary teaching, and dissent are complex. Boiled down to the simplest terms, the ultimate teaching authority resides in the pope and bishops. Their charism and authority are to be respected (see *Code of Canon Law* 752–753). In the face of challenge their teaching is to be given credence and acceptance unless a particular theologian or person has compelling reasons—for example, facts, arguments, experience not considered by the teaching authority—for dissent.

Dissent requires *reasons*, strong and very convincing. It is not justified by simple "opinion" or preference. Again, the presumption of truth or correctness is on the side of the legitimately constituted teaching authority in the church.

When the teaching authority is convinced after proper prayer, study, consultation and dialogue that it has arrived at the truth, it has the responsibility to speak and give guidance. It may not shirk that responsibility. It is the teaching authority's duty before God, and the pope and bishops owe it to the faithful to give dogmatic and moral guidance. People need such guidance, and many welcome it.

When the authority believes that the faithful are being harmed or confused by dissenting voices, it has the right to insist on its teaching and that those dissenting refrain from instructing contrary to that teaching. There are valid questions about how that authority is best exercised. But the official teaching authority does have the right to make clear that contrary teaching is in conflict with its own and not acceptable.

It may be that the dissenter or dissenters believe in conscience that the teaching authority has not correctly discerned what it is teaching. The dissenter may believe that the teaching authority has not considered all the facts, all the arguments and what scientific research and human experience are showing.

In such a case the dissenter may quietly urge the teaching authority to reconsider its position and teaching and argue his or her case in the academic forum or with the congregations or pope and bishops as the case may be.

Should the dissenter feel compelled to challenge publicly the teaching authority, the dissenter may be in good faith but, as Archbishop Daniel Pilarczyk of Cincinnati said in a pastoral letter, "The dissenter then does so at his or her own risk knowing and accepting the consequences."

Truth is not infallibly discerned by whim. The teaching authority has the obligation of using every means of arriving at and finding truth and being able to say, "Yes, this is in keeping with the constant accepted belief of God's church and people." Only then can it decide to proclaim that something is the infallible teaching and understanding of God's church.

In other words popes and councils do not make something

true by declaring it so. They proclaim a belief or fact they have ascertained to be the faith of the church and infallibly true.

Is the ordinary magisterium infallible?

The ordinary magisterium of the church can teach infallibly. As *The Teaching of Christ*, by Ronald Lawler, O.F.M. CAP., Thomas Lawler and Donald Wuerl, points out,

> Long before special councils had solemnly defined that Jesus is truly God, or had specifically and solemnly proclaimed that God knows us and loves us, these and many other essential elements of Catholic faith and life were taught by bishops everywhere in their ordinary magisterium as the revealed Word of God. To say that the bishops teach infallibly in such cases is in effect to say that they do what Christ commanded them to do: They serve as recognizable witnesses of a meaningful faith, so that men, hearing them, can believe God.

Or, as the Vatican II *Dogmatic Constitution on the Church* (25) puts it:

> Although the bishops, taken individually, do not enjoy the privilege of infallibility, they do, however, proclaim infallibly the doctrine of Christ on the following conditions: namely, when, even though dispersed throughout the world but preserving for all that amongst themselves and with Peter's successor the bond of communion, in their authoritative teaching concerning matters of faith and morals, they are in agreement that a particular teaching is to be held definitively and absolutely. This is still more clearly the case when, assembled in an ecumenical council, they are, for the universal church, teachers of and judges in matters of faith and morals, whose decisions must be adhered to with the loyal and obedient assent of faith.

The fact is that it practically takes an act of the extraordinary magisterium to affirm or make clear exactly what the ordinary magisterium does or has taught over the centuries.

Where does the belief in original sin come from?

For centuries theologians have been arguing over the nature of original sin itself. The words *original sin* do not appear in the Bible, nor does a specific assertion that baptism takes away original sin.

Genesis describes the sin of Adam and its effects on creation. Saint Paul also writes about the sin of Adam and its effect on Adam's descendants. He teaches that Christ has conquered sin and that in baptism we enter into the victory of Christ by entering into his death and dying to sin. Over the centuries Christians have used the words *original sin* to describe the sin of Adam *and* the effects of his sin that have been transmitted to us by birth as part of our human condition.

What is that condition and what are those effects? We become part of a humanity alienated from God. We enter a world greatly affected by sin. In that condition we do not live in the friendship and love of God.

What this all means is argued and disputed even now by theologians, but, basically, original sin is a lack of grace; the effects of this sin that we "inherit" are a darkened mind, weakened will and disordered emotions.

In Matthew Jesus commands the apostles to baptize all nations. John records that Jesus told Nicodemus we must be born again of water and Spirit. In Acts Peter tells the crowd they must reform and be baptized so that their sins may be forgiven and they can receive the gift of the Spirit.

Baptism restores us to the friendship of God, supplies an initial power to believe, joins us to Christ and his church, and brings us a sharing in the life of God—grace. It does something *positive*.

Now how do you describe all that in simple language? The theologian, catechist or teacher is confronted with the problem of trying to describe spiritual realities and divine mysteries in human terms. That is difficult, perhaps impossible, to do.

If we conceive of original sin as a condition we inherit from our first parents, that does convey *some* idea of reality.

Because of baptism we are liberated from the negative effects of the condition into which we are born; the effects are to some degree "taken away" and "removed." Original sin in this sense is taken away. And it is from the Scriptures that this belief and way of speaking are drawn (cf. *Catechism of the Catholic Church* 388–409).

In the case of the teaching about baptism, one could hardly say that it is not "backed up by the Scriptures." The church and theologians draw out the implications of what the Scriptures state, the consequences of what Genesis and Paul say about Adam, his sin and baptism. They formulate what is expressed there in narrative form.

Much the same thing occurs with church teaching about Jesus and the Trinity. From what Jesus says and the evangelists record, Christians draw out the conclusions that there are three Persons (Father, Son and Holy Spirit) in one God, that Jesus is the Son become incarnate, that there are two natures in the one divine Person who became incarnate (Jesus), and that Mary is the mother of God. These teachings are not *directly, specifically stated* in the Scriptures. Yet, practically all Christendom proclaims them in the Nicene Creed.

Finally, it should be remembered that the apostles' teaching was originally communicated orally; it was preached. It was many years before the first written Gospel appeared, and it wasn't until sixty or seventy years after the death of Christ that John's Gospel was completed. For years and even centuries after that, Christians argued over which books were to be accepted as inspired.

Not all the apostles wrote, but they all preached. The rule of faith was the preaching, the oral word, of the apostles. It was the church that discerned what writings were inspired and gave the judgment of authenticity on these works. The written Scriptures themselves came out of the tradition of the church.

Paul spoke of what had been handed over to him, how he learned the teaching of Christ and the apostles and what had happened to them. John wrote at the end of his Gospel that not everything Jesus said or did had been written down by him. Peter warned of the difficulty of interpreting Paul and the Scriptures.

The early Christian writers and fathers of the church repeatedly appealed to the tradition of the church and to the apostles and what had been given over by them in teaching and stating the belief of the church.

In other words tradition and Scripture must be taken together as the rule of Christian faith and belief. Tradition interprets the Scriptures.

What is excommunication?

There are two kinds of excommunications. An imposed or declared excommunication takes place by a public statement of the proper authority: "John Doe is excommunicated because _____." *Ipso facto* or *latae sententiae* excommunication means if you commit a certain crime or sin (and if all the conditions under law are present), you are by that very fact excommunicated.

All excommunications are meant to be medicinal. They are a kind of shock therapy meant to make sinners aware of the seriousness of their sins and their spiritual conditions and call them to conversion.

An excommunicated person (Canon 133) is forbidden (1) to have any ministerial part in the celebration of the Sacrifice of the Eucharist or any other sacraments of public worship; (2) to celebrate the sacraments or sacramentals and to receive the sacraments; (3) to exercise any ecclesiastical office, ministries or acts of governance.

Some other provisions of the law forbid the exercise of certain privileges, outlaw the reception of any dignity, office or function in the church, and invalidate acts of governance.

Automatic excommunication is incurred for the following sins: (1) apostasy, *(ipso facto)* heresy, schism (Canon 1364.1); (2) violation of the sacred species (Canon 1367); (3) physical attack on the pope (Canon 1370.1); (4) absolution of an accomplice in a sin against the sixth commandment (Canon 1378.1); (5) unauthorized ordination of a bishop (both the one ordaining and the one ordained are excommunicated) (Canon 1382); (6) direct violation by a confessor of the seal of confession (Canon 1388); (7) procuring an abortion (Canon 1398); (8) recording by a technical instrument or divulging in the communications media what was said by a confessor or a penitent in sacramental confession whether performed by oneself or another (added in 1988).

Because excommunication is a medicinal penalty, it must be absolved when the person truly repents. Sometimes remission of the penalty is reserved to the Holy See, for example, when a confessor directly violates the seal of confession. The usual place to begin the process for removing the excommunication is in the sacrament of confession or with the authority who imposed the excommunication.

For further information and detail consult *The Pastoral Companion*, by John M. Huels, O.S.M., J.S.D.

What Is the Society of Saint Pius X?

The story and identity of the Saint Pius X Society is very much involved with that of Archbishop Marcel Lefebvre. Lefebvre was a French archbishop who rejected much of the Second Vatican Council. He rejected the new order of the Mass, insisting on retaining the liturgy of the Eucharist as it came from the Council of Trent and the Missal approved by Pope Pius V in 1570.

Lefebvre founded a group of followers called the Society of Saint Pius X. He was eventually suspended by Pope Paul VI for ordaining priests when forbidden to do so. Later he was excommunicated by Pope John Paul II for ordaining bishops from the Society of Saint Pius X without papal approval.

Many of the Society of Saint Pius X followed Lefebvre into schism. Its members remain outside the authority of the Holy See well after the death of Lefebvre in 1991, still rejecting the changes of Vatican II and celebrating the Mass in Latin and according to the Missal of Pius V.

The society was named for Saint Pius X because Pius X, at the turn of the twentieth century, opposed what was known as "modernism" in the church. Lefebvre saw himself and his followers as opponents of a new kind of modernism.

In 1988 a group from the Society of Saint Pius X who did not wish to follow Lefebvre into schism formed the Fraternity of Saint Peter. In communion with the church its priests celebrate the Eucharist according to the old Tridentine rite.

What is the church's position on evolution?

In 1950 Pope Pius XII wrote in his encyclical *Humani Generis:*

> For these reasons the teaching authority of the church does not forbid that, in conformity with the present state of human sciences and sacred theology, research and discussions on the part of men experienced in both fields take place with regard to the doctrine of evolution, in as far as it inquires into the origin of the human *body* [emphasis added] as coming from preexistent and living matter—for the Catholic faith obliges us to hold that souls are immediately created by God.

Pius XII insisted on the immediate creation of souls, the spiritual element that distinguishes humans from mere animals. He did not find the theory of the evolution of the human body incompatible with Catholic faith or the Bible.

Of recent note, in an address to the Pontifical Academy of Sciences (October 22, 1996), Pope John Paul II said:

> Today, almost half a century after the publication of the encyclical, new knowledge has led to the recognition of more than one hypothesis in the theory of evolution. It is indeed remarkable that this theory has been progressively accepted by researchers following a series of discoveries in various fields of knowledge. The convergence, neither sought nor fabricated, of the results of work that was conducted independently is in itself a significant argument in favor of this theory.

He went on to say, "Revelation teaches us that [humanity] was created in the image and likeness of God (cf. Genesis. 1:27–29)."

Later he repeated again the teaching of Pius XII:

If the human body takes its origin from preexistent living matter, the spiritual soul is immediately created by God.... Consequently, theories of evolution which, in accordance with the philosophies inspiring them, consider the spirit as emerging from the forces of living matter, are incompatible with the truth about man. Nor are they able to ground the dignity of the person.

Can a Catholic believe in karma and reincarnation?

In his book *World Religions* Father John T. Catoir talks about Hindu belief and the place of reincarnation and karma in it. Hindus, he says, believe that the goal of existence is nirvana or annihilation. A person's goal in existence is to become completely absorbed in God, to lose any individuality. *Nirvana* means for an individual to become taken up into God like a drop of water disappearing into an ocean.

If a person has not achieved that goal and the secret of nirvana at the end of his or her present life, life must be repeated. The soul must keep taking on a new form until perfection and nirvana are achieved. The form the soul takes will depend on how well or poorly the individual has gained awareness of true self.

Catoir quotes Garuba Parana in stating the law of karma concerning this cycle of life: "A man reaps at that age, whether infancy, youth or old age that which he had sowed in his previous birth. A man gets in life what he is fated to get, and even a god cannot make it otherwise." Many see in this belief, because of the fatalism present in it, that to try to eliminate or alleviate suffering and pain is futile: They are inevitable. Individuals are only getting what they rightly deserve.

Dominican Father Benedict Ashley, author of *Theologies of the Body: Humanist and Christian*, says,

The fundamental reason that a Christian can't accept the concept of reincarnation is because of the doctrine of Resurrection, which means that we get our present body back in some form at the end of time. In the Buddhist and Hindu beliefs about reincarnation, the self is a soul and the body is something it puts on and takes off like a garment.

Simply put: Karma and reincarnation cannot be reconciled with Catholic faith. They deny heaven, hell and the Resurrection.

How did Jesus exist before the Incarnation?

Briefly, the Son of God, Second Person of the Trinity, exists from all eternity, one with the Father and Holy Spirit. Before the Incarnation, this Second Person of the Trinity was without a human body and human nature. At the moment of the Incarnation (when Mary consented to be the mother of Jesus) and by the power of the Holy Spirit, Jesus was conceived by Mary. At that moment the Second Person, the Son, took to himself a human nature. In the Angelus we say, "and the word became flesh...and dwelt among us." In the creed we say, "He was born of the Virgin Mary and became man." Thus, in the person of the incarnate Son of God both the divine nature and human nature are united. Jesus as Son of God always existed. From the moment of his conception (in the womb of Mary), the Son became human. (Cf. *Catechism of the Catholic Church* 461–483).

What is the church's teaching about the resurrected body?

The church is quite definite about the fact of the Resurrection, and in several of the creeds it proclaims the resurrection of the body. Teaching about the nature of this resurrection and the *risen body*, however, is much less definite.

That should be understandable since none of us has yet experienced resurrection or been able to talk with anyone who has. We can rely only on what little the Gospels tell us about the risen Jesus and how the apostles experienced Jesus in the flesh.

As a consequence, theologians speculate and theorize a

great deal about this risen body that will be ours. Yet, final and complete answers are few.

What *A New Catechism (Dutch Catechism)* says of resurrection is quite representative of what most theologians would say:

> All men will rise again like our Lord. The new birth will be completed. The Bible speaks, in splendid imagery, of the dead coming up out of the earth. This does not mean that the molecules of which our body was once formed will be reorganized as at the hour of our death. It is not a matter of reconstituting our earthly body.... What takes place is the perfecting of our spiritual body, of which Paul speaks ardently and at great length in 1 Corinthians 15:31–50, showing that we must not think of the resurrection as a return to the flesh and blood of our mortal frame.... We are not to think so much of the biological body as of the body which has the life of the new creation. The biblical phrase "coming out of the grave" means that we shall be our own selves—the same as before, but with a difference, just as Jesus after his resurrection was the same, but also different, so that his apostles knew that it was the Lord, but did not recognize him at first.

The *Catechism of the Catholic Church* has an extended treatment on the topic of bodily resurrection in Part One, Article 11 (988–1019).

Why do Catholics believe in immortality?

The resurrection of the dead and life after death is essentially a matter of *faith*. It does not rest on the arguments of philosophers, whether ancient Greeks or moderns. We believe in the resurrection of the dead because Jesus rose from the dead. The apostles and disciples are witnesses of Jesus' Resurrection.

Nevertheless, there are arguments that can be drawn from Greek and other philosophers that show belief in human immortality is reasonable. These arguments rest largely on the nature of the human person itself and our ability to have abstract thought, memory and recall. There is in us something that, despite growth and the constant replacing of human cells in the body, makes us always the same person. Our ability to distinguish good from evil, to recognize truth and beauty, to reason and theorize argues that the principle of life in humans is different from that in other animal species.

Nonetheless, Jesus and the apostles did not call on the Greek philosophers to argue for or prove that there is in humans something that lasts after bodily death. It is the word of Christ and the witness of the apostles that give us the basis for our belief in the resurrection. Jesus told the good thief dying on the cross next to him, "This day you will be with me in paradise." Paul told the Corinthians, "...the one who raised the Lord Jesus will raise us also with Jesus and place us with you in his presence" (2 Corinthians 4:14).

Speaking of the immortality of the soul, the *Catechism of the Catholic Church* has this to say:

> The church teaches that every spiritual soul is created immediately by God—it is not "produced" by the parents—and also that it is immortal: it does not perish when it separates from the body at death, and it will be reunited with the body at the final Resurrection. (366)

Further, ideas of immortality—a life after bodily death—go far beyond the early Greek philosophers to other peoples and cultures. The Egyptian pyramids give evidence of a belief in some kind of life after death. Native Americans believed in life after death—some buried things with the dead that the living anticipated would be useful in the next world.

Plato, Aristotle and other Greek philosophers may not have had the benefit of revelation and their ideas of soul and immortality may be imperfect, but these people were not stupid. They had great intellect and insight. Their ability to reason was truly remarkable. That is why they influenced the thinking and writings of theologians such as Saint Augustine and Saint Thomas Aquinas. We can wonder what they might have achieved intellectually if they had the benefit of modern technology and scientific instruments to gather physical facts and information.

What happened to the good people who died before Jesus' Resurrection?

The fact is we just do not know. Some theologians have taught that the just who died before the Resurrection of Christ were in a state between the hell of the damned and the paradise of the blessed. It has been described as a state of natural happiness, but not the joy of the beatific vision of God. In the terminology of medieval theologians, this state was the Limbo of the Fathers.

We often translate the biblical term *Sheol* as "hell." Our tendency is to think in terms of the place of the damned when we see or hear that word. But *Sheol* in the Scriptures had a much broader meaning. It meant simply the world of the dead. In early Christian writings and prayers, that is the sense in which we often read *hell*—not just as the hell of the damned.

The article in the creed that proclaims that, after his death, Jesus descended into hell is relevant to this point. Many explain this article by saying Jesus went to the place of the dead to "free" the just. Thus, the *Catechism of the Council of Trent* says,

> We profess that immediately after the death of Christ His soul descended into hell and dwelt there as long as His body remained in the tomb.... Hell here signifies those secret abodes in which are detained the souls that have not obtained the happiness of heaven.

What do we mean by *sola fide*?

Sola fide means "faith alone." This term is often used in discussions about the differences in Catholic and Protestant beliefs over the nature and means of salvation. *The Church's Confession of Faith: A Catholic Catechism for Adults*, first published by the German Bishops' Conference, then in English by Ignatius Press, devotes at least thirteen pages to the question of faith and justification and a study of Protestant and Catholic interpretations of Scripture concerning justification.

The authors of this catechism investigate the cause of disagreements not only between Catholics and Protestants but also among Protestants themselves. They go back to the time of Luther and Trent and attempt to place the dispute in its historical context.

Early on in examining the question, they state: "The original and fundamental meaning of these concepts is no longer immediately intelligible to us. We must exert ourselves to discover their original sense."

After speaking of some of the causes of misunderstanding and the distortions of polemics, the catechism says,

> We can understand that many controversies arose through semantic and even real misunderstandings and were only apparent oppositions. When we look instead to what was meant by the contradictory formulations, and especially to the personal acts of faith, we see in many questions an amazing nearness and deep commonality.
>
> The ecumenical discussion of the last decades has led to great progress in the doctrine of justification. Many Catholic and Protestant theologians are today of the opinion that the doctrine of justification need no longer separate the two churches.
>
> Two aspects of the doctrine must be conceived together: the grace of God and the cooperation of man rendered possible by it in faith and action. The Catholic and Protestant doctrines about this relation do not exclude each other in principle; they do not indeed coincide but they are open to each other.

The German catechism observes that in the past Catholics and Protestants often spoke past each other or at each other rather than to each other. The authors of the catechism speak of the need for patient dialogue in which old prejudices and misunderstandings are removed and both sides strive to obtain a deeper mutual understanding.

Of course, not all Evangelicals and Catholics will subscribe to the theologians' conclusions. Some initial reactions on the part of several Evangelicals were highly critical of their colleagues. One response headlined, "A Camouflage for Catholicism" and another voiced the fear that, unless answered, the document will bring an end to evangelicalism and the Reformation.

The Catholic church has not changed its teaching on grace and justification (cf. *Catechism of the Catholic Church* 1987– 2029).

Does Pope John Paul II contradict Pius XI in his views on Catholicism as the one true faith?

According to the *New Catholic Encyclopedia,* Pope Pius XI wrote *Mortalium Animos* in 1928 to explain why Catholics could not participate in the Lausanne Conference of 1927. Catholics could not accept the postulates of that conference that denied the church of Christ already visibly existed in the world and reunion could be achieved without identity in doctrine. According to the *New Catholic Encyclopedia*, the postulates of the conference involved modernism in theology, indifferentism in ecclesiology and relativism in doctrine. Catholics could not participate with those principles as starting points.

It should be noted, however, that this same Pius XI ordered Catholic universities to institute courses in Eastern Orthodox spirituality and theology. He urged esteem for Orthodox theology, spirituality and customs. It was this same Pius XI, the *New Catholic Encyclopedia* tells us, who declared that knowledge and fraternal charity are essential preliminaries to reunion and that prejudice and ignorance were responsible for past failures. In 1937 Pope Pius XI approved the attendance of unofficial Catholic observers at the Faith and Order Conference in Edinburgh.

Under Pope Pius XII, Pius XI's successor, an instruction from the Holy Office in 1949 gave formal recognition to the ecumenical movement and encouraged Catholics, especially priests, to pray for its success. It gave Catholics with proper approval permission to meet with non-Catholics as equals and discuss matters of faith and morals. It also permitted common recitation of the Lord's Prayer or some other prayer approved by the church.

Pope John Paul II is hardly starting something new in encouraging Catholics—and other believing people—to pray and dialogue in an effort to find unity.

From New Testament times on there have been stresses and strains threatening church unity. To read the Acts of the Apostles is to learn of the struggles and disagreement over doctrine and practices between Paul, with his Gentile followers, and Jewish-Christians. Those disagreements were resolved in what we often call the Council of Jerusalem, where opposing factions prayed and discussed.

The following centuries gave birth to their own schisms and heresies—from Arianism through the separation of East and West and the Protestant Reformation to today. How did the church and Christians try to resolve—even if unsuccessfully—their disagreements and again find unity? Through ecumenical councils. There they prayed, discussed and debated. Isn't that what Saint Paul and the Christians at Jerusalem did?

That is what Pope John XXIII had in mind. He invited observers from other Christian denominations to the Second Vatican Council. The Vatican II *Decree on Ecumenism* urged that we appreciate goodwill where it exists. It recognized those things Catholics and other Christians and believers often have in common and that God can be at work in the lives of those who may not be in complete union with the church.

Vatican II recognized that in the case of rifts and separations "often enough men of both sides were to blame" (cf. *Catechism of the Catholic Church* 817–822).

Against that background Pope John Paul II is very much in line with what Pius XI and his successors have said and done. John Paul II has recognized that in the course of history there is blame enough to be laid on the doorsteps of all. He has apologized for the failures of the church and our forebears that helped bring on separation.

John Paul II, like the bishops of Vatican II and Paul VI, has urged prayer and dialogue. He has promoted discussions by Catholic theologians with those from other Christian denominations in an effort to find where we share common beliefs and where we really disagree. John Paul II urges prayer together as a beginning point in the quest for unity.

Vatican II and Pope John Paul do not espouse indifferentism or suggest differences do not matter. They have not and do not suggest compromising Catholic doctrine. They do suggest that at times dialogue may reveal differences are not so real as may have been imagined.

Pope John Paul II in a recent encyclical, *Ut Unum Sint* (That They All May Be One) again insists on the special role and ministry of the pope as Bishop of Rome among Christians. John Paul II is not about to "give the store away" when it comes to the teaching of Christ and the church. He recognizes ecumenism is not an easy process, but he sees it as an effort to do the will of Christ.

What is a miracle?

One definition of a miracle is this: a sensible fact beyond the natural power of every created agency and manifested as an immediate and extraordinary intervention of God's omnipotence.

There is an interesting discussion of miracles in a little booklet from Franciscan Herald Press, *The Miracles of Jesus Then and Now*, by Alfons Weber. Weber says that, in the biblical sense, miracles were occurrences that allowed people to surmise that God was at work among them. People living in the biblical period did not think in terms of natural law and would not be concerned about determining if scientific explanations were possible for wonderful events. To them there were all kinds of signs that God was present and acting among them. The sudden break of a storm, an unexpected physical recovery, a seemingly impossible victory in battle would be regarded as miraculous.

This is not to say that there are not happenings in Scripture where we can apply the criteria of today and say, yes, God worked a miracle. In Matthew 11:21–22 Jesus himself speaks of miracles done at Chorazin and Bethsaida. And events such as Jesus healing a man with a withered hand (Mark 3:1–6), curing a paralytic (Mark 1:40–45) or raising Lazarus to life (John 11) meet the criteria we would use today in declaring a miracle has taken place.

The miracles of Jesus pointed to the fact that the reign of God was being established. They pointed to the identity of Jesus and were evidence for and calls to belief (cf. *Catechism of the Catholic Church* 515).

Miracles today continue to be signs of salvation, calls to belief, signs that Christ is able to overcome death, hunger, evil, and that the kingdom of God is present to us (*Catechism* 548–549, 1335).

Is it foolish to pray for miracles? We should not be asking God to miraculously perform what we should be doing for ourselves—such as wrestling with the great problems and terrible diseases and disasters of our time. Likewise, we shouldn't be asking God to intervene in trivial affairs. But if we are believing people, we can surely ask God to intervene in the calamities and helpless situations of our lives, to work a miracle or miracles among us. At the same time that we ask for miracles, we must truly have great faith and be willing to accept the will of God, whatever it is.

Do saints "produce" miracles? Not in the sense that a saint works a miracle by his or her own power. *God* works miracles, sometimes at the intercession or prayers of a saint (*Catechism* 434).

Do Catholics still believe in purgatory?

The Sacred Congregation for the Doctrine of the Faith in 1979 issued an instruction called *The Reality of Life After Death*. It insists on belief in the Resurrection and life everlasting as part of the Catholic faith. It also talks about this life to come, heaven, hell and purgatory.

At the same time the instruction is very restrained when trying to describe these realities. It urges restraint on the part of others who write about and attempt to explain them. It urges them not to, as it were, allow their imaginations to run wild. That is exactly the kind of thing that causes confusion and creates problems of faith.

The key paragraph in regard to purgatory is this one:

In fidelity to the New Testament and tradition, the Church believes in the happiness of the just who will one day be with Christ. She believes that there will be eternal punishment for the sinner, who will be deprived of the sight of God and that this punishment will have a repercussion on the being of a sinner. She believes in the possibility of a purification for the elect before they see God, a purification altogether different from the punishment of the damned. That is what the Church means when speaking of hell and purgatory.

The instruction urges, "When dealing with man's situation after death, one should especially beware of arbitrary imaginative representations since excess of this kind is a major cause of the difficulties that Christian faith often encounters."

At the same time it adds: "Respect must, however, be given to the images employed in the Scriptures. Their profound meaning must be discerned, while avoiding the risk of attenuating them, since this often empties of substance the realities designated by them."

This instruction simply realizes that in talking about heaven, hell and purgatory we are attempting to describe realities the living have never experienced. That is not easy to do. And much of the time we are saying, "It is like this or that."

After saying that the doctrine of purgatory was "incipiently present in Judaism" and can be deduced or inferred from certain New Testament texts, *The Church's Confession of Faith: A Catholic Catechism for Adults*, first published by the German Bishops' Conference, shows how belief in purgatory goes back to the days of the catacombs and is evidenced in the inscriptions there.

Trying to explain the nature of purgatory, it reminds us that the word means simply a place or state of purification. It explains,

The talk of purgatorial fire is an image that refers to a deeper reality. Fire can be understood as *the cleansing, purifying and sanctifying power of God's holiness and mercy.* The encounter with the fire of God's love that takes place in death has a purifying and transforming power for the man who has indeed decided for God in principle but who has not consistently realized this decision and has fallen short of the ideal. God's power straightens, purifies, heals and consummates whatever remained imperfect at death. Purgatory is God himself as purifying and sanctifying power for man. We can understand the doctrinal declarations of the Church against this background.

This catechism says of those being purified, "Their pain before God's face is that they are not yet pure enough to be able to be wholly filled and beatified by his love."

One of the difficulties we face in trying to discuss all this is that we are talking from our own human perspective of time about what the dead are experiencing in eternity, which is outside the realm of time. So we can only speculate on how all this takes place or "how long" it may take.

So Catholic teaching is as follows: (1) Purgatory is an integral part of our belief and faith as Catholics. To deny it would mean we are not completely professing the faith of the church. (2) If a person completely in union with the will of God dies and is perfect in his or her love, that person has no need of purgation or purification. There is no need for purgatory, this person immediately enters into heaven, the state of complete happiness in God. (3) We should not think of purgatory as a kind of temporary stay in hell. Purgatory and hell are different. And the pain of each is different in kind.

For the latest official statement on the church's understanding of purgatory, you will want to consult the *Catechism of the Catholic Church* 1030–1032.

What is the Purgatorial Society?

Purgatorial societies come in different forms. All take their inspiration from our faith and confidence that we can help the dead still going through purification to come to final unity with God.

In some cases parishes or religious orders invite people to contribute for a predetermined number of Masses to be celebrated throughout the year. As they contribute they enroll or list friends and relatives to be included among those for whom the Masses are said.

In other cases, around the commemoration of All Souls, it is announced that stipends for Masses for the dead will be received and dead friends and relatives will be remembered in those Masses.

The total amount of offerings will be divided by the amount of the usual Mass stipend and as many Masses celebrated for all enrolled.

There may be other plans, but the basic idea is that of people pooling stipends to remember the dead in Masses and prayers through the year.

Can a Roman Catholic in good standing be a Mason?

The 1983 *Code of Canon Law* no longer imposed excommunication for joining Masonic associations. Some then concluded that membership in the Masons was now generally unobjectionable. The Congregation for the Doctrine of the Faith was asked about this in November 1983. It answered that, although there was no longer excommunication for membership in the Masons in the new Code, "joining them remains prohibited by the church. Catholics enrolled in Masonic associations are involved in serious sin and may not approach Holy Communion."

The reasons for this prohibition become clear in a report made for the U.S. bishops by William Whalen, a Purdue University professor, who has written books on secret societies and the beliefs of other religions and sects.

Whalen strongly insisted that Masonry involves a real religion that does not accept Christ as God or the Scriptures as the revealed word of God. To be a Catholic and a Mason, he said, is contradictory. The same would hold true of Rosicrucians. There is at least implicitly a strong strain of pantheism (the heretical belief that the universe is God) in Rosicrucianism. And reincarnation seems another of its doctrines.

Catholics are not the only ones hostile to membership in the Masons (and Rosicrucians). Whalen also cited Pentecostals and Mennonites and branches of Lutheranism and the Salvation Army that discourage or prohibit membership.

Is the Knights of Columbus a secret society?

Russell Shaw, the director of public information for the Knights of Columbus, answered in this way:

> Is the Knights of Columbus a secret society? No. A secret society is one whose membership, leaders, organization, program and purposes are secret. The members of the Knights of Columbus are encouraged to advertise their membership by publicly wearing the emblem of the Order and explaining the organization to anyone who might be interested.
>
> As for the rest of it—leaders, organization, program, purposes—these are matters of record, repeatedly publicized in K of C literature (for example, *Columbia*, a monthly magazine with a circulation of 1.5 million readers) available to anyone who asks for it.
>
> There are nevertheless two aspects of the Knights of Columbus that might be described as private, if not exactly secret. (1) Attendance at business sessions is restricted to members. This is a common practice among groups of all sorts. (2) The initiation ceremonies ("degrees," the K of C calls them) are not made public, and members assume an obligation not to divulge them to nonmembers. This, too, is the practice of some other groups; its purpose is to sustain the mystique of the K of C and foster a sense of fraternity among members. Since the latter number 1.5 million practicing Catholic laymen as well as many priests, bishops and cardinals, people can safely take it for granted that there is nothing untoward about the ceremonies.

There is nothing secret about the knights' works of charity and faith. And they are known for their loyalty to the church and Holy Father.

What is the canonical status of the religious group Opus Dei?

A fact sheet distributed by the Office of Communication of the Prelature of Opus Dei describes it as, "A personal Prelature... international in scope, serving the universal church by way of insertion into the local church."

Founded in Madrid on October 2, 1928, by Blessed Josemaria Escriva, its membership is listed at nearly eighty-four thousand people around the world. Its headquarters are in Rome. Its ordinary (bishop) has ordinary hierarchical jurisdiction in carrying out the prelature's specific purposes. According to the fact sheet,

> Lay members therefore remain dependent on the local bishop as ordinary faithful of the diocese in which they live, and they likewise retain full freedom and their own responsibility in all matters in the secular sphere. Priests of the Prelature are drawn from the lay membership and serve the members, cooperators (which include non-Catholics) and their friends. Diocesan priests who wish to share in its spirituality may be associated with Opus Dei in the Priestly Society of the Holy Cross, but continue fully under their bishop.

The fact sheet also states that in our country some members of Opus Dei, in cooperation with others, conduct apostolic works in major cities. Elsewhere, members are engaged in universities, high schools, vocational institutes, medical dispensaries and training centers for workers and farmers. Members are men and women, married and single of every class and social condition.

Opus Dei's stated purpose is to "spread in all sectors of society a profound awareness of the universal call to holiness and the exercise of a personal apostolate in the ordinary circumstances of everyday life and more specifically through one's ordinary work."

According to an article written by Sister Camille D'Arienzo in Brooklyn's diocesan newspaper, *The Tablet*, there is a three-tiered hierarchy in Opus Dei.

Those on the highest level assume full responsibilities for internal working.... On the middle rung are people who have taken private vows, including that of fidelity to the teaching magisterium of the Church. On the third level are those who sympathize with the program and are preparing to enter it.

Referring to an interview with Father Angel de la Parte Paris (not a member of Opus Dei), Opus Dei is geared to "the intellectually endowed.... It attracts established medical doctors, scientists, lawyers." De la Parte Paris speaks from his experience of Opus Dei in Spain.

Pope John Paul II appears to have high regard for Opus Dei. The Vatican's chief spokesman, named by the pope, is an Opus Dei member, Joaquin Navarro-Valls. On May 17, 1992, Pope John Paul II beatified the group's founder, Monsignor Josemaria Escriva de Balaguer.

Critics of Opus Dei say it is too secretive, elitist and separatist. They would have it show greater concern for social problems and the effects of unjust structures on the poor.

What are theologians?

Webster's *Ninth New Collegiate Dictionary* defines *theology* as "the study of religious faith, practice and experience: especially the study of God and his relation to the world." It defines *theologian* as "a specialist in theology."

In Catholic usage when we speak of theologians, we usually imply some special training, education or expertise. In speaking of theologians we are speaking of writers and eachers who concern themselves with God, God's attributes and relations to the universe. Catholic theology itself is divided into five areas: dogmatic, moral, pastoral, ascetical and mystical.

Our Sunday Visitor's *Catholic Encyclopedia*, edited by Peter Stravinskas, states, "The theologian must possess a doctorate or at least a licentiate degree." And a "theologian's function is to explain and defend the church's official teachings and to express better some of the church's teachings in the light of today's terminology and discoveries."

The Catholic theologian examines God and our relations with God and each other in the light of faith and revelation. The Catholic theologian reasons concerning all these things with guidance from the church's teaching authority, the magisterium.

The authority of the theologians can come from several sources. It may come from education and training—their knowledge and the strength of their reason and intellect. It may come from the missions or approvals they are given to teach by universities and the recognition of their peers. It may come from the church's approval of their teachings or missions to teach and write given by the church, otherwise known as canonical mandates. Canon 812 of the *Code of Canon Law* requires such mandates for those who teach theological disciplines in institutions of higher studies.

The theologian's mission is not to mislead or lead people astray. The theologian's task is to help us better understand the mysteries and revelation of God and their implications for our lives. Early Christian theologians explored questions such as, What does it mean to say Jesus is both God and man? Later theologians pondered over how Mary could have been conceived free from sin. Today's theologian may ask when and if it is morally permissible to disconnect life-support systems.

Two relevant works are *The Ecclesial Vocation of the Theologian*, issued by the Congregation for the Doctrine of the Faith, and *The Vocation of the Theologian*, by Monika Hellwig.

Why must clergy and religious wear certain clothing?

According to the *New Catholic Encyclopedia*, special clerical dress outside of church did not exist much before the sixth century. Special clothing seemed to evolve because the clergy gradually came from philosophers and ascetics and they already had distinctive clothing.

Even then centuries passed without any definite regulations. The Council of Trent (1545–1563) merely urged dress conformable to the cleric's order and propriety. Nothing was specified in regard to color. Apparently black did not take over until the seventeenth century.

Pope Sixtus V (1585–1590) ordered the cassock for sacred and public functions. In the United States, the Third Plenary Council of Baltimore (1884) determined that clerics were to wear the Roman collar and cassock at home and in the church.

Outside, the Roman collar and a coat of black or somber color reaching to the knees were to be worn. J. A. Shields, in the *New Catholic Encyclopedia* account, says this prescription was never formally revoked but it has always been interpreted to mean clerics should conform to the style of conservative laymen.

The present *Code of Canon Law* simply says clerics are to wear suitable ecclesiastical garb in accord with the norms issued by the conference of bishops in accord with legitimate local custom (284).

In *The Code of Canon Law: A Text and Commentary*, John E. Lynch, C.S.P., informs us that on January 27, 1976, the prefect of the Sacred Congregation for Bishops recognized that it is proper for clergy and religious to wear clothing suitable to the occupations in which they are engaged, recreation, for example.

Lynch also states,

> It would certainly be within the spirit of the law in the United States today to limit the use of clerical attire to situations in which the cleric is on duty, actually functioning as a cleric, or attending formal gatherings in the diocese. He could, for example, wear sport clothes while traveling or attending class.

In many instances religious habits and dress reflect the common clothing of people in the founder's time. The current *Code of Canon Law* rules, "Religious are to wear the habit of the institute made according to the norm of proper law as a sign of their consecration and as a testimony of poverty" (669). The order's own constitutions or rule approved by Rome will describe that group's habit.

In 1972, a letter from the Sacred Congregation for Religious and Secular Institutes said secular clothes are permitted when wearing a habit would impede the normal activities of the religious.

There are, of course, good reasons that can be offered for clerical and religious garb. Of course, though religious dress may identify the wearer as priest or religious, it isn't clothing that confers virtue and holiness. As Shakespeare says in *Measure for Measure*, "*Cucullus non facit monachum*" ("The cowl doesn't make the monk").

Do priests wear skullcaps?

Any Catholic priest may wear a skullcap. This head covering goes by different names. It is sometimes called a *solideo, calotte, pilleolus* or *sub-mitrale*. It is most often spoken of as a *zucchetto*.

Originally, it had a very practical purpose. Clerics wore a hairstyle called the tonsure. The hair on the crown of the head was cut and shaved. A skullcap was then often worn to keep the head warm.

While some priests may continue to use a skullcap for utilitarian reasons, members of the hierarchy must use the zucchetto as a liturgical vestment. Its color will tell you the person's office. The pope wears a white zucchetto; cardinals, red; bishops, purple; and abbots and other clergy, black. Prelates must remove the zucchetto from the Sanctus of Mass until after Communion and whenever the Blessed Sacrament is exposed.

According to John C. Noonan, Jr., in *The Church Visible*, the zucchetto did not develop from the Jewish yarmulke but has a development all its own.

What is the significance of the ring that bishops and cardinals wear?

According to John C. Noonan, Jr., in *The Church Visible*, the bishop's ring is a sign of authority. In the earlier *Code of Canon Law*, clerics who were not bishops were forbidden to wear rings.

As a symbol of episcopal authority the ring first appeared

in the third century. By A.D. 637 Saint Isidore of Seville would write, "To the bishop at his consecration is given a staff; a ring likewise is given him to signify pontifical honor or as a seal for secrets." The bishop's ring would later also take on the symbolic meaning that he was wedded to the church.

The cardinal's ring is given by the Holy Father at a Mass on the day following the consistory that named one a cardinal.

What is an Agnus Dei?

According to *A Handbook of Catholic Sacramentals,* by Ann Ball, Agnus Deis are small discs of wax taken from the paschal candle and blessed by the pope on the Wednesday of Holy Week in the first year of his pontificate and every seventh year following. On one side of the disc is stamped the figure of a lamb representing Christ the paschal lamb sacrificed for our redemption.

The Agnus Dei is frequently encased in leather or silk and sometimes surrounded by lace and fancy embroidery.

The ceremony of blessing takes place after the Agnus Dei (Lamb of God) of the Mass. In the ceremony the pope dips the wax discs in a mixture of water, balsam and chrism. When the pope blesses the Agnus Dei, he prays for protection from fire, flood, storms and plagues and for safety in childbirth.

Ball further tells us that packets of Agnus Deis are placed in the miters of cardinals and bishops who come for them the Saturday of Easter Week.

What is necessary for a church to become a basilica or shrine?

An indult or proclamation of the Holy See makes a church a basilica.

The old *Code of Canon Law* (in effect until 1983) declared that the title *basilica* could not be given to any church except by apostolic indult or immemorial custom. Indult or custom would determine the "privileges" of the basilica.

Commentators on the old code listed four *major* basilicas—all in Rome. They are St. John Lateran, St. Mary Major, St. Paul Outside the Walls and St. Peter's. Basilicas are distinguished by a papal altar and *porta sancta* (holy door) opened by a papal delegate in jubilee years.

Two *minor* basilicas are listed, created by grants of popes. Both are in Assisi: the Basilica of St. Francis of Assisi and the Basilica of St. Mary of the Angels. They are also termed by some as patriarchal basilicas.

Some churches granted the title of minor basilica in the United States include: Mission Dolores in San Francisco, California; Our Lady of Sorrows and Queen of All Saints in Chicago, Illinois; Assumption of the Blessed Virgin Mary in Baltimore, Maryland; and Our Lady of Gethsemani in Trappist, Kentucky.

The old code was completely silent about shrines. However, the new *Code of Canon Law* is silent on basilicas but contains five canons on shrines!

Canon 1230 says that the term *shrine* means a church or sacred place that, with the approval of the local ordinary, is frequented by the faithful as pilgrims.

Canon 1231 states that for a national shrine the approval of the episcopal conference is necessary. For an international shrine the approval of the Holy See is required.

How does a church get its name?

Canon law is minimal on the naming of churches. Canon 1218 says only that each church is to have its own title, which cannot be changed after its dedication. Commentaries then direct the reader to the current liturgical books that are more explicit on the titles of churches, and which rules are to be followed. The Ritual for the Dedication of a Church states that every church to be dedicated must have a titular. This titular may be the Blessed Trinity, our Lord Jesus Christ invoked according to a mystery of his life or a title already accepted in the liturgy, the Holy Spirit, the Blessed Virgin Mary (likewise invoked according to some appellation already accepted in the liturgy), one of the angels, or a saint inscribed in the *Roman Martyrology* or in a duly approved appendix (to the martyrology). A blessed may not be a titular without an indult from the apostolic see.

The ritual also indicates a church may have only one titular unless it is a question of saints who are listed together in the calendar of observances (for example, Cosmas and Damian, Peter and Paul). The ritual then gives to the bishop the responsibility of dedicating to God new churches built in his diocese.

From a canonical point of view, the bishop alone has the authority to establish a parish. Part of the act of establishing a parish would include the dedication of that parish to God under a particular title. It is, therefore, the bishop who has the final say about the name of a new church. In practice the bishop sometimes asks the founding pastor to recommend a name. The pastor may sometimes consult the members of the new parish on a patron or title.

But sometimes the bishop has his own list of favorite names or wants to be sure names are not duplicated. It may be that someone who contributes greatly to the building of a church requests that it be dedicated under a particular title.

It is hard to say how particular churches came to be titled in the course of history. After the definition of the Immaculate Conception (in 1854), many churches were named for Mary under this title. The same was true of the dogma of the Assumption (an ancient dogma solemnly defined in 1950). Often enough, after a new saint is canonized, a church will be named for that saint, for example Saint Elizabeth Seton or Saint John Neumann.

When religious orders build churches, those churches may be named for their founders or saints of their orders.

In some ways naming a church is like naming a baby—lots of people can get into the act.

How are bishops selected?

Canon law 377 states it clearly: "The Supreme Pontiff freely appoints Bishops or confirms those lawfully elected."

Over the centuries there were different methods of election. Almost everyone, for instance, has heard of how Saint Ambrose was made bishop of Milan by acclamation of the people. And in some instances treaties between the Vatican and different countries gave their governments rights of nomination or presentation of candidates for bishop.

The Second Vatican Council determined that such rights should not be granted in the future. It also asked that where rights of nomination or presentation had been granted in the past the civil authorities would waive them.

The *Code of Canon Law* (377.2) legislates that at least every three years the bishops of an ecclesiastical province or a bishop's conference are to draw up a list of priests suitable for the episcopate and send the list to Rome. Each bishop individually has the right to make known worthy candidates.

According to the code, in the case of appointing diocesan bishops, the papal legate, after consultation with different people, suggests candidates (377.3). Canon 377 further specifies that in the case of an auxiliary bishop, the diocesan bishop proposes a list of at least three candidates.

The law further declares (403) that when pastoral needs require it, a diocesan bishop may request one or more auxiliary bishops. It also states that in serious circumstances, the Holy See may give a diocesan bishop an auxiliary with special faculties or a coadjutor with the right of succession. There is nothing to preclude the diocesan bishop's requesting such an appointment.

To sort through these lists and assist the pope in making his decision, there is the Vatican Congregation for Bishops. In the end it is the pope who decides the appointment of bishops and the terms of their appointments.

There are many factors that affect the decision whether or not there is true pastoral necessity for an auxiliary bishop. But there is no "magic number" of people that determines such appointments. The age and health of the ordinary and the geographical size of a diocese may be among considerations.

In recent years both the requests of the dioceses of Cleveland and Joliet for auxiliaries were denied. The Vatican Congregation for Bishops wanted to avoid a proliferation of auxiliary bishops in the United States.

The length of time it takes to appoint a diocesan bishop depends on the situation. Is the see open because of a sudden or unexpected death? Because of a previous bishop's retirement? Are special skills and talents necessary? Particular language abilities, familiarity with the diocese's culture? Pastoral and administrative experience?

Considering the fact that a person appointed may be in office many years, the Holy See may well want to take its time in finding the right bishop.

Why do Catholics eat fish on Friday?

There is and has been no *law* that Catholics must eat fish on Friday. Over the centuries custom and law have been that Catholics abstain from *meat* (the flesh of warm-blooded animals) on certain days (chiefly Fridays).

Many eat fish in the place of meat, but that is a matter of choice. They might just as well eat eggs, cheese or beans if they want protein in the diet on days of abstinence.

Many have suggested that some popes wanted to give the fishermen a boost, but there is no historical proof for that. And, *de facto*, abstinence of one kind or another has its roots in the Old Testament and forbidden foods in the Mosaic law.

The entry on fast and abstinence in the *New Catholic Encyclopedia* will tell you that abstinence among Christians is mentioned in the *Didache* written in or around A.D. 90. So it is hardly an invention of a pope in the Middle Ages. The days of fasting and abstaining, however, have changed and varied from place to place and from one set of times and days to another.

The reason for observing Friday as a day of penance (abstinence) should be fairly obvious. It was the day of Christ's death.

What is the church's position concerning penance and abstinence during Lent and throughout the year?

In 1966 Pope Paul VI reorganized the church's practice of public penance in his apostolic constitution on penance (*Poenitemini*). The 1983 revision of the *Code of Canon Law* incorporated the changes made by Pope Paul. Not long after that, the U.S. bishops applied the canonical requirements to the practice of public penance in our country. To sum up those requirements, Catholics between the ages of eighteen and fifty-nine are obliged to fast on Ash Wednesday and Good Friday. In addition, all Catholics fourteen years old and older must abstain from meat on Ash Wednesday, Good Friday and all the Fridays of Lent.

Fasting, as explained by the U.S. bishops, means partaking of only one full meal. Some food (not equaling another full meal) is permitted at breakfast and around midday or in the evening—depending on when a person chooses to eat the main or full meal.

Abstinence forbids the use of meat but not of eggs, milk products or condiments made of animal fat.

Each year in publishing the Lenten penance requirements, the U.S. bishops quote the teaching of the Holy Father concerning the seriousness of observing these days of penance. The obligation to do penance is a serious one; the obligation to observe, as a whole or "substantially," the days of penance is also serious. But no one should be scrupulous in this regard; failure to observe individual days of penance is not considered serious. Moral theologians remind us that some people are excused from fasting and abstinence because of sickness or other reasons.

In his apostolic constitution on penance, Pope Paul VI did more than simply reorganize church law concerning fast and abstinence. He reminded us of the divine law that each of us in our way do penance. We must all turn from sin and make reparation to God for our sins. We must forgive and show love for one another just as we ask for God's love and forgiveness.

The *Code of Canon Law* and our bishops remind us of other

works and means of doing penance: prayer, acts of self-denial, almsgiving and works of personal charity. Attending Mass daily or several times a week, praying the rosary, making the Way of the Cross, attending the parish evening prayer service, teaching the illiterate to read, reading to the blind, helping at a soup kitchen, visiting the sick and shut-ins and giving an overworked mother a break by baby-sitting—all of these can be even more meaningful and demanding than simply abstaining from meat on Friday.

Observing the specified days of fast and abstinence is the minimum for doing penance. And the *Code of Canon Law*, following what Paul VI wrote, urges that all Fridays of the year be days of penance. Our bishops, referring to the words of the pope, remind us that fast and abstinence on the days prescribed should be considered the minimal response to the Lord's call to penance and conversion. "People," we are reminded, "should seek to do more rather than less."

In that spirit we are encouraged to abstain from meat on all Fridays of the year. Some bishops have further suggested that abstaining from meat on Fridays throughout the year is a fitting sign of our solidarity with hungry people throughout the world. For most people of the world, eating meat is a luxury.

What are the responsibilities of a parish council?

Canon law permits the existence of a parish council. It also allows the bishop to mandate that the parishes in his diocese each have a parish council. If the bishop has not mandated a parish council, a pastor may himself decide to establish a council in his parish.

The purpose of the parish council is to assist the pastor in the pastoral care of the parish. But the council is a consultative body. It advises and offers its opinion. It does not have legislative or decisive power. The governing of the parish is, by law, in the hands of the pastor.

Since the bishop may enact norms governing parish councils in his own diocese, you would really have to ask a particular diocese for or about any norms governing parish councils there.

In the absence of a canonical pastor, the bishop appoints an administrator of a parish. Again, you would have to consult any diocesan norms for administrators or letters of appointment to know their authority.

The *Code of Canon Law*, however, does require that all parishes have a financial council. The duties of this council are to be spelled out in diocesan statutes. It is those statutes that will determine the competence of the council. The pastor can certainly use this council in numerous ways and the wise pastor will make much use of the members' skills and knowledge in determining budgets, expenditures, salaries and contracts.

Is it mandatory to name children after saints?

The 1917 *Code of Canon Law*, in force until 1983, obliged a pastor to require a Christian name be given to a child presented for baptism. If the parents insisted on a name not regarded as Christian, he was to add a Christian name chosen by the parents. A Christian name was understood to be the name of a saint or Christian virtue, or something similar, for example, Mary, Joseph, Faith, Charity, Hope.

The present *Code of Canon Law* puts the matter in negative terms and places the obligation on parents and sponsors as well as the pastor. All of them are to see that "a name foreign to a Christian mentality" is not given (855). What would be a name foreign to a Christian mentality? Something like Lucifer, Zeus or Satan would come under the canon.

Why do the holy days of obligation vary from place to place?

Over the centuries traditions and customs regarding feasts or holy days of obligation have varied from nation to nation. They have also varied within the United States. In the early years of colonization, dioceses such as San Francisco and New Orleans followed the liturgical calendars of the founding nations: Spain and France. Under British rule the Roman Catholics of the United States observed thirty-six feasts of obligation kept in England. In 1777 Pope Pius VI reduced the holy days of obligation for England and its colonies to eleven. And in 1789 Bishop John Carroll of Baltimore, the first U.S. bishop, removed the obligation from the feast of England's patron, Saint George.

In our own time, before Vatican II, the U.S. bishops had obtained approval to observe just six of ten feasts of obligation in the 1917 *Code of Canon Law*. After Vatican II, with the publication of the 1983 *Code of Canon Law* and the earlier revision of the liturgical calendar, there was much discussion in this country of what feasts or solemnities should be observed as days of obligation. Canon 1246.2 of the new code permits the bishops' conference, with prior approval of the Apostolic See, to suppress the obligation of some feasts in the code or transfer their celebration to Sundays.

The U.S. bishops chose to remove the obligation from the feasts of Saint Joseph and Saints Peter and Paul. They also transferred the observance of the solemnities of Corpus Christi (the Most Holy Body and Blood of Christ) and Epiphany to the following Sundays. As a conference they decided to continue celebrating Christmas (December 25), the Solemnity of Mary (January 1), the Ascension (Thursday of the sixth week of Easter), the Assumption of the Blessed Virgin (August 15), All Saints (November 1) and the Immaculate Conception (December 8) as feasts of obligation.

That, however, did not end the matter. The observance of some feasts, such as the Assumption and All Saints, presented particular difficulties when they fell on Saturdays or Mondays.

Priests found themselves trying to celebrate multiple masses to permit people to satisfy both Sunday and feast-day obligations. People got confused over what Masses would satisfy what obligations. The day of the feast or Sunday was not finished when they were attending Mass for the other. It was not only confusing but physically taxing for priest and people. What was this doing to the spirit of devotion?

So, as a conference, the U.S. bishops decided, with Vatican approval given July 4, 1992, that when the solemnity of Mary, the Mother of God (January 1), the Assumption (August 15) or All Saints (November 1) falls on a Saturday or Monday it is not of obligation to attend Mass for the feast.

Yet some western U.S. dioceses apparently felt more was needed and had problems celebrating the feast of the Ascension on a Thursday. As the missalette and liturgical calendar note, the celebration of the Ascension has been transferred from Thursday to the following Sunday in Alaska, California, Hawaii, Idaho, Montana, Nevada, Oregon and Washington.

Further, according to the April 9, 1992, issue of the *Catholic Messenger*, of Davenport, Iowa, Bishop Joseph Ferrario of Hawaii obtained permission of the Holy See to observe only two feasts—other than Sundays—as days of obligation in Hawaii. Those feasts are Christmas and the Immaculate Conception (patroness of the United States). According to the news report this makes Hawaii's practice conform to that of the South Pacific Islands. Ferrario suggested thinking of the suppressed and transferred feasts, together with other major feasts, as "holy days of celebration."

Do East and West agree on the dates for Christmas and Easter?

Differences over the feast of Easter and when to celebrate it have existed since at least the second century. In recent times there has been a desire on the part of many to have a common, fixed date for Easter. And along with that there are people advocating the adoption of a new unchanging calendar. With such a calendar the days of the month would always fall on the same days of the week.

In an appendix to the *Constitution on the Liturgy*, the fathers of Vatican II recognized these wishes and said,

> The sacred Council is not opposed to assigning the feast of Easter to a fixed Sunday in the Gregorian Calendar, provided those whom it may concern give their assent,

especially other Christians who are not in communion with the Apostolic See.

The council also said it does not oppose measures to introduce a perpetual calendar into civil society, provided it retained a seven-day week with Sunday and introduced no days outside the week, so that the present sequence of weeks is left intact. In its *Decree on the Catholic Eastern Churches*, the council said,

> Until all Christians agree, as is hoped, on one day for the celebration of Easter by all, in the meantime as a means of fostering unity among Christians who live in the same area or country, it is left to the patriarchs or to the supreme ecclesiastical authorities of the place to consult all parties involved and so come to an unanimous agreement to celebrate the feast of Easter on the same Sunday. (20)

In other words the council was careful to respect the customs and traditions of the Eastern churches and had no desire of forcing a fixed common date for Easter upon the Eastern churches. And while the church hopes for a common observance of Easter, it hopes it comes about by the agreement of all Christians.

What determines the date of Easter or when Lent begins?

The Council of Nicaea, in 325, determined that Easter should be celebrated the first Sunday after the first full moon of spring. To determine the beginning of Lent, count back six Sundays before Easter. The Wednesday before the first of these Sundays is Ash Wednesday.

Why do we celebrate Christmas?

Why do citizens of the United State celebrate Lincoln's or Washington's birthday? They were great men who had a tremendous influence on the people's history and lives. We celebrate Jesus' birth because it was such a tremendously important event in the history of the human race. His birth was the turning point of all history. By being born and coming among us, he brought salvation to the whole world.

Neither Scripture nor tradition tells us the day of the year that Jesus was born. And historians even disagree on the exact year of his birth. There are different theories about why the feast celebrating his birth was assigned to December 25. That day could have been chosen for mixed reasons.

In the Julian calendar, however, the calendar in use when the feast was established, December 25 was the day of the winter solstice. By imperial decree that day had been dedicated to the pagan sun god. Many believe that the church wanted to impose a Christian meaning or significance to this day and replace the pagan celebration with a Christian feast. At the time the feast was established, Christian writers were already referring to Jesus as the Sun of Justice. That made this day also appropriate for the feast.

Is there a hierarchy in lay ministries?

Any discussion of the church's hierarchical structure and exercise of ministries should begin with what Saint Paul wrote about gifts in chapter 12 of 1 Corinthians. There he said:

> Now there are varieties of gifts, but the same Spirit; and there are varieties of services, but the same Lord; and there are varieties of activities, but it is the same God who activates all of them in everyone... All these are activated by one and the same Spirit, who allots to each one individually just as the Spirit chooses.... If I speak in the tongues of mortals and of angels but do not have love, I am a noisy gong or a clanging cymbal. And if I have prophetic powers, and understand all mysteries and all knowledge, and if I have all faith, so as to remove mountains, but do not have love, I am nothing. (12:4—13:2)

The word *hierarchy* can be used in different senses, as a look in *Webster's* dictionary will make evident. For instance, we can talk about a hierarchy of values, a corporate hierarchy or a hierarchy of responsibilities. When we talk about the hierarchy of the church, it generally refers to the structure of the church, or those in ordained ministries or exercising authority and jurisdiction.

In the structural sense the church is divided into the laity and sacred ministers, legally called clerics (see canon 207). In this sense those who belong to the hierarchy are deacons, priests and bishops under the pope.

Even those who are officially instituted into the ministries of reader and acolyte (as candidates for priesthood) do not belong to the hierarchy in this canonical sense. And that means that those who receive ministries as laypersons do not belong to the hierarchy.

One could, in a certain sense, speak of a hierarchy in extraordinary and special ministries or a ranking of ministries according to their involvement in the celebration of the Eucharist and nearness to serving the priest and the altar. But that does not increase anyone's personal worth or determine anyone's holiness or sanctity.

We all have a common dignity as children of God and a common responsibility for carrying out the church's mission in our own way and according to our state. Remember, too, how Jesus admonished his disciples when they asked for special treatment: "Whoever wishes to be great among you will be your servant..." (Mark 10:43).

Ministries, like the gifts of which Saint Paul speaks, should not be a source of pride or boasting, not a reason for lording it over others! In the end the most important is the hierarchy of holiness. Our true glory comes from how completely we love God and do the service of love for each other.

How can a priest retire?

Priests may retire from active ministry for a variety of reasons. Like other people they get old, weak and sick. They are unable at seventy to stand in a classroom for five or six hours a day. They do not have the energy to run a parish of a thousand families. Some are forced into nursing or retirement homes for the same kind of help other old people need.

Few, unless they are blind, deaf or bedridden, stop praying or celebrating the Eucharist. Many who are able continue to give what help they can in parishes, convents, old people's homes and other institutions.

There are a lot of heroic priests out there who have labored many years with little attention then or now. Many parishes are glad to have a retired priest take up residence there and offer help with daily and Sunday Masses.

Old age does not pass a priest by simply because he is a priest.

Who oversees the formation of priests?

On the highest level the education of seminarians is the concern of the Vatican Congregation for Catholic Education. The Congregation for Institutes of the Consecrated Life and Societies of Apostolic Life also sees to the formation of candidates for the priesthood in the case of religious orders. In the United States, on the national level, the U.S. Bishops' Committee on Priestly Formation looks to the education and formation of future priests.

Of course, the local bishops and the major superiors of religious orders are responsible for their students and how they are being taught and formed.

There was a study of seminaries and theology schools and formation centers initiated by the Congregation for Catholic Education in 1981 at the mandate of Pope John Paul II. Bishop John A. Marshall of Burlington, Vermont, was in charge of the study. A report on the visitation and study of freestanding theologates, collegiate seminaries and clusters was written by Msgr. Richard Pates, executive secretary of the U.S. Seminary Study. It was published in the April 20, 1990, issue of *Origins*, a publication of the U.S. Catholic Conference.

According to Monsignor Pates's report, Bishop Marshall was assisted in the study by forty American bishops, fifteen major superiors of religious men and ten other representatives of religious seminaries. Seventy representatives of seminary rectors, spiritual directors, directors of field education, professors and deans were members of teams that conducted seminary visitations. There were 221 on-site visits of the institutions educating students for the priesthood.

Bishops, seminary presidents or rectors, together with religious superiors involved, received reports from the visitation committees on strengths and weaknesses with committee recommendations. These reports were finally sent to the appropriate Vatican congregations. The Vatican reviewed the reports and sent a commentary with directives to be implemented to the bishops and religious superiors. Studies of individual seminaries continue to be made.

Why are married ministers from other Christian denominations allowed to be ordained, yet priests cannot marry?

Pope John Paul II and the Holy See do not see the male and celibate requirements for ordination as unjust. A Roman rite Catholic who seeks ordination knows and accepts the condition of celibacy in advance. Married ministers from other Christian denominations who enter into full communion with the Catholic church were married before the question arose of ordination to the priesthood in the Roman rite. The church sees some special good to be served by ordaining these minister to the priesthood. Surely the pope sees a good for the whole church—not just a personal good—to be served by such an ordination.

Obviously, Pope John Paul II is convinced of the wisdom and value of requiring Roman rite priests to be celibate. He believes the church is unable by the will of God to validly ordain women. It does not seem likely anything will happen to change the convictions of the pope in either case.

Whether one agrees or disagrees with the pope and his convictions, consider these few things:

- There are at least two elements in a vocation to the priesthood. One is a personal call of the individual through grace. The second is the call of the church to service and priesthood, manifested finally in the call of the bishop to ordination.

- The church is obliged to call only those it feels will best serve the needs of the people of God.

- At this time the pope now charged with leading the people of God believes that celibacy is a necessary value and quality for ordination and priestly ministry in the Roman rite.

- Whether persons agree with the judgment of the pope and bishops in an instance like this, they ought at least to listen to the reasons being given, try to understand them and then give the pope and bishops credit for believing their judgments are correct and faithful.

- We should all be engaged in a search for truth and what will best serve the good of the people of God. Priesthood should be thought of first and above all else as a call to sacrifice, service and true ministry. In establishing requirements of ordination, the church must follow what it believes Christ himself instituted. The church must weigh the felt call to the priesthood of any person against who it believes can best serve the welfare of God's people.

What is Catholic feminism?

According to *Webster's Ninth New Collegiate Dictionary*, *feminism* is defined as the theory of the political, economic and social equality of the sexes and organized activity on behalf of women's rights and interests.

Catholic feminism is simply the belief that men and women are equal in the church and religion as well as the rest of life. A Catholic feminist is anyone who argues and works for that recognition and to give women equality in the church.

Trying to say how feminists may differ among themselves in their beliefs and goals may be like trying to say how Democrats and Republicans may differ among themselves on goals and policies. Some goals of some feminists may be questionable or goals with which other feminists could not agree. Most Catholic feminists differ from many other feminists, however, in opposing abortion and supporting the right to life. Some Catholic feminists dissent from church teaching on particular questions of sexual morality and other issues, but that would not be particular to them as women or feminists. It is also true of some men.

A report sponsored by the Catholic Commission for Justice, Peace and Development of the New Zealand Catholic Bishops' Conference ("Made in God's Image") listed many of the concerns of women in the church: ordination of women to the priesthood, the use of inclusive language in liturgy and worship, the opportunity for laypersons (including women) to preach, balanced representation of competent men and women on all diocesan management and advisory boards and parish finance committees, women as ministers of the sacraments of reconciliation and anointing, the installation of women as lectors, pastoral care for the divorced and remarried, the use of women in training and forming seminarians, and equal pay and employment opportunity.

Most feminists are concerned about wife and child abuse, child care and working women, and forcing separated and divorced husbands to provide support for their children.

In their response to the "Made in God's Image" report ("Discerning Aspirations Congruent With the Gospel"), the New Zealand Bishops' Conference stated that the report stood on its own and permission to publish it did not mean that the bishops agreed with all the report's contents. At the same time they promised to undertake theological reflection on the research and report. This theological reflection, they said, will genuinely try to discern which aspirations expressed in the research are congruent with the church's commitment to the gospel.

Women, whether feminists or not, have legitimate grievances in the social and political order. And, as has been suggested by any number of bishops, they have many legitimate goals for greater equality and recognition in the life of the church.

What is the history of the Infant of Prague?

Something of the history of the statue of the Infant of Prague is in the *Dictionary of Catholic Devotions,* by Michael Walsh. The statue was brought to Prague by a Spanish princess and donated there to Our Lady of Victory church in 1628.

The replicas of the statue are frequently dressed in royal robes. In the infant's left hand there is a globe with a cross on it. That symbolizes Christ is ruler and redeemer of the whole world. He has redeemed it by the cross. The right hand of the infant is raised in blessing.

According to *Signs and Symbols in Christian Life,* by George Ferguson, two rings linked or placed one above the other symbolize earth and sky. The two rings on the infant's fingers further tell us he is Lord of heaven and earth and he blesses all.

Does a Communion service on Saturday fulfill the Sunday obligation?

A person has not fulfilled the obligation of the law to attend Mass by attending a Communion service. But the obligation can be dispensed in certain circumstances.

In certain unforeseen or unanticipated circumstances, the lawgiver would not intend to bind a person or persons to fulfillment of a law. The church may not want to bind the persons attending the Communion service to anything more and would excuse them from any further obligation.

There are moral theologians who would excuse those caught in such a situation on the basis of substantial observance. They would say substantial observance should be applied to the obligation to attend Mass on Sundays just as the church itself applies it to the laws of fast and abstinences. To miss one day is not a grave matter. Thus, to miss Mass on one occasion for good reason would not be a substantial failure to observe the law.

The pastor might very well see certain circumstances as good reason to dispense those present from any further obligation. In light of the priest shortage, some dioceses are developing guidelines that address these situations.

Can a person spread the gospel without preaching?

In his *Apostolic Exhortation on Evangelization in the Modern World (Evangelii Nuntiandi)* given December 8, 1975, Pope Paul VI wrote,

> Above all the gospel must be proclaimed by witness. Take a Christian or a handful of Christians who, in the midst of their own community, show their capacity for understanding and acceptance, their sharing of life and destiny with other people, their solidarity with the efforts of all for whatever is noble and good. Let us suppose that, in addition, they radiate in an altogether simple and unaffected way their hope in something that is not seen and that one would dare to imagine. Through this wordless witness these Christians stir up irresistible questions in the hearts of those who see how they live: Why are they like this? Why do they live in this way? What or who is it that inspires them? Why are they in our midst? Such a witness is already a silent proclamation of the Good News and a very powerful and effective one. Here we have an initial act of evangelization.... All Christians are called to this witness, and in this way they can be real evangelizers.

Adding anything to this statement may be something like trying to embroider a rose. However, this must have been part of the insight of Saint Francis of Assisi when he invited one of his early followers to go preaching with him. They walked through a town and returned where they were staying without speaking a word. When the companion asked why they had never preached, Francis responded that they had indeed given their sermon by offering their wordless example.

Many who request instruction in the Catholic faith do so because of the example of some good Catholic or Catholics who had drawn them. It might have been a relative, a coworker, a business acquaintance or someone else, but almost always it was a person living his or her faith who attracted them. That is evangelization at its most basic level (cf. *Catechism of the Catholic Church* 849–856).

What are the corporal and spiritual works of mercy?

The works of mercy are actions done out of love of God and neighbor to assist others in spiritual or physical need.

The *corporal acts of mercy* are to feed the hungry, to give drink to the thirsty, to clothe the naked, to visit the imprisoned, to shelter the homeless, to visit the sick and to bury the dead.

The *spiritual works of mercy* are to admonish the sinner, to comfort the afflicted, to forgive offenses, to bear wrongs patiently, to counsel the doubtful, to instruct the ignorant and to pray for the living and the dead.

What is tithing?

According to Father Louis Hartman, C.SS.R., in the *Encyclopedic Dictionary of the Bible*, tithing was an ancient Semitic custom. It was observed differently at different times in Israelite history. Although John McKenzie in his *Dictionary of the Bible* calls tithing a religious tax, Hartman says it was not viewed as a tax but as a gift made at a religious sanctuary and it was never a ten-percent "income tax." The tithe applied to farm products—firstfruits and the firstborn of flock and herd. It was made on new grain, new wine and new oil. The tithes given at a local sanctuary were eaten in a festive meal before God. And every third year the tithe was to be put in storehouses and used for orphans, widows, aliens and the poor.

According to the *New Catholic Encyclopedia*, the early Christian church had no tithing system. It viewed tithing as abrogated by the law of Christ. However, by A.D. 585, the Council of Macon legislated tithes and other local councils made similar laws. The earliest practice was to give tithes of the fruits of the earth. In the thirteenth century tithing was extended to profits and wages, and different rules were made about what was tithable and what was not. The practice did not continue very long in Europe; it was never general practice in the United States.

The present *Code of Canon Law* (222) says, "The Christian faithful are obliged to assist with the needs of the church so that the Church has what is necessary for divine worship, for apostolic works and works of charity and for the decent sustenance of ministers," and, "They are also obliged to promote social justice and, mindful of the precept of the Lord, to assist the poor from their own resources."

So there is no church law about tithing or how much a person is to contribute to the parish or the larger church. Obviously, though, we do have a responsibility to contribute to the support of our parish and pastor and those who minister with him. And in our order of priorities, they should come high.

But the amount we contribute to our parishes must be weighed against the real and actual needs of our parishes and against how much we are able to contribute without impoverishing ourselves.

A parish that is deeply in debt and must maintain a parish school obviously needs more from a parishioner than one that is debt-free and has no school to support.

And a person committed to tithing should not necessarily give everything of the tithe to the parish. There are other people and organizations that have a legitimate claim on our charity and should share in our contributions. There may be poor people whom we want to help personally. There are soup kitchens that need our alms to feed the hungry. There are organizations depending on us to give medical care and assistance to the poor or to conduct medical research. People starving in foreign lands have some claim on our charity.

Our contributions—or part of them—should be used to help the sick, suffering, starving and dying now rather than be placed in a savings account to gather interest.

Give what you believe to be a fair amount to maintain your church and parish, and donate the rest to the people and charities you decide are the most important and that you especially wish to help.

Does the church have a policy about filming movie scenes in churches?

As a rule, dioceses do not have a formal set of rules concerning the use of churches for movie or TV filming. The decision to give permission would generally be the responsibility of the pastor or a religious superior. Those consulted pointed out that it would obviously be wise for a pastor or the one in charge of the church to ask for a copy of the script in advance or at least carefully inquire into the nature of the film to make sure the film does not include material that would be sacrilegious, offensive or inappropriate in a sacred place.

Whenever filming takes place in a church, those who have the care of the church should remove the Blessed Sacrament while filming is going on.

A film rating is usually not determined until the film has been completed and studied by a review board. But a pastor could get a sense of the moral quality of the film by questioning its makers and insisting on reading the script. Yet, scripts can be and are changed as filming proceeds.

If a pastor foresees a given film could possibly be controversial or embarrassing to the Catholic community, he would be prudent to seek the advice of diocesan authorities. And a diocesan authority should be informed about possible filming in Catholic churches because of the press coverage to be expected.

CHAPTER FOUR

$$\dagger$$

Pastoral Puzzles

In his book The Challenge of Faith, *popular spiritual author Father John Powell tells the story of how he almost lost his faith.*

Before leaving for the Jesuit novitiate, Father Powell wanted to express thanks to a neighbor for all that he'd done for Powell and his family over the years. After Father Powell had said thank you and the two men had exchanged some small talk, the neighbor found out where Father Powell was going and said: "Don't go. You'll be wasting your time and talent. There is no God. You'll be pouring your life down a drain."

Shortly after he arrived, sure enough doubts naturally began to appear. "What if the man across the street was right? What if there is no God?" His prayers seemed to go unanswered. In the midst of despair, ready to give up, he went to see the Master of Novices who said simply, "Be patient." Eventually, after a brief spell of disbelief, Father Powell experienced it—the "touch of God." Rather than becoming an occasion of danger, the crisis of faith became an opportunity for him to grow in faith.

In a similar way, through his book The Seeker's Guide to Being Catholic, *Mitch Finley speaks to the situation of many*

Catholics today. Instead of having all the answers, they find themselves asking more questions. Faith that once used to be as solid as a rock at times appears to feel like sand through fingers. Speaking of this condition he writes,

> *Being Catholic today means being a seeker, a pilgrim, a person with questions, doubts, and insecurities. Most Catholics no longer think of the Vatican as an answer machine and their faith as a security blanket. Rather, to be Catholic is to embrace a faith that sometimes requires you to take chances and stick your neck out.*

The call then is not to certitude but to faith—to trust in our relationship with Jesus and his church. In this regard the Catechism of the Catholic Church *states:*

> *The world we live in often seems very far from the one promised us by faith. Our experiences of evil and suffering, injustice, and death, seem to contradict the Good News; they can shake our faith and become a temptation against it. It is then we must turn to the* witnesses of faith... *(164–165).*

Those witnesses—Abraham, Mary, the saints—reassure us that in our moments of doubt, while there may be no "answer," there is constant love of God all around us. The challenge and gift is opening ourselves to that love.

•

What fate awaits those who die outside the church?

There is a scene in *Brideshead Revisited*, by Evelyn Waugh, in which an elderly family member lies dying. He has lived a life without God for many years. But, just before he dies, he is seen making the Sign of the Cross.

Waugh's point is, of course, we must never give up on the mercy and grace of God. We do not know what God does in the last moments of a person's life. We should trust and go on praying for those near and dear to us.

There is also a story about Saint John Vianney, the Cure of Ars. A concerned friend had consulted him about the fate of a dear one who had jumped off a bridge and committed suicide. The Cure responded that between the bridge and the water God overtook the man.

We must not despair. God is wonderfully good and merciful. With hope and love we can place those who seem removed from God in his caring hands.

Why does God allow people to suffer?

As Pope John Paul II indicated in his apostolic letter *On the Christian Meaning of Human Suffering,* there is always a certain amount of mystery in suffering. That is especially true of natural disasters. Suffering may be easier to explain when it results from the misuse of human freedom.

In the cases of Mary and Jesus and their suffering, we might recast the question as, "Once God gave human beings a free will, how could God not allow them to suffer?" Mary was forced to ride an ass sixty-four miles from Nazareth to Bethlehem because the emperor was free to demand it. Just as God gave Mary a free will and the ability to say yes to being the mother of Jesus, God gave the emperor a free will that enabled him to decree a census with difficulties for other people. Just as Jesus was able to say, "Not my will but yours be done," his persecutors were able to cry, "Crucify him!"

Suffering can come to others from humans' misuse of freedom. But, again, when God chooses to let us be human, to make choices for good and evil, how could God constantly step in and say, "No, in this case I will not let you do this!"? To take away the freedom of the evildoer takes away the merit and the glory of the saint who freely says, "Yes, whatever it costs me, I will be faithful to God's will."

Take all the pain out of Mary's life and what meaning does she have for us as the protodisciple of Jesus? What does she then have to say to the mother today who risks her life to give birth to a child? What meaning does she have for the wife and mother who lives in poverty? For the mother who suffers watching her child waste away from cancer?

If God had not allowed Mary to experience hardship, pain

and suffering, what would she have to say to us about these things? What inspiration could she have for us if God had said to her that she would never have to worry about anything again, never lack for anything, would always have a comfortable existence and a life of plenty?

Mary could experience what she did because she was one of us just as Jesus was one of us. Mary can be praised and honored because she accepted pain and suffering to do God's work.

Can suffering be redemptive?

Some assert that all sickness is the work of the devil. But what did Jesus say when told about Pilate murdering some Galileans and mingling their blood with that of the sacrifices they offered?

Jesus asked if, because these Galileans had suffered in this way, the people thought they were greater sinners than all other Galileans. And he answered his own question, "By no means!" Jesus went on to ask if the eighteen who were killed when the tower of Siloam fell on them were more guilty than everyone else who lived in Jerusalem. Again he answered himself, "By no means!" (see Luke 13:1–5).

In John 9:1–3 when one of Jesus' disciples asks him if a man blind from birth was blind because of his own sins or the sins of his parents, "Jesus answered, 'Neither he nor his parents sinned; it is so that the works of God might be made visible through him.'" Jesus promptly went on to give the man sight.

We cannot automatically make sickness and suffering the result of personal sin or pronounce it the work of the devil. At the same time God does not expect Christians to be complacent in the face of pain and illness. The followers of Christ can never be indifferent to the suffering of another. Referring to the parable of the Good Samaritan, Pope John Paul II, in his apostolic letter *The Christian Meaning of Human Suffering*, asserts, "Suffering, which is present in so many different forms in our human world, is also present in order to unleash love

136

in the human person.... The person who is a 'neighbor' cannot indifferently pass by the suffering of another."

Surely God blesses the work of doctors and nurses, therapists and pharmacists—all who minister to the sick and look for cures. And surely God blesses families and friends who visit and care for the sick. In most parishes visiting the sick and bringing spiritual care to them is an important way of carrying out the corporal and spiritual acts of mercy.

When the priest anoints a sick person, he prays that God will give that person healing and strength. The priest asks God to show the sick person mercy and compassion and restore him or her to health. So God does expect us to struggle against sickness and disease.

And what of the redemptive value of suffering? Many who have endured physical affliction could speak of the graces they discovered in sickness. Saint Ignatius of Loyola would surely tell how he discovered God, how his whole life was changed during his recuperation from a broken arm and leg suffered in battle. Francis of Assisi would tell how God came to him in the midst of sickness and imprisonment.

Through sickness God often stops us in our tracks and turns us around. We are forced to take time to reflect on our values and goals in life. In sickness we experience our own weakness and helplessness. We are invited to seek out God as our hope, our strengthener, our consoler and comforter.

In the midst of sickness we see the love and goodness of God in those who minister to us and make Christ present in our lives.

There are also graces for those who care for the sick. Here we receive the opportunity to practice charity. We are given the opportunity of finding Jesus in the sick. We cannot, then, be passive in the face of suffering. We must, again like Jesus, seek to heal and make whole, relieve the pain and anguish of the sufferer. As the pope phrases it, "At one and the same time Christ has taught man to do good by his suffering and to do good to those who suffer. In this double aspect, he has completely revealed the meaning of suffering."

Out of pain and suffering God can and does draw good.

How can a good God allow evil?

The existence of evil is a mystery. Everyone, including Pope John Paul II, who has written about the existence of evil and suffering starts out by stating evil and suffering are mysteries and does not pretend to offer a complete or definitive explanation for the why of them. This is especially true concerning natural catastrophes and physical evils, such as sickness and disease. We cannot completely "explain" why a good God allows such evils.

But, often what appears to one person as evil is accepted as good by another. The child who wants to go on a picnic sees rain as evil. The farmer blesses God for it. The forest fire threatening a house is evil to a homeowner. To an ecologist it is part of nature's way of renewing old forests. The flooding river that damages buildings in a town may seem evil to the residents, but the farmers on the outskirts might be happy for the deposit of new rich soil on the land.

As the story of the Tower of Babel in the book of Genesis instructs us, one of the things we humans have to contend with is pride and a feeling of self-sufficiency. Natural upheavals as well as sickness and disease keep us aware that we are not self-sufficient or the masters of the universe. They remind there is a power higher than ourselves and we are very much dependent on God.

Earthquakes, floods, hurricanes, volcanic eruptions and droughts, as well as pain and suffering, also tell us that this is not paradise in which we live, that this is an imperfect world and we can never expect complete happiness and fulfillment here. They remind us that we can reach our ultimate goals and achieve complete happiness only in the realized kingdom of God.

God has quite a different view from ours. We must trust that what seems evil to us will eventually be for the good.

What was the fate of Judas?

In *Basics of the Faith: A Catholic Catechism*, Alan Schreck says,

> The Catholic Church teaches that we cannot judge or de-
> termine whether any particular person has been con-
> demned to hell, even Hitler or Judas Iscariot. The mercy
> of God is such that a person can repent even at the point
> of death and be saved.

Many have expressed concern over the reported "despair" of
Judas. Scripture does not explicitly use this word concerning
Judas, however. And other than to define it, not many manu-
als or catechisms speak much of it, either. *An American Catholic
Catechism*, edited by George Dyer, says despair seems to be,

> Besides a distortion of faith itself, more a psychological
> or emotional crisis, perhaps generated by past sins, than
> a mortal sin in itself. Obviously despair is a grievous
> matter.
> But it is difficult to conceive how a person who de-
> spairs could fulfill in this act the other conditions requi-
> site for mortal sin. It is particularly difficult to believe
> that a person who despairs does so with full consent of
> the will or in a radically free act.

Why does God sometimes seem absent to those who pray?

Those who write about spiritual dryness or aridity offer various reasons for this condition. They suggest looking first for
natural explanations, such as sickness, lack of sleep, worry
over family problems and overwork. Or, they say, it may de-
rive from emotional problems. Other causes offered are habits
of sensuality, habitual venial sin, vain curiosity, lukewarmness
in serving God and superficiality. If a person discerns that one
or more of these causes is present, they must deal with and
remedy them.

Writers, however, such as Adolphe Tanquerey in *The
Spiritual Life: A Treatise on Ascetical and Mystical Theology,* also
recognize aridity can have a providential purpose. After

describing aridity as a privation of the sensible and spiritual consolation that makes prayer and the practice of virtue easy, he speaks of why God may see fit to visit a person with aridity.

Tanquerey says that God acts thus to detach persons from created things and even the happiness that comes from devotion so that they may learn to love God for God's sake alone. God thus humbles a person by making him or her see that consolations are not a right but free gifts from God. Spiritual dryness also effects purification from past faults, present attachments and self-seeking.

Serving God without emotional reward and by sheer willpower can bring real pain and suffering. The pain endured for the sake of God becomes an act of expiation.

Tanquerey urges those suffering aridity to remember that it is more meritorious to serve God without warm emotions than when experiencing great consolation. They should also remember in order to love God it is enough to will to do so. The most perfect act of love is bringing our own wills into conformity with God's will.

Tanquerey urges persons in aridity to unite themselves to Jesus in the Garden of Olives praying, "Not my will but yours be done." Above all, persons suffering spiritual dryness must not lose heart and abandon prayer, piety and devotion.

Many saints, such as Saint Teresa of Avila and Saint John of the Cross have experienced the pain of spiritual dryness. Saint Teresa speaks of aridity in *Interior Castle*. Saint John of the Cross explains it in *Ascent of Mt. Carmel*, writing about the dark night of the soul and the passive night of the senses.

What does it mean to be scrupulous?

Scrupulous people lack two things: the ability to judge well and a sense of humor. They have great difficulty in making good, reasonable judgments—at least about themselves and their own moral acts. And they have difficulty in coming to any kind of final decision, accepting it and living with it. They can decide something rationally but not emotionally. They have to keep digging up old "sins" (which are very often non-sins) and rehashing them and their circumstances. They have to decide over and over again whether they have done everything "right" so that God cannot catch them up.

Scrupulous people live in constant fear and distrust. They fear the wrath and punishment of God. Perhaps it is because of an image of God they acquired in childhood as all-avenging judge of human beings, an image they may have absorbed from teachers or parents. They do not accept God as a loving, merciful, compassionate, forgiving parent. They are forever anxious and worried, depressed and frightened.

One of the signs of equilibrium is the ability to laugh, especially at yourself. Perhaps one way to gain this ability is to ask yourself what you would say to a friend who came and told you your story as his own. Perhaps then you could say: "You know, you really are being ridiculous about this. You worry about things that ordinary good people do not consider serious at all. Other sensible people accept that they have really tried to be honest with God and themselves and they now accept God's forgiveness."

People who suffer from scruples should:

1. Accept their confessors' judgments and abide by them. Follow their advice.

2. Accept that they are, like all of us, in need of God's healing and mercy.

3. Read and pray often over the parable of the Prodigal Son, the stories of the woman taken in adultery and of Mary Magadalene washing the feet of Jesus. Realize that this is the same Jesus and the same Father to whom we come asking for love, mercy and forgiveness.

4. Ask Jesus to help them to accept forgiveness and to trust in his words of forgiveness.

5. Realize that Jesus did not ask those he forgave to keep repeating their confessions of guilt over and over again. Once they repented, once they asked for forgiveness, he simply gave it and asked them to go and sin no more.

141

6. Accept that they did their best to confess as required and that God doesn't ask any more than that.

7. Accept that they cannot judge the things they did years ago by the knowledge and understanding that they have now. The things they did years ago have to be judged by what they understood at the time. Guilt is not retroactive.

8. Accept that the more they keep going over what they did and said years ago, the more confused they are likely to become now. If they were satisfied in the past that they were doing the best that they could, they should be done with it all.

9. Accept this agony as proof of their faith! If they did not believe and care, it would not be the trial and agony that it is.

We must all surrender to the love and goodness of God. Trust in God. When and if you achieve that, you will find peace. Pray with Jesus, "Father, into your hands I commend my spirit."

An audiobook that may be helpful is *Helps for the Scrupulous*, by Russell Abata, C.SS.R. *Understanding Scrupulosity: Helpful Answers for Those Who Experience Nagging Questions and Doubts*, by Thomas M. Santa, C.SS.R., can also be helpful.

Did Jesus know everything?

The question of what Jesus knew and when he knew it still occupies the discussions of theologians. In his commentary on the Gospel of Matthew, Alexander Jones reminds us that in the Incarnate Son there are two planes of knowledge. One is total and divine. The second is limited and human.

As Jones expresses it, direct communication between the two is established only by Jesus' "infused knowledge." This knowledge (of his divinity and messianic character) is given Jesus in proportion to the needs of his redemptive work. Jesus did not need the knowledge of the time of the world's ending or the destruction of Jerusalem to accomplish the work given him.

Beyond that Jones notes the constant practice of the Son was to claim no knowledge beyond that which the Father had instructed him to use.

According to the *Collegeville Commentary*, the Son's knowledge is put in a category of its own—above that of men and angels. But as man, Jesus knew only what he had learned in the normal human way and those things that were revealed to him for the needs of his mission. Apparently the time of the final manifestation was not among those things.

Nor did the disciples need to know. Even in his glorified state, after the Resurrection, Jesus refused them that information.

Does God have a memory?

In the Eucharistic Prayers of the Mass we ask God to "remember" his people, those for whom we pray, those who have gone before us in death and those gathered together in the celebration of the Eucharist. There are also pleas in the Psalms that God remember his compassion, his kindness of old, and that he remember not our frailties and sins of our youth. And Mary praises God because he has helped Israel his servant, "remembering his mercy" (Luke 1:54).

Yet in all these prayers those who speak use human language to describe the way we perceive God acting in our lives (see *Catechism of the Catholic Church* 26–49).

In fact, of course, God is different from us. God's way of knowing is different from ours. The theological dictionaries remind us that whenever we speak of God we do so by analogy. That means (whether we include the phrase or not) we are always saying that God is "something like" and God's knowledge is "something like..."

From our point of view—our experience of God—we think and speak of God acting in the past and present and how God will act in the future. But God exists and acts in eternity. Theologian Ludwig Ott, in his *Fundamentals of Catholic Dogma*, tells us that in eternity "there is nothing past, as if it were no longer, nothing future, as it has not yet been. In it there is only 'is,' that is, the present." He further writes that in God's knowledge there is no progress from known to unknown; there is no succession: "God knows all in one single individual act." With God, "The difference between past, present and future does not exist...since for God all is present."

An American Catholic Catechism, edited by George J. Dyer, puts it in similar terms:

> Present, past, and future are temporal distinctions that are directly meaningful only to a mind in time knowing in the present. If God truly transcends the world, and if the world and its total order depend on God, then God knows whatever is in the world at any point of its temporal order. It is all "present" to him, not as though he and it were subject to some one identical temporal measurement, as when we say that something is present to us, but in the simple coincidence of the divine causal knowledge with all that proceeds from it, as when we say that action and effect are simultaneous.

In other words, from God's point of view everything is now. That applies not just to the knowledge of God but also to all the divine acts, including those of the will. So, in theological terms, we can hardly speak of God as having memory. If everything is present—is now—God has no need of memory, or of us to remind God of something forgotten or of which God is not mindful. And if God is truly eternal, we can hardly speak, from God's standpoint, of "when." God's decisions are all just as much in the "now" as his knowledge.

Our human intellect is limited. It can take us only so far in understanding the infinite, divine life of God. We will always be confronted with mystery in trying to understand God.

Can God forgive someone who has had an abortion?

God can forgive anything because God is God—because as Saint John proclaims, "God is love and he who remains in love remains in God and God in him" (1 John 4:16).

The proof of God's readiness to forgive is in all those parables in the Gospels, such as the story of the Prodigal Son and the parable of the Lost Sheep. It is in the very actions of Jesus, proclaimed in Scripture and homilies at Mass—how Jesus forgave the woman taken in adultery, Mary Magdalene, Saint Peter, the good thief, the very ones who crucified him.

How can those in the church community forgive? The community must be willing to forgive if it is to imitate Jesus, to act in his name. The apostles (disciples of Jesus) were sent forth to preach and bring the forgiveness of sins! The church's business is forgiveness! We dare not withhold mercy and forgiveness from others if we ourselves desire forgiveness. After all, do we not pray in the Lord's Prayer that God forgive us as we forgive others?

Also, if we are to imitate Jesus, we must be willing to forgive ourselves as Jesus forgives us, to accept the forgiveness that Jesus holds out to us. In its own way, to think God cannot forgive is a terrible kind of pride and almost an insult to God! It is to place limits on God's mercy and forgiveness.

Imagine the young woman caught up in such circumstances. Have pity on her. Imagine the fear, the shame, the despair she experiences; her sense of hopelessness; all those things that lead to such bad and regrettable decisions. If we could be moved to pity, how much more will God have pity! As with any serious sin, those who have had an abortion must strive to understand what they have done and why, and to avoid serious sin in the future.

How does the Father beget the Son?

We are always limited creatures trying to understand an infinite God—a being far beyond our comprehension and intelligence. To understand him as God understands himself would make us God or the equals of God.

145

In speaking of Jesus we must always remember we are talking about the second person of the Blessed Trinity—God the Son—become incarnate. In Jesus, the Son, are united two natures: the divine and human. The divine person possesses two natures.

In the divine nature the Son exists from eternity. He always was, is and shall be. There never was a time when the Son did not exist and never will be a time when he will not exist. From eternity or in eternity, the Son is begotten of or proceeds from the Father; to use comparisons that limp—as a thought proceeds from or is begotten by the mind (not *made*, not created) or light proceeds from the sun. Just as the Father is *always* there, the Son (Second Person) is always there being begotten by the Father.

In time the Second Person, the Son, took to himself a human nature—he became flesh, he became man, Jesus. In his *human nature* the Son (Jesus) did not exist forever. It is this event we proclaim in the Angelus prayer and celebrate at Christmas—"And the Word became flesh and dwelt among us." Jesus, in whom are united the divine and human natures, began to exist in time.

What promises does God make?

If you look at a concordance of the Bible, you will find dozens of references to texts about God's promises. Many of them will concern God's faithfulness to his promises of the covenant with Abraham, Moses and his people.

One of the more prominent discussions of this is in Saint Paul's first letter to the Corinthians (10:13). *Today's English Version* of the Bible translates them,

> Every test that you have experienced is the kind that normally comes to people. But God keeps his promise, and he will not allow you to be tested beyond your power to remain firm; at the time you are put to the test, he will give you the strength to endure it, and so provide you with a way out.

These words in context refer to temptations against faith in times of trial and persecution.

Also, in the course of John's description of the Last Supper (John 13–16), Jesus spoke of preparing a place for his disciples in his Father's house, that whatever they would ask in his name he would do, and that he would send them the Holy Spirit to be their advocate. He promised them peace. But he also spoke to them of the suffering they would have to endure. Lastly, Jesus promises at the end of Matthew's Gospel (28:20), "I am with you always, until the end of the age."

Did Jesus really think God had abandoned him on the cross?

Father Raymond E. Brown, s.s., in *The Death of the Messiah* (Volume II) devotes some fifteen pages to Jesus' death cry in the Gospels of Mark (15:34) and Matthew (27:46).

Brown indicates that since the time of the fathers of the church through contemporary times, exegetes have tried to explain the words of Jesus, "My God, my God, why have you forsaken me," in various ways.

Many exegetes will remind us that Jesus' words are the opening words of Psalm 22. The evangelist expects his readers to recognize these words as such. The reader is to realize that the speaker in the psalm goes on to recall God's help in the past, to ask his help now again and proclaim God "did not despise or abhor the affliction of the afflicted; he did not hide his face from me, but heard when I cried to him."

The passage is, at least implicitly, a proclamation of trust and confidence. Alexander Jones gives this explanation of Jesus' words in *The Gospel According to Saint Mark*. He refers to the word *forsaken* ("abandoned") as a "poetical expression of the pain to which God 'abandoned' the psalmist without, however, having turned his face away."

Brown would have us remember Christ became like us in all things but sin. Jesus was truly human. He had human emotions, human reactions. Jesus experienced real pain, real sorrow. Brown, after discussing other views, writes,

147

Overall, then, I find no persuasive argument against attributing to the Jesus of Mark/Matthew, the literal sentiment of feeling forsaken expressed in the psalm quote. The interpretation of this prayer at the end of the Passion Narrative should follow the same course as the interpretation of the opening prayer of the Passion Narrative in Mark 14:35–36 and Matthew 26:39.

There are many who would reject the literal meaning that Jesus really wanted the hour to pass from him, and was not eager to drink the cup of suffering. They could not attribute to Jesus such anguish in the face of death. If one accepts literally that anguish at the opening moment when Jesus could still call God, "Abba, Father," one should accept equally literally this screamed protest against abandonment wrenched from an utterly forlorn Jesus who is now so isolated and estranged that he no longer uses "Father" language but speaks as the humblest servant.

Brown sees the prayer of Jesus "to the One who had the power to save him from death" in the Epistle to the Hebrews (4:14–16, 5:7–10) supporting the view that Jesus does indeed feel forsaken. Says Brown, "It is on the cross that Jesus has learned even more fully 'obedience from the things he suffered.' It is here that he has made 'strong clamor,' and it is here that he will be 'heard from [anxious] fear' and made perfect."

Is this world the best God could make?

Rather than viewing the question of creation from our own vantage point, perhaps we ought to start with God's purposes. The world God made best suited his purposes of expressing his goodness, sharing his life with others and his own glorification.

God's great gift to humans is freedom. It is in our ability to choose good that we are made more in God's image and likeness than lower creatures. The ability to choose good also means the possibility of choosing evil. It is in choosing that we are able to "merit" reward. It is in choosing that we are able to love and be loved by others. Those goods in

God's plan are what are important.

Commenting on the statement of the Fourth Lateran Council that all creatures were created good by God, Adolphe Tanquerey in *A Manual of Dogmatic Theology* writes,

> However, it does not follow from this that the world God created is the most perfect. For since God's goodness and power are infinite, they cannot be exhausted through a finite work; therefore, God could make other creatures who would be more perfect. Nevertheless, we can state that the world is relatively the best, inasmuch as God chose the best means to attain the end He had proposed to Himself in creating.

And Ludwig Ott, in *Fundamentals of Catholic Dogma*, in commenting on the thesis that God was free to create this world or any other, states,

> The world now existing does not possess the highest conceivable measure of perfections. Neither did God owe it to Himself to create the best world, because His perfections and happiness cannot be increased even by the best world. If one were to deny God's freedom in choice between this or that world (libertas specificationis), one would limit His omnipotence, which extends to all that is intrinsically possible.

When we deal specifically with suffering, we are always faced with mystery.

What is "the dark night of the soul"? Does it cause people to abandon the sacraments or leave the church?

The "dark night" was for saints a feeling of abandonment, of being alone. They were assailed by doubt. But faith enabled them to believe and remain convinced that—even though they did not feel the presence of God—he was with them and could be relied on.

Most who leave the church do not do so because they experience "the dark night of the soul" described by some of the saints. Many have problems with individual beliefs or doc-trines.

Faith begins with and is essentially a *commitment to a person or being*. The Christian (Catholic) believes, first of all, in God and Jesus. He or she is committed to Jesus and the Father. *Belief in what Jesus taught and is taught in his name and with his authority* follows after the commitment to Jesus.

It would indeed be hypocrisy for a person to receive Communion if he or she did not really believe in the Eucharist. And we can't encourage a person to receive the Eucharist when the rest of that person's life is not in conformity with what is symbolized and professed in receiving the Eucharist.

But we should support such people in what faith they do have and encourage them to pray for enlightenment and the gift of complete faith. We should take people where they are, as Jesus did in his lifetime. In this case that would mean to encourage them to pray, to read the Scriptures, to attend Mass. With the grace of God, goodwill and an open heart, people often find their way back to faith and are enabled to make a commitment to God, where previously that commitment was never real.

Many people go to church as children and learn to pray and worship without ever making a real, personal act of commitment and belief for themselves. Until reaching adolescence or early adulthood, they never consciously asked themselves if they believed in Jesus and his church. They never actually said, "Yes, I do believe."

Teachers, pastors and parents can teach, instruct, encourage, explain, but in the end each individual person must make his or her own assent and commitment to God. No one can do that for us.

How can we get along with fundamentalists?

You are not alone in your problem. The sometimes zealous proselytizing of fundamentalists may be annoying, but we should be sensitive to their good qualities—their charity, their respect for the Scriptures and their zeal in promoting what they believe is the word of God.

A desire to better understand the Scriptures is one good thing that can result from confrontations with Bible-quoting enthusiasts. But generally, little is accomplished by carrying on a kind of debate with fundamentalist friends or relatives. Usually they are concerned more with making points than listening to and understanding what you have to say.

The best response would be to say something like, "Listen, I have heard many times what you have to say. I respect your conscience and your goodwill. I would like to think that you also respect mine. Obviously, we are not going to come to an agreement. And I do wish this to be a pleasant occasion for both of us. I do not wish to argue: That will be fruitless for you and me. So let us make this a time of friendship and family. If we can't do that, there really isn't much reason for us to come together."

If you wish to know more about fundamentalism, read *Fundamentalism: What Every Catholic Needs to Know*, by Anthony Gilles, or *Fundamentalism: A Pastoral Concern*, by Eugene LaVerdiere, s.s.s.

Should an abused wife forgive and forget her husband's abuse?

To forgive does not mean you have to forget. Sometimes our hurt and pain have been so great we cannot just erase the memories of them. We will very likely remember how we have been wronged and try to avoid a repetition of it if we can.

Forgiveness means we rise above the hurt we feel and wish the wrongdoer well in the Lord. We renounce hate and the desire for revenge. We love the one who has hurt us. That doesn't mean we have to get all warm and emotional. It means we wish the other person well despite the injuries and offensive conduct. It means we try to be decent and civil despite provocations.

Marital counseling or therapy can help an abusive person find healthier ways to express anger or frustration. It can also help a victim of abuse to deal with anger and resentment and

151

provide some constructive ways to respond to put-downs and verbal abuse. There are many degrees and perceptions of abuse. If you are subject to serious verbal or physical abuse, seek help immediately through family, friends, your church or an organization such as Women Helping Women.

What happens to us when we die?

Even though we believe in the resurrection of the dead, the loss of those we love brings grief and sorrow.

In 1979 the Congregation for the Doctrine of the Faith spoke to some of these concerns in a *Letter on Certain Questions Concerning Eschatology*—sometimes referred to as a statement on life after death. The congregation said it was making this statement because of confusion over the article in the creed concerning life everlasting, discussions of the existence of the soul, the meaning of life after death and what happens to the soul between the death of the Christian and the general resurrection.

The congregation acknowledged that, "Neither Scripture nor theology provides sufficient light for a proper picture of life after death." In other words our knowledge and understanding of what happens after death is limited and imperfect.

At the same time it stated that the church believes in the resurrection of the dead and understands the resurrection as referring to the whole person.

Concerning the soul, it says,

The Church affirms that a spiritual element survives and subsists, an element endowed with consciousness and will, so that the "human self" subsists. To designate this element, the Church uses the word "soul," the accepted term in the usage of Scripture and tradition. Although not unaware that this term has various meanings in the Bible, the Church thinks there is no valid reason for rejecting it: Moreover, she considers that the use of some word as a vehicle is absolutely indispensable in order to support the faith of Christians.

The *Catechism of the Catholic Church* says,

> Death puts an end to human life as the time open to either accepting or rejecting the divine grace manifested in Christ. The New Testament speaks of judgment primarily in its aspect of the final encounter with Christ in his second coming, but also repeatedly affirms that each will be rewarded immediately after death in accordance with his works and faith. (1021)

Should lapsed Catholics be encouraged to return to the church?

We should encourage our friends to take up their religion again as fully as possible. Suggest they begin attending Mass and praying regularly for guidance and the assistance of God. Many have marital issues that must be overcome before they can fully return to the church. If asked, encourage friends to talk to the priests of their parishes or other priests who might be helpful and understanding. Offer whatever support you can, and assure your friends that they will be in your prayers. You might recommend *Faith Rediscovered: Coming Home to Catholicism,* by Lawrence Cunningham. Also, you might send a friend's name and those names of others for whom you pray to *Another Look*, 3031 Fourth Street, NE, Washington, DC 20017. This is an outreach ministry of the Paulist Fathers. Without mentioning your name they will send a bulletin gently inviting your friend to "take another look." It will contain the personal experience stories of others who have taken another look and found happiness in returning to their faith. It will offer the persons receiving it the opportunity of removing their names from the mailing list if the bulletin is not wanted.

The best way to encourage those who have fallen away is by our own lived faith and example. Judgmental words and repeated invasions of privacy will not be well received. Pray for those you know who have left the church, and do your best to be a model of Christian charity.

Do those in heaven see what is happening on earth?

The Tablet (a Catholic magazine published in England) carried a description of the ordination of Bishop Crispian Hollis. The reporter wrote, "Cardinal Hume [now deceased archbishop of Westminster] preached a brief homily in which he imagined the saints in heaven, the Church triumphant, 'jostling with each other to catch a glimpse of the new bishop, to find out what he's like.'"

Theologians commonly teach that the deceased in heaven have some awareness of the people they knew and loved on earth, what is happening concerning them and events that interested them in life. The good things that happen to those they loved would be a source of happiness to those in heaven.

In that sense remarks such as, "Your mother is looking down at you," are true. But we must remember we are trying to express in human language and terms supernatural realities. To imagine those in heaven watching earthly events on a heavenly television screen or peering through the clouds with telescopes at their friends on earth is hardly a scientific way of expressing how they acquire knowledge of what is happening here. The truth is simply expressed in the best way most people know how to express it.

Is it possible to be married in heaven?

It has been the church's belief, deeply embedded in Scripture, that we who are now living will, after we die, be united with those who have gone before us. So the widowed can certainly be consoled with the knowledge that dying in the Lord they will indeed be "united" with their good Christian spouses. And their presence and love will be an added source of happiness to the happiness you will experience in knowing and living in the love of God himself.

As we grow older, we discover that life is usually not a matter of blacks and whites. Further, time and progress bring us face-to-face with new questions and situations. After Jesus' death the early church members realized they had lots of questions Jesus had not directly answered. And reflecting on the things Jesus said and did gave rise to new questions.

Some of the questions we have, and the church before had, deal with matters of "dogma" or doctrine—truths about God and God's way of acting with us and in his world. Who is God? What makes him different from us and the creatures he made? What is the life of God like? How is the Son "different" from the Father or distinct from the Father? How can there be three Persons in one God?

Other questions deal with the morality of the things we do—questions about right and wrong. What was to be done about Christians who lapsed from the faith under persecution? What is a Christian to do when ordered by the state to take up arms in its defense? Can war be just? Is it lawful to demand or take interest for loaning money to someone else? Must a person undergo painful and uncertain treatment for a sickness? Can a childless couple make use of in vitro fertilization, or use the services of a surrogate mother?

In both areas the church depended on theologians and moralists to offer answers and guidance. Where there was agreement of practically all the theologians, who were often bishops at the same time, what they taught became confirmed in one way or another by the teaching authority of the church. When the church's common belief or understanding was seriously questioned, the general councils and popes declared what was of divine faith.

In some cases there was (is) no general agreement or understanding concerning matters of belief. For instance, there were many different ideas about what happens to an unbaptized infant. In such a case a Catholic considers the *reasons* a theologian offers for an *opinion* (for example, the existence of Limbo) and is free to hold the opinion that seems most convincing.

In the area of morals the church generally does not make *infallible* statements. If church authority has made a non-infallible pronouncement, that certainly enjoys the presumption of truth and must be followed unless a person has grave and persuasive reasons for dissenting.

What happens if the church has offered no official teaching concerning a moral problem? What happens if the situation is so new and different the church and theologians of the past have not discussed and considered the moral and ethical problems involved? What happens if new developments arise and call old solutions into question?

In such situations we are accustomed to hearing various voices proclaiming different opinions about what is right and wrong, what is permitted and what is not permitted. In such a case, again, we look to see if the church (the Holy See, the bishops) is giving any direction. We look to what moral theologians—the specialists and experts—are saying. If there is general agreement among them, that gives us good guidance for making our decisions. If there is disagreement among them, we look to the reasons they offer for their positions and opinions.

We may find that one group or a particular theologian offers more convincing and compelling arguments than others, or arguments that others have not taken into consideration, so that we say we are convinced of *that* opinion or teaching. We are convinced that it is correct and we follow it. We may find that theologians are divided on an issue and that one opinion is as probable as another. In such a case we may follow either opinion or any opinion that seems truly probable.

And always we weigh what the theologians and moralists are saying against the Scriptures themselves and the tradition and the magisterial teaching of the church in making our conscience decisions and understanding the faith of the church.

Is it appropriate to say a Mass for a pet?

In considering the fate of animals, we might keep in mind Saint Paul's words to the Romans (8:18–25). There Saint Paul says that creation itself will be "set free from its bondage to decay and will obtain the freedom of the glory of the children of God." The second letter of Peter also tells us, "We await new heavens and a new earth" (2 Peter 3:13). With that in mind, some believe that you could allow for some transformed animal life in the new creation.

As Catholics, however, we believe that in this creation only human beings are capable of entering into the Resurrection of Jesus and the kingdom of God. We also believe that only human beings are capable of sin and need forgiveness and purification. We do not believe that plants or animals are capable of supernatural life before or after death.

Some, therefore, judge it without purpose and inappropriate to offer a Mass for a deceased pet.

When a priest (or cardinal) blesses a fishing fleet, the prayer is for those who will sail in the ships, that they will be kept safe and that their efforts to catch fish will be rewarded and prove fruitful. The prayer of blessing reads, in part, "Bless this boat, its equipment and all who will use it. Protect them from the dangers of wind and rain and all the perils of the deep. May Christ, who calmed the storm and filled the nets of his disciples, bring us all to the harbor of light and peace."

In the blessing ceremony for animals, the church recalls the place of animals in God's plan of creation, the role of humans as stewards of creation and how animals assist humans in their work and provide food, clothing and companionship.

The blessing prayer asks,

> O God, you have done all things wisely; in your goodness you have made us in your image and given us care over other living things. Reach out with your right hand and grant that these animals may serve our needs and that your bounty in the resources of this life may move us to seek more confidently the goal of eternal life.

While we do not believe that animals can lead a supernatural existence, we as Christians should surely respect them as part of God's creation giving praise and glory to God by their existence. And we should treat them with respect and kindness. That is the kind of vision expressed in Saint Francis of Assisi's Canticle of Creatures.

How can we get along with Jehovah's Witnesses?

First of all, we must see the good in each person. Although we may believe they are mistaken in the choices they have made and in very simplistic interpretations of Scripture, they are very likely people of goodwill. They are trying to live very moral and religious lives. And they are making great sacrifices and performing many acts of self-denial to do this. We certainly ought to admire and respect their dedication to serving the Lord.

Next, we should try to understand where they are coming from. We should have a general idea of what the Jehovah's Witnesses believe and their religious practices. The chapter on Jehovah's Witnesses in *Separated Brethren,* by William Whalen, might be helpful.

Another helpful book is *The Catholic Answer to Jehovah's Witnesses: A Challenge Accepted,* by Louise D'Angelo.

We should also make every effort to increase our own understanding of the Scriptures and our faith. We can do that by general reading. There are lots of books that explain particular books of the Bible or the Scriptures as a whole. There are also many fine explanations of the Catholic faith available, such as *Believing in Jesus,* by Leonard Foley.

If you are discussing religion with a Jehovah's Witness, do not let yourself get "trapped" into arguing about individual and isolated verses of the Scriptures—it will be unproductive. For example, to debate individual verses from Revelation, without understanding or agreeing that the whole book deals in symbols and allegory, will get you nowhere. That would be like trying to make *Star Wars* into a straight historical work and arguing about the literal meaning of passages in it.

Rather, try—if you can—to keep such discussion focused on the "big" questions, such as:

1. Why do Witnesses deny the divinity of Christ when the New Testament writers themselves insist Jesus is God? Particularly, Saint John attests to Jesus' divinity in the conclusion of his Gospel. And why, if they deny Saint John's Gospel, do they attach so much importance to Revelation, also authored by John?

2. Why do Witnesses insist on their own particular translations of words and verses when scholars of all faiths who have studied the original languages of the Bible and customs of the people agree on other meanings contrary to the Witnesses' interpretation? And isn't this strange, especially, when the founder of the Witnesses and his successor knew none of the languages in which these works were written? (One of them was forced to admit in court that he did not know the Greek alphabet.)

3. Why put so much confidence in the interpretations of these men, when other interpretations made by them have already been proved incorrect by the mere passage of time (for example, the world would end or Armageddon would come in 1914)?

4. Why do just some Old Testament laws bind and not others if Christ did not institute a New Testament? (You might carefully read Deuteronomy and Leviticus for examples to use.)

For the rest, to sustain your own faith, you might join a study club or take a correspondence course on the Bible. You may also want to consider taking a class offered by your local parish or university in the Scriptures. And you might find support by joining a prayer group.

Should a Catholic attend the wedding of a Catholic marrying outside the church with no dispensation?

It is not easy to answer such questions with just a yes or a no. Each case is individual and requires a particular judgment about what is the best or most charitable thing to do. There are a lot of factors to be weighed and questions to be answered before a person makes a decision to attend the marriage of a Catholic marrying outside the church.

Among the questions to be answered are: Will the person getting married take your attendance as approval of what he or she is doing? Will your decision to attend encourage the person to go ahead and marry contrary to God's law and enter a sinful union? Or does the person know and realize your attendance will only be a sign of caring and friendship?

If you do not attend will it only embitter that person and drive him or her farther from the church, thus making any future effort to be reconciled with the church and God harder and more unlikely? Will failing to attend cause division and enmity in the family? What action—attending or not attending—is most likely to keep open communication with the person and, in the end, have the most spiritual effect?

That is one set of considerations. Another is: What effect will your attending or not attending the wedding have on other people, especially those for whom you have the most responsibility? If you attend will your children or other family members take it to mean that you see nothing wrong with what the other person is doing?

Is it likely to encourage others to do the same thing in the future? In other words will it give genuine scandal? Or will the other family members understand that you are not approving of sinful conduct but are merely showing friendship and caring by attending the ceremony?

The closer the relationship, of course, the more pressure to attend and the more significant the act of attending or not attending.

Keep in mind that, outside of close family relationships, attending or not attending a wedding is not noticed very much. The parties do not stop to ask questions about why so-and-so did not come. We frequently exaggerate the importance of going or not going and the likelihood of giving real offense by not attending.

Also, to be fair, those marrying outside the church must have some consideration and understanding for the consciences of their friends and relatives. They should not expect or demand them to do what they believe is wrong. Friendship and love are, after all, two-way streets.

Where the relationships are closest, kindness and a show of affection are more likely to have the best spiritual effect in the long run. A parent who has hope of eventually leading the child back to God and church, for instance, might choose, after letting a child know he or she believes what the child is doing is wrong, to keep communication open and to show love and concern—even by attending the ceremony.

In all these cases we have to respect the prudential decision a person makes and accept that it is made in good conscience whether the person decides to attend or not to attend.

Should people have their children baptized though the parents no longer attend Mass?

It is not always easy to predict what a pastor or associate pastor will decide or do. Priests put different emphasis on various facts and considerations. The ritual for baptism and various directives from the Holy See, however, indicate that infants (children) should not be baptized if there is not *good reason* to believe that they will be raised and formed in the Catholic faith. It is possible that a pastor may seriously question whether your children will be educated and instructed in the Catholic faith if you yourself do not practice your religion. He may further question what will happen if your spouse is not committed to raising the children in the faith.

Your pastor will urge you to return to the practice of your faith and religion. Would you really respect him if he did not? And he will suggest that attending Mass would be an indication that you do wish to actually raise your children in the faith.

Nevertheless, the sense of various directives and instructions from bishops is that requests for baptism from individuals like yourself are not automatically to be refused. Where the pastor can discern that a parent does intend to provide for the Catholic education and formation of his children, they should be baptized.

How should you approach your pastor? Calmly. Ready to explain your own unreadiness to share in the Eucharist and life of the parish and your reasons at the same time for wishing to have your children baptized. You should also be able to respond to how you intend to provide for their religious formation and practice while you do not practice the Catholic faith. You should be able to explain that you are seeking more than the benefits of a Catholic school education and a conveying of acceptable values: that you want your children to have a *life* in God nourished by prayer, sacraments and hearing the word of God.

This may be the time to examine why you really wish to have your children baptized. And that means reexamining your own life and your own relationship with God. What is it that you are seeking for your children that you are not seeking for yourself? And if you wish or seek these things for your children, why not also for yourself?

How should we treat a wealthy person who shuns acts of charity?

Many modern Good Samaritans have found the people they help less than grateful, cheerful and pleasant. Teachers, social workers and medical workers know that the poor, sick and lonely are not always thankful, patient or self-effacing and can even be very demanding.

A person doing acts of charity should recall the reasons for the charity—the love of God and a desire to imitate the generous love God bestows on all of us.

In his first letter John reminds us, "In this is love, not that we loved God, but that he loved us and sent his Son to be the atoning sacrifice for our sins. Beloved, since God loved us so much, we also ought to love one another" (1 John 4:10–11).

Charity is certainly done more easily when it is received with gratitude and exclamations of appreciation. But the real test of love is in giving when kindness is taken for granted or even with indifference or surliness. Our charity is most like God's when we give without expecting return, when we give unconditionally without demands on the recipient, when we can pray as Christ did for his persecutors, "Forgive them, for they know not what they do."

Consider, too, that some people may be financially well-off but have great need to experience affection, personal interest, human warmth and friendship. And the apparently stingy persons may be driven by fear of exhausting their savings in sickness. They may fear being left alone and without savings if catastrophic illness occurs.

Mother Teresa would have told us this kind of charity comes only with practice and grace. It comes only with reminding ourselves of the motives for our charity. It comes only with prayer and reflecting on the goodness God has first shown us.

This was the experience of Saint Francis of Assisi who saw Christ in the leper *after* he had embraced and kissed him. Francis wrote of his experience in his testament:

> The Lord gave me, Brother Francis, the grace of beginning to do penance in this way: that, when I was in sin, it seemed extremely bitter to me to look at lepers, and the Lord himself led me in among them and I practiced mercy with them. And when I came away from them, what seemed bitter to me, was changed to sweetness of spirit and body for me.

What happens to those who commit suicide?

In the vast majority of cases, suicide is a not a coldly planned, completely rational act. In most instances the person who commits or attempts suicide is acting out of great emotional stress or overwhelming depression. Reason is clouded and not functioning normally. The very attempt is a kind of distress signal, a cry to be noticed, a plea for assistance.

Even after the person has harmed himself or herself, there may come a change of heart. For example, an elderly woman had slashed her wrists and neck while sitting in her easy chair. But she had quite evidently experienced remorse. She had somehow walked or dragged herself to the kitchen door looking for help, only to collapse and die before someone found her.

In such cases guilt and responsibility are greatly diminished. And in cases of suicide pastors usually do not deny Christian burial.

Now, suicide as a coldly calculated, freely committed act is another matter. Father Bernard Häring in *The Law of Christ*, echoes what other moral theologians have long said. Suicide, the arbitrary taking of one's life, is among the most grievous sins against bodily life. It is contrary to the deepest instinct of self-preservation.

On the religious level it is a "manifestation of the most extreme and arbitrary self-assertion, of spite and desperation." Häring writes that this sin violates the very majesty and sovereignty of God; the suicide has not the will to serve and to suffer according to God's will. The suicide sees no meaning in his or her life and suffering.

The *Catechism of the Catholic Church* says:

> Suicide contradicts the natural inclination of the human being to preserve and perpetuate his life. It is gravely contrary to the just love of self. It likewise offends love of neighbor because it unjustly breaks the ties of solidarity with family, nation, and other human societies to which we continue to have obligations. Suicide is contrary to love for the living God. (2281)

We are living in times when human life is being greatly devalued. Euthanasia and mercy killing appear on the ballot each year in some areas, to be acceptable and lawful. There is much talk about whether or not ordinary lifesaving or preservation measures should be used for the aged and terminally ill. A prominent medical journal published an article by a doctor about how he had assisted a person to die with a lethal injection. That may explain why some people see suicide as an easy and acceptable escape from sorrow and pain.

It is important for Christians to insist on the value and dignity of human life under all circumstances. We must be sensitive to the suffering and pain of others and reach out to them.

How should we treat children marrying outside the faith?

Blaming others because their children marry outside the church and take up a non-Christian religion might well be like blaming the father of the prodigal son for the son's abandoning his home and family ways (see Luke 15:11–32).

Our grown children are adults with minds and wills of their own. They must answer to God for their own actions and choices. None of us can know why they have chosen to do what they have. Only they themselves and God know whether the decisions they have made have been for conviction, convenience or weakness. Their parents cannot make an act of faith for them. Parents cannot live their childrens' lives for them and they must accept that, and so must the rest of the family.

What parents can do is imitate Luke's father of the prodigal or Saint Monica with her son, Saint Augustine. Continue to love these children. Keep the lines of communication open. Offer a constant example of a faith-governed life. Do acts of penance and pray for their return to the practice of their Catholic faith.

How should we deal with distractions at Mass?

Father John Huels, O.S.M., wrote an article dealing with frustrations that people in religious communities experience in celebrating daily Masses ("Daily Mass: Law and Spirituality," *Review for Religious*, July/August, 1991). One person is bored because there is little variety or change. Another feels exhaustion because other members of the community want every liturgy to be celebrated with the solemnity of Sunday liturgies. One comes to the liturgy viewing his or her attendance primarily as an act of personal devotion. Another regards attendance as an act of duty, fulfilling an expectation of the religious community and church. And still another sees attendance as vital to building and holding community together. Dealing with other people's needs and expectations can frequently be an uncomfortable, messy business. It may call for compromises with which no one, in the end, is completely satisfied. It almost always calls for tolerance if the purposes of a group or community are to be fulfilled.

Parents may be bringing crying babies to church because it is the only way they can attend Mass on Sunday. Besides wanting to fulfill an obligation, they are fulfilling their spiritual needs. They find it necessary to maintain a bond with the rest of the parish and church. The irritation occasioned by the baby's wails may not vanish with that realization, but the rest of us may be able to accept it and bear with it more easily.

It may also be frustrating when a celebrant (or lectors, for that matter) can be only partially understood. If the celebrant mumbles, acoustics are bad or there is no adequate loudspeaker system, an effort should be made to correct what is wrong. But foreign accents are not easily changed or overcome.

In such a situation we might remind ourselves of the universality of the church and that our worship and charity embraces all. Our celebrating with a person of another nation, tongue or culture acts out the faith and love that unites us.

It would be easier to rise above such frustrations were we celebrating with the many people of different languages, customs and liturgical expectations gathered with Pope John Paul II in Saint Peter's Basilica. These things would be taken for granted there. Sometimes we are called to do that on the level of local community and parish as well.

None of this is meant to excuse sloppy, irreverent, poorly celebrated liturgies. We all must bring the best from within to worship and celebrate God's goodness. But we all have to accept human limitations even as we expect God to accept them.

What are the signs of the end of the world?

Scripture scholars and commentators have long been wrestling with the passages that refer to the end of the world. They come up with different possible answers to what Jesus meant or how these passages are to be interpreted and explained.

Remember that in A.D. 70 Jerusalem fell under Roman siege. The destruction and suffering were terrible. When the Romans finally took the city, the Temple was destroyed and much of the population had fled. It was the end of an era or world as the Jews knew it and the beginning of a new world.

Without quoting here all the texts surrounding those above and going into them separately, we can say there is agreement among commentators that Jesus in these passages is talking about two different events. The first is the fall of Jerusalem with the destruction of the Temple to come. It seems impossible to say precisely when each of the Gospels was written. But it may be that each of them, if not one or the other, was written after the fall of Jerusalem and the destruction of the Temple.

The second happening about which Jesus is speaking is the end of time and the Second Coming.

As the evangelists have recalled Jesus' words, it is not always easy to distinguish when he is speaking of the fall of Jerusalem and when his words are about the end of the world.

Given these uncertainties, exegetes offer different explanations of Jesus' statement, "This generation will not pass away till all these things happen": (1) Jesus is here referring to the end of Jerusalem. Those in Jesus' generation did indeed witness the signs and the fulfillment of Jesus' words. They saw the end of an old world and the beginning of a new world. (2) "This generation" means the human race. The human race will not pass away until all that Jesus says takes place.

In commenting on the passage in Luke, Eugene LaVerdiere, s.s.s., says it means, "At that time, heaven and earth will pass away (21:31a) but two realities will surely remain: this generation (21:32b), that is the human race, and the words of the Lord (21:33), which will then be fulfilled."

In view of the difficulties in these passages, both these approaches seem to have merit and sound reasonable.

Will those living at the end have to die before entering heaven?

In the letter to the Romans, Saint Paul states, "Death spread to all, because all have sinned" (Romans 5:12). However, in 1 Thessalonians when writing about the Parousia, Paul says, "Then we who are alive, who are left, will be caught up in the clouds together with them [those who have died] to meet the Lord in the air" (4:17).

The book of Genesis, in speaking of the descendants of Adam, states of Enoch, "Enoch walked with God; then he was no more, because God took him" (5:24). And Sirach says, "Enoch walked with the Lord and was taken up, that succeeding generations might learn by his example" (Sirach 44:16). Hebrews says, "By faith Enoch was taken so he did not experience death; and 'he was not found, because God had taken him'" (11:5). We also have 2 Kings 2:11 to consider, "As they continued walking and talking, a chariot of fire and horses of fire separated the two of them, and Elijah ascended in a whirlwind into heaven." Finally, 1 Maccabees 2:58 states, "Elijah, for his burning zeal for the law, was taken up to heaven."

There are a variety of explanations by scriptural exegetes of these different texts. They range from explaining them by simply repeating legends without authenticating them, to saying the sacred authors are using euphemisms for death or dying, to simply accepting the texts as statements that Enoch and Elijah actually did not die.

In *Fundamentals of Catholic Dogma*, Ludwig Ott takes the Bible texts as simple statements that Enoch and Elijah did not die. After talking about the universality of death, he says, "Individual human beings can, however, by special privilege, be preserved from death." He says that those of the just who are living when Christ comes again will not die but will be immediately transformed or changed. He notes that Saint

Thomas Aquinas gave as his opinion that Paul did not wish to deny altogether that they would die but implied that their death would be for a very short time. Ott calls this explanation, "exegetically hardly tenable."

As for escaping the punishment of original sin, if it is assumed that these will not experience death, they have endured the greatest punishment for original sin—an initial deprivation (before baptism) of sanctifying grace. It may be relevant to note also that, even though the Blessed Virgin was conceived and born without the effects of original sin, traditions do not agree whether she experienced bodily death. Some argue that if Jesus himself died Mary also would have died. Yet Pope Pius XII, in proclaiming the dogma of Mary's assumption into heaven, rather carefully avoided making any pronouncement about whether she had first died or not. He said simply, "It is a truth of faith revealed by God that the immaculate, ever Virgin Mary, the Mother of God, was assumed body and soul into heavenly glory after the completion of her earthly life."

How should we treat a child's cohabitation outside of marriage?

It is heartrending for any parents to see a loved child reject the faith and values precious and dear to them. It is important not to take a son's or daughter's abandonment of the church and faith as a personal rejection of or judgment on you. Many parents in your place tend to ask, "What did I do wrong?" You did not necessarily do anything wrong. We—including our children—each have our own will and responsibility. We all make our own decisions and must answer for them ourselves. You should not, then, blame yourselves for your children's decisions.

Many parents today are facing the same situation. It has become somewhat common for young people to live together outside of marriage. Not only parents are asking what they should do, but also priests and bishops.

That is why Pope John Paul II addressed himself to this

situation once when speaking to the Italian bishops. He lamented that unmarried people living together is one of the main social conditions causing the disintegration of the family, and asked the bishops to improve family life.

Yet, he also asked the Italian bishops to take a "patient and loving" attitude toward couples who have not had church marriages. He said, "Pastors should never tire of telling people who live together that they should not consider themselves separated from the church." And, "Even though it is impossible to admit them to Eucharistic communion, they are not to be excluded from our affection, benevolence and prayer."

The pope advised, "Approach people living together with discretion and respect, and strive through patient and loving action to remove the impediments and smooth the road toward regularizing the situation."

This is also good counsel for parents. Your child surely knows that you do not approve of these living arrangements. You must also express that you continue to love and care for your child. Write, phone and invite your child to visit.

By keeping the lines of communication open, you also keep open a way for your child to return to the practice of the faith without seeming to have "caved" to parental authority. By maintaining contact, you will continue to have some good influence. And continue to pray for your child without ceasing.

Was John the Baptist born free from original sin?

In his account of the Visitation, Saint Luke says, "When Elizabeth heard Mary's greeting, the child [John] leaped in her womb" (Luke 1:41). Luke earlier states that when the angel of the Lord appeared to Zechariah—while he was offering incense—and announced the coming birth of John, Zechariah proclaimed, "He will be filled with the holy Spirit even from his mother's womb" (Luke 1:15). Some infer from these texts that John was cleansed from original sin in his mother's (Elizabeth's) womb and, thus, born without original sin. One is free to believe this, but it is not a necessary conclusion nor is it a matter of faith, something that must be held.

While some believe John was freed from original sin while still in his mother's womb, the church proclaims as a matter of faith that Mary, the mother of Jesus, was conceived without original sin, that she was never from the first instance touched by original sin.

How can we be happy in heaven without the things we love here on earth?

A Broadway play and movie forty years ago pictured heaven as a place where everyone from God and the angels to saints wear white robes at a joyful fish fry. We all know that was a fantasy, the imagination running wild. We all are pretty well sure that heaven is not a fish fry.

The trouble is that most of our real knowledge about heaven is theoretical. We know heaven is a life of great joy and happiness in which we are completely fulfilled. But we have no way of describing that from our present experience.

In the Gospels Jesus compares heaven to a wedding banquet. This is because banquets and weddings (like fish fries) are occasions of great merriment and enjoyment. But few of us take those descriptions so literally that we worry about whether roast beef or chicken, peas or corn, port or sherry will be on the menu.

You will definitely find and know your friends in heaven. If the Mystical Body, communion of saints and family of God mean anything, we can be sure we will enjoy and find happiness in our relationships in a way higher than on earth.

Such earthly pleasures as playing the piano may seem very important now but will not likely have that same importance in eternity. But whatever is necessary for our happiness, God will somehow satisfy.

Heaven, life after death, is a *different* kind of life and existence. The principal joy of life with God is in loving God and being loved by God. The joy comes from hopes fulfilled. Stop imagining life after death and heaven as simply a continuation of life as you know it now beyond the clouds or on some other planet.

Who judges us at the end—Jesus or God the Father?

The Gospels contain different images to picture or express the reality of God's final judgment. The Gospel of Matthew 13:24–30, for instance, uses the parable and employs the image of a wheat field to describe the fact of God's judgment. At harvest time the householder has the weeds separated from the wheat and burned.

But perhaps our most common image of judgment is in Matthew 25:31–46 where Jesus describes the Son of Man seated on a glorious throne. He is surrounded by the angels; the nations of the world appear before him.

Like a shepherd separating sheep and goats, he lines up the saved and lost to his right and left. They are rewarded or punished on the basis of the charity they rendered Jesus in the poor and hungry.

But we must remember that Jesus and the evangelists are using images and comparisons that we can understand to convey supernatural and spiritual realities.

The basic truth being conveyed is that, in the end, all human beings are subjected to the judgment of God. The justice, goodness and love of God are manifest to all. The goodness of God triumphs.

Those who have loved the Lord are united to him in glory. The kingdom of God triumphs and prevails over sin. Saint Paul calls this "the day of Christ" (Philippians 1:6, 10; 2:16) and "the day of the Lord" (1 Thessalonians 5:2; 1 Corinthians 1:8). In Luke it is called the day of "the Son of Man" (17:24).

As the catechism for the German Bishops' Conference (*The Church's Confession of Faith: A Catholic Catechism for Adults*) puts it, "The end of time will reveal that Jesus Christ is and was from the very beginning the grounding and central meaning of all reality and all history, the alpha and the omega, the first and the last, the beginning and the end (Revelation 1:8; 22:13)."

Everything will be measured by and against him at the

end. Thus he is the judge of the living and dead. And, again as the German bishops remind us, these are images rather than descriptions.

While discussing the matter of God's judgment, it should be noted that theologians speak of a private judgment of each individual that takes place at the moment of death. The dead do not await the final judgment to know whether they are saved or lost.

Once again, the German bishops have put the matter well:

> This judgment should not be imagined as an external judicial proceeding. It must be understood as a spiritual event. Faced with God's absolute truth as disclosed in Jesus Christ, a man will see the truth of his life. The masks will fall away; the distortions and self-deceptions will vanish. It will become finally clear to each man whether he has won his life or lost it. He will then enter either into life with God or into the darkness that is distance from God.

Are we made in God's image?

Someone once said that God made us in his own image and likeness and we, as it were, return the favor by making God in our own image and likeness. There is some truth in that.

We are indeed made in God's likeness. And by looking at God's creatures we can learn much about God. That is true not just of humans but of all creation as well. Francis of Assisi would sing his beautiful Canticle of Creation because he saw in creatures signs of God's power, beauty, goodness and providence.

Human beings, at their best, give us an insight into God's love, mercy, compassion, forgiveness and justice. Jesus is, of course, the best image of God and gives us insights into the nature of God through his deeds and words. But even then, the human nature of Jesus, like all human natures, is limited. The triune God transcends all understanding.

Because God is a spiritual being and we cannot see, hear or touch God in his divinity, we cannot perfectly describe him and how he lives and acts. We are often reduced to saying God or the way he is or acts is "something like" things we physically experience.

The authors of Genesis talked about and described God and his actions in experiential ways rather than in abstract terms. They did not talk about omnipotence, but they described the mighty, wonderful things God did and related how God was more powerful than any other being. They did not use philosophical and theological language to describe God and spiritual realities. Nor did they possess God's complete revelation. God revealed himself to humans over a long period of time and that revelation was completed in Jesus.

So the writers of Genesis often use concrete and anthropomorphic terms to describe God and his actions. They give God human characteristics and describe God acting as a human being would. They humanize God and make God a kind of superhuman being.

Just as fablers and dramatists make elephants dance and trees talk, the authors of Genesis describe God walking in the garden and talking to Adam and Eve. And, because in their own experience people rested after they worked, they describe God as resting after the "work" of creation. God certainly did not need to rest, to recuperate from physical labor and exhaustion. One reason to describe God resting was to reinforce the idea of the Sabbath rest.

They conveyed their theology in story form. In reminding us the world was made by God, the writers are saying God transcends human beings. All of us humans are made by God. God made man and woman good. Further, just as we experience temptation, the first man and woman experienced temptation. They disobeyed God and introduced sin and evil into God's creation. Everyone who comes after the first man and woman experiences and suffers from the evil they brought into the world. That is the main thrust of what the authors of Genesis were trying to tell us.

Scriptural exegetes have long recognized the difficulty of trying to take every detail in Genesis in a literal sense. Those authors of Genesis had an idea much different from ours of what the world and universe are like. They had no telescopes, space satellites or ships to put them on the moon. They described the universe as it appeared to them. The sky was like a ceiling, something like the dome on a modern football or baseball stadium. Above the dome and under the earth was water. It rained because there were holes in the dome.

The writers did not worry about details such as how light came to be before God made the sun. They were not teaching science or cosmology. They were theologizing. So it would be a mistake to take Genesis as a literal description of the earth and the act of creation.

As far is theology is concerned, God certainly could have made everything as it is today in one act of will. Or God could have initiated an evolutionary process in which plants and animals grow and take new shapes and forms. God could have initiated creation with gases and matter that cooled and solidified. And there could have been a "big bang" event that sent new bodies hurtling into space. What the church insists upon is that God created from nothing whatever was first and that God by a special act of creation put into us the soul or spiritual element that makes us humans what we are.

Much of how the world or earth as we know it came into being will have to be determined by scientists drawing on everything from anthropology and archaeology to astronomy and space study. Whatever the details, they will not in the end diminish the truth that God made the world and everything in it.

Why is it said that when Gregorian Masses have been celebrated on thirty consecutive days the person goes right to heaven?

The custom of offering thirty Masses on thirty consecutive days with a belief they have a special value goes back to Pope Saint Gregory the Great. He said he was assured his friend Justus was delivered from purgatory after Gregory had had thirty Masses offered for him. The church does not and cannot say that after the offering of Gregorian Masses a person will certainly be freed from purgation. But in 1884 the

Congregation for Indulgences declared the belief of people in the efficacy of the series to be "pious and reasonable." And before he became pope Benedict XIII said, "The reason for the special value of this custom lies in the merits of Saint Gregory, who obtains by the great efficacy of his prayers the satisfactory virtue for these thirty Masses." A long, continuous belief in the church is that prayers and Masses offered for the dead are of benefit to those who have died in a state of grace but remain in a state of purgation. Exactly how God applies the merits of Christ and the "treasury of the Church" in answer to these prayers has long been a matter of theological discussion.

One long-held theory speaks of different fruits of the Mass. These fruits are called: (1) general fruits that go to the whole church independently of the celebrating priest's intention, (2) special fruits that go to the benefit of those persons (living or dead) for whom the Mass is offered in a special way and (3) personal fruits that benefit the priest and faithful celebrating a particular Mass.

The present *Code of Canon Law,* following Pope Paul VI's *Firma in Tradtione* (issued *motu proprio*—on his own initiative—in 1974), sees a Mass offering as a donation freely given by the faithful primarily out of their concern for the church and their desire to support its material needs.

Father John Huels, O.S.M., addresses the question in his commentary on the canons concerning Mass offerings. He says they should be understood as gifts to the church or its ministers on behalf of some intention, much as a donation or bequest is made to any charitable institution in the name of some person, living or dead. The obligation of the priest accepting an offering is to apply a Mass according to a definite intention.

Huels observes that the code does not explain what it means to apply a Mass according to a definite intention. He then states, "The traditional theory of the special fruits of the Mass which the priest applies for the benefit of the donor's intention is widely discredited by contemporary theologians and, moreover, is not fostered in recent ecclesiastical documents on the subject." Rather importantly, he notes that the canons on applying intentions do not depend on any particular theological theory.

With that in mind it is interesting to observe that the secretary for the Congregation for the Clergy, Archbishop Gilberto Agustoni, in commenting on the congregation's February 22, 1991, *Decree on Collecting Mass Intentions*, seems to accept the theology of special fruits. He says in his March 22, 1991, commentary,

> Nor can we forget that Catholic doctrine has constantly taught that the fruits of the Eucharistic Sacrifice can be attributed to various purposes: first of all to those whom the Church herself names in the "intercessions" of the eucharistic prayer, then to the celebrating minister (the so-called ministerial fruit), then to *those making the offering*, etc.

Archbishop Agustoni's remarks here are not a definitive doctrinal statement; they represent his own theology. They do, though, reflect the lack of theological agreement on exactly how the offering of a Mass benefits people for whom the offering is applied. In any case the church carefully regulates the giving and accepting of Mass offerings so that there should not even be the appearance of a kind of trafficking or commercialism regarding them.

Whatever theology of Mass offerings people follow, while believing that God does respond to our prayers and Masses for the dead, we must remember we cannot constrain or force the goodness, mercy and justice of God. God is free to respond in any way to our prayers. A loving and good God will not abandon those who died without friends and relatives endowed with money as well as concern and love for them. We cannot "buy" our own or anyone else's way into heaven.

We should remember that in every offering of the Eucharist we pray for *all* the dead and living in the name of the church. And all the dead are frequently included in the prayers of intercession after the Gospel. Many people, in gratitude for God's goodness, have Masses offered for all the poor souls who do not have anyone to pray for them or who have been in purgatory the longest.

The special value in having a series of Gregorian Masses comes not from the dollars given but from the love and sacrifice behind them. The offering for the Masses should be seen, as the church sees it, as a generous way of providing for the needs of the church and the support of priests.

In this case it will probably be a way of providing especially for missionary priests because few pastors are eager to take on the obligation of celebrating a Mass for the same particular intention on thirty consecutive days. Parish priests have requests from many parishioners for Masses. And pastors have a special obligation of celebrating Mass for all the people of the parish on Sundays and other specified days.

Did God create life on other planets?

Until the sixteenth century there was little speculation about other worlds or life on other planets. After all, until Copernicus and Galileo came along, didn't everything revolve around the earth? Weren't earth and human beings the center of the universe?

According to Father John P. Kleinz in a series of columns (1981) in the *Catholic Times*, the diocesan newspaper of Columbus, Ohio, medieval scholars couldn't see "how rational beings outside Earth could fit into the doctrine of the unity of the human race redemption of all humankind by Christ." As studies and knowledge of astronomy grew, Kleinz said, a noted German scholar, Father Joseph Pohle, wrote in 1884 the most complete theological treatise until that time on living rational beings beyond earth, *The Galaxies and Their Inhabitants*. Pohle concluded not only that such creatures were possible and appropriate but also that they must exist!

Kleinz notes further a theologian's comments in 1955 after a flurry of European speculation occasioned by reported sightings of flying saucers. People were even asking whether the church should be ready to send missionaries into outer space. Dr. Michel Schmaus of the University of Munich said then that, if there are other rational beings in outer space, Christ would be their head (Saint Paul wrote that Christ is the head of the universe and God has made him Lord of all) but not necessarily their redeemer (if they needed a redeemer after an original sin).

It might be that redemption through Christ could be preached by some messenger of the faith without Christ making any visible appearance among them, said Schmaus. Or it would be possible that God did not give these creatures any supernatural goal.

In an appendix to his book *The Wide World, My Parish,* the Dominican theologian Yves Congar said,

> The only certainty that theology contributes here is that, if living beings endowed with understanding exist elsewhere, they too are in God's image, for he is creator of Mars and Venus just as he is of Earth.... Could there have been an incarnation in one of these inhabited worlds? Could the Word of God have taken flesh there and become a Martian, for instance?... Or could the Father have been incarnated there, or the Holy Spirit?

God certainly would not have to follow the earthly scenario in creating other worlds and rational creatures. God could have created hundreds or thousands of first creatures on another planet. God could have offered them the same opportunities for supernatural life and happiness we have been given.

Given the same test as humans, other rational beings might have passed it and there may have been no original sin among them.

Asking if God will come in judgment to other planets is being guilty of what Father Kleinz talked about in regard to C. S. Lewis, the Anglican theologian and author of the space novels *Out of the Silent Planet* and *Perelanda.* Lewis wrote of races on other planets who were free from the doom of original sin, and he wanted us "to stand firm against all exploitation and all theological imperialism." If we do not, "we might be forcing on creatures that did not need to be saved that plan of salvation which God has appointed for man."

179

Why is it forbidden to take Communion to a friend in a nursing home?

A certain order should be maintained in the handling and distribution of the Eucharist. That is why Communion is supposed to be given by an ordained deacon or priest or a duly appointed extraordinary minister of the Eucharist.

It would be better to think about how all the Catholic patients could be served rather than anticipate complaints because one patient was able to receive Communion more often than the others—if they are able to receive at all.

Try to get the pastor and diocese concerned about ministering to all the Catholics in the home and suggest that one way of doing so would be to appoint people like yourself as Eucharistic ministers.

CHAPTER FIVE

THE BIBLE

As the graduation party came to a close, the father called his son over. "Son," he said, "I just want you know how proud I am of you. Your mother and I could not have asked for a better child than you. Our expectations have been exceeded. I only want to wish you the best next year in college and want you to know that we'll always be here for you. What I'm going to give you now is but a small sign of our love."

It was the moment he'd been waiting for. He thought for sure his dad was going to give him the keys to a new car. Instead, his jaw dropped when his dad reached over to the bookcase and handed him a Bible. "You've got to be kidding me," the son exclaimed. "You call this a gift?" With that he brushed by his father and stormed out of the room. Their relationship was never the same.

Years later, after the son had married and moved away, he was called back home to help his mother with funeral arrangements for his father. One night while sorting through his father's personal effects, he saw the Bible he'd been given so long ago. It was lying on his father's desk. For some reason he felt the urge to go over and pick it up. He opened the cover and his jaw dropped. There *was the check in the exact amount for the new car he'd wanted so long ago.*

If only he'd opened it sooner.

Quoting Vatican II's Dogmatic Constitution on Divine Revelation, *the* Catechism of the Catholic Church *has this to say about Scripture in the life of the church:*

> *"And such is the force and power of the word of God that it can serve the Church as her support and vigor and the children of the Church as strength for their faith, food for the soul, and a pure and lasting font of spiritual life." Hence "access to Sacred Scripture ought to be open wide to the Christian faithful."... The Church "forcefully and specifically exhorts all the Christian faithful...to learn 'the surpassing knowledge of Jesus Christ,' by frequent reading of divine Scriptures. "Ignorance of the Scriptures is ignorance of Christ"' (131, 133). "*

•

When and where did the word *Bible* originate?

The word *bible* comes from the Greek word *biblia*, which means "books." The singular is *biblion*, "book."

So "The Bible" suggests in English *"The* Book" (or *"The* Books," since the Bible is actually a collection of books edited and printed in one volume).

The term "The Book" was used for Scripture long before the church ever determined officially and finally exactly all the books that were to be accepted as the inspired word of God (formally defined by the Council of Trent in 1546).

Already in 2 Maccabees 8:23, the sacred writer tells us, "After reading to them from the holy book and giving them the watchword, 'The Help of God,' he [Judas Maccabeus] himself took charge of the first division and joined in battle with Nicanor." Second Maccabees was probably written around 80 B.C. so the inspired writings were already being called "The Book" or "The Holy Book" (Holy Bible) at that time.

You may also trace the use of "The Book" (Bible) back to Moses, depending on how you translate the Hebrew. In some translations, *Today's English Version,* for instance, Exodus 31:24 tells us that Moses wrote God's law in "a book" and he told the priests in charge of the Covenant Box (Ark of the Covenant), "Take this book of God's law and place it beside the Covenant Box of the Lord your God, so that it will remain there as a witness against his people." Elsewhere the Scriptures speak of "the book of the Law" or "the book of the covenant."

Obviously from very early times, inspired writing(s) was referred to as "The Holy Book" or "The Book" (Bible).

What does the church mean when it says the Bible is without error?

Especially in these later centuries there has been much discussion about what it means to say that the Bible is inerrant. The discovery that certain biblical texts describe natural events in terms that do not conform to scientific evidence or facts forced Scripture experts and the church to think through again what it means to say there is not error in the Bible. The fathers of the Second Vatican Council struggled with the meaning of inerrancy and how best to express it during their sessions. *The Dogmatic Constitution on Divine Revelation* stated the fact of inerrancy this way: "The books of Scripture must be acknowledged as teaching firmly, faithfully and without error that truth which God wished put into the sacred writings for the sake of salvation." Each phrase is important in understanding this statement. The Scriptures express without error *that truth* which *God wishes* put in them *for the sake of our salvation.*

The council members were not saying that statements about astronomy, geography, biology or zoology are always errorless.

Further, a number of authors of popular catechisms or instructional materials follow the explanation of inerrancy given by Father Norbert Lohfink of the Pontifical Biblical Institute in Rome. Lohfink's point is that in talking about inerrancy you must always take the Bible as a whole. It is the Bible taken in its complete and unified form that is inerrant. Individual statements and books must be tested against the overall teaching of the Bible (cf. *Catechism of the Catholic Church* 106–107).

In developing Lohfink's thought in *The Theology of Inspiration*, John Scullion, S.J., says the Bible changes with the addition of each new book. God reveals the truth in stages. Each new book as it appears develops, adds to, modifies or corrects passages of earlier books.

The early books of the Old Testament express ignorance or doubt about life after death. Job, for example, says: "But mortals die, and are laid low; humans expire, and where are they? As waters fail from a lake and a river wastes away and dries up, so mortals lie down and do not rise again" (Job 14:10–12).

It is in the New Testament that Jesus reveals the life of the Resurrection. William Anderson explains in *In His Light*,

> To quote the Book of Job as a proof that we have no life after death is to miss the gradual unfolding message of the Bible. The individual message of the Bible passages must stand the test of the constant teaching of the Bible which is the inspired, revealed truth that the Bible teaches free from error.

From all that, you can see the danger of pulling individual verses out of the context of a passage, a chapter, a particular book or the Bible as a whole. That can create a great deal of misunderstanding and misinterpretation.

How can we be sure what the Bible means?

Each book or part of the Scriptures must be interpreted in light of its kind or genre of writing. A parable is a parable. It is not history but a story. You must interpret it to discern the point or lesson that is being made or given. A moral teaching is a moral teaching; for example, fornication is sinful. There is nothing symbolic or figurative about that. That is literally true. To understand what you are reading, you must know the kind of writing with which you are dealing and the particular forms being used by the human authors. And you must be aware of the rest of the Scriptures as well.

Some believe that simply praying before picking up the Scriptures to read them guarantees we will correctly understand them; but you would not try that with Einstein's theory. And why do people then disagree with each other about the meaning of many biblical passages when they have all prayed beforehand to understand them correctly? God does not dispense from using ordinary effort and common sense.

There are many Catholics today engaged in prayer and study groups who are praying over and seeking to understand and apply the Scriptures to their lives. While there are troublesome or unclear passages, most of us, even without being learned theologians, know what God is saying to us and how we are to live.

Even so, just as with many other things in life, we may never know the exact meaning of certain passages or expressions we find in the Bible. Life offers us absolute certitude in very few things. We must often live with ambiguity and uncertainty. The church has declared or defined the exact meaning of very few particular biblical texts. And even the second letter of Peter tells us,

> So also our beloved brother Paul wrote to you according to the wisdom given him, speaking of this as he does in all his letters. There are some things in them hard to understand, which the ignorant and unstable twist to their own destruction, as they do the other scriptures (3:15–16).

Nevertheless, we know and agree for the most part on what the Bible and Jesus teach us and what they say to us about salvation and how to please God. To assist us in our understanding, we have the church and its magisterium—a living rule and guide of faith. The church and the magisterium came even before the New Testament was written. It was the church, the living authority in the church, that established and discerned with the help of the Holy Spirit what writings were inspired and contain what has been handed down to us from the apostles. Peter and the apostles preached the Good News, proclaimed what Jesus said and did before any book of the New Testament was written. This same church and the successors to the apostles act as guardians and keepers of the tradition and authentic interpreters of the teaching committed to writing under the inspiration of the Spirit.

There are scores of wonderful books about the Scriptures, who wrote the particular books, when they were written, the forms of literature that they are and the times and peoples they describe. A good way to start reading and studying would be to pick up a Bible and read the introductions at the beginning of the Old and New Testaments and before each book. Also, the Liturgical Press has a series of individual books of the Bible with a section-by-section or line-by-line commentary or explanation that should be very helpful.

What is the difference between Catholic and Protestant Bibles?

As Melvin Farrell, s.s., points out in *Getting to Know the Bible*, the Bible has a somewhat complicated history. The differences between Protestant and Catholic translations of the Bible are in the Old Testament or Hebrew Scriptures. The books of the Bible were written as individual books or writings. They were in response to different needs or situations and had purposes of their own. They emerged from different authors and traditions. Father Farrell tells us that until the Babylonian exile, which took place from 587 to 538 B.C., there were three different traditions concerning sacred writings among the Israelites: Northern, Southern and Deuteronomist. After the exile the three traditions were merged. One volume of sacred writings resulted with the Pentateuch (first five books of the Bible) at its heart.

With the passage of time other books came to be regarded as sacred or inspired. But not everyone agreed about which books were inspired.

Jews in Palestine formed a list of some thirty-nine books written in Hebrew. Egyptian Jews (Jews of the Diaspora) added writings of their own, such as Tobit, to this list and produced a Greek translation of forty-six books called the Septuagint. Thus, there came to be a Palestinian Canon and the Septuagint, also known as the Greek or Alexandrian Canon.

After the Temple in Jerusalem was destroyed by the Romans in A.D. 70, the Jews felt a need to preserve and gather traditions to pass on to those who would come after them. Around the end of the first century, the Jews of Palestine settled on a Palestinian Canon.

In the meantime the early Christians were reading and writing in Greek. They were producing sacred writings of their own. The books they wrote in their liturgies and instruction were in Greek. They followed and accepted the Greek or Septuagint version of the Hebrew or Old Testament Scriptures.

Although all Christian lists were not immediately the same, there was a list of Christian inspired writings by A.D. 150. Councils in 393 and 397 listed twenty-seven books as belonging to the New Testament or Christian writings. By his death in 420 Saint Jerome had produced the Latin Vulgate translation, which became the official Bible of the church.

When the Reformation came along, Martin Luther translated the Palestinian Canon rather than the Vulgate of Jerome. Leaders of the Reformation for the most part followed Luther's German translation of the Bible, accepting the Palestinian Canon.

The Council of Trent (1545–1563) took up the question of the inspired writings and authoritatively defined the canon as the books now contained in the Catholic translations of the Bible, following the Greek (Alexandrian) Canon.

Today many Protestant translations of the Bible contain the additional Catholic books calling them by the name of Apocrypha. Catholic scholars use the term *deutero-canonical* for these books unique to the canon used by Catholics and Orthodox.

Why have some of the names of the books in the Bible changed?

A lot of hands were involved in shaping modern editions and translations of the Bible. The names used for books sometimes depend on the translators or editors and what language they used and how they divided the manuscripts. For instance, did the translator treat Kings and Chronicles as one or as separate works?

Working from different languages, did the translators use Greek or Hebrew forms of titles, names and spellings? To exemplify, did the translator follow the Greek and say *Isaias* or the Hebrew and write *Isaiah*? Did translators, as they did in the case of the Douay Bible, take over the Greek, titling and writing "Paralipomenon" or go directly back to the Hebrew and use the name "Chronicles"? Did the translator, as in the case of the Douay Bible, think of a manuscript (Kings 1, 2, 3 and 4) as one writing following the Greek system or as separate, 1 and 2 Samuel and 1 and 2 Kings?

The *New American Bible* translation is most often read in Catholic church celebrations. The translator of this version, like those of the Jerusalem Bible, went back to the original languages or oldest existing forms of the biblical texts.

In doing so, said Pope Paul VI, in an introduction to the *New American Bible* version,

> The translators have carried out the directive of...Pius XII in his famous encyclical *Divino Afflante Spiritu*, and the decree of the Second Vatican Council (*Dei Verbum*), which prescribed that "up-to-date and appropriate translations be made in the various languages by preference from the original texts of the sacred books," and that "with the approval of Church authority, these translations may be produced in cooperation with our separated brethren" so that "all Christians may be able to use them."

Much of this information—and more—you will find in *The Bible: An Owner's Manual*, by Robert R. Hann.

Have there been any advances made in scriptural scholarship?

Some advances and discoveries have made the Bible and its message clearer to us.

- Manuscripts ranging from nearly whole books of the Bible to fragments or sections of a book have been discovered. Sheets of papyri, parchments, and metal or clay scrolls often have given us copies of scriptural books or passages older than those we had before. Because they were older, these texts are closer to the original manuscripts and thus generally freer of mistakes in copying and additions by copyists.

- We have learned more about the languages used by the inspired authors. A better understanding of words and expressions used by the writers, and how they were understood by the people of the writers' time, leads to a clearer meaning or understanding for us of what the sacred writers were saying.

- Writings contemporary with the biblical writings have taught about the "literary forms" (styles of writing) used by biblical authors. To realize that the sacred author is using an allegorical style or is writing in the style of historical fiction makes a difference in how we interpret and understand a particular book or section. A poem (psalm) conveys its message in a way quite different from a family history or genealogical table.

- Scientific methods of dating manuscripts and materials tell us better when books or sections of them were first written.

- Nonbiblical manuscripts written prior to or contemporary with some biblical books have been found. Again, these other writings tell us something about the literary forms that the Bible writers used. They also tell us about the customs, ways of living and ways of thinking proper to people living in biblical times. These nonbiblical writings supply historical information about events mentioned in the Bible or taking place at the same time. They give us more information about nations and people who figure in the biblical narrative.

- In 1947, an Arab boy discovered a huge cache of ancient manuscripts in a cave by the Dead Sea. Among them were very old texts of biblical writings. Some were writings of and used by a religious group called the Qumran Community. These "Dead Sea Scrolls" were composed at various times between 250 B.C. and A.D. 68. From them we learn much about the religious climate at the time John the Baptist appeared and Jewish belief and religious practices when Christianity began.

- Archaeological discoveries, some by accident and some by scientists working systematically in planned digs, have been going on for centuries. They are taking place right now. The *Biblical Archaeology Review* reports on what is being discovered by archaeologists.

In past years it has reported on what appears to be the synagogue where Jesus preached in Capernaum. It also looked at the type of furniture found in a house in Jerusalem burnt by the Romans in A.D. 70. As a result, we learn more about the way of life of people who lived in the first years of the church and what it was like for the people of Jerusalem as the city burnt around them.

Another issue reported on discoveries at Lachish, a city conquered and destroyed by Sennacherib in Judah in 701 B.C. Inscriptions depict how war was waged, how captives were tortured and how prisoners of war were put to death. Inscriptions and reliefs in the Assyrian palace at Nineveh show how men and women dressed at the time, and depict Jews being driven into captivity. Clay tablets holding the Annals of Sennacherib contain his own account of his victory at Lachish and how the beaten King Hezekiah sent him "his daughters, concubines, male and female musicians...[and] a personal messenger to deliver the tribute and make slavish obeisance." All these things throw light on the events described in 2 Chronicles and 2 Kings.

For further information try *A Guide to the Lands of the Bible* and *The Synagogues and Churches of Ancient Palestine*, by Leslie Hoppe, O.F.M., and *The Cultural World of Jesus* (three volumes) by John J. Pilch.

Are there "lost" books of the Bible?

There are books similar to those in the Bible but rejected by early Christians and the church as not scriptural or inspired by God. The Christian communities looked to the bishops and fathers of the church as great teachers for guidance concerning what writings should be accepted as inspired by God.

The Bible-like books that were rejected are called *apocryphal* (Greek for "hidden" or "concealed") Gospels by the Catholic church. The followers of Jesus simply did not accept some or all of what was in these writings as being in conformity with what they knew about Jesus and his teaching. At least in part, they did not reflect what the disciples and apostles had taught and preached about Jesus and the things he said while among them.

In the case of New Testament apocryphal Gospels, some of them are a kind of partisan literature advancing heretical teachings or viewpoints. Others are described as a combination of piety and curiosity. In the case of the pietistic books, their authors may never have intended them to be accepted as Scripture.

Some of the apocryphal writings purported to give secret revelations not contained in the accepted books of Scripture—revelations of the kind some self-designated mystics or prophets may give out even today. They claimed to possess a secret wisdom open only to the followers of the writer or a select group.

Some of the pietistic writings attempted to fill in details about the life of Mary or Jesus not contained in the recognized Gospels. In these writings there may be factual material mixed with fantasy and imagination. What is called the *Infancy Gospel of Thomas* has stories about the childhood of Jesus. It has a tale, for instance, of Jesus making living pigeons out of clay models.

"But," says Joseph Kelly in *Why Is There a New Testament?*, "in general this gospel presents him as a detestable little brat who shows off his miraculous powers and often uses them vindictively. Jesus withers the arm of a man who disturbs his game, strikes dead a child who runs by and accidentally bumps into him, and inflicts blindness on bystanders who criticize him for killing children."

You can see why few would have seriously thought this writing to be Scripture, and why many would not make copying it by hand part of their life's labor before the invention of printing.

You can find entries about the apocryphal Gospels in almost any encyclopedia or Catholic dictionary of theology or the Bible. Various books about the apocryphal writings are available in public libraries and bookstores.

Does the church define the meaning of biblical texts?

An essay by Father Raymond E. Brown, s.s., and Sandra Schneiders, I.H.M., on hermeneutics (interpretation) in the *New Jerome Biblical Commentary* speaks at some length on this topic. The authors make at least six points in speaking of the church's role as keeper of the Scriptures:

1. In some instances the church simply gives directives or guidelines on how to interpret or understand the Scriptures. Later findings and research in biblical criticism may lead to revised or new directives for better understanding.

2. The magisterium sometimes uses particular texts to support or illustrate its teaching without intending to define their literal meaning. One example of this would be Genesis 3:15, "I will put enmity between you and the woman, and between your offspring and hers," in *Ineffablis Dei* on the Immaculate Conception.

3. The church does not claim the power to infallibly determine details of such things as geography or chronology. The scope of its authority is matters pertaining to faith and morals.

4. The church has officially commented on the meaning of very few passages.

5. When the church has commented on the meaning of certain passages, it has most often done so in negative fashion—to reject as false an interpretation because of its implications for faith and/or morals. The Council of Trent, for instance, rejected the Calvinist interpretation of John 3:5, "No one can enter the kingdom of God without being born of water and the Spirit," that would make it only a metaphor. So, too, did the church condemn those who disassociated John 20:23, "If you forgive the sins of any, they are forgiven them; if you retain the sins of any, they are retained," from the power to forgive sins in the sacrament of reconciliation.

6. Using some texts to support church teaching does not mean the church intends to define their meaning.

When were Adam and Eve created?

Biblical exegetes and anthropologists alike would tell you only "events" such as the creation of the earth and the first human beings (Adam and Eve) and the time between Adam and people such as Noah belong to prehistory. They predate the keeping of any written records or histories. What we have is a *popular* account of the origins of creation and the human race. People fashioned accounts like these to give some explanation of the world and human beings as they experienced them. The Hebrews used stories of the surrounding peoples but brought them into line with their faith in Yahweh.

The creation story in Genesis is, of course, an imaginative account of the origin of human beings rather than a scientific description or explanation. The point of the author in this story is that both man and woman have been made by God, God is their creator and they are very different from the rest of creation. Man and woman, human beings, are made in the image and likeness of God.

Pauline Viviano, writing in the Scripture commentary series from the Liturgical Press on the Old Testament, in *Genesis* says one of the most puzzling aspects of these verses is that God, Yahweh, forms woman from a *rib* of the man. There are no passages in other ancient literature from the East to suggest a particular idea or meaning the author has in mind. Viviano, however, advances an idea to be found in Bruce Vawter's earlier work, *On Genesis: A New Commentary.* Vawter says that in the Sumerian language the word that meant "rib" also meant "life." He believes that there is some kind of play on words that is taking place (as happens, for instance, in the New Testament when Jesus tells Simon his name will be Peter [rock] and on Peter [rock] he will build his church).

The time of the appearance of the first humans on earth, then, is more a question for anthropologists and scientists than Scripture exegetes. Perhaps the best estimates or guesses will be in encyclopedias or reference books.

Where is the Garden of Eden?

Any attempt to make an exact geographical location of the Garden of Eden presumes that the author of the Book of Genesis is giving a literal, step-by-step account of creation and the events that followed.

Most Catholic biblical scholars today do not believe that the Genesis account is that kind of writing. The author could just as well have placed the scene of Eden in Europe or North America. He placed it in the East because he was of the Eastern world.

Bruce Vawter in his book *On Genesis: A New Reading,* says that we must remember that the geography in Genesis is primitive and "done by someone who was not personally familiar with it."

John C. Gibson, in his book *Genesis,* writes,

The identity of the other two rivers, Pishon and Gihon, and the lands associated with them, Havilah and Cush, has been endlessly debated, not only by modern scholars but by the rabbis and Christian Fathers of earlier times, and with no agreement among them. It may well be that they are for the author fictional places like the

194

land of Nod to which Cain flees (Genesis 4:16) which was also in the mysterious East. The descriptions, half real, half imaginary, will then be meant to conjure up a picture of a country in, but not quite of, the known world, a country which we would all like to reach but which is always just out of reach over the next range of mountains or beyond the horizon. And this, I think, is exactly the impression the author wishes to leave with us. Eden is a country where men and women ought to be, it is accessible to them, but for a reason which he is about to give, no human being has yet got to it.

Trying to locate geographically the Garden of Eden is a waste of time and misses the real point of what the Genesis author is saying. It is like reading about Shangri-La in James Hilton's *Lost Horizon* and then trying to determine exactly where it is in the mountains of Tibet.

Why does Adam blame Eve for the sin in the Garden of Eden?

The telling of the story of Adam and Eve was influenced by the biases of the culture and times in which the human author lived.

But readers should not get lost in the details and mistake them for the real point of Genesis. The Genesis account is not the memoirs of Adam or Eve: They left no diaries. It is not a historian's account of witnesses and descendants. It is not a newspaper reporter's firsthand account of what he or she saw happening in the garden. It is not the result of an interview given by Adam or Eve after all these events took place.

Genesis is a theologian's attempt to explain the sorry plight of humankind in the writer's own time, to explain why there is so much sin and evil in a world made good by God.

That theologian was not familiar with theological and philosophical terms common in the twentieth century and did not speak in abstract terms. So the author explained the origin of evil and sin in a way people of that earlier time would understand—in narrative or story form, through the actions of people.

Arguing whether the fruit Adam and Eve ate was an apple, a peach or a plum will be—if you excuse the expression—fruitless! Whether Adam or Eve ate first really is not the point. What the author, inspired by God, is trying to say is that God did indeed make the world and everything in it, that God created humankind good just as God made the world good. There is sin and evil in the world because the first humans disobeyed God and introduced evil into God's creation.

There actually are probably at least two Genesis authors whose accounts were put together by a later editor. Were any of these contributors sexist? Maybe.

Where did Cain find a wife?

Genesis is not a history book. An editor has stitched together several writings and, in some cases, descriptions or versions of the same events. The author and editors are not chiefly concerned with passing on history, and they certainly are not writing history in a scientific way. Their main purpose is to convey theology or explain questions such as, "How do human beings relate to God?" and "Why is there evil, pain and suffering in the world?" The stories they relate are for the purpose of explaining these things in their relationship to God.

They are not trying to provide a list of all the generations of human beings and descendants of Adam and Eve long after the human race first appeared on the scene of time. They are not trying to give their readers a neat, complete and accurate family tree.

After the creation accounts, Genesis goes on to speak of Cain and Abel, descendants of Cain, the birth of Seth from Adam and Eve, children of Seth, and in chapter five, verse four says, "Adam lived eight hundred years after the birth of Seth, and he had other sons and daughters."

Obviously there had to be female descendants, daughters of Adam and Eve, the first human beings—whether or not their names are given—if sons of the first humans were to be able to marry and reproduce. Sons and daughters of the first humans had to intermarry.

But the names of all the children of Adam and Eve, how many there may have been and who married whom isn't really important to the writer. Humankind is important to the writer. People will be talked about only insofar as they enable the author to show how sin came into the world and the terrible things it produced and continues to produce!

How could God ask Abraham to sacrifice Isaac?

Commentators approach that story in two ways:

1. The sacred writer wants to make the point of Abraham's complete and unquestioning faith and tells the story as an illustration of that point. Explanations of why God should demand this test are not the author's concern; he will not be distracted from the lesson he wishes to make. In the face of terrible consequences, in the face of an act that seems bound to frustrate and make uncomfortable the promise God has given him of becoming the father of uncountable peoples, Abraham trusts and will be obedient to God no matter what the consequences. Obviously, the narrator believes that God's action in the story is in keeping with his wisdom and goodness.

2. The sacred writer does indeed want to make clear Abraham's faith, but employs an account that was used earlier to make another point—God rejects human sacrifice!

To appreciate that you must realize that God set Abraham apart and made a covenant with him. He would become the founder of a nation, the father of all Israelites.

Abraham was surrounded by "pagans." In Abraham's world and among his neighbors human sacrifice was a common thing. Archaeological digs have turned up ovens in which infants were roasted to death in sacrifice. Archaeologists working in Canaan have repeatedly found infant skeletons buried beneath the thresholds of city gates and houses.

The infants were buried there as sacrifices, Bruce Vawter writes in *On Genesis: A New Reading*, "to ward away evil and ensure divine protection."

So, to Abraham this would not be an unusual practice. In his experience it was a commonplace thing, certainly not unthinkable. The first and second book of Kings, as well as Exodus, refer to human sacrifices among the nations surrounding Israel. And it is also clear that even the descendants of Abraham also practiced human sacrifice. They did not see it incompatible with their worship of God.

Therefore, the sacred writer not only extols the faith of Abraham but also teaches the Israelite descendants of Abraham that *God does not will or want human sacrifice!* God rejects human sacrifice. Israel is to be different from the nations who offer human lives to God.

Bruce Vawter suggests that part of our problem is that we do not grasp or appreciate the terms and language that the author of this passage uses. We do not appreciate the "casual way in which God and man converse in these patriarchal stories."

Vawter continues:

> That *God said* to Abraham that he should take his son and *offer him up as a holocaust* means that to a man of proved religious sensitivity it once came as an inner conviction that his highest duty required of him to destroy his only heir in service of some greater good. That later *the Lord's messenger called to him from heaven* and told him no such thing was desired of him means that this same man arrived at a new conception of what is pleasing to God, or even, if you will, a new conception of God himself.

Interpreted in this way, the story takes on quite a different twist, doesn't it?

What is God's name?

The work of a translator is to try to reproduce in another language as accurately as he or she can what is in the original. In most languages there are different names or expressions used to designate God. In English, for example, we speak about God, the Lord, our creator, the supreme being, the maker of all, and we use still other expressions.

Hebrew also has and had different ways of speaking about God or naming him. For instance, the Hebrews used the word *El*, which is best translated as "God." It was a word also used by other Semites to mean a being or beings above human beings (like the pagan gods). When Moses asked for God's name, God told him he was *Yahweh*, or "I am who am," or "He who is." The Hebrews also used the word *Adonai*, which is translated "Lord." Sometimes the Old Testament writers spoke of *Yahweh Sabaoth*, which seems to be a shortening or abbreviation of *Yahweh elohe sabaoth Israel*. According to my reference books that would be translated something like "Yahweh, the God of the hosts of Israel." Or shortened, "Yahweh, the God of hosts."

So when modern translations use variously Yahweh, Yahweh Sabaoth, God or Lord, they are trying to reflect what is in the most ancient manuscripts and original language. Rather than translate *Yahweh* into "He who is" or "He who causes to be," they leave it in the original because it is a proper name. By comparison, if a person's name is *Salvador* in Spanish, we leave it in the Spanish form when speaking English. We don't, as a rule, translate it to *Savior*.

In the case of the name Yahweh, by the third century B.C. Jews had stopped pronouncing the word when they saw it written. This name was regarded as too sacred to be spoken. Further, in writing Hebrew the vowels of *Yahweh* were not used, only the consonants. So on an old manuscript the reader would see *YHWH* when the author referred to Yahweh. A reader coming upon this name was not to pronounce it, but to substitute aloud the word *Adonai*. As a reminder of this, manuscript copiers would place the vowels *a, o, a* of *Adonai* under the consonants of *Yahweh*, *YHWH*. Later copiers did not understand what had been done and moved the vowels up between the consonants to read *YaHoWaH*. That was made by the translators of many old English Bibles into *Jehovah*—a word or name never used by the original authors.

Why does God appear so cruel in the book of Exodus?

The story of the plagues in Exodus is more complicated than we might at first believe. Commentators make it clear that the story or stories of the plagues went through many hands and tellings before they got to the final editor of the book of Exodus and eventually Cecil B. DeMille's epic movie, *The Ten Commandments*.

Evidence of different hands is to be found in the text itself. James F. Leary in *Hear O Israel: A Guide to the Old Testament*, says that in Exodus four different oral traditions have been woven together. According to John F. Craghan, in the "Exodus" chapter of the *Collegeville Bible Commentary*, one source sees the plagues as God's punishment on Pharaoh because he refuses to let Israel depart Egypt. Another of the sources sees the plagues more as signs and wonders given to make it clear Moses and Aaron represent God (Yahweh).

There are also certain inconsistencies in the final telling of the story. For instance, Craghan asks, if all the cattle were killed in the fifth plague how were they affected by the boils and hail of the sixth and seventh plagues? And where did the firstborn cattle come from that were struck dead in the tenth plague?

It also seems clear the tenth plague and its story are quite separate from the accounts of the other plagues.

At least some commentators would see at the basis of the Exodus account a series of real natural events and phenomena. They are seen by some as recurring disasters of the natural order—crops being devoured by insects, cattle struck by disease, hailstorms pelting land and creatures, the land being overrun by pests and the Nile being polluted. Some would theorize these phenomena resulted from the impact of a comet striking in the region or a volcanic eruption.

Behind these events, perhaps in the midst of them, God, Yahweh, is acting. As Father D. Ryan says, in the "Amos" chapter of *A New Catholic Commentary on Holy Scripture*, edited by Father Reginald Fuller, the Israelites did not distinguish between what God permits and what God directly causes. Everything that happened was attributed to God. They did not distinguish between primary and secondary causes—everything was done by Yahweh.

In *The Old Testament Without Illusion*, John L. McKenzie says the scribes who put these stories down were writing a theological explanation of existing reality—Israel was the people of God.

James F. Leary finds in the recurrent theme of the Exodus, "Let my people go, that they may serve me," the theological statement of Israel's transference of loyalty from Pharaoh to Yahweh. Leary further states, "The narration of the plagues builds on the same theme, namely that God's purpose to save Israel from slavery and to make the Hebrews his ambassadors to the nations will not be thwarted even by the great powers of the day."

McKenzie suggests that behind the Exodus account are songs and an old literary form called a cultic recital. The scribes' telling of Exodus was something like writing the history of the war of 1812 from the "Star Spangled Banner." Moses is a figure around whom legends have formed like legends formed around King Arthur of Britain and his Camelot.

Of the tenth plague, the death of all Egyptian firstborn males, McKenzie says, "Scholars are sure the story arose from the Passover ritual," which came from the offering of the firstborn of men, flocks and herds in the spring. At an early date the theme of liberation was added to the original Passover feast. The sparing of the Israelite males and later their ransom with an animal sacrifice was an assertion that Israel never practiced human sacrifice like some of its neighbors.

Does God as portrayed by the Israelite scribes of Exodus appear cruel and vengeful? What kind of God is this who calls for pestilence, destruction and death? Even Christians sometimes have such a view of God—even after all Jesus said and did. Men of the Middle Ages cried, "God wills it," and marched off as Crusaders to sack, pillage and burn.

Men of the Inquisition burned heretics in the name of God. Today there are those among us who want to see hurricanes, forest fires, earthquakes and floods as punishing acts of God.

And some insist God shows he is angry with sinners by visiting some of them with AIDS.

Lawrence Boadt sums up things rather well in *Reading the Old Testament: An Introduction*: "The tenth and final plague stands apart. Although it may seem coldly brutal to us, Israel saw the death of Egypt's firstborn as God's clear choice on behalf of his people and his life-and-death concern for their freedom."

He also says,

> Behind the greatly magnified accounts of the Lord's victory that we find in the present text stands an authentic memory of Israel. The doubts over the possibility of any miracle at all simply misses the point. Scientists will tell us quite readily that every plague, from the animal locust swarms to the virulent outbreaks of skin diseases, can be found naturally in northern Africa.... The miracle does not stand on any of these factors. In fact, ancient peoples, dependent on oral storytelling, who cherish traditions of a god acting in a special way and breaking in upon their normal way of life with astounding suddenness, almost always magnify the details and accent the heroic aspects.
>
> The miracle is only in the *timing* of such fortunate events, a timing that cannot be explained in any way except by design or because of prayer. A refugee band such as Israel just does not escape the power of the Egyptian army unless God chooses to protect and guide it. The very words the Old Testament uses for such miracles mean more properly "signs" or "wondrous, unexplainable things." They suggest that the event in question can only have divine direction because it is beyond human control. For the ancient Near East, there were no lucky chances or accidental happenings; all things were the result of the divine will. When the ordinary pattern changed dramatically, then it was a sign to be read and understood by all.

Father Hilarion Kistner, o.f.m., editor of *Homily Helps*, in reacting to this question said:

> God, even when inspiring the sacred writers, does not remove their ways of thinking, feeling and imagining. He uses them as they are. We need sometimes to modify their message with the fuller and clearer revelation of late times. Both Old Testament and especially New Testament passages make us realize that God is not cruel and vindictive: "God sent his only Son into the world so that we might live through him. In this is love, not that we loved God but that he loved us and sent his Son to be the atoning sacrifice for our sins" (1 John 4:9–10).

Why is there so much violence in the Old Testament, when God forbade killing?

Scripture scholars would begin to deal with this question by examining the description of Moses' encounter on Mount Sinai. They would ask, is this indeed a literal account of how the commandments were received or did an author, centuries later, convey the law through an imaginative literary device? In other words, did God actually write the Ten Commandments on tablets of stone or is the whole account a way of saying the law came from God?

The Israelites surely did not understand the commandment not to kill to be absolute. That seems evident from the rest of the law in Deuteronomy: It prescribes the death penalty for such crimes as adultery or raping a betrothed virgin. The killing referred to in the Fifth Commandment is murder. The Israelites surely did not understand the commandment to forbid them from engaging in war with the consequences of killing enemies. Nor did they understand the commandment not to steal to forbid taking booty. Even today, those who are opposed to the death penalty for even heinous crimes, by and large, accept the right to kill in self-defense.

Next, we must remember the Israelites were products of their time. They were very much influenced by the nations around them and their legal codes, practices and mind-sets.

As Lawrence Boadt remarks, in *Reading the Old Testament: An Introduction:*

> Modern people are shocked by such brutality, but it is necessary to remember that the ancient world did not share our outlook. Their ethical principles often placed national survival above any personal goods, and identified success in war or politics with the will of their god or gods.

Just as the Crusaders cried, *"Deus vult!"* ("God wills it!"), the Israelites thought of themselves as engaged in a holy war. Deuteronomy instructs that before the soldiers go into battle the priest is to come before them promising that God goes with them. Even in our own time, nations sometimes think of themselves as engaged in holy wars.

Beyond that, Israel conceived of itself and its loyalty to God as greatly endangered by the peoples around them and any contact with them. Thus, intermarriage was forbidden and prophets proclaiming false gods were to be put to death. The Israelites were instructed in Deuteronomy that if their own wives, brothers, sons, daughters or friends were to entice them to serve false gods, they were to kill them!

Still further, the survival of enemies presented more than a religious threat. Israel was a comparatively small people. The presence of enemies nearby or allowing enemies surrounding them to recover strength and rearm would constitute a continuing military threat.

As the Israelites saw it, the religious and military threat was to be eliminated as part of God's will for Israel—by destroying the threat completely.

The Israelites, like their neighbors who followed the same practices, put much of this in a theological garb. Victory came through God, victory was to be dedicated to God and Israel should not profit from the victory; the victory should be dedicated as a sacrifice to God. The destruction of enemies and their cattle would be a sign that Israel warred in the name of God, putting its trust in God alone and sought nothing for itself. Israel was not very different from peoples of our time who insist, "God is on our side!"

Very pertinent to this discussion are the remarks of *The Collegeville Bible Commentary*, edited by Diane Bergant and Robert J. Karris, on Deuteronomy 20:1–20:

> The theology of divinely willed and directed wars was an ancient Near Eastern commonplace. What we read here and elsewhere in Deuteronomistic literature is an explanation of Israel's battlefield experiences and memories. It hardly describes actual strategy and tactics.

In other words the author of Deuteronomy presents what is more Israel's idea of what God commanded and approved than what God actually commands. And just because certain brutal events are recorded in the Scriptures does not mean God sanctioned or commanded them—whatever the justification and primitive moral sense of those who participated in them.

Jesus, in the Sermon on the Mount, went further than the Hebrew Scriptures and Mosaic Law. He tells whoever is angry with his brother will be liable to judgment (Matthew 5:21–22).

Who was Caleb?

Caleb is in the books of Numbers and Joshua. Caleb was the son of Jephunneh of the tribe of Judah. Numbers lists him among the twelve Moses sent to reconnoiter the land of Canaan (chapters 13 to 14). They were told to report on the population of the land, their military strength and the fertility of the soil.

All recognized the bounty of the crops. But none besides Caleb urged trying to take possession. The others were fearful and defeatist. Caleb urged going up to seize the land. When the people threatened revolt and rejection of Moses and Aaron, Caleb with Joshua urged fidelity to God and to trust that God will be with Israel. The two were then threatened with stoning!

Because of Caleb's "different spirit," God promises to bring him into the promised land along with Joshua while those rebelling will wander in the desert without entering the land.

In Joshua 14—15 Caleb reminded Joshua, who had succeeded Moses, of God's promise. Joshua then gave Hebron to Caleb, and Caleb drove out the Anakim people. Caleb then gave his daughter to Othniel for capturing Kirath-sepher.

Is the book of Job fact or fiction?

The message of Job is true. The vehicle for the message is probably a story woven around an actual person from the past, a heroic and holy man who suffered greatly in patience and acceptance of God's will. But the dialogue and cast of other characters are the author's "creation."

This story is not preserved in the Bible for its own sake. It is not history but a vehicle for theology. The author is wrestling with the question of why good people suffer, why bad things happen to good people. And the answer he gives comes from the lips of Job.

Those who are disturbed by the notion that the Bible contains fiction might be helped by remembering the story of the Good Samaritan. It is easier to recognize that it is not important whether a man literally went down to Jerusalem and fell among thieves, and that a priest and Levite passed him by while a Samaritan came to his aid. It was not historical details that concerned Jesus. He was using a story—whether true or made up—to make a point. Why should it shock us that some Old Testament writers may have been doing the same thing?

Why does the book of Sirach refer to wisdom as "she"?

The word for wisdom is feminine in both Hebrew and Greek. It is simply a common literary device. Even in daily speech and conversation, we personify inanimate and abstract things.

For example, we speak of a ship as "she." We talk about "mother" church and proclaim the church as the "bride" of Christ. Our country or government becomes "Uncle Sam" and Great Britain "John Bull." Saint Francis sang of "Brother Sun and Sister Moon." And we refer to "mother earth."

Sirach, like other wisdom books, simply personifies wisdom and endows it with human characteristics as we do when we speak of experience as a hard teacher or say that a religious has taken lady poverty for a bride. It is a manner of speaking. The author or authors of Sirach were as much at home using this device effectively and beautifully as we are today.

However, it is worth noting Father Lawrence Boadt's remark in *Introduction to Wisdom Literature: Proverbs:*

> Several passages treat wisdom as though it were an independent being close to God (Proverbs 1:20–33, 8:22–31, Sirach 24:1–31, Wisdom 9:9–11). This is primarily a literary device to express how the transcendent God becomes present in a personal and immanent way by communicating himself to our intelligence, understanding and faith. Without this development, Christianity's theology of Jesus as Son of God and Word-made-flesh could not have found such expression.

Who was Jael?

The story of Jael (Jahel) is told in chapters 4 and 5 of the book of Judges. In chapter 4 the Israelite judge Deborah commands Barak to lead an army of ten thousand Israelites against an army of Canaanites under the generalship of Sisera. The Israelites defeated the Canaanites. Of the Canaanites, only Sisera survived.

He fled on foot and made his way to the tent of Jael, wife of the Kenite Heber. Since the Kenites were at peace with the Canaanites, Sisera asked Jael to hide and feed him. Feeling safe from the Israelites, Sisera slept. Apparently Jael decided to throw in her lot with the Israelites. She murdered Sisera in his sleep by driving a tent peg through his head.

Jael's praise is then sung in the Canticle of Deborah in Judges 5:24–27.

Did Samson commit suicide?

The *Encyclopedic Dictionary of the Bible*, edited by Louis Hartman, C.SS.R., had this to say:

> Samson's death in the temple of Dagon at Gaza, which he brought down on himself and the assembled Philistines (16:23–30), was not an act of suicide, but rather a return to his mission, to which he had been unfaithful when he betrayed the secret of his strength to Dalila [Delilah], but which he in conscious response to his call and with a prayer to God on his lips, now fulfilled, even at the cost of his own life.

From this point of view Samson's death was like that of a martyr who dies in defense of some virtue, as in a person who leaps to death rather than be sexually violated.

The moralist Heribert Jone, O.F.M. CAP., calls this indirect suicide and says that while in itself it is forbidden, it may be permitted for a proportionately grave reason. Jone writes: "One kills himself indirectly if, without the intention of committing suicide, he knowingly and willingly does something which not only has an intended good effect, but from which death also follows."

It is presupposed that the good effect results from the action as immediately as does death. By example Jone then finds it permissible for a person to leap from a dangerous height to escape burning to death, or for someone in wartime to blow up an enemy fortification or ship even though the person foresees his or her own death in doing so.

Why were lepers treated so harshly?

The term *leprosy* in the Bible seems to have been given to a number of skin infections—not Hansen's disease, which some people call leprosy today.

Because these diseases were so infectious, the law in the book of Leviticus prescribed exclusion (quarantine) from the community to prevent their spread. The afflicted's rent garments, bare head and cries of "unclean" were to warn others of the presence of the disease and the possibility of contracting it.

The quarantine was not meant to be a punishment but a health measure, though it seems very likely people thought of the disease as a punishment for sin. The fear of catching the disease could lead people to act unkindly toward the diseased person.

While such actions are not to be excused, they were certainly not limited to the Jews at the time of Jesus. Nor was the desire to control and stop the spread of infection.

Our newspapers are full of examples of what fear can do to people in the presence of AIDS. Some doctors have refused to treat AIDS patients. Those who do frequently take great precautions.

Did the Jewish revolt against Rome influence the writing of the Gospels?

It is not easy to date exactly when each of the Gospels was written. And certainly there were multiple reasons for each of the Gospels. But it does appear that Saint Paul was already dead by the time the first Gospel was put into written form. The first of the Gospels, Mark, was written sometime near A.D. 65 when Jewish zealots were revolting against Roman rule. Jewish-Christians were at odds with their own as well as being caught up in Roman persecution. The Roman reaction to the zealots produced the destruction of Jerusalem and the dispersal of the surviving Jews in A.D. 70.

This event marked the definitive separation of the Jewish-Christians from the rest of the Jewish community. Families became split and Christians were put out of the synagogues. The author of Mark wanted to explain, among other purposes, that following Jesus demanded suffering and pain.

Matthew, writing about A.D. 85 for a community made up in large part from those with Jewish roots, wanted to help them make sense of the pain of persecution and separation from their own.

Luke, writing around A.D. 85 for a Gentile audience, was

less concerned with these events. John, in 90 or 100, was further from these events and had his own theological concerns.

For more on the Gospels and Scriptures in general, you might read the introductions to them in study Bibles or one of the many commentaries on the Gospels and Bible.

What are the symbols of the four evangelists?

The key to these symbols of the evangelists we see in paintings or carved into pulpits or lecterns is the differing ways in which the four Gospels begin.

The symbol for Matthew is a winged man (sometimes described as a divine man). This figure is used because Matthew teaches about the human nature of Jesus and begins his Gospel by tracing the human ancestry of Christ.

A lion with wings represents Mark and his Gospel. Mark's Gospel opens with John the Baptist crying out in the wilderness. The Baptist's cry is like the roar of a lion. An added reason for the lion is that Mark's Gospel stresses the royal dignity or character of Jesus.

Artists have chosen to represent Luke and his Gospel with a winged ox. Luke begins with the scene in the temple where animal sacrifices are being offered. Luke also explains the sacrificial character of Jesus' life and death.

John's symbol is the eagle. In the prologue to his Gospel, John's vision soars into the heavens and he gazes into the mysteries surrounding the Incarnation of Jesus with the piercing eyes of the eagle. Throughout the Gospel he reaches the loftiest heights of theology.

The images for these symbols apparently come from the first chapter of Ezekiel. Here the prophet describes a vision in which the hand of the Lord came upon him. In the vision there were figures "something like four living creatures." They had a human form, and each had four faces: those of a man, a lion, an ox and an eagle (Ezekiel 1:3–10).

What does *synoptic* mean?

Synoptic comes from the Greek word *synopticos*, which can be translated "seen together" or "seen with." Matthew, Mark and Luke are called the synoptic Gospels because large sections of these writings when put side by side (seen together) reveal remarkable similarities. Similar patterns in narrating events emerge, and sections in two or all three of them are almost identical, word for word.

That is true because the writers or editors probably gathered material from some of the same sources. Most likely, these were written accounts of particular events (a narrative of the Passion, for example) or collections of Jesus' sayings in circulation before a writer or editor collected as many as he could to include in his own telling of the Good News. Before the Gospels took their present final form, the evangelists or editors may have borrowed from each other.

John's Gospel is distinguished from the synoptic Gospels because it is so different from all of them. The writer of John may not have known or been aware of the other accounts. He used different sources and has his own distinct approach and style. His writing is highly theological. He follows his own order and chronology in telling the story of what Jesus said and did.

Why do the Gospel accounts differ on some details, such as the thieves crucified with Jesus?

Ask ten witnesses to an automobile accident what happened and what will you get? Ten different accounts of the same incident. All will describe the same event. Many of the details will be the same. But some will include details that the others omit or tell the story from a perspective different from that of others.

With that in mind it may help you understand why the Gospel accounts are not always the same.

They are different because they are the works of four different writers or editors, each with his own viewpoint of what Jesus taught, said and did. Each is writing for a particular church or group of readers. Each has his own theology. Each wants to explain the meaning of Jesus and what he did as he sees it. And so the incidents and facts he selects are chosen with these things in mind, to support the points he wants to make.

Further, you must remember each evangelist is working from the oral accounts and written descriptions or written collections of Jesus' sayings that have come into his possession. Often the same materials are known to several or all the evangelists. Sometimes each has his own particular sources and traditions from which to work. Each evangelist will give his account using the facts about Jesus as he receives them.

Why do Matthew and Mark differ from Luke in their accounts of the thieves who were put to death with Jesus? Possibly because they are working from different accounts. Some recalled the taunts, the insults. Others recalled more vividly the mercy that Jesus showed on the cross and often repeated how Jesus prayed for his enemies and promised paradise and forgiveness to one of the thieves who asked for mercy.

Obviously, each evangelist is telling the story of Jesus' passion and death trying to make clear its significance and meaning as he saw it.

Mark and Matthew wanted to show how the Old Testament prophecies and psalms were fulfilled and stress how the scribes, Pharisees and robbers as well as the passersby taunted and ridiculed Jesus.

Luke wants to stress the mercy and forgiveness of Jesus and the coming of God's kingdom among us. The dialogue between the "good" thief and Jesus is very important to this.

Did Saint Paul write all the letters that bear his name?

As James Leary observes, in *A Light to the Nations*, the question of authorship in both the Hebrew Scriptures and the New Testament is very complicated. In our time and culture we expect that the person named as author of a work is responsible for its entire contents. If the listed writer took material from other sources or had the help of another person, we expect the title page or other explanatory material to tell us that. For example, the title page may read, "By John Doe as told to Jane Smith," or, "By John Doe with Jane Smith."

Even so, presidents or governors or candidates for political office employ speechwriters. One writer or a team of writers drafts a speech for the official or candidate who may edit it, then give it as his own, taking ownership of what the speech says. Similarly, the pope may have a group of theologians prepare an encyclical for him. When it is edited by him, he signs it as his own letter.

In the Mideast world, especially among the ancients and in biblical times, a person's name on a writing did not necessarily mean that that person wholly authored it. In some instances, says Leary, it could mean that the writing was dedicated to a person who had been a leader or hero of the community. It could mean that this work represented that person's thought or teaching. A disciple or writer might take on the persona and use the name of a well-known and respected individual to lend that person's authority to his own writing. A person's name on the writing could be a kind of statement that a disciple was rendering the thinking of a teacher or a school of thought based on the teaching of an apostle.

In some cases the earliest manuscripts of a particular writing bore no name or signature. Later, the writing came to be attributed to a particular individual for various reasons.

Whatever the case, we should remember our faith is not in the author or attributed author of a particular book of the Bible. In some instances we know a book went through the hands of several editors or a compiler. Our faith is in what the church has judged to have been written under the inspiration of God.

Drawing again on what James Leary says,

Modern scholars, after a complex process of textual analysis, conclude that not all thirteen letters attributed to Paul actually came from his hand. Some of the documents were probably written after the apostle's death by his disciples who deliberately imitated his style. They wrote to present his teaching, applying it to new situations and issues faced by a more complex and structured Church. All thirteen letters are definitely related to Pauline teaching. Each mirrors the gospel according to Paul.

Different experts and exegetes make cases for an author other than Paul for different epistles. Leary states that most agree Paul himself authored 1 Thessalonians, Galatians, 1 and 2 Corinthians, Philemon, Philippians and Romans.

He speaks of 2 Thessalonians, Colossians and Ephesians as Deutero-Pauline or doubtfully authored by Paul.

Leary says that 1 and 2 Timothy and Titus were written after Paul died, between A.D. 110 and 120.

Hebrews was very likely a sermon written down rather than a letter. The title used on the earliest manuscripts was simply "To the Hebrews." The author seems to have been known to the original readers, as 13:18–24 indicates. But who was that author? "Tradition" has been divided. Among those suggested are Paul himself, Barnabas, Luke, Clement, Apollos, Silvanus (Silas), Philip and Priscilla. The church father Origen said, "Who it was that really wrote the epistle, God only knows."

Does Saint Paul talk about the rapture?

After exhorting the Thessalonians to live moral lives, in the first part of chapter four, Saint Paul turns to a question that must have been of some concern to the Christians of Thessalonica. Apparently they, like most early Christians, expected Jesus to return during their own lifetimes. They expected to be among those who would meet the Lord at his coming and be taken by him into the kingdom of heaven. But, just as Christians today are concerned about the salvation of parents and friends, brothers and sisters, wives and husbands who died before them, early Christians worried about the dead.

What would happen to those they loved who died before

the coming of Christ? Would only those alive at Jesus' second coming share in the kingdom? That is the basic question Paul addresses in 1 Thessalonians 4:13–18. Paul's basic point is to reassure the Thessalonians that the just who are now living have no advantage over the just who have already died. All will share in the life and joy of the Resurrection with Jesus.

Paul uses the concepts, images and ideas of his time to express that. He pictures the coming of Jesus much as an Eastern ruler or conquering king would come to a city he rules or has conquered. He comes in procession with an entourage. Trumpets herald his coming. The town citizens do not just wait for him to come to them but go out to meet him. Since those at the time of Paul thought of heaven as "up," Paul pictures Jesus coming down from the skies and the saved "rising up" to meet him. They will be caught up with Jesus in the clouds—a frequent Old Testament and apocalyptic sign of the presence of God.

Is this what is referred to as the *rapture* in certain Protestant denominations? Monsignor Raymond Bosler, writing on the rapture in the diocesan newspaper of Indianapolis, *The Criterion,* spoke of having checked nine different biblical encyclopedias (eight of them Protestant) as well as Protestant and Catholic general encyclopedias without finding the word *rapture* in them. He did find a third meaning of *rapture* in *Webster's Third New International Unabridged Dictionary:* the sense of Christ raising up the true church at the end of time to a realm above the earth to enjoy eternal bliss with the Lord.

Bosler's conclusion was that talk about the rapture as a kind of great snatch is a recent creation of televangelists. The idea of some favored beings snatched up into the sky before the end of the world to enjoy a time of bliss all their own is simply not in the text. Nor do other texts support the idea of a "raptured" few watching the horrors they escaped being visited on the rest of humanity.

What did Saint Paul mean by saying, "I do that which I do not wish"?

In his letter to the Romans, Saint Paul said, "I can will what is right, but I cannot do it. For I do not do the good I want, but the evil I do not want is what I do" (7:18–19). Paul is describing his own experience and the experience of us all. Often we recognize and aspire to what is good and beautiful, what is pleasing to God. Yet while we are drawn to the good, something else draws us away from it, and we in fact do the evil we would rather not do. You might say there is something of Robert Louis Stevenson's Dr. Jekyll and Mr. Hyde in all of us. Saint Paul speaks of these contending elements as spirit and flesh.

We want to do good but often fail to do it. We abhor evil yet in our weakness are attracted to it and fall—we sin. We need God's grace to do good, to live by God's law, to persevere.

What was Saint Paul's "thorn in the flesh"?

No one knows for sure what Paul meant when he spoke of the thorn in his flesh. Some speculated that he referred to carnal temptations. Yet Thomas O'Curraoin, S.P.S., in *A New Catholic Commentary on Holy Scripture*, says that was certainly not the case. He suggests it was a chronic humiliating malady with acute attacks, such as "marsh fever."

John McKenzie in his *Dictionary of the Bible*, is just as certain Paul did not mean an illness. He says that some interpret the thorn to mean persecution by former coreligionists. Jerome Murphy O'Connor, in the *New Jerome Biblical Commentary*, says the passage is widely interpreted to refer to a psychic or physical ailment, which, in Jewish tradition, would be caused by Satan or a demon.

But Murphy O'Connor rushes on to say the passage really suggests an external personal source of affliction. He writes that in the Old Testament thorns meant enemies. The thorn in Paul's flesh could have been the hostility coming from within his own communities.

216

Can we know we are saved?

Whenever the question, "Can I know that I am saved?" comes up, think of Joan of Arc before her inquisitors. She was asked if she was in a state of grace. She answered that she hoped she was, and if she were not, prayed that God would put her there. None of us can have "metaphysical certitude," absolute certitude, that we are "saved" or in the state of grace unless given a divine revelation of that fact. But we can have moral certitude that at a particular moment we are in the state of grace. We can be morally sure that at a certain time we are guilty of no grave, unrepented sin and are living in the friendship of God.

At the same time we cannot be absolutely sure that tomorrow or ten minutes from now we will not sin gravely or that death will overtake us when we are in the state of grace. That is why we must pray, struggle and do penance. That is why we must not overestimate our strength and ability to resist temptation and throw ourselves unnecessarily into the occasions of sin. Or, as Saint Paul put it to the Philippians (2:12), we must "work with anxious concern to achieve" our salvation. (See also the *Catechism of the Catholic Church* 1730–1748.)

This is not to say that we should become morbid or despair. We have, and must have, hope and confidence in the grace of God. But it does mean that we must not be presumptuous and think we can dare anything, do anything or risk anything believing—because of some inner conviction—that we are saved once and for all regardless of whether we obey God's law and will and that we cannot be lost. In speaking about himself to the Corinthians (1 Corinthians 9:27), Saint Paul wrote, "I punish my body and enslave it, so that after proclaiming to others I myself should not be disqualified."

What does the phrase "asleep in Christ" mean?

Both the expressions "asleep in Christ" and "fallen asleep" are found in the letters of Paul. Whether you wish to call "sleeping" or "asleep in Christ" a metaphor or a euphemism, it means "dead."

The *Oxford Annotated Bible* (*Revised Standard Version* translation) says in a footnote to 1 Thessalonians 4:14,

> "those who are asleep" was a common metaphor for the dead. The footnote refers to the Gospel of John 11:11–16, where Jesus dialogues with the apostles about the death of Lazarus. In verse eleven, Jesus tells the disciples, "Our friend Lazarus has fallen asleep." When the apostles fail to understand him, verse fourteen tells us, "Then Jesus told them plainly, 'Lazarus is dead.'"

We ourselves use various euphemisms to talk about the dead and death itself. We speak about those who "rest" in Christ or peace, and we say, "the Lord came and took her." "Asleep in Christ" would also help convey the idea that it is not the end of everything when Christians die. The Christian who dies has the resurrection and life afterward to anticipate.

Why do the Gospels trace Jesus' genealogy through Joseph rather than Mary?

There are differences in Luke's and Matthew's versions of the genealogy of Jesus. Some think that Matthew gives the genealogy through Joseph and Luke gives it through Mary. Father Raymond Brown, S.S., who spends more than thirty pages on the genealogy of Jesus in *The Birth of the Messiah*, like many others does not buy that theory.

Brown argues that tracing a genealogy through the mother was simply not normal in Judaism. And Brown says that Luke makes it clear elsewhere he is tracing the genealogy of Jesus through *Joseph*. Brown also finds it unlikely that the differences between Matthew's list and Luke's result from levirate marriages with Matthew giving the names of legal fathers and Luke the natural fathers. (Levirate marriages, from Deuteronomy 25:5–10, allowed that when a husband died childless, his next of kin would marry the widow in order to beget children and continue the deceased husband's lineage.)

"Most scholars today have rejected the explanation that both the Matthean and Lucan genealogies are family lists," writes Brown. "A possible solution, corresponding to what we have already seen, would be that Matthew's genealogy represents a popular tradition about the Davidic lineage (to which the names of Joseph and Jesus have been joined), while Luke's genealogy may be the family list of Joseph's ancestors."

Brown says that among the early church writers there was disagreement about whether Mary was from the Davidic line. Luke tells us that Mary was betrothed to a man of the house of David whose name was Joseph. The text and the grammar of the text make it unclear whether Mary herself was of the house of David.

Further, Luke 1:5 tells us that Mary's kinswoman Elizabeth was of the daughters of Aaron, which would seem to argue against Davidic descent. The names of Anna and Joachim are not to be found in the Scriptures themselves. These names of Mary's parents come from tradition.

Brown holds that the intent of the genealogies is theological—the evangelists want to convey that Jesus is the expected Messiah, the son of Abraham and the son of David as well as the Son of God (Luke). Brown says: "While the genealogies tell us how to evaluate Jesus, they tell us nothing certain about his grandparents or his great-grandparents. The message about Jesus, son of Joseph, is not that actually he is also (grand)son of either Jacob (Matthew) or Eli (Luke)."

How did Matthew know the temptations of Jesus?

Henry Wansbrough, o.s.b., discusses the temptation in his entry on Matthew in *A New Catholic Commentary on Holy Scripture*. He calls the passage a highly formalized account in the style of rabbinic controversy.

Wansbrough speculates that Jesus himself recounted the facts of his temptation to his disciples. He also sees it possible that, aware of the fact of Jesus' temptation at this time, the disciples, and ultimately the author of Matthew, gathered the elements of the temptations Jesus faced throughout his messianic mission into this account of the temptation—at the beginning of his public life.

Still another possible explanation is that Matthew gave us

a midrashic account of the temptation. He interprets or explains the significance of the temptation by describing it in terms of earlier Old Testament events—for example, the testing of Israel in the desert during the Exodus.

Wansbrough did not go into the question of witness to the Agony in the Garden. But the most obvious explanation would be that Jesus shared the experience with his disciples following the Resurrection.

Why does John's Gospel say that John the Baptist did not know Jesus?

In the 1986 edition of the *New American Bible* translation (the one we hear proclaimed in church most of the time) John 1:29–34 reads:

> The next day he saw Jesus coming toward him and said, "Behold, the Lamb of God, who takes away the sin of the world. He is the one of whom I said, 'A man is coming after me who ranks ahead of me because he existed before me.' I did not know him, but the reason why I came baptizing with water was that he might be made known to Israel." John testified further saying, "I saw the Spirit come down like a dove from the sky and remain upon him. I did not know him, but the one who sent me to baptize with water told me, 'On whomever you see the Spirit come down and remain, he is the one who will baptize with the holy Spirit.' Now I have seen and testified that he is the Son of God."

Translators and commentators do not agree on the translation or meaning of these verses. The editors of the *New American Bible* footnote verse thirty-one with the statement, "This gospel shows no knowledge of the tradition (Luke 1) about the kinship of Jesus and John the Baptist." They are convinced that the Gospel of John in its present form is not the work of the apostle John, but that the author-editor is a later disciple among the followers of John who was not an eyewitness to the events he records. Somewhat removed in time and perhaps by place from Jesus, he would have been unaware of a blood relationship between John the Baptist and Jesus.

Dom Ralph Russel says of these verses, in *A New Catholic Commentary on Holy Scriptures,* that it is literally possible the Baptist did not know Jesus if he had spent his childhood in the desert. But he says the words of John can also mean he did not recognize Jesus as the Messiah and Son of God.

In *The Gospel of John* William Barclay states that John must have been acquainted with Jesus because they were, after all, relatives. He says, "What John is saying is not that he did not know *who* Jesus was, but that he did not know *what* Jesus was. It had suddenly been revealed to him that Jesus was none other than the Son of God."

Peter Ellis in *The Genius of John: A Compositional-Critical Commentary on the Fourth Gospel,* also seems to share this view. He writes, "The Baptist does not mean that he did not know Jesus at all, but that he did not know him for who he truly was, the Lamb of God."

A careful look at the entire context of John's words about not knowing him suggests that Barclay is right. In other words, while John personally knew Jesus as his cousin, he did not realize or know that Jesus was the Messiah, the one he was to proclaim. Now he knows because he had been told previously he would see the Spirit come down and remain upon the Messiah. He has now seen the Spirit come upon Jesus and recognizes him as the Messiah, the Son of God.

At the risk of beating this question to death, *Today's English Version* brings that understanding right into the translation of this section. It quotes the Baptist in this way: "I did not know who he would be," and, "I saw the Spirit come down like a dove from heaven and stay on him. I still did not know that he was the one, but God, who sent me to baptize with water, had said to me, 'You will see the Spirit come down and stay on a man; he is the one who baptizes with the Holy Spirit.' I have seen it," said John, "and I tell you he is the Son of God."

What exception did Jesus allow for divorce?

Read *Marriage in the Catholic Church: Divorce and Remarriage,* by Theodore Mackin, S.J. While concluding we simply cannot know exactly what the "exceptive clause" in Matthew means, he believes the phrase "except for adultery *(porneia)*" was added to Jesus' words by Matthew trying to interpret the mind of Jesus.

There are a number of various explanations suggested by others.

Porneia referred to what was called in rabbinic terms *erwat dabar* (Deuteronomy 24:1). In Catholic terminology that would be an invalidating condition or impediment to marriage, for example: consanguinity (blood relationship), affinity (relationship by marriage) within a forbidden degree or the slave status of the girl's father at the time of the wedding. In Jewish law it did not invalidate the marriage but offered grounds for dissolving it.

The question of divorce is raised in Matthew because Matthew wrote largely for converts from Judaism who wanted to know if the rabbinic tradition still holds. Matthew has Jesus saying it is legitimate to dissolve a union that was really not a valid marriage.

Another explanation frequently put forth is that *porneia* indicates an incestuous union (brother and sister, for example, or uncle and niece) that not only may but must be ended.

Or, it is suggested the husband is practicing polygamy, has taken a second wife.

Many Protestants and Eastern Catholic churches interpret *porneia* to mean adultery or sexual misconduct on the part of the wife. Mackin finds that a double standard inconsistent with Jesus' way of acting elsewhere in the Scriptures and inconsistent with his demands for forgiveness and mercy.

Whatever the case, the magisterium of the church continues to understand Jesus' words to forbid marriage while a person's partner in a valid, sacramental, consummated marriage still lives.

As to the marriage of relatives, throughout history most peoples have had a taboo or believed that marriage between close relatives (father and daughter, brother and sister) is wrong and harmful to society.

The Catholic church, too, believes that marriage between very close blood relatives is morally wrong and even forbidden by natural law itself within the closest degrees of blood relationship.

There is some question concerning how far between relatives the natural prohibition extends. Society and the church have, over time, extended the forbidden degrees by their own legislation and authority.

In the case of church law, if marriage between certain relatives is not forbidden by natural, divine law, the church can dispense from its own law.

The church will never dispense where there is a case of relationship by direct descent—father and daughter, grandmother and grandson, and so on. The church sees that as beyond its power. Canonists believe that brother-sister marriages are also probably null by natural law.

In the case of collateral relationships (for example, cousins, aunt and nephew) the present code forbids marriage up to and including the fourth degree (first cousins). But it is possible to dispense within some of those degrees. The closer the relationship, the stronger and more serious must be the reason why marriage should be permitted.

To calculate the degrees of relationship may take some doing because we do not all use words such as *cousins* or *second* or *third cousins* in the same way. Sometimes you just have to sit down with one who understands the law and terminology and make a chart of who was whose father and mother.

Why did Jesus curse the fig tree?

To fully appreciate the story of Jesus cursing the fig tree, we should bear several things in mind.

For one thing, the Old Testament prophets often performed symbolic acts to gain attention and convey their message. Jeremiah, for instance, was commanded by God to place

223

a yoke upon his shoulders, symbolic of the yoke of oppression its enemies would force on Israel (Jeremiah 27—28). Jeremiah was also ordered to break a potter's flask in the sight of the people, as a symbol of how God will smash Israel (Jeremiah 19).

The prophet Ezekiel packs his bags, digs a hole in the wall and departs through the hole carrying his baggage, symbolizing the exile to come.

The Hebrew Scriptures often use figs or the fig tree as a symbol of Israel. In Hosea, for example, we find God saying, "Like grapes in the wilderness, I found Israel. Like the first fruit on the fig tree, in its first season, I saw your ancestors" (9:10).

And in Jeremiah we find, "When I wanted to gather them, says the LORD, there are no grapes on the vine, nor figs on the fig tree; even the leaves are withered" (8:13). And, again, Jeremiah compares the repentant Israelites, who will return from the exile to a basket of good, edible figs, while he compares Zedekiah and the princes to a basket of bad figs that cannot be eaten.

Finally, we should put the Gospel incident back in context. Mark's story of the fig tree is sandwiched around his account of Jesus' cleansing of the Temple.

It is interesting to note that when Matthew tells of Jesus cursing the fig tree he omits the fact figs were not yet in season. Admittedly, this is a bothersome detail and something of a distraction. But it should not lead us away from the point. Whatever is to be said about figs being in season Jesus wants to teach a lesson in the here and now. He cannot wait around for two or three months until the fig crop is due!

The point, then, for the apostles is the fruitlessness of the Temple worship and piety at Jesus' time. Like the fig tree's abundance of green leaves, the activities of the Temple give the impression of religious vitality, but the Temple worship is barren. Henry Wansbrough, O.S.B., points this out in his commentary on Mark in *A New Catholic Commentary on Holy Scripture*.

As Wansbrough says, Jesus is hungry for the fruit of good

works. And later, commenting on the text in Matthew, he suggests Jesus' action is a warning to the religion's leaders not to reject the grace of God present in Jesus.

Jesus' action, then, is prophetic and symbolic. And in the dark days ahead, the apostles are to recall the power of Jesus' word. They are to continue to have faith in Jesus and act out of faith. Faith in Jesus and the power of their prayer will enable them to overcome all obstacles.

Why did Jesus say not to call him good?

The rich young man in Mark's Gospel was not thinking of Jesus as God or approaching him as divine when he spoke to him. As Father Alexander Jones writes, the man approached Jesus in his human capacity and it is on that level Jesus responded to him: "addressed as man, he replies as man."

From that point on the commentaries have different ideas to offer. One says Jesus is rebuking the rich young man for trying to flatter him and is telling the man to be sincere. Others, like Jones, see Jesus' words not as a rebuke but as a "springboard for instruction." Jesus wants the rich young man to realize and acknowledge that Jesus is also divine.

What did Jesus mean when he said he came to bring division?

In Luke's Gospel Christ says to the apostles: "Do you think that I have come to bring peace to the earth? No, I tell you, but rather division! From now on five in one household will be divided, three against two..." (12:51–52). How do we reconcile this saying with Christ's title, Prince of Peace?

The word *peace* has many senses. And Luke is speaking of two different senses when he recalls the song of the angels at Jesus' birth (2:14) and the words of Jesus to his disciples about himself as a source of division as they journey to Jerusalem (12:49–53).

The *Encyclopedic Dictionary of the Bible,* by Louis Hartman, c.ss.r., tells us that the Hebrew word *shalom,* usually

225

translated as "peace," is so rich in meaning there is hardly any single word in our modern languages that can express its full meaning and all its nuances. The translators who worked on the Greek Septuagint version of the Hebrew Scriptures had great difficulty in trying to translate *shalom*. Throughout the Septuagint they used twenty-five different ways of trying to render this word where it appeared.

Where *shalom* appears in the Hebrew Scriptures, it goes well beyond the idea contained in our English word *peace* or the Latin word *pax*. It means much more than the absence of war and strife. It has the sense of the final peace that is to come with the messianic age. It is the gift of the eschatological age and the Prince of Peace, who is to restore peace between God and Israel or humanity.

This peace comes with Jesus and is given to those who truly prove to be his disciples. According to John McKenzie, in his *Dictionary of the Bible*, *shalom* is the state of perfect well-being, an achievement not possible to the world. In the New Testament it becomes synonymous with *salvation*.

Commentators agree that in this sense *shalom* is not to be achieved without strife or painful divisions along the way.

It is peace in this sense that is promised in the angels' song. And this is the peace promised when Jesus tells his disciples, "Peace I leave with you; my peace I give to you. I do not give to you as the world gives" (John 14:27).

In Luke 12:49–53 Jesus and Luke are talking about peace in a much more limited sense: the absence of conflict, struggle and division. As they make their way to Jerusalem, Jesus is preparing the disciples for what is ahead. After the fact, Luke is attempting to explain to his community why their families have been split down the middle because of belief in Jesus, why they face rejection and even persecution.

The follower of Jesus cannot choose peace at any price: The true disciple of Jesus must be willing to proclaim him to the world even in the face of rejection. The journey of discipleship is not some calm and pleasant stroll with Jesus as we make our way to the New Jerusalem.

Jesus calls for a decision. No one can be neutral concerning him and the word. The disciple of Jesus cannot compromise about Christ or the gospel. As Jesus says, the wheat will be separated from the chaff (Luke 3:17).

What does "poor in spirit" mean?

William Barclay, in *The Gospel of Matthew,* notes that the beatitudes are a kind of literary form, like that found in the psalms of the Hebrew Scriptures with exclamations such as "Happy are those who do not follow the advice of the wicked, or take the path that sinners tread" (1:1), "Happy are those whose transgression is forgiven, whose sin is covered. Happy are those to whom the LORD imputes no iniquity" (32:1–2) and "Happy are those whom you choose, and bring near to live in your courts" (65:4).

Barclay stresses that in Aramaic, the language in which Jesus proclaimed these beatitudes, there is no verb. That means they are exclamations and not just statements. A translation closer to what Jesus would have said in the case of the first beatitude might be, "O the blessedness of the poor in spirit."

The importance of recognizing these beatitudes as exclamations, says Barclay, is that the beatitudes then become statements about the present and "not pious hopes of what shall be; they are not glowing but nebulous prophecies of some future bliss; they are congratulations on what is." This blessedness exists here and now and is not something into which the Christian will enter in the future, though it will find its consummation in the presence of God.

Further, the Greek word for blessed, *makarios*—Matthew's Gospel is in Greek—means to Christians a godlike joy. It is a joy that has its secret within itself, "that joy which is serene and untouchable, and self-contained, that joy which is completely independent of all the chances and changes of life.... The Christian blessedness is completely untouchable and unassailable."

Returning to the discussion of the first of the beatitudes, Barclay says, comparing it to Greek and Hebrew words, that the Aramaic word for "poor" had come to describe "the man who, because he has no earthly resources whatever, puts his whole trust in God."

Working from Greek, Hebrew and Aramaic, Barclay then says that "Blessed are the poor in spirit" means:

> Blessed is the man who has realized his own utter helplessness, and who has put his whole trust in God; there will enter into his life two things which are opposite sides of the same thing. He will become completely detached from things, for he will know that things have not got it in them to bring happiness or security; and he will become completely attached to God, for he will know that God alone can bring him help, and hope and strength.

Writing in his Milwaukee *Catholic Herald*, Archbishop Rembert Weakland, O.S.B., said this beatitude or blessedness refers to an interior disposition or an attitude that the disciple of Christ must have. He says it is a basic attitude on how one stands before God and applies to all followers of Christ. He says,

> The poor in spirit are those who acknowledge their dependency—in the very roots of their being—on God and God's goodness and love toward them. They know salvation does not come from themselves nor from their acts.... To know deep down in one's heart that one depends on God for everything is to be radically poor—poor in spirit.

Archbishop Weakland adds that when we are poor in spirit we realize our dependence on others, we are more open and forgiving toward others, wiser in estimating our strengths and weaknesses, more courageous, realizing that we will have God's help, and wiser also in judging true success. Lastly, the poor in spirit pray differently, truly asking that God's will be done.

The beatitude concerning "the meek" is not always translated the same. Sometimes it is translated as "the gentle" or "the humble." *The New Jerome Biblical Commentary* says "the meek" should be understood as those "slow to anger" or "gentle with others" and expresses a form of charity found in the meek and gentle Jesus. Alexander Jones, author of *The Gospel According to St. Matthew*, believes "the meek" should be understood in much the same sense as poor.

William Barclay says that no one English word can translate the sense of the third beatitude. Its sense is best translated,

> O the bliss of the man who is always angry at the right time and never angry at the wrong time, who has every instinct, and impulse, and passion under control because he himself is God-controlled, who has the humility to realize his own ignorance and his own weakness, for such a man is king among men!

One who is poor in spirit in Matthew's sense has indeed the best kind of "spirit"—courage, self-control, confidence in love and joy in life.

Did Jesus take the Nazirite vow?

Mark 14:25 does not imply Jesus took the Nazirite vow at the Last Supper or any time before that. The evangelist would make it much clearer if that were his intent. Most people interpret Mark 14:25 as Jesus making a simple statement of fact: He will not drink wine again before he dies.

Why did Jesus speak harshly to the Canaanite woman?

Many readers find difficulty with the passage concerning the Canaanite woman and her plea for help. Commentators struggle with trying to explain the reactions and words of Jesus. Alexander Jones does as good a job as any in *The Gospel According to St. Matthew*. He reminds us, at least implicitly, that tones and inflections do not come off the paper.

Jones suggests the words of Jesus are not as harsh as they read. Whatever Jesus says, the Canaanite woman is not put off. She seems to accept his response as an invitation to persist and try to top his remark.

Jones also asserts the Greek for *dogs* might well be translated as "pet" dogs or "little dogs" (puppies). Jesus is telling her the children of the family (Jews) come before the pets! All of this must be seen in the context of the hereditary enmity of Jews and Canaanites.

Jones sees this as a kind of small parable or allegory. Jesus insists that the priority of his mission is to the Jews. Yet Jesus responds to faith wherever he finds it. And in the Canaanite woman he finds *great* faith.

Who was the beloved disciple?

Many have tried to identify the person the Gospel of John calls the beloved disciple or the disciple Jesus loved.

Though many tend to think of John, nowhere does the Gospel text say that the disciple called "beloved" is named John. Some people believe that they can deduce the beloved disciple was John the apostle or another John who was a disciple of John the apostle. They believe this second John wrote or edited the Gospel according to John.

Tied in with the question of who is the beloved disciple, then, is the question of who actually authored the Gospel of John. Was it John the apostle? Saint Irenaeus, writing in the second century, stated that he was—even though the early manuscripts of this Gospel bear no author's name. For a long time after Irenaeus, it was simply accepted as fact that John the apostle, the son of Zebedee, was the writer of this Gospel.

More recent commentators hold that the tradition and viewpoint behind the Gospel come from John the apostle but that a later disciple of the apostle wrote or edited the Gospel. Some say there may yet be a third person involved who added the last chapter of this Gospel.

This gets further complicated because the Gospel of John tells us in 11:5 that Jesus loved Martha, her sister Mary and Lazarus, and 11:35 says that when Jesus wept over the death of Lazarus those present said, "See how he loved him." Some commentators say that the beloved disciple was Lazarus!

Was the beloved disciple the young man who ran away naked from the garden? The Gospel does not say that. And some guess that that young man was Mark or John Mark, who first accompanied Paul then became the companion of Peter.

Different commentators build different cases and offer various arguments why the beloved disciple was not John the apostle, the son of Zebedee and brother of James.

But that raises other questions to deal with. For instance, does that mean there were other disciples besides the twelve apostles present at the Last Supper? And if the beloved disciple is distinct from the apostle John, why do we not hear of him from anyone before the Last Supper takes place? If he is so beloved and someone different from the apostle, why doesn't Jesus take him to the mountain for the transfiguration? Why doesn't Jesus single him out to be near him in the garden when he prays—as he does Peter and the sons of Zebedee?

What do the experts on the Gospel of John say? Neal M. Flanagan, O.S.M., in *The Collegeville Bible Commentary*, writes,

> The beloved disciple seems to be a Jerusalem disciple with connections to the high priest. His presentation of Jesus—on the solid presumption that he either authored the Fourth Gospel or was extremely instrumental in shaping its literary form (19:35; 21:24)—is so different from that of the other three Gospels that he was hardly one of the Twelve, a title he rarely uses (only in 6:67–71 and 20:24). He is coupled with Peter, over whom he has a certain kind of spiritual precedence. At this present moment of scholarship, it seems best to accept the beloved disciple as anonymous, yet as a true disciple and eyewitness of the Lord, connected with Jerusalem, not one of the Twelve, whose different background and different Christian experience led him to produce, directly or indirectly, a version of the Good News strikingly different from that of Mark, Matthew and Luke. Historical as he is, the beloved disciple is also presented to us as an ideal, a model of what we should be as disciples ourselves—loved and loving.

Raymond Brown, S.S., in *The Gospel and Epistles of John: A Concise Commentary*, in regard to Saint Irenaeus's identification of the beloved disciple and author of the fourth Gospel as John the son of Zebedee, says,

Today, it is recognized that such late second-century surmises about figures who had lived a century before were often simplified, and that authorship tradition was sometimes more concerned with the authority behind a biblical writing than with the physical writer.

Accordingly, it is doubted by most scholars that any one of the canonical Gospels was written by an eyewitness of the public ministry of Jesus, even though (as the Roman Catholic Church teaches) the Gospels are solidly rooted in oral tradition stemming from the companions of Jesus. The beloved disciple was one of the latter, but the contrast with Peter (13:23–26; 18:15–16; 20:1–10; 21:20–23) and his appearance at scenes where the synoptic Gospels place none of the Twelve (19:26–27) suggest that he may not have been an apostle.

Michael J. Taylor, S.J., in *John—The Different Gospel*, after referring to the dispute over the identity of the author and the beloved disciple, says, "It might be best to say we simply do not know for sure who the author is."

On the other hand, Dom Ralph Russell, in *A New Catholic Commentary on Holy Scripture*, the oldest of these sources, argues strongly that John the apostle and son of Zebedee is both the author of the Gospel and the beloved disciple. He concludes,

So the beloved disciple fits the Gospel picture of John son of Zebedee, disciple of the Baptist and apostle of Jesus. Views that he was a wholly ideal figure, or an unknown young man, or Lazarus, must be brought to the touchstone of this evidence.

Does mention of the beloved disciple mean that God loves some more than others?

To understand how there could be a "beloved disciple," we must distinguish between the love proper to the Second Person of the Blessed Trinity (the Son) in his divine nature and the love that Jesus the Incarnate Son felt in his human nature. There is a difference between how we experience God's love while on earth and the happiness and fulfillment we can expect in eternity. Part of the joy of heaven rests in loving and being loved by God.

The Council of Florence (which began in 1438) defined that the degree of the happiness of the blessed in heaven is unequal. It is received in proportion to the diversity of merits.

God loves himself first because of God's own goodness. God loves others because they reflect and image God's goodness. The more God's creatures, the elect, live by God's will, the more like God they are, the more lovable they are and will be. Thus is the special lovability of Mary, the mother of Jesus. Her will is perfectly conformed to God's will.

In philosophical or metaphysical language, one manual of theology puts it this way: "The degree of God's love for creatures is one and the same in the inner-divine act; in the extra-divine created effect, however, it is different according to the grade of its amiability." To me that means we all start equal but the more we love God, are faithful to God's will and glorify God, the more God loves us in comparison to others.

We should note at the same time that all the theologians state the "inequality" of love distresses no one in heaven. All are as happy as they can possibly be. And there is no envy.

Speaking of our considering Jesus acting in his human nature, it does not strike me as strange that he should feel greater affection and love for those near to him by human relationships or friendship. It is natural that Jesus would feel greater love and affection for his mother, his foster father and disciples and companions who offered him friendship than those who put him to death or whom he never met. That is perfectly human (as well as perfectly divine).

Did Jesus see a value in friendship?

In the Gospel of John, Jesus speaks to his disciples of his own understanding of friendship:

> No one has greater love than this, to lay down one's life for one's friends. You are my friends if you do what I command you. I do not call you servants any longer, because the servant does not know what the master is

doing; but I have called you friends, because I have made known to you everything that I have heard from my Father. You did not choose me but I chose you. And I appointed you to go and bear fruit, fruit that will last, so that the Father will give you whatever you ask him in my name. I am giving you these commands so that you may love one another. (John 15:13–17)

In addition, it may interest you to know that there are nearly two pages of references in *Nelson's Complete Concordance of the New American Bible* to texts in both the Hebrew Scriptures and the New Testament concerning friends and friendship.

Some verses from the sixth chapter of Sirach may be of special interest:

A faithful friend is a sturdy shelter; he who finds one finds a treasure. A faithful friend is beyond price, no sum can balance his worth. A faithful friend is a life-saving remedy, such as he who fears God finds; For he who fears God behaves accordingly, and his friend will be like himself. (Sirach 6:14–17)

What does it mean to be born again?

The *Dictionary of Christianity in America* has an entry for "born again" and an attempt to define what it means when applied to certain Christian believers. The entry notes the expression is drawn from Jesus' words in John 3:3, where Jesus tells Nicodemus we must be born again from above. The dictionary then notes that the term has taken on a "broad and imprecise usage" in general American discourse. The term has come to mean any Christian "who exhibits intensity or overt self-identification or a keen sense of divine presence." The term is also applied to persons who attribute to God the cause for events in their personal lives.

This dictionary also says that in American understanding "born again" is associated with revivalism or any conversionist form of Protestantism and describes the direct experience of a person in a notable single event or a specificiable period when that person shifts his or her life focus from any other center to Jesus Christ.

In other words "born again" is often used to describe a conversion experience in which a person's life is transformed. Some might also call it an experience of being saved.

How could anyone do works greater than Jesus?

In attempting to understand the text from John 14:12, it is important to put it in the context of the entire chapter and Gospel and note especially the verses that follow. After Jesus says the person who has faith in him will do greater works than he, he explains, "because I am going to the Father. I will do whatever you ask in my name, so that the Father may be glorified in the Son. If in my name you ask me for anything, I will do it" (John 14:12–14).

In other words the disciples will do works "greater" than Jesus because of him and his grace. They will not be acting independently of him. He will do works through and in the disciples united with him.

In *The Genius of John: A Compositional-Critical Commentary on the Fourth Gospel*, Peter F. Ellis puts it this way,

> According to Chapter 17, Jesus accomplishes his work in an effective sense when he brings his apostles to believe that he has been sent by the Father (cf. 17:6–8). The work that the apostles will accomplish is to bring others to believe as they believe (cf. 17:18-23). By the time John wrote the Gospel at the end of the first century, many thousands had come to believe in Jesus; thus Jesus can say of an apostle who believes in him and brings others to believe in him, "And greater works than these will he do."

It is the work of spreading the Gospel over the world in the face of great obstacles that is the greater work done by Jesus through his disciples.

Why did Jesus say that Mary has chosen "the better part" though Martha worked so hard to serve him?

Preachers and writers love to dwell on the contrast between Mary and Martha, and some even assert that Mary was smarter because she chose to stay with Jesus and saw the importance of prayer over activity. But exegetes of the Scriptures tell us that is a minor theme and something of a side issue.

As Father Lawrence Brett pointed out in *Sharing the Word*, this episode must be put back in the context of Saint Luke's journey narrative. He notes that Luke's Gospel is the Gospel of women. Luke shows women sharing equally with men in the task of proclaiming Christ to the world. In this incident that Luke recalls, both Mary and Martha are heroines.

Following as it does the parable of the Good Samaritan and Jesus' commandment to love our neighbor, Luke shows Martha exercising this love and carrying out the role of the Good Samaritan who offers personal service, care, hospitality and love at very real personal cost. Moreover, it is actually Martha who is given the prominent role. It is her home. *She* has a sister, Mary. *She* is busy with the details of hospitality.

But Luke, following up on the previous things that have happened "along the way," has another point to make. In Jesus' time religion was the domain of men. *Men* studied and discussed the law. They took the active roles in the synagogue. In the Temple women could enter only so far. They could not go beyond the court of women. Now Mary takes a place at the feet of Jesus! She is seen in the role of a disciple, listening to Jesus (the rabbi, teacher) explain the Law and things of God.

Mary also draws our attention (and the attention of the community of Luke) to the fact that discipleship means *listening* to the word as well as *doing*.

Says Father Brett,

While we may contrast Mary and Martha, Luke would have us see them both together. It is the story of Martha *and* Mary, after all.

There is no conflict between listening and doing; each must accompany the other. The words of Jesus to Martha are a gentle reproach, not a harsh one. It is a reminder that one must first hear the Word of God in order to act upon it.... Martha is not reprimanded for her activity. She is sure, as we are, that God's blessings are given to "those who hear the Word of God and keep (or observe, by doing) it...." If Martha had a fault, it was an inability to see that Mary was not as unselfish as she.

We make much too much of what sounds like a reproach to Martha and miss what is much more important. The account is not meant, as Luke gives it, to be an insult to Martha or homemakers. Martha, as other texts will show us, was much loved by Jesus and was an important person in his life. If Jesus could speak freely to her, we find in John's Gospel that Martha could also speak freely and with a certain tone of reproach to Jesus, "If you had been here my brother would not have died!" (11:33).

What did Jesus mean when he said we must hate our father and mother?

The New American Bible translation (the one we hear most often in our Sunday liturgy) of Luke 14:26–27, the relevant text, uses the words: "If anyone comes to me without hating his father and mother..."

The translation in the *Today's English Version* is: "Whoever comes to me cannot be my disciple unless he loves me more than he loves his father and his mother, and his wife and his children, his brothers and sisters, and himself as well."

Jerome Kodell, O.S.B., in *The Gospel According to Luke* (part of the New Testament series of the Collegeville Bible Commentary), states that the Greek word used in this quotation really does mean "hate" or "hating." But, he adds, this is a Semitic exaggeration. Jesus, as quoted by Luke, is stressing that a person who would become his disciple must be ready to renounce *anyone* who stands in the way of a complete commitment to him—even the closest relative, such as father, mother, brother and sister. And later on in New Testament days, members of the early church really had to do that.

Kodell adds that *hate* in the sense of Jesus' words means "prefer less." And that is rather close to *Today's English Version,* choice of "unless he loves me more than."

It is important to see and interpret a passage like this in the context of the whole Gospel and all of the Scriptures. When we compare what Jesus says here with other things that he did and said, we realize that he did not literally, without any qualification, mean we must detest or hate our parents. In other passages he reminds us we must observe the commandments, including the commandment to honor and respect our parents, and he rebukes those Pharisees who exempt themselves from caring for their parents by declaring their wealth dedicated to the Temple.

Why must we become like children to inherit the kingdom?

To understand Jesus' words, "Unless you change and become like children, you will never enter the kingdom of heaven" (Matthew 18:3), we must put them in context. Jesus spoke these words to his disciples after they came to him asking who is of the greatest importance in the kingdom of God. He then called a child over and stood him in their midst. Jesus is speaking to persons concerned about status and position. These words are followed by, "Whoever becomes humble like this child is the greatest in the kingdom of heaven" (18:4).

Jesus is telling his disciples they must come to God (and to each other) with the attitude of children—who had no legal rights, rank or status. Children then, as now, were completely dependent on their parents. Everything they received was a gift. The kingdom is given as a gift of God—not a right, not something to which we are entitled. Position in the kingdom does not depend on inheritance or birth rights. The "greatest" in God's kingdom do not lord it over others; they serve.

Jesus then goes on to talk about the simple (childlike) faith that should characterize the disciple and the evil of scandalizing the simple and innocent ones.

What is the meaning of "Son of Man," a title for Jesus?

In the *Dictionary of the Bible*, by John McKenzie, and Louis Hartman's *Encyclopedic Dictionary of the Bible*, the authors relate that the title "Son of Man" appears to have its roots in mideastern mythology and the apocryphal books of Enoch and 4 Esdras.

In mythology Son of Man is the primordial man who becomes deified and returns in the final days to inaugurate the kingdom of God. In the apocryphal books of Enoch and 4 Esdras, the Son of Man appears before the Ancient of Days. He is the righteous one who reveals all hidden treasures. Chosen as judge he overcomes kings, the powerful and sinners. He is the light of and hope of peoples. People are saved in his name, and the saved will eat and drink with him in eternity.

In speaking of himself as the Son of Man, Jesus appears to have taken the title from the book of Daniel 7:13. In Daniel the prophet has a vision of four frightening beasts representing the Babylonian, Medean, Persian and Hellenistic empires. All come to destruction.

Daniel states that, as he watched, the Ancient One (Ancient of Days) took his throne with thousands upon thousands ministering to him. With judgment of the beasts the visions continue and Daniel sees "one like a Son of Man coming, on the clouds of heaven." From the Ancient One he receives dominion, glory and kingship. Nations and peoples of every language serve him. He receives an everlasting dominion that shall not be taken away and a kingship that shall not be destroyed.

In the synoptic Gospels (Matthew, Mark and Luke), Jesus, and only Jesus, uses this title concerning himself some seventy times. In John, Jesus applies the title to himself eleven times. The term emphasizes Jesus' humanity. It makes him capable of suffering, and as Son of Man he experiences his passion. He is indeed the Son of God, but as Son of Mary he is also Son of "man."

At the same time the title evokes the image from Daniel of Jesus as judge to come. His human experience and ability to identify with humankind makes him a most appropriate judge for human beings.

Did Jesus know when the end was coming?

Both William Kurz, S.J., in his exegesis of the Acts of the Apostles in the *Collegeville Commentary,* and Henry Wansbrough, O.S.B., in *A New Catholic Commentary on Holy Scripture,* say much the same thing.

Kurz suggests Acts 1:6–7 should be read against the background of Luke 12:35–46, Luke 17:20–37 and Luke 21:7–9. Remember Luke is the author of Acts as well as the Gospel according to Luke. In these Lukan passages we find the parable of the workers who are urged to be ready at any time for the coming of the master because no one knows when to expect his return. We also hear Jesus saying the time of the coming of the kingdom cannot be known—it "is already among you." Lastly, Jesus urges the disciples not to be deceived by the cries of the doomsayers crying the end is near.

According to Kurz, Luke uses the question of the apostles in Acts to indicate they still do not understand what Jesus meant by the "kingdom of God." Later on in Acts 2:3 he will show God's promise was about the coming of the Holy Spirit rather than an earthly kingdom.

The message is much the same in the Gospel—the apostles should not try to guess what cannot be known. They should rather focus on the power of the Spirit as a sign of living in the promised final day and use their power and the time left to them to witness to Jesus to the ends of the earth.

Wansbrough says the passage finds the apostles still looking for a worldly messianic kingdom and they will not understand what Jesus has been saying until they receive the Spirit. The message is stop looking for the imminent Second Coming of Christ. And the kingdom is not to be confined to Israel. Acts will later tell how the gospel was spread to Judea, Samaria and even Rome (the end of the earth).

What was Jesus referring to when he mentioned the "stumbling stone"?

Two texts from Isaiah have relevance. In Isaiah 8:11–15 the writer proclaims that the Lord of hosts will be a snare, an obstacle and a *stumbling stone* to both houses of Israel. And many in Jerusalem shall stumble and fall, broken, snared, captured. In 28:16 Isaiah says, "See, I am laying a stone in Zion, a stone that has been tested, a precious *cornerstone* as a sure foundation; he who puts his faith in it shall not be shaken" (italics added).

Psalm 118:22 reads, "The stone which the builders rejected has become the cornerstone." In the first and direct sense those words of the psalm refer to the nation or people of Israel. The powers or superpowers of the psalmist's world would have thought Israel of little importance or consequence and treated Israel with contempt. But, declares the psalmist, the Lord has chosen Israel to be the foundation or cornerstone of his kingdom, which will embrace all nations.

In a second and prophetic sense, the words of the psalm apply to Jesus as the foundation stone upon which the Father will build his kingdom. In the context of Luke's Gospel, Jesus has come up to Jerusalem where he will now suffer and die. He has driven the money changers and sellers from the Temple and aroused the anger and resentment of the chief priests, scribes and leaders of the people. Having just bested them in verbal jousting and gone one up on them by asking a question they dare not answer, Jesus now speaks over their heads to the people. He tells the parable of the wicked tenants who kill first the servants and then the vineyard owner's son who has come to collect the rent.

The people immediately get the point when Jesus says the vineyard will be taken away from the tenants and given to others. They understand that he is saying that many of the religious leaders will lose out on the kingdom. The poor sinners and Gentiles will enter in their stead. Luke also tells us the chief priests and Pharisees knew that Jesus was speaking to them.

After the people have voiced their dismay, Jesus drives home his point by quoting Psalm 118:22. Luke says he looked at them and asked, "What then does this Scripture passage mean: 'The stone which the builders rejected has become the cornerstone'?" And he follows that with words reminiscent of Isaiah, "Everyone who falls on that stone will be dashed to pieces and it will crush anyone on whom it falls."

Eugene LaVerdiere, s.s.s., in *Luke*, observes that Jesus here is not so concerned with the stone as with those who trip over the stone. A corner or foundation stone was no small thing. It would have been of great size and strength to support a building. Imagine what would happen today if a stone from a good-sized building fell on some passerby. Or think of yourself running and tripping over a large stone. How many bruises or broken bones—if you survived?

This is the spiritual fate Jesus is prophesying for the leaders and priests who will reject him (the cornerstone of God's kingdom) and hand him over to be killed. Everyone listening to Jesus got the point. And later, in the Acts of the Apostles (4:11), we will find Peter telling the Sanhedrin that Jesus "is 'the stone rejected by you, the builders, which has become the cornerstone.'"

And Peter, in 1 Peter 2:4–8, will urge his readers to come to the Lord as living stones to be built into a spiritual house. He then quotes Isaiah about laying a stone in Zion and refers to the rejected stone becoming the cornerstone. Saint Paul, in Romans 9:32–33, describing the relationship of Jews and Gentiles and what happened to Israel, will say that Israel stumbled over "the stone that causes stumbling" and quote Isaiah.

In other words the contemporaries of Jesus clearly understood that he was using metaphors and types. They had no trouble understanding that he was speaking of himself as the cornerstone of God's people and a living temple. And they realized clearly that in speaking of those who stumble over the stone he was speaking of those who reject him.

Is it wrong to call priests "Father"?

In the Gospel of Saint Matthew (chapter 23), we find Jesus commenting on and condemning the pride and hypocrisy of the Pharisees and Jewish teachers of the Law. He says they love the best places at feasts and reserved seats in the synagogues and they want to be greeted with respect in the marketplaces and be called "Rabbi."

Jesus says:

> But you are not to be called rabbi, for you have one teacher, and you are all students. And call no one your father on earth for you have one Father—the one in heaven. Nor are you to be called instructors, for you have one instructor, the Messiah. The greatest among you will be your servant. All who exalt themselves will be humbled, and all who humble themselves will be exalted. (Matthew 23:8–12)

The context makes it clear it is not so much *words* or titles that Jesus is criticizing as the *attitudes* behind them. Christ is condemning the attitude of those who love and covet titles and marks of distinction while abusing and misleading those they are to serve. Christ is warning his disciples against those who seek for themselves the respect that belongs first to God.

Is there any more reason to interpret this prohibition literally when it comes to using the title *Father* than there is for *Teacher* ("Rabbi") and *Master* ("Leader")? If this text means that we ought not call anyone Father—literally, so that word is never used of anyone but God—why should we not also understand it to mean that we ought not *ever* call anyone *Teacher, Leader* or *Master*?

Catholics interpret the text to mean simply that we should not give to men the honor, the faith, the reverence that belongs to God. We have no intention of doing that in calling our priests Father anymore that we do in speaking of parents as fathers, children's instructors as teachers or baseball managers as leaders. The title *Father* simply recognizes that the priest relates to the faithful as a father (small case) spiritually. He—acting for Christ—gives them the life of God in baptism and the Eucharist. He encourages, instructs, counsels, comforts in the sacrament of reconciliation—all as a good and loving father.

Saint Paul repeatedly addressed Timothy and Titus as his *sons,* despite the words of Jesus. In writing to Philemon (verse 10), Paul speaks of Onesimus as "my child...*whose father I have become during my imprisonment.*" Also, Paul tells Timothy in his second letter to him, "...the gospel, for which I was appointed preacher and apostle and teacher" (2 Timothy 1:11).

All this bears out what the church always tells us—that we must look at everything the Scriptures say. We must not lift isolated verses out of context to make them say things Jesus never intended to say. We must bring to the Scriptures good common sense and the guidance of the teaching church to which the Scriptures were entrusted.

Was the Last Supper a Passover meal?

This question has long puzzled Scripture scholars. The synoptic Gospels indeed seem to say that it was the Passover meal that Jesus celebrated with his disciples on Thursday before his death. Yet John rather clearly says that the Jews who brought Jesus before Pilate would not enter the praetorium because they did not want to contract ritual impurity and be unable to celebrate the Passover meal. And John (19:14) states that Jesus died on the preparation day for the feast of the Passover.

In speaking of the seeming clash between the synoptics and John, Father John McKenzie, S.J., says this celebrated difficulty has received no generally accepted solution.

Nevertheless, a number of efforts have been made to reconcile the accounts. One possible solution involves the day of the month on which Passover fell and the day of the week on which it occurred when Jesus was put to death.

To understand this explanation begin by thinking of a modern situation. Think of holy days of obligation such as the solemnities of the Immaculate Conception and All Saints. Both of these feasts are attached to a day of the month—December 8 and August 15. These feasts and days of the month can fall on any day of the week. When the feasts fall on a Saturday or Monday, they create particular problems. Priests and people experience difficulty in celebrating many Masses of obligation in close order. As a result, some bishops dispense from the obligation of the holy day; other bishops do not.

In the time of Jesus the feast of the Passover was celebrated on the fourteenth day of the month of the spring equinox called Nisan. The Passover meal was to be eaten that night. The Jewish day began and ended with sunset—not midnight. The Jewish Sabbath was celebrated from sunset of what we call Friday to sunset of Saturday.

It is theorized that because at the time of Jesus' death the foureenth day of Nisan fell on the Sabbath (between Friday sunset and Saturday sunset), the Pharisees and Sadducees differed in their practices of eating the Passover meal. The Pharisees were concerned that in preparing for and eating the Passover meal they might violate the law requiring rest on the Sabbath. To avoid that possibility, in the year of Jesus' death, they anticipated the eating of the Passover meal and ate it on Thursday night. The Sadducees, on the other hand, were more concerned about eating the meal on the day designated by law, the fourteenth day of Nisan, than with violating the Sabbath rest.

According to this theory then, Jesus and his disciples followed the practice of the Pharisees and ate the Passover on Thursday. Those at the praetorium followed the practice of the Sadducees, the political leaders, and ate it on Friday night when both the fourteenth of Nisan and the Sabbath had begun.

What do we know about Simon of Cyrene?

Tradition says little more than what is in the Scriptures about Simon of Cyrene. William Barclay in *The Gospel of Saint Mark*, notes that Simon, like any man in Roman-occupied territory, could be pressed into service by the military. Reminding us that Simon was from Cyrene in North Africa, Barclay suggests Simon was in Jerusalem for a once-in-a-lifetime pilgrimage to celebrate the Passover.

Barclay also identifies Simon of Cyrene with the father of the Rufus mentioned in Paul's letter to the Romans, 16:13, as do other commentators, because Rufus was a rare name. Barclay further speculates that the Simeon mentioned in Acts 13:1 is also Simon of Cyrene. Simeon is called Niger there, the name for a person "of swarthy skin who came from Africa." Barclay suggests that Simon (Simeon) was among those in Antioch sending Paul and Barnabas on the first mission to the Gentiles.

What does "INRI" mean?

At the time of Jesus, when a criminal was crucified the charge was placed on the cross. The Gospel of Matthew 27:37 tells us in the case of Jesus, "Over his head they put the charge against him, which read, 'This is Jesus, the King of the Jews.'" Mark 15:26 reads, "The inscription of the charge against him read, 'The King of the Jews.'"

The author of John relates,

> Pilate also had an inscription written and put on the cross. It read, "Jesus of Nazareth, the King of the Jews." Many of the Jews read this inscription, because the place where Jesus was crucified was near the city; and it was written in Hebrew, in Latin and in Greek. (John 19:19–20)

In Latin the inscription would read, "*Jesus Nazarenus, Rex Judaeorum.*" In Latin the letter *J* can always be represented by the letter *I,* so the letters *INRI* are first letters of those words— a kind of abbreviation that is meant to remind us of the inscription and can fit the narrow confines of the crucifix.

John goes on to say that the Jews wanted Pilate to change the inscription to read, "This man said 'I am King of the Jews.' Pilate answered, 'What I have written I have written'" (John 19:21–22).

Who were the thieves crucified with Jesus?

The Gospel of Luke (23:33–43) tells us that Jesus was crucified between two thieves. Luke does not give the name of either one. Three different collections of the lives of the saints, however, give their names as Dismas, traditionally the "good thief," and Gestas, the unrepentant thief.

They use as their source for this information an Arabic Gospel of the infancy. This book was very popular during the Middle Ages. It contains a legend or myth that two thieves waylaid the Holy Family on their flight into Egypt.

In character Dismas paid Gestas forty drachmas to leave the family unharmed. At this point the infant Jesus predicted the two would be crucified with him in Jerusalem and he would take Dismas with him into paradise.

Why did Jesus not want Mary Magdalene to touch him but urged Thomas to do so?

Jesus' words are translated differently in various English versions of the text. An older translation of the *New American Bible* renders the text (John 20:17), "Do not touch me!" The current *New American Bible,* as well as *Today's English Version,* has Jesus saying, "Stop holding on to me...." *The New Jerusalem Bible* translates Jesus as saying, "Do not cling to me." Scripture scholar William Barclay, in *The Gospel of John,* translates the words as, "Do not touch me," but suggests their meaning is, "Do not hold on to me." Father Hilarion Kistner, O.F.M., a Scripture scholar and former professor, says that all these translations are possible and acceptable.

Explaining these words of Jesus, Father Raymond Brown, in *The Gospel and Epistles of John,* comments that Jesus is simply telling Mary not to hold him back—he is about to ascend to the Father. His ascension will enable him to send the Spirit who will beget the disciples anew, making God their father.

George W. MacRae, in *Invitation to John,* says Jesus is warning Mary that she cannot hold on to the Jesus she has known— he is ascending to the Father. It is the risen Jesus that must now be the object of her faith. And the disciples can now become children of God with Jesus' father as their father. The proclamation of the risen Jesus will rest on what Mary has seen.

Whichever of these explanations we may accept, the seeming conflict with Jesus' later command to Thomas (John 20:27) disappears. His concern then is to establish the reality of the Resurrection.

What did Jesus mean when he said sins against the Holy Spirit will not be forgiven?

As William May notes in the entry on sin in *The New Dictionary of Theology*, theologians have long tried to define what the Scriptures mean by "sins against the Holy Spirit" or the "unforgivable sin." They speak of obduracy, presumption, despair, rejection of known truth, envy of the grace that others enjoy or final impenitence.

In most cases there is somehow a rejection of grace involved when speaking of sin unto death or sins against the Spirit.

The sin is unforgivable because the sinner is simply unrepentant. The sinner is hardened in alienation from God and does not desire forgiveness or want reconciliation.

What is the Gospel of Mark's "awful horror"?

The expression "awful horror" is translated in different ways in various versions of the Bible. The *Revised Standard Version* translates the expression as "devastating sacrilege." The old *Douay Version* speaks of the "abomination of desolation." Other translations are "devastating accursed thing" and "abominable and destructive presence."

The 1986 revision of the New Testament in the *New American Bible* translates Mark 13:14 as, "When you see the desolating abomination standing where he should not (let the reader understand), then those in Judea must flee to the mountains."

Commentator Alexander Jones says Jesus here is calling

to mind the passage in Daniel where he says that the leader of the invader "shall abolish sacrifice and oblation: On the temple wing shall be the horrible abomination until the ruin that is decreed is poured out upon the horror." Here Daniel is referring to the invasion by Syria under Antiochus IV in 168 B.C. Antiochus erected an idol and altar to Olympian Zeus in the Temple and set up a brothel in the sacred court. The flesh of swine was offered on the altar in the Temple and pagan altars were erected in surrounding cities.

Other references to the abomination can be found in Daniel 11:31 and 12:11 as well as 1 Maccabees 1:54 and 2 Maccabees 6:1–5.

In the context of Mark, Jesus is telling his listeners that a similar event or horror will take place in the last days. Jones sees the words fulfilled in A.D. 68 or 70 when the first Jewish zealots turned the Temple into a fortress and then the Romans destroyed the city and Temple.

Henry Wansbrough, O.S.B., exegeting Mark in *A New Catholic Commentary on Holy Scripture*, suggests that in inserting "let the reader understand" Mark is clueing Roman Christians to see here a reference to the emperor Titus, who had been acclaimed in Jerusalem after sacrifice to the standards of Rome in the court of the Temple. And later spoils from Jerusalem were paraded through the streets of Rome in A.D. 71. Wansbrough says this explains why the abomination is a "he" rather than an "it."

What does the Apostles' Creed mean when it says Jesus descended into hell?

In Latin the Apostles' Creed reads *"descendit ad infernos."* *Ad infernos* stands for the Hebrew word *Sheol*, which means "the underworld." The phrase *"descendit ad infernos"* has presented problems to teachers and translators for a long time. How is it to be understood? What is meant by *infernos*, which is often translated as "hell"?

In *A Book of Prayers*, published by the International Commission on English in the Liturgy (ICEL), a footnote to the

Apostles' Creed notes that the line *"descendit ad infernos"* has been subject to various interpretations. It says,

> Some have understood it as underscoring the assertion of death in the previous line. Others, following 1 Peter 3:19, have thought of it as beginning the resurrection sequence—our Lord proclaiming his victory to the souls of the departed. Still others have thought of our Lord going to do battle with Satan, thus guaranteeing the deliverance of the saints.

Noting that some confessional groups have officially espoused one or the other of these interpretations, the International Consultation on English Texts (an ecumenical group) said its task was not to take sides but to provide a text (English translation) open to all these views.

It did so by putting the translation in sense lines so that it reads:

> He suffered under Pontius Pilate, was
> crucified, died and was buried.
> He descended to the dead.
> On the third day he rose again.

This was the translation ICEL adopted and it is the translation you will find in our U.S. version of the sacramentary for Masses with children. It is also the translation that is used by Canada in the celebration of the Eucharist. (Canadians substitute the Apostles' Creed for the Nicene Creed.)

The *Catechism of the Catholic Church*, sheds further light on this (632–633).

Did Jesus rise or was he raised from the dead?

The work of the translator is to translate as accurately and clearly as possible what is in the original text. The translator's work is not to promote a particular theology; it is to be as objective as possible and to tell us what the original author or writer actually said. In Matthew 28:6 translators or groups of translators have the angel saying that Jesus "is risen" while others—the *New American Bible* translators among them—

have the angel saying he "has been raised."

At the same time there are other passages where it is clear the words must be translated either "is risen (or rose)" or "has been raised from the dead," as the case may be, and they are all in agreement.

It is also a fact that in credal statements or magisterial teachings Jesus is sometimes said to "have risen" and other times said to "have been raised."

The Teaching of Christ, by Ronald Lawler, Donald Wuerl and Thomas Lawler, explains the two ways of speaking thus:

> Faithful to the message of Scripture, the Church teaches both that the Father raised Jesus from the dead and that Jesus rose by his own power, "God raised him up" (Acts 2:24), "I lay down my life, that I may take it up again.... I have power to take it up again" (John 10:17–18).
>
> The explanation is this: It was by the power of God that the humanity of Jesus was raised from the dead. This power of the one God belongs to the Father and Son equally. When the resurrection is seen as the seal of the Father's approval, the glorification of Jesus' humanity is viewed as the work of the Father; when it is seen as a manifestation of Jesus' divine power and personality, it is viewed as the act of the Son himself.

John McKenzie, in his *Dictionary of the Bible*, notes that Saint Paul consistently sees and writes of the Resurrection as the work of the Father. He explains that Paul attributes the Resurrection to the Father as a part of general attribution of the redemption to the Trinity of persons in their respective roles. McKenzie says, "The resurrection of Jesus places him in a new life, and this new life comes from the Father who is the source of all life."

McKenzie states,

> Unless one wishes, as certain heretics have done, to understand these passages as meaning that Jesus received a personality which he did not possess in his incarnation, one must understand them to mean the titles which signify this redeeming work are not fully verified in him until he is raised up to the right hand of God.

What is "the great eschatological test"?

The Greek word *eschatos* means "last." When theologians and Scripture commentators write about "eschatology" or "eschatological" things, they are writing about the end of the world, theorizing about what will happen at the Second Coming of Christ.

Matthew, Luke and Mark have all recorded what Jesus said about the last days and his Second Coming. Luke quotes Jesus as saying:

> There will be signs in the sun, the moon, and the stars, and on the earth distress among nations confused by the roaring of the sea and the waves. People will faint from fear and foreboding of what is coming upon the world, for the powers of the heavens will be shaken. Then they will see "the Son of Man coming in a cloud" with power and great glory. Now when these things begin to take place, stand up and raise your heads, because your redemption is drawing near. (21:25–28)

Father Laurin Wenig (*The Spring of Life: Your Introduction to Sacred Scripture*), in commenting on the book of Revelation's account of the last days, calls the end of the world "the great KABOOM!" He says,

> It is a fascinating story of weird, dragon-like beasts fighting with damsels in distress. Roll all the evil leaders of history into one super villain and call him the "Antichrist." Give him an arsenal of laser beams, neutron bombs, atomic submarines and nuclear warheads. Give his victims water pistols as weapons. Those are the odds of evil versus good when we read the Book of Revelation. It makes the story of David and Goliath look like an episode of Sesame Street.

However colorful Father Wenig's description, it gives us some idea of the stress and agony to be endured by those who face the trials and events that precede the coming of Christ in glory and judgment. People will truly be tested and endure a great trial.

Many Scripture experts believe that Jesus' words in the

Lord's Prayer, "and lead us not into temptation...," would be better translated something like, "Subject us not to the trial/but deliver us from the evil one" (Matthew 6:13), as in the *New American Bible.*

In their opinion Jesus is then telling the apostles and us to pray that we be spared from the great trial and test of the last days—the eschatological test.

Where did Pentecost take place?

We are not really told where the apostles were when the Holy Spirit came on Pentecost. Acts simply says, "When the day of Pentecost had come, they were all together in one place" (Acts 2:1). It then goes on to say, "And suddenly from heaven there came a sound like the rush of a violent wind, and it filled the entire house where they were sitting" (2:2).

Why the presumption that the apostles were in the upper room where they had celebrated the Last Supper with Jesus? I should think because earlier (Acts 1:12) we are told that after Jesus ascended into heaven, "They returned to Jerusalem," and, "When they had entered the city they went to the room upstairs where they were staying" (1:13), and, "All these were constantly devoting themselves to prayer..." (1:14).

Artists, meditation writers and preachers, then, envision the apostles (with Mary and others) in the upper room of the Last Supper when the Spirit comes. But the text of Acts does not say they were in the upper room.

Furthermore, between that section of Acts and the description of Pentecost, Luke apparently takes the apostles and us out of the upper room for the selection of Matthias to replace Judas. We are told in Acts 1:15–26, "In those days Peter stood up among the believers (together the crowd numbered about one hundred twenty persons)." One hundred twenty people could not have fit in the upper room.

The Greek word used in Acts 2:2 *(oiken)* usually means *house.* It, like the similar Hebrew word *beth,* can be used for *temple.* But then it usually has a modifier, for example, "house of God." There is no modifier in Acts 2:2. And in later verses

Luke uses a different Greek word for *temple, hieron,* the same word he uses for *temple* in twenty-three other places.

It is safe to say the apostles were in some sort of house, not the Temple. Anything beyond that would be speculation.

Who is the Antichrist?

In his *Dictionary of the Bible,* Father John McKenzie says,

> The figure of Antichrist has been interpreted in many ways; but there are good reasons for doubting the long-established opinion that he signifies a real historical-eschatological figure. In Apocalypse (Revelation) the connection of the beast with Rome is too close for him to be anything else than the persecuting imperial power; and no better explanation of the cipher 666 has been proposed than that which finds it the sum of the numerical value of the Hebrew letters of the name Caesar Nero (KSR NRWN), the emperor (A.D. 54–68) who first put Christians to death.

McKenzie also says in connection with the first and second letters of John that there are many Antichrists and the Antichrist is a personification of the powers of evil occasionally focused in anyone who denies Christ. So in a sense the Antichrist comes many times. Many commentators hold that same opinion.

Who are the book of Revelation's living creatures?

As Wilfrid J. Harrington reminds us in *Understanding the Apocalypse,* the revelations of an apocalypse are made through the medium of visions. The seer attempts to put the visions in conventional language. He uses images, symbols and numbers.

Nearly everything is symbolic—but not all the details are significant. The seer is concerned with ideas, his purpose to convey the ideas he has received from God. Harrington warns against trying to make everything cohere or reducing the visions to pictures. The commentators on Revelation chapter 4 agree this text and its living creatures have some kinship with Ezekiel chapter one, where Ezekiel describes a vision that was given him on the banks of the river Chebar in Babylon.

Ezekiel, too, describes four living creatures identified in chapter ten as cherubim. They are different from John's living creatures in that each of Ezekiel's creatures had four faces and four wings.

In Revelation chapter four John describes the heavenly court and the worship that takes place there. Among those around the throne of God, John sees four living creatures. These creatures have six wings, suggestive of seraphim. One has the face of a lion, one of a man, one of an ox and one of an eagle. They imply nobility, wisdom, strength and mobility.

According to John J. Scullion, s.j., in a *New Catholic Commentary on Holy Scriptures*, they are symbols of the cosmos. Harrington says they are the four angels responsible for directing the physical world and symbolize the whole created cosmos. These creatures have eyes in front and behind—nothing escapes their sight. Since seven represents perfection, the six wings of the creatures tell us they are less than God.

The creatures sing, "Holy, Holy, Holy is the Lord God almighty, who was, and who is, and who is to come" (4:8). Their song is the unceasing song of nature in praise of its creator.

Later Christians would use the creatures as symbolic of the four evangelists. The eagle was identified with John because of his soaring mysticism; the lion with Mark because he speaks of the desert and of John the Baptist; the man with Matthew because he begins the Gospel with the human origins of Jesus; and the ox with Luke because he begins with the sacrifice offered in the Temple by Zechariah.

CHAPTER SIX

LITURGICAL PRACTICES

"**P**eople change." Yes, that's what he said. I'd asked my friend and colleague to capture what good liturgy should do for us and that was his reply. The more I think about it the more I find myself in agreement with his simple but powerful words.

The Catechism of the Catholic Church offers us something along these lines when it says,

> In the Church's liturgy the divine blessing is fully revealed and communicated. The Father is acknowledged and adored as the source and end of all the blessings of creation and salvation. In his Word who became incarnate, died, and rose for us, he fills us with his blessings. Through his Word, he pours into our hearts the Gift that contains all gifts, the Holy Spirit. (1082)

The transformation that liturgy opens up for us is by no means easy to achieve however. It is, as the Latin root of the word liturgy implies, "the work of the people." Matthew Kohmescher, in Catholicism Today: A Survey of Catholic Belief and Practice, speaks of it this way:

Good liturgy revolves around the creative use of... human in-struments: of silence (so that we can reflect on what has been said or done); of words (especially the words of the One whose presence we are celebrating); of music (which can express the fullness of our being and emotions so much better than the word all by itself); of gestures (which, like pictures, are worth a thousand words); and of symbols (the togetherness and union expressed in a family meal).

With so many ingredients it is not easy to get the recipe right all the time.

As the public expression of the church at prayer, especially as seen through the Mass and the celebration of the Eucharist, in observing and participating in the liturgy, we see what the church lives and believes—rightly or wrongly.

Seen in this light, one recognizes that structure, order and form are necessary to give us this foretaste of heaven. This concern, though, should never turn into a hollow "rubricism," where scrupulous adherence to the smallest of details gets in the way of what the liturgy offers and invites us into—conversion. In ending our conversation my friend left me by saying, "Let not perfection be the enemy of the good." Good, faithful, transformative liturgy is indeed difficult to achieve.

•

Why should we go to church?

Several years ago, when Communist oppression was being lifted in the Soviet Union, some interesting information about the church and the practice of religion under Communist rule began to emerge. One interview revealed that during the years of Communism Catholics gathered secretly on Sundays in Ukraine. Usually there was no priest. But they gathered to pray and recite the rosary in common. The person interviewed said they believed their coming together to pray so important that they regarded failure to attend a sin. This under all the difficulties and danger it meant to pray together!

Why was it so important to come together to worship?

Obviously, they felt a human need to express their dependence on God. To acknowledge that God, after all, is Lord of all and rules his creation with love. They felt a need to express that as a community. And they felt a need to draw on each other—as well as the Lord—for encouragement and strength to persevere in faith and serving the Lord.

People have felt these needs and the desire to give worship to God as a people far back in history. Though they may have believed in a plurality of gods or had rather crude ideas of God, they worshipped and offered sacrifices as families or tribes. The patriarch or leader acted as priest and mediator. Archaeologists find evidence of special worship sites everywhere from Stonehenge in England to the Incan temples of Peru. There are ruins of ground temples in Malta dating back to 2400 B.C. and the ziggurat (temple) in Ur of the Chaldees going back to 2000 B.C.

During the Exodus the Hebrews carried the Ark of the Covenant with them and "housed" it in a tent when they were not on the march. Solomon later built the Temple in Jerusalem as a fit place for the Ark and worship. Outside of Jerusalem were the synagogues where the Israelites came to pray and read the word of God together.

The early Christians—as Jesus commanded at the Last Supper—came together in their homes or house churches to celebrate the Eucharist and the love and goodness of God.

In the early centuries the places where the Christians worshipped were not public. They worshipped in secret because of persecutions. But after Constantine came into power in Rome the Christians began to build churches. Constantine himself began the construction of a church later called the Basilica of St. John Lateran. Constantine had churches built in Palestine as places associated with special events in the life of Christ and our redemption. The idea of special places to worship is very ancient.

Going to church on Sundays and other times to celebrate the Eucharist (going to Mass) began very soon after the Resurrection of Christ. That is evident from the letters of Saint Paul and the writings of the fathers of the church.

Celebrating the Eucharist is carrying out Jesus' command to "do this in memory of me." And it reminds us of Jesus' words that where two or more are gathered in his name he is in their midst.

How much of the Mass must be attended to fulfill the Sunday obligation?

The present *Code of Canon Law* reads, "On Sundays and other holy days of obligation the faithful are bound to participate in the Mass" (1247). It does not say *part* or *parts* of the Mass. The expectation is that the person will attend a complete Mass. *A Catholic Catechism* quotes the canon and states, "Those who deliberately fail in this obligation commit a grave sin."

Before Vatican II, moral theologians and canonists would talk about the three principal parts of Mass as the Offertory, Consecration and Communion. Anyone who missed any one of those parts, they wrote, would not have fulfilled the obligation of hearing Mass.

Today, canonists and liturgists do not use that terminology. They speak of the Liturgy of the Word, the Liturgy of the Eucharist and the Liturgy of Communion as the main divisions of Mass.

Moralists are more likely to speak of substantial observance of the law and what that might mean. They would assert the law imposes a serious obligation. But some would question whether a person seriously or gravely violates the law if on one occasion he or she does not attend Mass. Some would also acknowledge that to miss a few minutes would not generally be a serious matter. All Catholics must, however, be aware of the gravity of their obligation to attend Mass. To be absent for any or all of the Mass without cause could well be an indication of contempt for the Mass.

The Penitential Rite is part of the Mass. It takes place after the entrance song, right after the priest has entered the sanctuary and greeted the people. It can take different forms. One commonly used is the confession of faith (Confiteor) and Lord have mercy (Kyrie Eleison). Arriving after these prayers is arriving late for Mass.

Just as there can be excuses for missing Mass, there could be excuses for coming late or leaving early or missing part of the celebration. A parent might have to take a crying child from the church. A person may feel ill, or need to use the restroom. There would be no fault in leaving for such reasons. But to sneak a cigarette or step outside because of boredom would hardly be sufficient causes.

A hospital worker may have to leave early or a mother may have to hurry home to watch children while dad takes a turn at going to Mass. A traveler may have to catch a bus or plane. Surely such reasons would excuse from fault. But to be first off the parking lot?!

While an emergency may demand that a person leave before the end of Mass, one who has departed before the Consecration and Communion can hardly be said to have attended Mass. But the emergency may excuse them from further effort to go to Mass.

Is it acceptable to say the rosary during Mass?

The rosary is a beautiful form of prayer, combining both vocal and meditative prayer. Many people have grown rich in the spiritual life by praying the rosary. The church's documents on the liturgy, however, do not support the practice of reciting (in a group or privately) the rosary during the celebration of the Eucharist.

The *Constitution on the Sacred Liturgy* (30) states,

> To promote active participation the people should be encouraged to take part by means of acclamations, response, psalms, antiphons, hymns, as well as by actions, gestures and bodily attitudes, and at the proper times a reverent silence should be observed.

The Instruction on Music in the Liturgy says:

> The faithful fulfill their liturgical role by making that full, conscious and active participation, which is demanded by the nature of the liturgy itself and which is by reason

261

of Baptism, the right and duty of the Christian people. This participation: a) should be above all internal, in the sense that by it the faithful join their mind to what they pronounce or hear, and cooperate with heavenly grace, and b) must be, on the other hand, external also, that is such as to show the internal participation by gestures and bodily attitudes, by the acclamations, responses and singing.

In other words the church expects us to take part as much as we can in the prayers and ceremonies of the Mass. That is rather difficult to do while continuing to say the rosary or some other unrelated prayers.

May a eucharistic minister bless?

It is true that by canon or liturgical law some blessings are reserved to bishops, priests or deacons. They are usually blessings that take place in liturgical rites or blessings that set aside or dedicate (consecrate) things for sacred use.

The *Book of Blessings* (the official English version of the blessings in the Roman Ritual) states, "The blessing of throats [on the feast of Saint Blaise] may be given by a priest, deacon or lay minister who follows the rites and prayers designated for a lay minister" (1626).

Concerning the blessing and distribution of ashes for Ash Wednesday, it says,

> This rite may be celebrated by a priest or deacon who may be assisted by lay ministers in the distribution of the ashes. The blessing of the ashes, however, is reserved to a priest or deacon.

The term *lay minister(s)* would include eucharistic ministers. Considering the shortage of priests today, it is easy to understand why the church would make these provisions.

There are countless other ways laypersons bless themselves or others. Most of us, on entering the church on Sunday, begin by blessing ourselves. We make the Sign of the Cross with our fingers dipped in holy water to remind us of our baptism, and we ask God to bless us. Most Catholic families ask

God to bless their food and those gathered for the family meal. And when someone sneezes, many people automatically say, "God bless you!" No one thinks these things improper or presumptuous.

The general introduction to the *Book of Blessings* speaks of the ministry of blessing. After noting what this means in the case of bishop, priest, deacon, acolyte and reader, it says,

> ...other laymen and laywomen, in virtue of the universal priesthood, a dignity they possess because of their Baptism and Confirmation, may celebrate certain blessings as indicated in the respective orders of blessings by use of the rites and formularies designated for a lay minister. Such laypersons exercise this ministry in virtue of their office (for example, *parents* on behalf of their children)... (italics added).

It is good and proper, under the right circumstances, for laypersons to bless.

How were the readings picked for the three-year Mass cycle?

The Introduction to the lectionary explains that the three-year cycle is intended to provide a more varied reading of Sacred Scripture on Sundays and feasts.

Readings for Sundays and feasts are arranged according to two principles called "semicontinuous" and "thematic." For special seasons of the year or special feasts, the readings have been chosen to fit the season or feast—they are "thematic." For example, all of the readings for a liturgical season, such as Lent, or a feast, such as the Immaculate Conception, have been chosen to fit the season or saint's feast being celebrated.

The Gospels in Ordinary Time are for the most part continuous. In other words beginning after the nativity accounts of the Christmas season, the lectionary takes one version of the Gospel (Matthew, Luke or Mark) chapter by chapter up to the Passion and Resurrection accounts. On these Sundays the Old Testament reading has been chosen because it is in some way related to the Gospel text or has a similar point or theme.

During Ordinary Time the second reading New Testament texts (Letters, Acts) have not been chosen in relation to the Gospel. The lectionary simply presents them in a semi-continuous fashion so that we do hear and become familiar with them over a three-year cycle.

Can priests change the words for Mass and the sacraments?

Canon 846 of the present *Code of Canon Law* states that the liturgical books approved by competent authority are to be faithfully observed in the celebration of the sacraments; therefore, no one on personal authority may add, remove or change anything in them.

However, that canon must be read together with other liturgical laws and the liturgical books themselves.

The directives, or rubrics, in the sacramentary for Mass and the ritual books for the sacraments often explicitly permit adaptations of the rite or that the priest use his own words. There are also at times a number of prayers, greetings and introductions from which the priest may choose.

The Foreword to the sacramentary contains a quote from the April 27, 1973, circular letter of the Congregation for Divine Worship:

> Introductions are ways of leading the faithful to a more thorough grasp of the meaning of the sacred rites or certain of their parts and to an inner participation in them. Particularly important are the introductions that the General Instruction assigns to be prepared and spoken by the priest: the comments introducing the faithful to the day's Mass before the celebration of the Liturgy of the Word before the readings, and to the eucharistic prayer before the preface; the comments concluding the whole rite before the dismissal. Prominence should also be given to those introductions to the penitential rite and the Lord's Prayer. By their very nature such introductions do not require that they be given verbatim in the

form they have in the Missal; consequently it may well be helpful, at least in certain cases, to adapt them to the actual situation of the community.

Also, the entire Roman ritual that many knew as children and young adults has been revised with the renewal of the Latin rite liturgy. So if things sound different when a priest is anointing the sick, distributing Communion and so on, it is not necessarily a priest trying to modernize formulas on his own authority.

The church has revised the way sacraments are celebrated and administered. Whatever the revisions, though, when it comes to the essential parts of the sacramental rites and their forms, priests and ministers of the sacraments are not supposed to be revising them on their own or "winging it." The words of the Consecration are to be pronounced as they are established in the sacramentary. The formula for baptism that appears in the ritual is to be used without changes, and the formula for absolution that appears in the rite for the sacrament of reconciliation is not to be tampered with (although in danger of death the priest may use just the essential part of the absolution as provided for in the ritual itself).

In the case of the sacrament of reconciliation, there has been a revision of the form for absolution since Vatican II. It is now a bit longer. The priest prays:

God the Father of mercies, through the death and resurrection of his Son, has reconciled the world to himself and sent the Holy Spirit among us for the forgiveness of sins; through the ministry of the Church may God give you pardon and peace, and I absolve you from your sins in the name of the Father, and of the Son, and of the Holy Spirit.

What is the difference between Eastern rite and Roman Catholics?

We Catholics of the Roman rite, to the dismay of Eastern rite Catholics, tend to think of ourselves as alone in the Catholic church with only one way of praying and celebrating liturgy.

Actually there are two dominant rites in the church—the Roman (or Latin) and the Eastern. Each of these rites has what John Deedy's *The Catholic Fact Book* calls subdivisions, which are also called rites.

The different rites originated as the disciples and missionaries went forth to preach Christ to the nations and celebrated the Eucharist. They suited their preaching and way of celebrating the Eucharist to the language and customs of the people they were evangelizing. They responded to the religious instincts and mind-sets of the people they encountered.

Catholics of the East developed their own kind of spirituality, their own theology and theological emphasis; so did those of the Roman or Latin world of the West.

In the West there also developed different rites: the Ambrosian rite of Milan; the Mozarabic rite of Toledo, Spain; the Lyonndais rite of Lyons, France; the Braza rite of Braza, Portugal. Some religious orders had liturgical rites of their own.

One reason that the Roman rite and the Roman Missal became so common was that the Franciscans of the thirteenth century carried these with them as they spread over so much of the world.

In the Greek world (or East) some of the rites that developed were the Byzantine, Chaldean, Coptic, Syrian, Maronite, Armenian, Malabar, Alexandrian and Antiochene.

When the theological quarrels arose that divided East and West by the eleventh century, some Eastern Catholics remained in or later returned to unity with Rome and accepted the authority of the pope. These Eastern rite Catholics in union with Rome are called Greek Catholics. Those who separated and remain separate from Rome are called Orthodox.

In 1570, when Pope Pius V made a major effort to bring order and unity to the celebration of the Eucharist and liturgy, he allowed any rite that could prove its existence for two centuries to continue.

As Catholics from different parts of the world emigrated to the United States, they brought their own rites and customs and styles of architecture with them. Eastern Catholics also have their own code of canon law. Eastern rite dioceses in the United States have their own bishops and clergy. There is a listing of the Eastern rite dioceses with their bishops, clergy, religious and institutions in the *National Catholic Directory*.

Are lectors permitted to change the wording in the readings?

There are three English Bible translations approved for liturgical use by the Holy See and the U.S. Conference of Catholic Bishops. They are *The New American Bible; The Revised Standard Version, Catholic Edition;* and *The Jerusalem Bible*. No other English translations are authorized for use in the United States.

We are not supposed to make up our own translations of the readings of the lectionary. There is, however, some looseness in adapting or translating the readings for use in children's Masses. And, apart from the readings, there are places in the liturgical rites where the celebrant or minister is given a choice of prayers, told to invite, introduce or use other suitable words, without any specific formula being given.

It is not always wrong to insert a ceremony or the use of customary symbols into a liturgical celebration. After all, you do not find the Sunday collection in the rubrics of the Mass! And most agree it is appropriate to allow words from a family member after Communion at a funeral Mass.

Concerning the problem of readers changing words, R. Kevin Seasoltz says, in *New Liturgy, New Laws*,

> If observance of a law occasions rejection of the liturgy or the Church by a large segment of the community, surely the traditional teaching of *epikeia* justifies the nonobservance of the law. This affirmation is in keeping with the medieval axiom that sacraments are for people; people do not exist for the Church. For example, in communities that are aware of and committed to efforts to assure justice for women and minorities in the Church, the use of sexist language in the liturgy is often both irritating and alienating: In some instances it arouses deep hostility.
>
> Sometimes the bias against women is built into the

vernacular translation but not into the original Latin text. There is no reason why the words *"pro multis"* in the text of (eucharistic) institution within the anaphora need to be translated "for all men." To avoid harm and insult to the community, ministers have rightly changed the text and avoided sexist language.

Seasoltz was writing before those words were officially changed to "for all," but his explanation of why such things are sometimes done still holds true.

Why does the Nicene Creed lack inclusive language?

Changes in liturgy and translations of Scripture and liturgical texts almost always give rise to quarrels and angry exchanges. Saint Augustine did not care a bit for Saint Jerome's Latin vulgate translation of the Scriptures and let it be known he preferred the Old Latin translation. There are still those who prefer the Rheims-Douay translations of the Bible and distrust any translation made since. When the Church of England introduced its new book of worship, it met with resistance from many people. Some congregations go on using the old *Book of Common Prayer*.

So, whatever some may think, changes in liturgical books are not made casually or quickly. There are too many consequences and values involved. Simply to change from saying, "This is the Word of the Lord," to, "The Word of the Lord," can take years! Before those asking for a change can make it, permission from Rome is required, and pastors are instructed to explain the changes to parishioners.

Further, changes in liturgical prayers have ecumenical ramifications. Prayers such as the Nicene Creed, the Our Father and the Gloria appear not just in our Roman or Latin rite liturgy but in the liturgies of other Christian churches. Certainly there is a value in a common text and being able to pray together, a value of being able to express common beliefs in common language.

The International Commission on English in the Liturgy (ICEL) has been working on a new translation of the Roman

Missal (of which the sacramentary is a part) for some time. ICEL's work is overseen by a board of eleven bishops. Before changes are finalized and introduced in the liturgies of the English-speaking countries, they must pass the vote of the individual conferences of bishops. It may take years yet before changes under discussion are approved and implemented.

When changes are proposed, there will be some voices raised in loud opposition and others insisting that the proposed changes should be made. There will be some bishops and priests on both sides: That is the way of human nature. Some will advance the need for inclusive language; others will stress their desire for poetic, elevated, lyrical language.

We should all pray for true dialogue (people listening to each other and their reasons), people talking to each other in a civil way rather than shouting into the air and accusing each other of heresy.

At this time ICEL has a tentative text for the Creed. The proposed revision says, in part, "For us and for our salvation he came down from heaven, was incarnate of the Holy Spirit and the Virgin Mary and became truly *human*." Notice, *For us men* and *became man* are replaced by *For us* and *became truly human*.

Already questions are being raised about what *us* would mean to Catholics or other Christians who pray this prayer a generation from now! Writing in *The Catholic World Report*, Robert Hutchinson is one who raised these questions. He argued that you have three heresies in waiting and said that the Fathers of Nicaea added *anthropous*, "human beings," to prevent heretical interpretations, a reason "being recklessly ignored now."

Those who favor *men* in translations such as this insist that in English, as understood by everyone for hundreds of years, *man* or *men* in such contexts has been understood without any difficulty to mean any of the following: human, human beings, human race or humankind. In other words they maintain this is inclusive language already.

Obviously, these questions can be charged with emotion and more complicated than immediately realized.

Related to this debate, the *Catechism of the Catholic Church* contains the following passage:

> God transcends all creatures. We must therefore continually purify our language of everything in it that is limited, image-bound or imperfect, if we are not to confuse our image of God—"the inexpressible, the incomprehensible, the invisible, the ungraspable"— with our human representations. Our words always fall short of the mystery of God. (42)

A resource worth consulting on this matter is published by the United States Catholic Bishops: "Criteria for the Evaluation of Inclusive Language Translations of Scriptural Texts Proposed for Liturgical Use."

May the Gospel be recited from memory? Must we stand during the Gospel reading?

The *General Instruction of the Roman Missal* in front of the sacramentary calls upon all to stand for the reading of the Gospel. However, the celebrant of a Mass in a nursing home might tell all to sit or remain sitting.

Concerning the proclamation of the Gospel from memory, Father Thomas Richstatter, O.F.M., who teaches liturgy at Saint Meinrad Seminary, states:

> The practice is not sufficiently widespread to bring any official comment. The opinion of liturgists, professors of homiletics and professors of communication arts is mixed.
>
> Against the practice are those who say that it is a reading and should be read. They say there must be a connection between the reader and the written text, the Lectionary.
>
> Supporting the practice (I would be in this group) are those who say that the main thing for the practice is the overwhelmingly favorable reaction of the people. People put down their books and look at you. They say afterward that they never heard the Gospel with such clarity before.... The time it takes to memorize texts causes the

preacher to live with the word in such a way that it greatly improves the proclamation of the Gospel with meaning and conviction, and the homily is more likely to grow out of the sense of the text.

The more important issues are not the reading versus reciting on the part of the priest, bishop or deacon but rather reading versus listening on the part of the congregation. Faith comes by hearing, not by reading, Scripture says.

A newsletter from the U.S. Bishops' Liturgy Committee states,

> Just as the Church is obliged to faithfully proclaim the Bible as it has been passed on, the reader is obliged to faithfully proclaim the biblical text exactly as it appears in the Lectionary Mass.

Why do we make the Sign of the Cross at the Gospel?

We sign ourselves the same way the priest does when he begins to read the Gospel—on the forehead, lips and heart. We say at the same time, "Jesus be on my mind, on my lips and in my heart."

The signing of the book and self is a reminder of the respect and love we should have for Christ and his word. We should always have in mind the word and example of Jesus, keep him close to our hearts and be ready to proclaim him and his word to the world.

Balthasar Fischer, in *Signs, Words and Gesture,* puts it this way:

> The sign of the cross on the forehead, lips and heart also has to do with this Lord who is entering the assembly and will speak. Everyone present is saying as it were, "Now I must pay attention. It is my Lord who speaks. Since my Baptism I have belonged to him body and soul, in my thoughts, words and feelings."

In other words we are to be completely and entirely devoted to Christ.

Why do we use incense?

The use of incense goes far back in time. Incense was in common use in Near East countries, burnt for its perfume—perhaps an ancient kind of air freshener. From secular use it passed into religious service. People employed it in worship of their gods. According to one source, at a fete in honor of Baal, the Babylonians burned one thousand talents of frankincense. Incense also played a part in honor given to kings and the Roman emperor.

Among the gifts of the Magi was frankincense—a gift worthy of a king.

The book of Exodus refers to incense. In chapter thirty, Moses is told to make an altar of acacia wood for the burning of incense and Aaron is to burn incense morning and evening. Also, in Exodus 30:34–38 Moses is given a formula for incense to be used solely in the worship of Yahweh. It is to be made of equal parts of storax, onycha, galbanum and frankincense blended and ground into fine dust. The incense is to be placed before the commandments in the meeting tent. Elsewhere in the Old Testament incense was often burnt in connection with the burnt offerings of animals.

The sweet smell of incense and its rising smoke gave it a kind of natural symbolism. It became the image of something pleasing to God. So in Psalm 141 we have the plea, "Let my prayer come like incense before you."

Early Christians also found symbolic meaning in the use of incense. In the book of Revelation, for instance, John has a vision of heaven and a kind of heavenly liturgy where the twenty-four elders worship the lamb that was slain. The elders hold harps and gold bowls filled with incense, "which are the prayers of the holy ones" (5:8). In Revelation 8:3–4 an angel holding a golden censer is given a great quantity of incense to offer and the smoke of the incense goes up before God with prayers.

Among Christians today incense has ritual and symbolic meaning. Its sweet aroma symbolizes something pleasing and acceptable being offered to God.

Burning incense is also a sign of reverence and dedication.

Incensing the body at a funeral Mass is a sign of reverence for the body that was once the temple of God. In a more solemn liturgy incensing the book of the Gospels indicates reverence for the word of God and Christ himself who is the Word incarnate (*Catechism of the Catholic Church* 1154). Incensing the altar shows respect for Christ, whom the altar represents, and his sacrifice made present upon the altar. Incensing the Easter candle is, again, a sign of reverence for Christ, who is the light of the world. Incensing the Blessed Sacrament at Benediction is a sign of adoration and worship given to Christ, truly present upon the altar. It becomes a sign of our prayers rising to heaven.

May deacons preach?

The present *Code of Canon Law* (764) says that priests and deacons, with at least the presumed consent of the rector of a church, have the faculty to preach everywhere—unless the competent ordinary (the bishop of the diocese or the person's religious major superior) has removed or restricted this faculty or a particular law requires express permission.

So, unless there is a particular law in your diocese or the bishop has not allowed or somehow limited preaching by deacons or the deacon in your parish, it is perfectly within the law and proper for a deacon to preach in your parish with the permission of your pastor.

While preaching the homily after the Gospel is reserved to a priest or deacon, the code (766) also allows that, if it seems necessary or useful in certain circumstances or particular cases, laypersons may preach in a church or oratory. In this instance the preaching would be at a paraliturgical service or perhaps after a Mass.

Even further, the *Directory for Masses with Children*, from the Congregation for Divine Worship, says, if there are few adults present at a Mass for children, the pastor may allow one of the adults present to speak to the children after the Gospel. This is especially so if, the *Directory* says, the priest finds it difficult to adapt himself to the mentality of the children.

Permanent deacons are ordained only after at least two or three years of studying Scripture and theology. If they are permitted by the local bishop to preach, they will have had training in homiletics and preaching.

If a pastor is humble enough to admit that the deacon may be a better preacher than he or his associate(s), he deserves to be thanked and commended. There are reasons that might make it difficult for the priest himself to preach. For example, because of old age he may become tired by celebrating a long liturgy. Pain may make it hard for him to be on his feet for any length of time. Perhaps he has very little time to prepare a homily. Celebrating multiple Masses on Saturday evening and Sunday and traveling from one church to another to serve different communities may take all the strength he has.

All these things are going to become more common as our priests continue to become fewer and older. In places where the Eucharist cannot be celebrated every Sunday because a priest is not available, we will be very grateful to have a deacon preach the word of God.

What is an acolyte?

In his apostolic letter issued *motu proprio* ["of one's own accord"] "by which the discipline of first tonsure, minor orders and subdiaconate in the Latin Church is reformed," Pope Paul VI wrote:

> The acolyte is appointed in order to aid the deacon and to minister to the priest. It is therefore his duty to attend to the service of the altar and to assist the deacon and the priest in liturgical celebrations, especially in the celebration of Mass; he is also to distribute Holy Communion as an auxiliary minister when the ministers spoken of in canon 845 of the Code of Canon Law (old code) are not available or are prevented by ill health, age, or another pastoral ministry from performing this function, or when the number of those approaching the sacred table is so great that the celebration of Mass would be unduly prolonged. In the same extraordinary circumstances he may be entrusted with publicly exposing the Blessed

Sacrament for adoration by the faithful and afterward replacing it, but not with blessing the people. He may also, to the extent needed, take care of instructing other faithful who by temporary appointment assist the priest or deacon in liturgical celebrations by carrying the missal, cross, candles, etc., or by performing other such duties. (cf. canon 230; see also 903 in the *Catechism of the Catholic Church*)

That defines what this official ministry is.

Pope Paul VI also "in accordance with the venerable tradition of the Church" reserved institution in the ministries of reader and acolyte to men. But actual practice varies from place to place and even within the same diocese.

Why do people no longer bow their heads at the name of Jesus Christ at Mass and other times?

An older woman tells how the girls of her day always walked a new boyfriend past a Catholic church. If he tipped his hat when they went by, he was a Catholic and passed the test for courtship.

Obviously times have changed. Not many men usually wear hats. And people do not think much about making signs of reverence when riding buses and automobiles or rushing back and forth to work at lunchtime.

Ideas of reverence and suitable signs of reverence change and develop. Often they come out of one's culture. Some of the basic liturgical signs of reverence came from the courts of the emperors of old. In Rome when persons came into the presence of Caesar, they went to one knee saying, "Ave, Caesar" ("Hail, Caesar"). In the Eastern empire subjects would *salaam* (bow profoundly) in the presence of the emperor.

In other societies people prostrated themselves when they came before the ruler. Kisses, curtsies, bows of the head are all signs of respect in different societies. Among some people, walking on your knees is not only a penitential act but a sign of reverence.

Different people have different ideas of what shows due

respect and how often such signs of respect should be repeated to show the reverence due to someone or something. A lot depends on custom.

When liturgical rites and customs were revised in the Latin rite, following Vatican II, a common rule of thumb was to avoid repetition. In the priest's rubrics for the celebration of the Eucharist a good many kisses, genuflections, bows and Signs of the Cross were eliminated as repetitious.

That does not mean that the church wanted Mass celebrants (and/or other ministers and participants) to be less reverent. It may well be there was a hope the signs of reverence we do make would be more thoughtful and real expressions of reverence. Consider how thoughtful the reverence might be if people bowed their heads at every mention of the name "Jesus" as they recited the Litany of the Holy Name.

The *General Instruction of the Roman Missal* gives some idea of the proper signs of reverence. The instruction establishes the expected signs of reverence by the priest in the celebration of the Eucharist. Among them:

- Kissing the altar and the book of the Gospels.

- Genuflections after the showing of the Eucharist bread and chalice and before Communion.

- Genuflections before and after Mass if there is a tabernacle with the Blessed Sacrament in the sanctuary.

- Genuflections when passing in front of the Blessed Sacrament.

- A bow of the head when the three divine Persons are named together and at the name of Jesus, Mary and the saint in whose honor Mass is celebrated.

- A bow of the body toward the altar if there is no tabernacle with the Blessed Sacrament—and during certain of the celebrant's prayers.

Those directions offer norms for other times of prayer as well. The important thing is that we do not become so familiar with holy things that we lose proper respect for them, that our signs of reverence become so automatic and routine they lose their meaning.

When should we genuflect?

The double genuflection (on both knees) at certain times of the pre-Vatican II liturgy is no longer required by the rubrics of the new liturgy. Some individuals or countries may continue it out of piety and devotion.

According to Monsignor Peter J. Elliot, in *Ceremonies of the Modern Roman Rite*, genuflection on one knee is reserved for: (1) Our Lord present in the Eucharist on the altar, in the tabernacle, in the monstrance or in a pyx; (2) The cross during its veneration on Good Friday until the beginning of the Easter Vigil; and (3) A relic of the true cross exposed for veneration.

A bow of the body (deep bow from the waist) is made to the altar if the Blessed Sacrament is not on it or behind it. A bow of the head is to be made at the mention of the three Divine Persons, at the names of Jesus and Mary and the saint in whose honor the liturgy is being celebrated.

Should one kneel to receive Communion?

Prior to Vatican II it was regular practice to receive Communion kneeling at the Communion rail. Kneeling was regarded as the posture of reverence and humility appropriate for one receiving the Body and Blood of Jesus. A person expressed unworthiness in the presence of Jesus and gave adoration to God by kneeling. But kneeling did not become the way of receiving Communion until the eleventh century.

At the Last Supper Jesus and the apostles probably ate in the reclining position—a practice common among Jews at that time. In early New Testament times people celebrated the Eucharist in connection with meals in their homes. They probably observed the usual customs and took the customary postures of their time and place. After the persecutions ceased the Eucharist was separated from other meals. As Christians began to worship in churches, other customs came into use.

Those customs differed from one place to another.

Today, standing has pretty well taken over among us Latin rite Catholics in the United States. Besides allowing better "traffic control" (movement of people), standing is an expression that those celebrating the Eucharist are a pilgrim people (like the Jews of the Exodus). They must be spiritually on the move, always ready to follow where the Lord will call and lead them. The Eucharist is food for the way!

People of different groups and eras choose to express what seems most important to them through their liturgical gestures and practices. After all, liturgy is not a frozen tradition.

Respect the piety and try to understand the mind-set of those who insist on kneeling, and hope they are as generous in respecting those who stand.

It is wise to accept the decisions of authority about such practices. It is reasonable to have consideration of others by not disrupting the flow of the liturgy and creating chaotic celebrations.

What is the proper way to distribute Communion?

The directives in the *General Instruction of the Roman Missal*, in the front of the current sacramentary, indicate that the signs and practices surrounding the reception of Communion should make it clear that Communion is a sharing in the sacrifice being offered.

For instance, the singing of a Communion song is desirable because it expresses union of spirit by union of voices and gives evidence of joyful hearts and makes the procession to receive Christ's body more fully an act of community. What we do and how we act should reflect a certain amount of joy and the fact that what is happening is not just happening between God and one individual. What demeanor and tone of voice will express those things while preserving the reverence also urged by the instruction is something about which people may disagree.

For the priest (and other ministers), at the distribution of Communion, the sacramentary directs that "He takes a host for each one, raises it a little, and shows it saying, 'The Body of Christ.' The communicant answers, 'Amen.'" For Communion from the cup, "When he presents the chalice, the priest or deacon says, 'The Blood of Christ,'" and "The communicant answers: 'Amen.'"

In the West we usually think it proper to look at a person who speaks to us or to whom we are speaking. Since the minister of Communion is told to show the host to a communicant and speak to him or her and the communicant is told to respond to the minister's proclamation, that suggests that they look at each other and the host. They are making statements of faith to each other. A genuine smile might reflect the joy both should be feeling.

Why does the priest and/or deacon kiss the altar and Gospel book?

According to Joseph A. Jungmann, s.j., in his book *The Mass*, kissing is "a custom that has come down from ancient times." In his book on a related topic, *The Eucharist*, Johannes H. Emminghaus indicates the kiss probably has its roots in the court ceremonies and customs of the Roman Empire, where any object that was handed to the ruler had to be kissed first. The kiss was obviously a sign of reverence.

Beyond that, Emminghaus reminds us, the kiss is a bodily gesture that symbolizes a union that is desired or has been achieved—a sign of love and unity between friends or marriage partners.

In the liturgy both the altar and Gospel book represent Jesus. The kiss given to the altar or book is not just an act of reverence for the altar or book itself but also an act of reverence and love given to Christ himself. According to a liturgical dictum, "The altar is Christ." To kiss the altar expresses our desire to be one with Jesus, to be one with God.

In some of the Eastern rites, kissing the altar, at least at the end of Mass, is carried out with more ceremony and a touching personal prayer. For instance, in the Syrian liturgy the priest, upon kissing the altar at the end of the Eucharist, prays,

Abide in peace, holy altar of God. I do not know whether I shall be allowed to approach you again. May the Lord grant me to see you again in the Church of heaven.

Must we kneel at Mass?

At present there are differences in this practice in the United States as compared to Germany and other European nations. These differences probably go back to the revision of the *Roman Missal* and the introduction of the present sacramentary.

The *Roman Missal* says that the people should kneel at the Consecration unless prevented by lack of space, the number of people present or some other good reason.

The National Conference of Catholic Bishops, using the authority granted them by the *General Instruction on the Roman Missal*, determined that people should kneel from after the Holy, Holy, Holy (Sanctus) until after the Great Amen at the end of the Eucharistic Prayer.

In Europe many churches—even those with stone floors— do not have kneelers. In some, movable chairs are placed in rows too narrow to allow for kneeling.

There is some movement in the United States to discontinue kneeling. In 1990 delegates of the Federation of Diocesan Liturgical Commissions (FDLC) recommended that standing be the posture for the Eucharistic Prayer. Speakers pointed out that it is only in the United States that the people kneel for the entire Eucharistic Prayer. They recommended that when new editions of the Missal are printed they provide for standing during the Eucharistic Prayer.

Some churches and pastors have already taken the matter into their own hands. Pastors are teaching schoolchildren and asking their congregations to stand during the Eucharistic Prayer. Some cathedral renovations eliminate pews and kneelers in favor of movable chairs (without kneelers). Many other churches and chapels have been built or remodeled without kneelers.

Why the movement to eliminate or severely limit kneeling during celebration of the Eucharist? One reason given is that we in the United States should follow what other Catholics in the Roman rite do. Other reasons are theological rather than a matter of an aging Catholic population that finds kneeling difficult. Liturgists argue that kneeling for the Eucharist is a relatively recent practice. It took over in the Middle Ages as the liturgy became the action of clerics and the people were reduced to spectators. Kneeling is more a posture for private prayer. Since people said their private prayers while the priest celebrated the Eucharist, they chose to kneel.

Liturgists also argue that standing better expresses the spirit that should characterize those celebrating the Eucharist. It is a posture of joy, readiness to hear and be on the way—an Easter attitude, as Klemens Richter calls it, in *Sacramental Symbols: Answers to Today's Questions*. He writes that it is the attitude of freedom, of those liberated from sin and death, the posture of those awaiting the return of Christ.

Kneeling, of course, has its own significance. It is the attitude of respect, adoration, humility, submission, reverence and sorrow and petition.

It may be relevant to note, also, that the Latin texts of the four usual Eucharistic Prayers speak of standing around or near the altar—though it is the translation of the second Eucharistic Prayer alone that reflects that.

This matter generates strong feelings. Advocates of both kneeling and standing must respect the reasons and feelings of each other.

How does one prepare for Communion in the home?

Start with the most important thing: creating an atmosphere conducive to prayer and reverence. Sometime before you expect the priest or eucharistic minister to come, turn off the TVs and radios. Give the sick person time to pray and prepare him- or herself for reception of Communion.

Those who care for the sick may want to pray with them. Caregivers are usually allowed to receive Communion with the sick under the usual norms for Communion.

Presuming Communion is to be brought to the home, the ritual *Pastoral Care of the Sick* directs that those with the sick should be asked to cover a table with a linen cloth as the place where the minister will put the Eucharist until the time of Communion itself. There should be lighted candles on the table (except, of course, in cases where the sick person is on oxygen or other fire hazards are present in the home) and, where customary, a vessel of holy water. It is wise to put a spoon and glass of drinking water on the table, in case the sick person has difficulty swallowing the host.

If the sick person is well enough to assist, he or she is encouraged to join with the caregivers in choosing some of the prayers and readings for the Liturgy of the Word in which Communion will take place.

It is appropriate for one of the caregivers to meet the minister at the door of the home and lead the minister to the sickroom. Should the sick person want to go to confession, others should withdraw until the sacrament of reconciliation has been completed. Then the caregivers and family members present should join in the Liturgy of the Word, making the proper responses to the prayers and readings. It is good to give the sick person a bit of time to make a thanksgiving after Communion.

What is the proper way to have a home blessed?

The Roman ritual *(Book of Blessings)* provides blessings of a home for two occasions. One is the blessing of a new home, which can be done at any time. The other is a blessing for homes during the Christmas season, especially on the feast of the Epiphany, and the Easter season.

The directives for both situations say a priest, deacon or layperson may perform the blessings. If a layperson gives the blessing, the person is to use the rites and prayers designated for a lay minister. The *Book of Blessings* directs that the blessing should not be given unless those who live in the home are present—you do not just bless empty living quarters.

How does one arrange for the blessing? By calling the

parish priest and simply asking if he will come and bless the home. One can make as much of the occasion as one wishes. Some may offer some refreshment to the priest or invite him for dinner. If he is blessing a number of homes at the same time, he may simply want to perform the blessing and move to the next home.

In the event a priest or deacon is unable to come to the home, it is reasonable for the head of the household to bless the home in the presence of the family.

Is it acceptable to offer a small part of the host in Communion for the sick?

Any Catholic requesting the Eucharist at a reasonable time and in reasonable circumstances has a right to this sacrament. And the sick, especially, are in need of spiritual help and nourishment.

Giving the sick who have difficulty in swallowing only a part of the host has been taught in pastoral theology classes and has been common practice for a long time.

In *Ceremonies of the Modern Roman Rite*, Monsignor Peter J. Elliot (who has served in the Roman Curia) offers practical solutions for problems in ministering Communion. After stating that no attempt should be made to give the Eucharist to the irrational, the unconscious or those who cannot hold down solid or liquid food, he considers the situation of those who have difficulty swallowing.

He states that some solutions are to provide water immediately after Communion and to give the communicant only a small fragment of the host. For those unable to swallow solid matter, he recommends offering Communion with the Precious Blood from a sealed container.

How often can one receive Communion?

The new *Code of Canon Law* states in canon 917,

> One who has received the blessed Eucharist may receive it again on the same day only within a eucharistic celebration in which that person participates, without prejudice to the provision of Canon 921.2.

That means whenever, wherever, however a person has received Holy Communion, he or she may receive a second time on the same day if the person is participating in the celebration of Mass.

So, if the person has already received Communion in or outside of Mass, he or she may receive a second time if it is during a Mass in which he or she is participating. A person may not just walk in at Communion time and receive a second time. Canon 921.2, however, allows anyone in danger of death from any cause (a heart attack, missile attack or natural disaster) to receive Communion as viaticum a second time during the same day even if outside of Mass. In fact, the code strongly suggests that the person receive again in such circumstances.

Cases where these canons might most frequently apply are in which a person has attended Mass on Saturday morning and then attends a Mass on Saturday evening to satisfy the Sunday obligation. The person may receive at both Masses. The same applies for someone who attends a daily Mass in the parish and then attends a wedding or funeral Mass in the evening. Again, the person may receive in both instances.

Are chasubles, gold chalices and sitting in the chair necessary parts of the Mass?

The *General Instruction of the Roman Missal* indicates the celebrant conducts the opening rite from the chair. He reads the Gospel (and other readings, if necessary) from the lectern (ambo). The homily is given from the lectern or chair. The priest also directs the prayer of the faithful from the chair or lectern. For the Eucharist he takes his place at the altar. After Communion the celebrant may return to the chair.

The instruction states the celebrant is to be vested in alb, stole and chasuble. Outside a church (such as on a cruise ship), he may use a chasuble-alb (chasalb, a one-piece vestment) with a stole.

The instruction states that liturgical vessels are to be made from solid (not easily breakable) and noble materials (327–329). Chalices should have a cup of nonabsorbent material (wood would not be acceptable).

What should one do when the chalice is spilled?

A sacrarium is a special sink in the sacristy. It is special because it drains directly into the soil underneath the church rather than into a common drain.

The *General Instruction of the Roman Missal* states, "If any of the precious blood spills, the area should be washed and the water poured into the sacrarium." So, too, should the purificators used to cleanse chalices, patens and ciboria be washed in the sacrarium and the water drained into the earth.

If there should be no sacrarium, water from these washings may be poured on clean earth in a garden where it will not be stepped on. After the first washing altar cloths upon which the Precious Blood have been spilled may be allowed to dry and then washed in a normal way.

Can a eucharistic host be retained for home worship?

By canon law, the Blessed Sacrament *must* be reserved in cathedral or parish churches, and in churches or oratories attached to the houses of religious institutes.

The Eucharist *may* be reserved in a bishop's chapel and, with the local ordinary's (usually a bishop's) permission, in other churches, oratories and chapels.

The law in all cases requires that the Sacrament be kept in a church, chapel or oratory. And there are other requirements about a fixed and solid tabernacle.

The law also requires that someone be responsible for the custody and care of the Blessed Sacrament, and that a priest celebrate Mass at the place of reservation with some frequency. That is to make sure the hosts do not age and go stale or moldy.

The law does not permit reservation of the Eucharist in private homes. The purpose of reserving the Eucharist is to have the Blessed Sacrament available as viaticum for those near death, Communion outside of Mass and adoration of the Lord present in the Eucharist. Reservation in private homes does not very well fit those purposes, and it is difficult to guarantee that the Sacrament will be treated with proper respect.

John M. Huels, in *More Disputed Questions in the Liturgy,* notes that it would be within the law for a bishop to permit reservation of the Blessed Sacrament by a private person for an *urgent pastoral need.*

When would there be such a need? Perhaps a deacon lives miles from church and must bring Communion to sick Catholics in outlying districts. In such cases the bishop could permit private reservation with a statement of particular requirements.

Where should the tabernacle be?

At the Last Supper Jesus consecrated bread and wine and gave them to his apostles to eat and drink. No one suggests that anything remained to be kept and reverenced or put in a special place.

It was only with time that Christians began to reserve some of the consecrated Eucharist. And their purpose was to have the Sacrament available to give to the sick and dying. Thus, some place or container was necessary to reserve the Sacrament with proper dignity and reverence.

Once Christians began to reserve the Blessed Sacrament for the sick, they also began to adore Christ in the reserved Eucharist and spend time in prayer and reflection in the presence of the Blessed Sacrament. Associated with these periods of adoration and prayer came public eucharistic devotions, such as Holy Hours, processions in honor of the Blessed Sacrament and exposition of the Blessed Sacrament with Benediction following. These developments reflect that the faithful came to appreciate many aspects of the Eucharist over time.

All of these actions were distinct from the celebration of the Eucharist, where we reenact the Last Supper and make present again the sacrifice of Christ.

The bishops at Vatican II attempted to reemphasize the ancient, communal aspects of the Eucharist and Christ's presence. Today many liturgists and church leaders believe that it is confusing to call for Christ to become present in the Eucharistic Prayer when the Sacrament is already present on the altar in the tabernacle. It divides our attention.

When we are celebrating Mass our attention should be devoted to the eucharistic action and all that it implies and involves—not on the tabernacle.

Thus, the church urges that the places of celebrating Mass and reserving the Blessed Sacrament be distinct, that the altar and tabernacle be separated architecturally and structurally.

The U.S. Catholic bishops said, in *Built of Living Stones*, a document that gives guidelines on church art and architecture, that the tabernacle could be placed either "in the sanctuary, apart from the altar of celebration...or in a separate chapel suitable for adoration and for the private prayer of the faithful."

Speaking practically, a separate chapel will provide more quiet and foster greater reverence than the main body of church with people coming and going, choir practices and wedding rehearsals. St. Peter's in Rome and other great basilicas and cathedrals have had special Blessed Sacrament chapels in place since long before Vatican II.

If the parish wants to have special devotions, with a large number participating, the Blessed Sacrament can be exposed on the main altar and put back in the tabernacle afterward.

Can a priest say Mass alone?

Ordinarily at least one person should be present when a priest celebrates Mass. However, the law itself recognized there can be a just and reasonable cause for a priest to celebrate alone. And whether or not there is someone else present, the Mass would be valid.

Mere convenience or preference would not be sufficient reason to celebrate alone.

May anyone other than an ordained priest celebrate Benediction?

According to Canon 943 the minister of exposition of the Blessed Sacrament and the eucharistic blessing is a priest or deacon.

In special circumstances an acolyte, extraordinary minister of Communion or another person deputed by the local ordinary in accordance with the regulations of the diocesan bishop may expose the Blessed Sacrament for adoration. At the end of the period of veneration, that person may return the Sacrament to the tabernacle. Only the priest or deacon, however, may bless those present with the Blessed Sacrament.

Why do Catholics recite the creed every Sunday?

Although the creed is not recited at each and every Mass, it is proclaimed by the congregation at all Masses on Sundays, holy days and solemnities. We recite the creed partly to remind ourselves of who we are and what we are about. It marks our identity as Catholic believers.

This creed, as others, was born out of the quarrels and struggles of earlier centuries. It was meant to establish for ourselves just what we do believe about God and the saving acts of God in history.

There is, of course, always the danger that our recitation of the creed becomes mechanical, that we say the words without ever thinking what they mean or their significance for us as believers. The creed, like other prayers, should be a genuine proclamation of our belief in God and the truths God has revealed. By constantly reminding ourselves of what we believe, we should be moved to love and gratitude. We should be motivated to live as believers.

How long must one fast before receiving Communion?

Well into the late 1950s an absolute fast from midnight to the time of reception was of overriding importance. The law made no exceptions. Petitions for dispensation (for example, a priest with throat cancer who needed a glass of water after preaching so he could swallow) had to be referred to the Holy See.

In the 1960s the law began to change. The duration of the fast was reduced to three hours and eventually to today's present teaching: Canon 919.1 states that before receiving Holy Communion one should abstain for at least one hour from all food and drink except water and medicine.

The second part of the canon permits those advanced in age, those who suffer from an illness and the people who care for them to receive Communion even if they have taken something during the preceding hour. The diocesan bishop can even dispense the faithful from fasting when appropriate.

No one should simply ignore the requirement, however. It is there as an expression of reverence and to maintain the sacred character of the Eucharist.

The Eucharist is indeed a "holy meal." The point is to keep it holy. Saint Paul early in the history of the church warned against taking the Eucharist after overindulging in food and drink (see 1 Corinthians 11:17–34).

At the same time, though, moralists might say that if the celebrant of the Mass skips the homily or if someone decides there will be none of the usual hymns, people can take the hour in a *moral* sense. They can proceed to Communion even if their fast has been a few minutes short of the hour.

The weak and aged may surely take advantage of what the church allows them whether at church or in the sickroom.

What is the proper fast for Ash Wednesday and the Fridays of Lent?

The law of abstinence (observed on Ash Wednesday and the Fridays of Lent) binds all those who have completed their fourteenth year. It forbids eating meat.

Fasting on Ash Wednesday and Good Friday binds all those who have reached their majority, that is, all those who are eighteen years old. And it binds until the beginning of the sixtieth year (the day after one's fifty-ninth birthday).

Fasting on these days permits one full meal and two smaller meals that, together, do not equal another full meal. Those who must fast may not eat between meals, but they may have liquids. Milk and fruit juices are permitted to those fasting, as well as beer, coffee, tea and soft drinks between meals.

What should be said when ashes are distributed on Ash Wednesday?

The sacramentary and *The Book of Blessings* (translated from the Roman ritual) permit a choice of formulas for both the blessing of and sprinkling with ashes on Ash Wednesday. At the distribution of ashes the minister may say, "Remember, you are dust and to dust you will return," or, "Turn away from sin and be faithful to the gospel."

Ministers decide what they believe will be more meaningful or effective with their communities and under the circumstances in which they celebrate liturgy. One minister may believe it more important to remind those receiving the ashes of our mortality and the judgment to come. Another may feel it more important to stress the call to penance and to live the gospel because, hearing it as often as we have, we have come to take it so lightly.

Are parishes supposed to veil both crosses and statues during Lent?

The custom of veiling crosses and images during the last part of Lent has changed over the centuries. According to Adolf

290

Adam, in *The Liturgical Year,* in the eleventh century a cloth, called the "hunger cloth," was suspended in front of the altar beginning with the fifth Sunday of Lent. At the beginning of Lent public sinners were excluded from church. The hunger cloth may have been an acknowledgment that we all are sinners and are partaking in a "fast of the eyes." By the end of the thirteenth century, statues, crosses and pictures were veiled. Bishop William Durandus in Southern France explained the custom by saying Jesus veiled his divinity during his passion and that the Gospel of the Fifth Sunday of Lent ended by telling us, "Jesus hid himself and went out of the temple" (John 8:59). Later writers would tell us the veiling was to remind us of Jesus' humiliation and to imprint the image of the crucified Christ more deeply on our hearts.

In 1969 the *Commentary on the General Norms for the Liturgical Year* and the new Roman calendar said, "crosses and the images of the saints are not to be covered, henceforth, except in regions where the episcopal conferences judge it profitable to maintain this custom."

A note following the texts for the Mass of Saturday of the fourth week of Lent in the sacramentary reads:

> The practice of covering crosses and images in the Church may be observed, if the episcopal conference decides. The crosses are to be covered until the end of the celebration of the Lord's passion on Good Friday. Images are to remain covered until the beginning of the Easter Vigil.

May a Catholic receive Communion at an Orthodox Mass?

Canon 844.2 says that, as often as necessity requires it or genuine spiritual advantage recommends it, and provided that the danger of error or indifferentism is avoided, the faithful, for whom it is physically or morally impossible to go to a Catholic minister, may receive the sacraments of penance, Eucharist and the anointing of the sick from non-Catholic ministers in whose churches these sacraments are valid.

It is very unlikely that a Catholic living in ordinary circumstances in a large city would find it physically or morally impossible to receive the Eucharist from a Catholic minister. Therefore, it is not permissible to receive the Eucharist at an Orthodox wedding. Even if all the conditions seemed to be present, a Catholic might stop to ask or consider how members of the other church might feel about a nonmember receiving Communion in their church.

Is the traditional Latin Mass still valid?

The traditional Latin Mass is often called the Tridentine Mass. After Vatican II it was permitted to use the vernacular (in our case English) in celebrating the liturgy. In 1970 the new sacramentary and *Novus Ordo* (New Order of Mass), based on the decisions of Vatican II regarding the Mass, were put into use. To identify the Latin Mass with the Tridentine Mass, though, is not quite correct. Latin may be used in celebrating Mass according to the New Order, and a Latin text for the ordinary prayers and Eucharistic Prayers can be found in our English sacramentary.

For the sake of some people still attached to the Tridentine Mass, near the end of the 1980s, the Holy See allowed bishops to permit the use of the Tridentine rite under certain conditions. Among those conditions were that celebrants would follow the latest edition of the old Roman Missal published in 1962.

Also, those who petition for this permission must have no ties with groups that call into doubt the lawfulness and doctrinal soundness of the form of Mass approved by Pope Paul VI in 1969.

The basic doctrines of the church cannot and do not change. But surely the church and papacy have seen any number of changes over the centuries. Any good history of the church will show that. Even the Tridentine Mass differs in language and rites from the way the Eucharist was celebrated in New Testament times before the fourth-century introduction of church buildings. The appearance of the first *Code of Canon*

Law in 1917 and the revised code in 1983 testify to changing laws as changes in society and cultures take place.

What is a Gregorian Mass?

In his *Dialogues* Pope Saint Gregory the Great, who reigned from 590 to 604, says that he had requested that Mass be celebrated on thirty consecutive days for the soul of a monk named Justus. It is further said that at the end of the thirtieth Mass, Justus appeared to his brother and physician Copiosus to tell him that he had now been delivered from purgatory. An inscription in the Church of Ss. Andrew and Gregory tells us Saint Gregory was also assured that Justus had been freed from purgatory. Thus, the custom of offering thirty Masses on consecutive days (Gregorian Masses) became popular in Europe until the time of the Reformation.

A sermon by Pope Benedict XIII, in 1720, four years before he was elected pope, gave new life to the practice. He said,

> The reason for the special value of this custom lies in the merits of Saint Gregory who obtains by the great efficacy of his prayers the satisfactory virtue for these thirty Masses.

The Sacred Congregations of Indulgences declared the confidence of the faithful in Gregorian Masses pious and reasonable. And the constitutions of some religious orders direct that Gregorian Masses be celebrated for every deceased member. Gregorian Masses must be celebrated on thirty consecutive days without interruption. It is not necessary that the same priest celebrate each Mass, but the Mass must be said for just one particular deceased person.

Not every priest or community will accept the responsibility of celebrating Gregorian Masses. It is not always easy to celebrate Mass for the same intention thirty days in a row. Pastors have an obligation of celebrating Mass for their parishes on Sunday. Priests get sick. Other people want Masses said for their intentions.

Why do we receive palms on Palm Sunday?

The palm is a symbol of victory and triumph. It is associated with the rejoicing that comes with victory. Thus, saints, especially martyrs, are often depicted carrying the palm of victory—they have triumphed over sin and won the victory of heaven.

All the Gospels recall the triumphant entry of Jesus into Jerusalem before his passion and death. The Gospels tell us that the crowds lined the road, welcoming Jesus to the city. And they laid branches from the trees or reeds on the road before Jesus. John recalls, "...they took branches of palm trees and went out to meet him, shouting, 'Hosanna! Blessed is the one who comes in the name of the Lord...'" (12:13).

In the first part of the liturgy on Passion (Palm) Sunday, we commemorate and reenact Jesus' triumphant entry into Jerusalem. Palms are blessed and given to those present to carry in procession. In the blessing of palms the priest says, "Today we honor Christ our triumphant King by carrying these branches. May we honor you every day by living always in him."

Some of the palms blessed on Passion Sunday are later burned to provide ashes for use in the Ash Wednesday liturgy the following year.

Who should wash the parishioners' feet on Holy Thursday?

The washing of feet in the Mass of Holy Thursday reminds us of the service Jesus did to his disciples on the first Holy Thursday (at the Last Supper). It has a long and varied history in the ceremonies of the church and was part of an early baptismal rite. It was also an act performed by monastics in service of the poor and each other. The Council of Toledo in 694 required the washing of feet on Holy Thursday, directing that every bishop and priest was to wash the feet of his subjects. In the Missal of Pope Pius V (1570), the washing of feet was placed at the end of the Holy Thursday Mass.

The sacramentary puts the washing of the feet after the

Gospel telling how Jesus washed the feet of the apostles (John 13:1–15)—and the homily.

The rubric in the sacramentary states that those who have been chosen for the washing of feet are lead by the ministers to chairs prepared in a suitable place. Then the priest goes to each and, with the help of the ministers, pours water over each one's feet and dries them.

In other words the priest performs the washing of the feet with the assistance of other ministers. That does not seem unreasonable if there are a basin and towels as well as a pitcher of water to handle. The rubric, however, does not envision several people going around washing feet apart from the priest.

Can a baby be baptized during Lent?

Canon 856 of the *Code of Canon Law* says that although baptism may be celebrated on any day it is commendable to celebrate it ordinarily on Sunday or, if possible, at the Easter Vigil. The code also encourages baptism during the celebration of the Eucharist so that the relationship between baptism and Eucharist will be clearly seen.

The baptism ritual says much the same thing. And pastors are told that, in the case of adult baptisms, they should ordinarily arrange it so that the Rite of Election (enrollment in the Catechumenate) begins on the first Sunday of Lent and baptism (and the other sacraments of initiation) be celebrated at the Easter Vigil.

If Lent has or is about to begin, it is close enough to Easter to baptize only at the appropriate time of the Easter Vigil or in the Easter season. This is true of healthy infants as much as of adults.

Why do bishops wear miters?

Signs and Symbols in Christian Art, by George Ferguson, describes the miter as

> ...a tall headdress worn by cardinals, archbishops, bishops and some abbots. It is a liturgical hat and has a plain

and simple form as well as a more ornate and precious form with embroidery and stones.

The *Dictionary of the Liturgy,* by Jovian Lang, O.F.M., describes the miter this way:

> The front and back are stiff, shaped like inverted shields ending in a peak which are pressed apart when the miter is on the head. These two pieces are sewn together at the lower part, but a cleft separates them on the top.... Two wide lappets hang down from the back over the shoulders.

The miter is a sign of authority. When worn at Mass it is taken off for the Eucharistic Prayer. The "horns" of the miter are reminders of the rays of light that came from the head of Moses when he received the Ten Commandments and are also symbolic of the Old and New Testaments. According to Lang the use of the miter originated in Rome in the eleventh century.

Is "Here Comes the Bride" suitable music for a church wedding?

Principles to be followed in choosing wedding music are often set in guides prepared by archdiocesan worship and liturgy offices. The guidelines urge good taste and call for music appropriate to the liturgy and a church. They recommend that much of the music be sung by the entire congregation. And the music is to be sacred rather than secular in character.

Guidelines from the Rockville Centre, New York, diocese state,

> Music, instrumental or vocal, by text or context that does not speak to the religious dimension, or even negates it, is inappropriate. The texts of songs used in the liturgy should support the meaning of the rite, and be grounded in scriptural themes. Of primary importance is what we are celebrating: the mystery of God's love and human love in a covenant relationship. For these reasons, popular songs are not permitted in the wedding liturgy. Often times a couple will request a song that is "their"

song. After discussion, it may be determined that this song is best suited at the wedding reception.

In the judgment of practically all liturgical ministers and pastors, "Here Comes the Bride" does not meet the test of those or other guidelines. And this is not just a recent judgment. Pastors and liturgists even before Vatican II were protesting or outlawing the use of this march because it comes out of the secular rather than sacred realm. (By the way, the piece commonly called "Here Comes the Bride" is the wedding march from Richard Wagner's opera *Lohengrin*. It is the music sung by the chorus as Lohengrin and Elsa are about to enter the wedding chamber.)

To use what may sound like an exaggerated or even far-fetched comparison, what would most Catholics feel or think if they came to a funeral in church and someone began singing "Pore Jud (Is Daid)" from the Broadway musical *Oklahoma!*? That is the same kind of judgment many liturgists and pastors make in regard to "Here Comes the Bride."

May a layperson give a eulogy at a funeral Mass?

Number 141 of the *Order of Christian Funerals, Approved for Use in the Dioceses of America, by the National Conference of Bishops and Confirmed by the Apostolic See* states:

> A brief homily based on the readings should always be given at the funeral liturgy, but never any kind of eulogy. The homilist should dwell on God's compassionate love and on the paschal mystery of the Lord as proclaimed in the Scripture readings. Through the homily, the community should receive the consolation and strength to face the death of one of its members with a hope that has been nourished by the proclamation of the saving word of God.

Obviously, eulogy here means a talk that, in effect, canonizes the deceased and ignores the reality of sin and the need we all have of God's mercy and forgiveness. Liturgical law stipulates the homily is to be given by a priest or deacon.

It is important to realize, however, that the same *Order of Christian Funerals* (170 and 197) permits a friend or member of the family of the deceased person to speak at the final commendation following Mass or outside of Mass at the burial site. Number 170 reads,

> Following the prayer after Communion, the priest goes to a place near the coffin.... A member or friend of the family may speak in remembrance of the deceased before the final commendation begins.

Number 197 says substantially the same thing for when commendation takes place apart from Mass.

What is the church's teaching regarding cremation?

With the changes in church legislation now permitting cremation—if it is not chosen as a means of denying the resurrection or Christian doctrine—more and more questions about the practice are emerging. The *Order of Christian Funerals* (appendix two on cremation) makes it clear the church still strongly prefers burial of the deceased body, but allows for cremation. Cremated remains should be treated with respect always, in all their handling and during any ceremonies.

When a choice has been made for cremation it is recommended it take place after the funeral liturgy. When cremation and committal take place before the funeral liturgy, with the approval of the diocesan bishop, the liturgy may be celebrated with the ashes present.

Number 427 says in this case:

> The cremated remains of the body are to be placed in a worthy vessel (urn). A small table or stand is to be prepared for them at the place normally occupied by the coffin. The vessel containing the cremated remains may be carried to its place in the entrance procession or may be placed on this stand or table sometime before the liturgy begins.

Finally, the remains should be buried in a grave or put in a mausoleum or columbarium (place at a cemetery for cremains)—not kept in a home, or scattered on the ground somewhere or on a body of water.

Why are funeral Masses prohibited during Holy Week?

It is important to realize that a death during Holy Week results in special, stressful problems for both the family and the parish priest.

For the family, tragedy and grief come when everyone else is preparing to celebrate a joyous feast. Children may be coming home from college or distant cities to be with parents and relatives. Reunions and get-togethers may have been planned well in advance. Travel schedules and plane reservations are difficult to change. Now all the plans are upset. The family has to deal with that as well as the grief it feels.

Because of the special problems a death occasions right before Easter, the family may rightly want to have burial take place before the feast, whether death comes on Tuesday, Wednesday or even Thursday. Delaying the funeral to Monday so that a Mass may be celebrated could just prolong all the nervous tension and cause other significant problems.

Pastors need to think of that and be sympathetic and as accommodating as possible.

On the other hand, funerals and burials create unique difficulties for a parish and pastor during the last three days of Holy Week (the sacred triduum). The church has to be decorated, arranged and rearranged for the particular services or liturgy of each day. The pastor has to prepare homilies and study the once-a-year rehearsals with ministers and singers in the church. In places where a priest serves two different congregations, difficulties multiply.

Just as a pastor must be sympathetic, families need to remember the pastor's problems and be considerate in what they expect of him.

Further, church legislation does not permit a funeral Mass on any of the days of the Easter triduum (Holy Thursday, Good Friday or Holy Saturday). At the same time, it does not forbid burial from the church. The *Order of Christian Funerals* says that the rite for the funeral liturgy outside the Mass may be used on these days. It also says that this liturgy (outside of Mass) is *ordinarily* celebrated in the *parish church*. But it may also be celebrated in the home of the deceased, a funeral home or a cemetery chapel.

So, if burial is to take place on Holy Saturday, the body could be brought to the parish church and the prayers and rites outside of Mass be celebrated there.

Family considerations combined with time limitations and the availability of the church may make it very difficult to make such a burial service work. It may well require some give-and-take on the part of the family and pastor. Both have to approach the situation understanding each other's difficulties.

When a burial outside of Mass is necessary, it would be proper and desirable to have a memorial Mass for the deceased shortly after the holiday is past. That would give everyone an opportunity to express more fully their love for the deceased, gather in prayer for the person, show support for the family and offer sympathy and consolation to the mourners. Easter week, while we are rejoicing in Christ's Resurrection and the promise of our resurrection, is a marvelous time for such a memorial Mass.

Whenever death occurs priests and pastors should be mindful of the exhortation in The *Order of Christian Funerals*. They should show loving concern for the family of the deceased person. As much as possible, they should involve the family in planning the funeral celebrations and choosing between the available options.

Why do modern churches have fewer statues?

When pastors and congregations began to implement the decrees of Vatican II, they often experienced a need to remodel and adapt their churches and worship spaces. With the advent of concelebrated Masses and fewer side-altar celebrations, the need for side altars became less. With the emphasis on participation in the liturgy, proximity to the altar and visibility of the celebrant and ministers became important. When pastors, architects and designers looked to the conciliar documents and decrees of implementation for direction and guidelines they found statements on art and environment in worship and worship spaces. In the *Constitution on the Sacred Liturgy*, they were told to seek noble beauty rather than sumptuous display.

The *Constitution* told them,

> The practice of placing sacred images in churches so that they may be venerated by the faithful is to be maintained. Nevertheless, their number should be moderate and their relative positions should reflect right order. For otherwise the Christian people may find them incongruous and they may foster devotion of doubtful orthodoxy.

Are flags allowed in churches?

The U.S. bishops, more than fifteen years ago, reminded parishes and pastors of what is contained in their statement *Environment and Art in Catholic Worship*. There it said that, because ours is a truly Catholic church, symbols identifying particular cultures, groups or nations are not appropriate as permanent parts of the liturgical environment.

Such symbols (flags, for example) might be appropriate for a particular occasion or national holiday, the Bishops' Committee on the Liturgy said in its December 1982 newsletter. But it added that these symbols should not regularly be part of the environment of common prayer.

In 1991, at the time of the Persian Gulf War, the Cincinnati Archdiocesan Office of Worship, noting the presence of flags in church sanctuaries on a permanent basis, reminded people that this is inappropriate in view of the global character of the church, which transcends all boundaries.

That office suggested the flag might be displayed in other places, such as near the main entrance or on a flagpole outside the church. The director of the office added that even the state flag of Vatican City should not be displayed in the sanctuary.

$$\dagger$$

MORALITY

Consider *these two quotes from distinguished English Catholics. The first comes from John Henry Newman (1801–1890), cardinal, man of letters and former leader of the Anglican Oxford Movement. Referring to life in his day, he opined: "I read my Bible to know what people ought to do and my newspaper to know what they are doing."*

The second comes from G. K. Chesterton (1874–1936), famous novelist, essayist and apologist for the Christian faith. He comments: "It is not that Christianity has been tried and found wanting. It is that it has never been tried at all."

If only we were able to bridge better what we know we are called to do with what we do! That is the challenge of Christian morality. We must be careful, however, not to make morality a "to do list." Ultimately morality is more about relationship than behavior. Christians act the way they do because they are in relationship with Jesus the Christ, not the other way around. The beginning question for morality then is not, "What should I do?" but more "Who do I want to be?" Echoing the truth of Genesis and reality of the Incarnation, we proclaim that we want to be alter Christus, *"other Christs," images of God.*

The Catechism of the Catholic Church *begins its examination of the moral life by quoting a sermon of Saint Leo the Great. It reads:*

> *Christian recognize your dignity and, now that you share in God's own nature, do not return to your former base condition by sinning. Remember who is your head and of whose body you are a member. Never forget that you have been rescued from the power of darkness and brought into the light of the Kingdom of God. (1691)*

•

Is it possible never to sin?

The desire to lead a truly sinless life is the starting point for living in the grace of God and becoming a saint. The example of many saints in the past and very holy people around us today demonstrates that with prayer and desire we can succeed in the struggle for sanctity and avoid all grave sin.

Yet we also know from the saints how difficult that struggle can be. Saint Paul refers to our proneness to sin and identifies with us in the tension we feel between what he calls the Spirit and the flesh. In Galatians 5:16–17 he writes,

> Live by the Spirit, I say, and do not gratify the desires of the flesh. For what the flesh desires is opposed to the Spirit, and what the Spirit desires is opposed to the flesh; for these are opposed to each other, to prevent you from doing what you want.

Saint Francis of Assisi was always conscious of his own weakness and admonished admirers not to praise him because it was always possible he would seriously fail. Once he was so severely tempted to sin against chastity that he threw himself into a rosebush and rolled in its thorns to overcome the temptation.

Adolphe Tanquerey in *The Spiritual Life,* reminds us that the saints themselves commit venial sins of frailty by allowing themselves to be momentarily betrayed through thoughtlessness or weakness of will. He does not excuse such failings and says they, like all sins, are to be deplored. He simply recognizes the human condition.

Because we have been so affected by original sin, Saint James reminds us, "All of us make many mistakes" (James 3:2). The Council of Trent declared that even for the just person *without a special privilege of grace* it will be morally impossible to avoid all venial sins throughout his or her whole life.

We must not become discouraged, give up hope or abandon the struggle with temptation. A high degree of holiness or perfection can be reached if we are faithful to God's grace. Because of our proneness to sin, we must pray and practice self-denial and mortification. We must make frequent use of the sacraments of reconciliation and the Eucharist.

Father Tanquerey suggests that in addition to these means of grace we use the daily examination of conscience—looking back over what faults or sins we have committed and asking ourselves how or why we failed. After discovering the circumstances and reasons that led to sin, we can plan how to avoid the occasions and situations that led us to fall. Then, being faithful to prayer and living in the spirit of penance, we can detach ourselves from the habits of sin that impede our growth in the love of God and true holiness.

God never gives up on any of us, and we must not give up on ourselves.

How can we be free to love God when we are commanded to do so?

Asking why we are commanded to love God is something like asking why Newton pronounced a law of gravity.

There is a law of gravity because that is the nature of our universe and creation. If Newton had never discovered and proclaimed the law of gravity, it would remain true that there is an attraction between the earth and bodies near its surface. That is the way God made things.

Whether Jesus or Deuteronomy ever proclaimed we must love God and our neighbor, it would remain true that we exist to love God and one another.

The old catechism asked, "Why did God make me?" The answer was, "God made me to know him, to love him, to serve him, and to be happy with him in heaven."

We can only know happiness if we realize our purpose in life, if we fulfill the purpose for which we are made. We are created to love and give glory to God. Only through union to God in love can we ultimately be happy and fulfilled. To be turned from God in sin, to despise or fail to love is to be emotionally torn apart. God is love: To be separated from God is agony.

We should think of the two great commandments—in fact, all of the commandments—not so much as laws in a legal sense but as statements of principles or guidelines. Thus, to be happy and enter into the joy of God's kingdom, you must love God and each other. To be true to your purpose and the way you have been created, you must live and act in love of God and one another.

The fact that God proclaims these laws makes it easier for us to understand who we are, what we are about and how we must live in order to find eternal happiness. It is to state plainly what you already perceived when you said, "It seems that one would just naturally feel drawn to love God." We are. And to resist, to turn away from God, can mean only pain in the end, though we have the capacity, the freedom to do just that.

How do we fulfill the commandments to love God and neighbor?

Concerning the love of God, Jesus tells his disciples at the Last Supper, "If you love me, you will keep my commandments" (John 14:15), and, "Remain in my love. If you keep my commandments, you will remain in my love, just as I have kept my Father's commandments and remain in his love" (John 15:9–10).

When it comes to love of neighbor, Jesus tells his disciples at the Last Supper, "This is my commandment: Love one another as I love you. No one has greater love than this, to lay down one's life for one's friends" (John 15:12–13).

In other words Jesus is the living example of what it means to love both God and neighbor.

Jesus practices what he preaches in the compassion he shows the suffering and sorrowful, the forgiveness he extends to sinners—to even those who nail him to the cross. You will see his love of God acted out in his faithfulness to the will of the Father. He acts out his love in giving his own life for the salvation of the world.

Jesus explains the meaning of the love of neighbor in the parables, particularly the parable of the Good Samaritan in the tenth chapter of Luke and the parable of the Prodigal Son in the fifteenth chapter of Luke.

Jesus also explains the meaning of love in his description of the Last Judgment in Matthew 25:31–46. He tells his disciples that when they feed the hungry, give drink to the thirsty, clothe the naked, visit the sick and those in prison, they do these things to him and will be admitted into the kingdom of heaven. When they fail the hungry, the naked, the sick and imprisoned, they fail to show love to him and will be condemned for their lack of love.

To better understand the meaning of love, read the description of the way the first Christian community in Jerusalem lived (Acts 4:32–37). Pray over the first letter of John as he offers the test of love:

> We know love by this, that he laid down his life for us— and we ought to lay down our lives for one another. How does God's love abide in anyone who has the world's goods and sees a brother or sister in need and yet refuses help? Little children, let us love, not in word or speech, but in truth and action. (1 John 3:16–18)

Finally, while James speaks of treating the poor and shabbily dressed in the same way as we treat the wealthy and well dressed and of the necessity of good deeds in the context of faith, we could just as well substitute the word *love*.
Recall his words,

> If a brother or sister is naked and lacks daily food, and one of you says to them, "Go in peace; keep warm, and

eat your fill," and yet you do not supply their bodily needs, what is the good of that? So faith by itself, if it has no works, is dead. (James 2:15–17)

What is an act of perfect contrition or an act of perfect love?

When we speak of an act of contrition being perfect, we are talking about the motive for contrition. This contrition is perfect because it proceeds from a perfect motive—the love of God. The sinner grieves because he or she has offended the all-good, loving and lovable God. The sinner deeply regrets having offended God much as a husband might grieve because he has offended the wife he deeply loves. The sinner realizes that sin is inconsistent with love. Because sin offends God and interferes with perfect union with God, it is to be lamented and eliminated.

Love is perfect when we love God for God's own sake—because God is good and first loved us. Love is perfect when we make God the center of our lives. Then we try to please God in everything we do. Our first reason for loving God is because God is lovable and we can only be happy and fulfilled by loving God and being loved by God. Again, our first motive for loving is God's own goodness rather than what God can do for us (see *Catechism of the Catholic Church* 1452).

Contrition is imperfect when the motive is imperfect: The reason we are sorry for our sins is that sin brings punishment.

Where does the saying about "the sins of the fathers" come from, and is there any truth to it?

In the book of Exodus (20:5), after the commandment not to carve idols, we read:

For I, the Lord, your God am a jealous God, punishing children for the iniquity of parents, to the third and the fourth generation of those who reject me, but showing steadfast love to the thousandth generation of those who love and keep my commandments.

Euripides is supposed to have said, "Visit the sins of the fathers upon the children." Horace is reported as saying, "For the sins of your fathers you, though guiltless, must suffer." Shakespeare, in *The Merchant of Venice*, says, "The sins of the fathers are to be laid upon the children."

Also in the Bible both Jeremiah and Ezekiel refer to a saying common among Jews: "The parents have eaten sour grapes, and the children's teeth are set on edge" (Ezekiel 18:2 and Jeremiah 31:29). They referred to a proverb by which the people were claiming they were being punished for their ancestors' sins rather than their own.

From one point of view, the saying is true. Later generations can suffer greatly as a result of their ancestors' sins. This is what we are talking about when we describe the effects of the sin of Adam and Eve. Certainly in our own time, later generations have suffered much as a result of wars waged by their parents and grandparents. If we misuse the earth, destroy the rainforests of South America, pollute our own rivers and air and poison the soil with toxic waste, those who come after us will pay a heavy price.

But Ezekiel's reason for citing the proverb was to challenge his own generation of coreligionists who were exempting themselves from guilt, picturing themselves as innocent victims of what their ancestors had done.

Ezekiel demands they face up to their own sinfulness and convert. Therefore, he confronts them by saying,

> What do you mean by repeating this proverb concerning the land of Israel, "The parents have eaten sour grapes, and the children's teeth are set on edge"? As I live, says the Lord God, this proverb shall no more be used by you in Israel. Know that all lives are mine: it is only the person who sins that shall die. (18:2–4)

And he goes on to say, "A child shall not suffer for the iniquity of a parent, nor a parent suffer for the iniquity of a child; the righteousness of the righteous shall be his own, and the wickedness of the wicked shall be his own" (Ezekiel 18:20). After further calling for conversion he says, "Therefore I will judge you, house of Israel, all of you according to your ways, says the Lord God" (Ezekiel 18:30).

Jeremiah (31:29–30) also challenges his hearers, "In those days they shall no longer say, 'The parents have eaten sour grapes, and the children's teeth are set on edge.' But all shall die for their own sins; the teeth of everyone who eats sour grapes shall be set on edge."

And, to round things out, we might recall that Deuteronomy 24:16, in stating the law, prescribes, "Parents shall not be put to death for their children, nor shall children be put to death for their parents; only for their own crimes may persons be put to death."

A great deal depends on the point of view taken by the authors or speakers and whether they approach sin from the viewpoint of its effects or guilt. The point is that, while we may be affected by the sins of those who have gone before us (or even contemporaneous with us), we do not inherit moral guilt. While we suffer because of others' sins, we can be innocent and pleasing in God's eyes.

What Is the Heroic Act?

A practice of piety called the Heroic Act has been encouraged by the Theatine Order. It is called heroic because of the complete selflessness involved in the practice. According to T. C. O'Brien in the *Encyclopedic Dictionary of Religion*, persons who make the Heroic Act offer to God any and all indulgences they might gain as well as expiatory works, and all prayers offered for them after death.

The Heroic Act should not be confused with Saint Louis Marie de Montfort's act of total consecration to Mary or the offering made by "victim souls."

De Montfort urged that the most perfect devotion to Mary was in consecrating self entirely to her, and Jesus through her, becoming a slave of Mary. That means completely consecrating self to Mary for all eternity—body, soul, spiritual and material possessions, the atoning value and merits of our good actions and the right to dispose of them, past, present and future.

310

The act of victim souls is to accept suffering without reservation in union with the self-offering of Christ in atonement for sin. O'Brien remarks that this offering is not to be made lightly or easily permitted by a spiritual director. The same is true of the Heroic Act and total consecration. They should not be spur-of-the-moment actions, but thoughtful and mature acts.

Is AIDS God's punishment for sin?

We cannot speak of AIDS as God's punishment for sin unless we also want to speak of emphysema as God's punishment for smoking, fallen arches as God's punishment for being overweight, or clogged arteries and heart trouble as God's punishment for eating too much butter and fatty foods.

AIDS is caused by a virus, one that can be transmitted through a number of activities, some immoral and some not. People have gotten AIDS from contaminated blood transfusions or even an infected dentist. If it were God's special punishment, why would the innocent, such as the newborns of AIDS mothers or a nurse pricked by a contaminated syringe, get AIDS?

There is a kind of built-in natural punishment for abusing our bodies and violating nature. But we ought not think of God sitting on high waiting to zap one particular group of people for a particular kind of immorality. For what particular sin is cholera the punishment?

In 1985 an editorial writer in *The Long Island Catholic* made an interesting observation about calling AIDS God's punishment:

> AIDS, of course, has been associated with homosexual activity or drug addiction. But it is simply nonsense to say that this is God's punishment for the people who act in these ways. Otherwise what shall we say when, at some future time, a cure is found—that God has changed his mind about these ways of behaving?

About that same time, the National Conference of Catholic Bishops' Administrative Committee issued a statement, *The*

Many Faces of AIDS: A Gospel Response. Archbishop Daniel Pilarczyk explained,

> The statement urges Catholics to respond to disease and suffering as Jesus did—not as an occasion for blame or condemnation, but as an opportunity to show God's love to those who are afflicted. It deplores prejudice and discrimination, and especially any form of violence, directed against persons with the AIDS virus or members of high-risk groups.

Almost all bishops and religious writers who have spoken to this question have said much the same thing: Our attitude should be one of compassion, mercy, caring and charity.

What was the sin of Sodom?

Whatever the original concepts behind the words *sodomy* and *sodomite*, there seems little or no doubt about what the author of Genesis had in mind in speaking of the sin of Sodom.

The writer of the comments on Genesis in the *Collegeville Bible Commentary,* Pauline A. Viviano, says, "There is no doubt about what the Yahwist believed that evil to have been. It is what accounts for the presence in all our modern languages of *sodomy.*"

A footnote to this text in the *New American Bible* states:

> Israelite tradition was unanimous in ascribing the destruction of Sodom and Gomorrah to the wickedness of these cities, but tradition varied in regard to the nature of this wickedness. According to the present account of the Yahwist the sin of Sodom was homosexuality [homosexual behavior] (Genesis 19:4–5) which is therefore also known as sodomy; but according to Isaiah (1:9–10, 3:9) it was a lack of social justice; Ezekiel (16:46–51) described it as disregard for the poor, whereas Jeremiah (23:14) saw it as general immorality.

It seems obvious Sodom was guilty of many sins and was thought of as a cesspool of vices. Part of the horror at the act of the Sodomites is the inhospitableness behind it. This abuse of travelers and strangers was a crime. The obligation of hospitality explains but does not justify Lot's act in offering the crowd his daughters instead of his visitors—once under his roof he owed his guests protection.

Finally, we know what the Israelites thought of homosexual behavior from Leviticus 20:13, "If a man lies with a male as with a woman, both of them have committed an abomination; they shall be put to death; their blood is upon them."

The Catholic church teaches that homosexual orientation itself is no sin, but that homosexual acts are by definition sinful (see *Catechism of the Catholic Church* 2357–2359).

What is the church's moral position on sex-change operations?

There are cases where a child is born with "ambiguous" genital organs. The child seems partly male, partly female. If the characteristics of one sex seem predominant it is permissible to help the child by surgery to live as a person of that sex. Where there is no predominance, Father Kevin O'Rourke, O.P., says in *Medical Ethics: Common Ground for Understanding*, parents should raise the child as belonging to the sex in which it is most likely to function best. Again, surgery will be acceptable if it will be helpful or necessary for this.

There are other cases, however, where a person who is physically or biologically a male speaks of himself as a woman trapped in a man's body. There is a kind of hatred of the person's own anatomical sex. The man or woman wants to be a member of the opposite sex. This is called Gender Dysphoria Syndrome.

Some psychiatrists propose reconstructive surgery to remedy the pain and anguish of such confusion of sexual identity. By surgery they would construct pseudosexual organs of the opposite sex. The man would be given the genital appearances of a woman, or a woman those of a man. Other characteristics would be altered with synthetic hormonal treatment. The surgery is called sexual reassignment.

Those who write on this subject acknowledge the psychic pain and anguish of those who experience this conflict over sexual identity. They urge that such people be treated with compassion. But with Benedict Ashley, O.P., O'Rourke writes in *Health Care Ethics* that transsexualism is a medical diagnosis with no definite meaning. There are no definite medical symptoms or dynamic giving rise to symptoms. Further, complete change cannot be achieved through surgery. The altered male will not be able to ovulate or conceive. The altered female will not be able to produce sperm or physically father a child. So it is that Father Thomas O'Donnell, S.J., in *Medicine and Christian Morality*, states that in his opinion such surgery does not actually change the sex of the individual.

For those who would agree with that conclusion, the moral question becomes quite evident: Is it morally acceptable to make this artificial substitution in order to try to help an individual adjust to a psychological aberration for which present psychiatry seems to have no adequate cure? Clearly, O'Donnell says, it is not morally acceptable for a number of reasons. Among those reasons is the fact that reconstructive surgery is not really a cure. The sex of the individual is not really changed. That was recognized by a New York court that refused to alter the sex designation on a transsexual's birth certificate. It called the surgery simply a mutilation.

O'Rourke and Ashley see this kind of reconstructive surgery as an effort to make a person's illusions or fantasies become reality. They say it is no favor to help the person live out an illusion. These authors conclude, "Thus it seems this type of surgery is intrinsically outside the limits of ethical medicine since its purpose is not genuine treatment of a psychological illness, but an illusory adjustment involving a destructive loss of bodily integrity."

O'Donnell sums up his evaluation by saying, "In the context of Catholic teaching, such a mutilation would clearly seem to involve a totally irresponsible lack of that due stewardship of human life and the integrity of one's person that the fact of creation demands."

Are images of Jesus and the saints idols?

A story by Stephen Vincent Benet titled "By the Waters of Babylon" chronicles a traveler finding the ruins of a previous civilization. Throughout the story the hero kept coming across an idol of the god Ashing. At story's end the reader discovers Benet has looked into the future and the city of New York, after some great catastrophe. The idol is simply the ruins of a bust of George Washington. People can misinterpret, misconstrue and fail to understand what others are doing or have done.

The General Council of Nicaea II (A.D. 787) declared that it is permissible to show images of Christ, the Mother of God, angels and the saints reverent homage but not adoration which is due to God alone. The council said that the reverence shown to such images is veneration referred to the prototype. The Council of Trent renewed and repeated what Nicaea II had said. Trent again stressed the relative character of any such reverence.

Are those who carry photos of spouses or children in their wallets or display them on their desks "worshipping" them? Are all those tourists going out to see the Statue of Liberty in New York, the Lincoln Memorial in Washington, D.C., or the faces of the presidents on Mount Rushmore guilty of idolatry?

Those statues, like pictures of George Washington in so many courthouses, are ways of honoring heroes from the past. They put us in touch with great people in our history. They become occasions for teaching children about the past and offering examples of great citizens.

Stained-glass windows, statues and paintings have long served these same purposes in the church. Crucifixes, statues of the Good Shepherd or Sacred Heart remind us of Jesus' sacrifice and love for us. Statues of Mary and the saints recall the heroism of the saints and suggest to us what we should strive to become (*Catechism of the Catholic Church* 2129–2132).

They are occasions for telling the children of today about the real saints and heroes of the past, for telling children what it means to live out their faith and religion. To all of us they offer the occasion to reflect and pray on the action of God in our lives. They help us to better sentiments of piety, call upon us to express our own faith and love. In honoring the saint we honor God who has worked such good and holy things in and through the saint.

How does the church distinguish between art and pornography?

In talking about obscenity, Supreme Court Justice Potter Stewart said that he couldn't define it but he knew it when he saw it. Many of us could say much the same thing about pornography. Whether we can define it in exact terms, most of us can recognize it when we see it. We can usually recognize the intention of those who produce and sell pornographic works and their intended appeal to buyers and viewers.

The Catholic bishops of California, in *Human Dignity and the Sacredness of Sexuality: Statement of the California Catholic Conference on Pornography* (May 29, 1986), spoke of pornography in connection with the Greek expression from which the word comes. They said it was coined to describe sexually arousing depictions of women being displayed or used as sexual slaves. They then went on to quote Margaret Mead's definition, "Words or acts or representations that are calculated to stimulate sexual feelings independent of the presence of another loved and chosen human being."

The statement goes on to say,

Both definitions suggest that pornography demeans women (and often enough, men, too, and children of both sexes) and profanes the most sacred aspect of sex, its relationship to love and the hope of human life. Such degradation of persons and distortions of human love and sexuality undermine those beliefs and values which form the foundation of the family and are essential to the healthy survival of truly human communities. In sum, pornography threatens the innate dignity of individuals and erodes the moral fiber of society.

The *Catechism of the Catholic Church* (2354) says much the same and terms it a grave offense.

Incidentally, the Attorney General's Commission on Pornography used a similar definition, saying pornography means material that "is predominately sexually explicit and intended primarily for the purpose of sexual arousal."

In 1988 the bishops of Wisconsin issued *An Ethical Evaluation of Pornography and a Call for Legislative Action*. In summarizing official statements and Catholic moral teaching, they divided pornographic works into four categories and assessed each category.

The first category was sexually violent material. This, they said, includes sadomasochistic depictions and, more destructively, the "rape myths" presenting a woman upon whom a man violently forces himself "eventually becoming aroused and ecstatic about the initially forced sexual activity, and usually portrayed as begging for more."

They noted that some of the sexual activity is coupled with extreme violence, such as disfigurement or even murder. Calling this kind of material evil and repulsive, they noted among other effects that it contradicts the inherent orientation of sex to human love. It depicts physical assault and abuse in a favorable and alluring light and misleads actual or potential aggressors.

The second category named was nonviolent material depicting degradation, domination, subordination and humiliation. This type of pornography presents some people as existing solely for others' sexual pleasure and assaults the dignity of the subordinated party.

The third category was nonviolent and nondegrading materials. Materials in this category present explicit sexual activity between consenting equals usually outside any context of marriage, love, commitment or even affection. These materials raise the issues of promiscuity and public morality and sometimes foster an atmosphere of alluring intrigue, infidelity and promiscuity.

The fourth category was nudity, especially when it becomes highly provocative in connoting sexual activity. Significantly, in relation to the question, the Wisconsin bishops say here,

Such nudity, if it excludes force, degradation or sexual activity, may be artistic, aesthetically transforming the raw facts into expressive form. However, it may at times border on the provocative and in such cases should be assessed as such. This material, moreover, can have a negative impact on children, or sexual relationships, and on the general moral climate.

True, some of the great painters have painted nudes. And there are nude figures in paintings hanging in churches and the Vatican museums. After some of them were painted and hung, later authorities came along and had other artists paint things such as fig leaves to cover exposed body parts. So it is evident people, including church people, can have different ideas of what is modest or artistic, as opposed to obscene and pornographic, in particular cases.

Most of us have little trouble differentiating a nude painting by Titian or a sculpture by Michelangelo from a *Playboy* centerfold and determining the painter's or photographer's intentions. We know what *Playboy*, *Hustler* or *Penthouse* is trying to sell to potential buyers.

Is it a mortal sin for an adult Catholic to see movies that are morally offensive?

Sins are committed by individuals. Each person must judge whether a movie will be an occasion of sin for him or her. To do so, one can read reviews, consult others, judge from my one's experience. Each person must form their own conscience and follow it.

A good source for information is the reviews and classification of the U.S. Bishops' Office for Film and Broadcasting. While they are reliable, they are personal or group opinions. Individual reviewers or classifiers within the office may not agree on the worthiness, message or moral effect of a picture. Such judgments are subjective.

Different people and different reviewers, for instance, have had different interpretations of countless movies. Accordingly, they differed in their moral evaluations of the films.

318

Elements in a story can be morally offensive without the picture being an occasion of sin. Just because a character murders his brother and marries his widow and the dead man's son seeks revenge (*Hamlet*) does not mean the play would be an occasion of sin.

According to the head of the Office for Film and Broadcasting, the office does not intend to censor pictures. The office offers information and evaluations so people can make their own informed decisions.

In the end each person must judge and follow his or her own conscience.

Does the church approve of psychic consultations?

There is a great deal of interest today in the powers and forces that exist in this world of ours. Things that would have seemed outlandish to rational people's imaginations just a hundred years ago—even fifty or twenty years ago—are now taken for granted. It is not unreasonable to believe that "there is more in the world than meets the eye."

We know so little about the human mind. Scientists tell us that our conscious life uses up the tiniest portion of the millions of brain cells that we have. Why does God give us so much brain capacity that we seem not to need?

Some people claim to, and even seem to, have a sixth sense by which they can tune into what is going on in a subject's life. This is something that we can neither prove nor dismiss out of hand.

The church is extremely cautious about this sort of thing. We have no business consorting with "spirits"—any invisible world that has nothing to do with God and belief, with repentance and submission to his will. God does not intend for us to know the future—or to know anything about him or the "invisible world"—except those things necessary and useful to our salvation. That is, we ought to seek to know God's will for us and the power to carry it out. For the Church's official response to this subject, consult the *Catechism of the Catholic Church* (2115–2117).

People who have special gifts, if they are really of God, should lead us to God and help us repent of our sinfulness, willfulness and self-centeredness. They should help us rely on God and God alone and to discover his will.

An additional consideration is that God's special gifts are not for sale. This is what makes me particularly concerned and suspect either fraud or a bad attitude on the part of "gifted" people who charge a fee. It is not wrong to watch a TV show that features such performances, or to find them remarkable. But it is not wise to spend money to engage the services of such a person.

What is the origin of the seven capital sins?

As commonly listed today, the seven deadly or capital sins are pride, envy, anger, sloth, avarice, gluttony and lust. They are inclinations that unchecked give rise to many sins. They are called *capital* sins because they are the fountainheads from which other sins flow.

According to Henry Fairlie in *The Seven Deadly Sins*, classifying the deadly sins had its origin in the monastic movement and "the list was first framed in the cloisters of Eastern Europe." John Cassian of Marseilles (360–435) introduced the rules of Eastern monasticism to the West, including the notion of eight deadly sins. These sins were not identical with the list used today.

Cassian's list of sins was modified by Pope Gregory the Great in the sixth century. It is his list that we use today. Gregory defined the deadly sins in such a way that they can be applied to the ordinary conditions of life rather than seen just as temptations that must be resisted by those in monasteries.

Fairlie notes it was once required in England that pastors preach on the deadly sins four times a year. That may explain why we find the parson in Chaucer's *Canterbury Tales* ("The Parson's Tale") preaching to the pilgrims on the seven deadly sins, inviting them to consider the extravagance of their clothing, the richness of their food, the raising of their children, greediness of landlords, deceit of merchants and the backbiting of gossips.

Is it a sin to miss Mass on Sunday?

The church has not abolished the law requiring Catholics to participate in the celebration of Mass on Sunday and holy days of obligation. Canon 1247 reads, "On Sunday and other holy days of obligation the faithful are obliged to participate in the Mass...."

The *Catechism of the Catholic Church* reminds us, "The Sunday Eucharist is the foundation and confirmation of all Christian practice" (2181). It goes on to say,

> For this reason the faithful are obliged to participate in the Eucharist on days of obligation, unless excused for a serious reason (for example, illness, the care of infants) or dispensed by their own pastor. Those who deliberately fail in this obligation commit a grave sin.

Note, there is a precept to participate in Mass on Sundays and holy days of obligation and it binds gravely. At the same time there can be serious reasons that excuse a person from observing the law.

Manuals of theology published before the present *Code of Canon Law* spoke of moderately grave reasons that would excuse. Besides illness, distance from the church, police duty, the need to shut down mills that run around the clock, the grave displeasure of a spouse or parents, the demand of an employer, fire and flood emergencies, care of the ill and being on a journey were listed as examples of such moderately grave reasons.

At least one of these manuals offered that "One may miss Mass for the sake of a pleasure trip once or twice if he has no other opportunity during the year or if it is the last opportunity he will ever have for a certain excursion."

It is also pertinent to note that when the church revised the rules concerning penance and fast and abstinence, it introduced the concept of substantial observance. Explaining Pope Paul IV's apostolic constitution *Paenitemini,* and a reply concerning it from the Sacred Congregation of the Council concerning substantial observance, John M. Huels, O.S.M., wrote,

> The substantial observance of the laws of fast and abstinence does not pertain to individual days but to the whole complexus of penitential days, i.e., one only sins gravely who, without an existing excuse omits a notable part, quantitative or qualitative, of the penitential observance which is prescribed as a whole.

Some moralists have argued that the same norm of substantial observance should be applied to the precept of Sunday Mass. They suggest that to regularly and habitually violate this law would indeed be a grave matter. But they believe to miss Sunday Mass on one or the other time without an excusing cause would not be a serious sin—unless done with contempt of the law. It may be that some people translate this to say it is no longer a sin to miss Mass on Sunday, but that is not what these moralists are saying. It is important to note that a Catholic who misses Mass without serious excuse under the mistaken impression that he or she is entitled to a "freebie" could well be guilty of contempt for the Mass.

Also, the *Code of Canon Law* does not set any age at which a person is no longer obliged to attend Mass on Sundays and holy days. The presumption is that as long as we are able we have a duty to worship God and nurture ourselves spiritually through participating in the Mass. Whatever the reasoning of the lawgiver, the law obliges as long as a person is reasonably able to observe it.

Obviously, however, there are age-related factors that make it very difficult (even impossible) for a person to attend Mass on a particular Sunday or even all Sundays. People in such circumstances or situations are excused from observing this church law.

Some practical examples: An elderly person may have great difficulty walking, have no car or have no one willing and able to drive him or her to the church. Another senior citizen may be unable to sit long without having to go to the bathroom. An older person who is completely exhausted by the effort of getting to church, comes home feeling ill for the rest of the day or must go back to bed right away is excused. If rain, exposure to very cold weather, or snow-covered walks threaten injury, catching cold or the flu, an older person is excused.

People must look at themselves and their own particular problems and circumstances and make the judgment whether they are excused from attending Mass on this one Sunday or all Sundays. Making this judgment or decision should not be an agonizing affair. It is largely a matter of using common sense.

What are we to consider as "servile work" on Sunday?

A change in social and economic systems has taken place over nearly all of the world. True, there may be labor that is still literally the work of slaves or comparable to slave work. But nearly everywhere slavery has been abolished as well as feudal systems with indenture to masters. What was once "servile work" is no longer necessarily the work of slaves and servants but work performed by anyone in society. And servants and slaves do not need protection from heartless masters who would work them to death every day of the week, including Sunday, unless there were a law to stop them.

As a consequence, the new *Code of Canon Law* does not even employ the term *servile labor*. Canon 1247 says simply,

> On Sundays and other holy days of obligation the faithful are bound to participate in the Mass; they are also to *abstain from those labors and business concerns which impede the worship to be rendered to God, the joy which is proper to the Lord's Day, or the proper relaxation of mind and body* [italics added].

Note the shift in emphasis in the new code. As Father Thomas Richstatter, O.F.M., points out in *The Code of Canon Law: A Text and Commentary*, the focus in the 1917 code was on the kind of work. The new Code directs our attention to the purpose of the celebration of the day and the joy and leisure necessary for that celebration.

Observing this law is largely a matter of personal judgment and conscience. The individual will know when he or she is living in the spirit of the law and observing its essentials. Participating in the Eucharist is surely part of observing the Lord's Day. But what kind of work and business interferes with the joy and relaxation of mind that should characterize the Lord's Day may be different for you and me. A business executive might well find it relaxing to spend some time mowing the grass or building a cabinet, while a farmer or carpenter would find that work. A salesperson might find it fun to do gourmet cooking, while a restaurant chef could find it tiring to fix bacon and eggs for breakfast. And if hard and tiring work (mentally or emotionally tiring as well as physically tiring) is necessary, we will have to judge for ourselves how much of that labor we can perform without contravening the purpose of this law.

It is wise to use part of Sunday for prayer, Mass, spiritual reading or reflection. If there is some work that must be done and it can be done in a reasonable amount of time, do it. If sewing, washing the car, cutting the roses back seems more hobby than work, it is not destroying Sunday observance to spend a reasonable time for that. If you are a family person, there should be time for family events, time to be spent with each other, time to listen to and get to know one another better, and to have fun together. You should not go back to work on Monday feeling more dispirited than when you left on Friday or Saturday.

In closing, you may find helpful Pope John Paul II's recent thoughts on this issue and others related to the Lord's Day in his 1998 apostolic letter, *Celebrating the Lord's Day*. Likewise, in commenting on the observance of Sunday, the *Catechism of the Catholic Church* says that Sunday is traditionally consecrated to Christian piety, good works, and humble service to the sick and elderly. The *Catechism* urges Christians to devote time and care on Sunday to their families and relatives and to use the day for reflection and meditation that furthers the growth of the interior life (2184–2188).

When and to what extent are
violations of canon law sinful?

In the civil order we have all kinds of courts, ranging from municipal courts to the U.S. Supreme Court, to judge when, how and to what extent particular laws bind or have been violated. Because it often takes several courts of appeal and years to decide cases, it is evident that law can be a complicated matter.

Ecclesiastical (canon) law as well as civil laws can present complications. At times those faced with administering church law must appeal to the Commission for the Authentic Interpretation of the *Code of Canon Law* for a clarification or statement of how particular laws bind.

Moralists and canon lawyers do not always agree on just how and to what extent ecclesiastical laws create moral obligations.

In general church law obliges in the way the legislator intends it to bind. Ecclesiastical laws do, in general, bind in conscience. And the rationale underlying this is obedience to the legitimate authority of the church, which has power to make laws for the common good.

But it is not always clear to what extent the legislator intends to bind under pain of sin. To judge that, look to gravity or seriousness of what a particular law enjoins. To impose a grave or serious obligation, the object of the law itself must be something serious. It would seem that when the law uses words such as *precept* or *obliged* it is implicit that the legislator (ultimately the pope) intends to oblige in conscience—under pain of even grave sin.

It is important in judging the seriousness of an obligation to consider the difference between laws that are "very serious and oblige at a given time (such as marriage laws) as distinct from those laws which are considered to involve serious matter, but command a whole series of action (such as those involving Sunday Mass, days of fast)." Following official teaching accompanying the changes in fast and abstinence laws, moralists would not see the violation of one such instance as a grave matter.

325

It is important to distinguish between juridical obligation and moral obligation with regard to ecclesiastical laws. Also, there are situations in which facts may appear true on the surface but are actually not so—situations in which a person might have recourse to the internal forum of conscience.

For instance, a person may appear to be validly married but knows without a doubt that the marriage is in fact invalid. He or she knows the partner never intended to enter a true and binding marriage but cannot prove it in a church court. In such a case, by entering a second—but genuine—marriage, the person might juridically violate canon law but not be morally guilty.

Finally, the theologian noted that dispensations from ecclesiastical law can be obtained for just and reasonable causes. That possibility, he said, indicates ecclesiastical laws are not absolute and "there can often be sufficient reasons for being excused from the obligation of the law, even when a dispensation is not (or cannot be) obtained. Laws are for people, for the common good; people are not for the law." It is accepted fact that a person who is ill is excused from attending Mass on Sunday, as an example of what the theologian means.

Bernard Häring writes, in *Faithful in Christ*, about the use of terms and expressions in canon and ecclesiastical law, that we must keep in mind what they mean or meant in the original context from which they were borrowed or derived. For instance, the expression *sub grave* might mean the legislator is simply pointing out the importance of a larger or more general obligation that we already have from divine law. The legislator may mean to say this ecclesiastical law is directed to fulfilling that obligation. For example, a law legislating works of penance may be meant to help us fulfill the divine obligation of penance and conversion through these particular acts rather than to create a new obligation arising from the ecclesiastical law itself.

Also to the point is a section in the Canon Law Society's commentary on literary forms in the *Code of Canon Law*. Not every canon states a law. When the legislator intends to state a law it should be clear that he is doing just that.

When there is doubt about the law, a person is not bound. And when it comes to burdensome things, the law should be taken in its narrowest sense. When the law is favorable, it should be interpreted in its broadest sense.

How common is mortal sin?

Some wonder aloud if, as a people, we are losing all sense of sin today. Others believe that in the past we exaggerated the amount of sin or presumed guilt where there was none.

Today the discussion of sin has been complicated by what theologians call "the fundamental option." That term refers to a person's basic orientation toward or away from God. Mortal sin is a rupturing of our relationship with God, a definite turning away from God. Most moralists would say that people do not just keep flip-flopping in and out of grace or friendship with God. That is what leads many to say that mortal sin is much rarer than was often supposed. Others perhaps exaggerate the "difficulty" of mortal sin by saying that it practically never happens.

Thomas Sullivan, in a *Chicago Studies* article, "Ten Questions about Religious Education," asked, "Is it dangerous to teach people about fundamental option?" Sullivan answers himself by saying it is always dangerous to teach material to students who are not mature enough to assimilate its meaning. He says some explanations of the fundamental option can be so oversimplified that they might suggest that no single act, however disordered, can ever be a mortal sin or express a change in a person's basic relationship with God. He calls this a caricature of the fundamental option.

Furthermore, Sullivan says that usually our moral lives are a series of interconnected actions. An action that changes the direction of our lives will not ordinarily be an isolated act but will be related to the rest of our lives.

He gives the example of a married man who has an adulterous weekend with a coworker. He says that man surely does not understand the fundamental option if he argues that what he did cannot be a mortal sin. Sullivan says that such an action would appear to be the ratification of a whole series of illicit flirtations and can certainly be expressive of a change in fundamental option.

Certainly we are obliged to follow our consciences. But our consciences must be informed. In judging good or evil we must take into account what Scripture and the church teach, and church teaching must be presumed true until sufficient reasons are given to call it into doubt. Personal knowledge, feelings or opinions are not presumed to carry the same or greater weight than church teaching. A person must have convincing reasons to act contrary to the magisterial teaching.

It is much easier to judge our own guilt or sinfulness than that of others. Even then it is sometimes hard to know whether we are guilty of self-deception, or we may fail to realize the influence of compulsion or other factors that lessen guilt.

Are there serious sins that are not mortal sins?

The *Introduction to the New Order of Penance* issued by the Sacred Congregation for Divine Worship, February 7, 1974, continues to speak only in terms of grave (or mortal) sin and venial sin, as well as the necessity of confessing every grave sin a person can recall after an examination of conscience. It speaks of mortal sin as the sin through which we depart from the fellowship of the love of God and says we are recalled by the sacrament of penance to the life lost through such sin.

Further, the *Statement on Basic Teachings for Catholic Religious Education* from our own National Conference of Catholic Bishops, January 11, 1973, also refers to mortal sin by which a person may rupture his relationship with the Father. And it says religious instruction must not be silent about the reality of sin, the kinds of sin and the degree of gravity and personal willfulness that indicate mortal sin.

None of these documents speaks of serious sin as a separate category. The recent *Catechism of the Catholic Church* retains this traditional distinction as well (1854–1864).

Practically all the catechisms today, including the *Catechism of the Catholic Church,* are careful to emphasize that knowledge and awareness as well as deliberateness and willingness or freedom are essential elements in determining the existence of grave sin. If the texts go into the subject at any depth, they remind us how difficult it can sometimes be to determine the degree of knowledge and deliberateness necessary and actually present for a mortal sin. They will recognize that emotional problems and the influence of external conditions can significantly reduce or take away a person's freedom and responsibility.

An *American Catholic Catechism*, edited by George Dyer, argues that a single act—for example, adultery, serious injustice—properly understood, can embody the rupture of a relationship with God and be mortally sinful. Dyer writes,

> Properly understood, the individual action is not an abstract, atomized occurrence that happens in a five-minute span. It is the culmination of an experience involving doubts, vacillation, thought, desires, deliberations over a period of time. When the individual act is placed in a fuller, more realistic context, it seems that it can be mortally sinful.

Concerning the introduction of a class of sin called "serious" but somehow between mortal and venial, the *American Catholic Catechism* fears confusion—unnecessary confusion. It observes that there are indeed many degrees of freedom involved in sins that are not mortal and suggests that some people may think or take the term *venial* to mean unimportant. If that is the case the author says this threefold division can be a practical way of calling attention to the inaccuracy and great danger of such an equation. No sin is unimportant, and as long we recognize that, the threefold distinction seems unnecessary.

There is mortal (deadly) sin. What makes it deadly is not so much the serious or grave matter, but the fact that one freely and deliberately chooses to do the thing involved means breaking off from the love and friendship of God. But no one who is trying to live for God does that very casually or lightly. It is unlikely to be something we do every day or many times a day.

Unless we know we are in a state of spiritual death, have turned from God in such a way that we have broken the bond of love by committing a *mortal sin,* we can receive Communion.

How can we decide when going to confession whether a mortal sin has been committed? Look at the gravity of the things involved in the decisions and choices we have made and the things we have done and consider the freedom and deliberateness with which we acted. That may not always be easy to determine. Sometimes all we can do is confess what we have done and leave the judgment to God. But the general tenor of our lives, the way we act toward the Lord and his law will give us some indication of whether we are turned to the Lord in grace or not and whether a particular action was probably done with full awareness and choice.

Are diocesan parish priests required to take the vow of chastity?

Bishops, priests and deacons are clerics. Canon 277 of the present *Code of Canon Law* governing Western rite Catholics obliges clerics to observe perfect and perpetual continence and celibacy for the kingdom of heaven and that they "can adhere more easily to Christ with an undivided heart and can more freely dedicate themselves to the service of God and humankind."

Canon 1037 requires that unmarried candidates for the permanent diaconate and candidates for the priesthood must publicly assume before God and the church the obligation of celibacy if they have not professed vows (including chastity) in a religious institute. Married men who are ordained to the permanent diaconate and become widowed may not remarry without a dispensation from the Congregation for the Discipline of the Sacraments and Divine Worship.

In the rite of ordination, responding to the questioning by the bishop, those to be ordained deacons manifest their intention to commit themselves to celibacy. Some moral theologians would call this acceptance of the obligation of continence and celibacy an implicit vow.

Of course, all Christians are called to chastity. *A Concise Dictionary of Theology* defines chastity as:

> that virtue which enables human beings to integrate sexuality within their whole personality according to their vocation in life: for the celibate, through abstention, for the married, through fidelity and for single persons, through self-control.

The violation of chastity by anyone is a sin if all the conditions of sin are present.

Clerics who attempt marriage are automatically suspended and face other penalties, including dismissal from the clerical state (canon 1394).

Clerics who live in concubinage or continue in other external sins against the sixth commandment that produce scandal are to be suspended. If they persist in their offenses, they can finally be dismissed from the clerical state.

In the cases of other offenses against the sixth commandment committed by force or threats or publicly or with a minor under the age of sixteen, the cleric is to be punished with just penalties, not excluding dismissal from the clerical state if the case so warrants.

That is the church law in regard to the obligation of chastity and celibacy. In the case of conduct that is criminal in the civil law, the violator is also, of course, subject to civil penalties.

Does the church permit homosexuals in the clergy?

Church law states:

> Clerics are obliged to observe perfect and perpetual continence for the sake of the kingdom of heaven and therefore are bound to celibacy which is a special gift of God by which sacred ministers can adhere more easily to Christ with an undivided heart and are able to dedicate themselves more freely to the service of God and humanity. (Canon 277)

Part of the formation process for ordination to the priesthood is the discernment of the church and the seminarian whether he has the will (intention) and the ability to live a chaste and celibate life. Seminaries and religious orders do not accept any person who does not intend to be chaste and give indication that he can live purely and chastely. This requirement is the same whether one's *sexual orientation* is homosexual or heterosexual. Both must be able and willing to avoid genital sexual *behavior*. Chaste and celibate homosexuals may be priests.

Is it immoral to live with a person of the opposite sex?

For many people the word *cohabitation* carries with it the implication of engaging in sexual relations. Therefore, we must first establish what we mean by cohabitation with the opposite sex.

Are male and female students in a college dormitory cohabitating? A brother and sister sharing an apartment or house? Is a live-in housekeeper or nurse caring for an elderly person cohabitating? A housekeeper caring for a widower and his family?

The mere fact of sharing the same house or apartment might not be sinful. But certainly an unrelated couple considering such an arrangement would have to answer how they are going to avoid the occasion of sin and the temptations they could expect to experience. They would certainly also have to answer how they are going to avoid scandal from living together: giving others, especially children, the impression morals do not matter and anything goes.

On those accounts most Catholic moralists would object to two healthy unrelated single persons of the opposite sex sharing the same apartment or house and living alone.

Is it possible to be unfaithful in marriage in ways other than adultery?

Men and women can sin against their marriage partners in more ways than by committing adultery. They owe each other more than simply having marriage relations with each other. We can gather that much from reading what Saint Paul says about love and family relationships, for example, 1 Corinthians 13:1–3 and Ephesians 5:21–6:4.

Partners owe each other *time* together. They owe each other emotional support, comfort and solace. They owe it to each other to share in the day-to-day parenting of their children. Obviously, this just begins to name some of the things husbands and wives owe each other.

Vanity is a form or manifestation of pride. And both sexes can be vain and proud. Vanity indicates self-centeredness, and the word sometimes has overtones of silliness and selfishness. Vain husbands and wives may put their personal desires and selves above the legitimate needs of their partners and families.

How might vanity manifest itself? The vain and insecure spouse may try to assert his or her self-worth at the expense of the other—perhaps by belittling remarks in public (or in private), trying to make the other look uneducated or of inferior intelligence.

The vain husband or wife may feel above sharing in housework or expect to be waited on hand and foot.

The vain spouse may be so concerned with appearances that he or she spends extravagantly on status symbols or self-enhancement. A wife may spend lavishly on clothes, jewelry or other things irrespective of the welfare of others in the family. Or the vain husband may insist on the most expensive automobile, the latest in electronic or computer gadgets or computer and sporting equipment.

The vain wife may be so concerned with her appearance (not wanting her lipstick smudged, her hair mussed) she coldly rejects the embrace or kiss of her husband. The vain husband may punish his wife with coldness for some imagined embarrassment.

What sexual acts are considered sinful in marriage?

It is impossible to treat fully the morality of sex in marriage in a brief answer. In his book *What They Ask about Morals,* Monsignor J. D. Conway provides a general rule:

> Generally anything is morally good in marriage if it brings husband and wife closer together, increases their mutual love, sharpens their need for each other, and intensifies their pleasure in each other—it is good as long as it does not frustrate the other purpose of marriage: procreation.

Whatever is done should express real love. Neither husband nor wife should ask of the other actions that are repulsive or truly distasteful or debasing and demeaning. Real love rules out acts of perversion and abusing a partner for a twisted kind of pleasure or satisfaction.

The *Catechism of the Catholic Church* (2360–2400) addresses expressions of love between husband and wife.

Is masturbation sinful?

The *Catechism of the Catholic Church* affirms that the act of masturbation in itself is serious matter for sin.

> "The deliberate use of the sexual faculty, for whatever reason, outside of marriage is essentially contrary to its purpose." For here sexual pleasure is sought outside of the "the sexual relationship which is demanded by the moral order and in which the total meaning of mutual self-giving and human procreation in the context of true love is achieved" (2352).

Using one's sexual powers outside of intercourse within marriage is disordered. It is self-love rather than love for a spouse and the fruit of married love.

For anything to be a mortal sin, however, two other elements are required: sufficient freedom (willfulness and consent) and knowledge or awareness. It is not always easy to judge how much freedom and consent—or awareness—are present in an act. The *Catechism* says:

To form an equitable judgment about the subjects' moral responsibility and to guide pastoral action, one must take into account the affective immaturity, force of acquired habit, conditions of anxiety, or other psychological or social factors that lessen or even extenuate moral culpability (2352).

Is it wrong to pray for money?

As Jesus taught in the Lord's Prayer, there is a certain order to be observed in our prayers. Most important, we should pray to honor and praise God, to thank God for all his goodness and providence. But Jesus also encouraged us to make known our needs to God—our physical needs as well as spiritual. So it is that we can pray for our daily bread.

If we pray for bread and the necessities of life, why should it be wrong to pray for a job to earn them? Or to pray for the means to obtain them in some other way? Would it be sinful for a starving person to ask a passerby for money to buy food? Then why would it be wrong to ask God to provide money for food, clothing or a place to rest? To pray to obtain money to pay lawful debts is surely nothing selfish or disordered.

Should parishes promote games of chance at their fund-raisers?

There is not one church position on sponsoring bingos, raffles and games of chance as means of raising funds for Catholic schools and churches. On the subject of gambling itself, Catholic moralists would say it is morally permissible—as long as it does not interfere with a person's fulfilling his or her obligations of justice and charity. The *Catechism of the Catholic Church* (2413) says pretty much the same thing, arguing that forms of gambling "are not in themselves contrary to justice. They become morally unacceptable when they deprive someone of what is necessary to provide for his needs and those of others." As long as the gambler can afford the potential loss, it is not wrong to play poker, buy a lottery ticket, take a chance on an automobile, place a bet on the Kentucky Derby or play bingo.

We do know, however, that any number of social and personal problems can result from gambling. Some poor people do waste needed resources on lottery tickets. People can become addicted to gambling to their own and family's harm. With numbers betting can come battles over turf. Gambling casinos can bring a variety of social evils and contribute to social decay.

That is why governments usually try to regulate gambling. It is also why many people oppose state lotteries as a form of revenue raising. In 1994 the active bishops of Florida issued a statement opposing the legalization of casino and riverboat gambling. Most bishops and pastors would prefer other means of fund-raising to bingo and raffles.

Some bishops have outlawed gambling as a church fund-raising means in their dioceses. Before his retirement in 1992 Bishop Warren Boudreaux of Houma, Louisiana, had directed that by 1996 gambling be eliminated as a parish fund-raiser. He urged pastors and parishes to encourage tithing and to institute stewardship programs in place of festivals and bingo.

In 1985 Bishop Ernest Unterkoefler approved a diocesan pastoral council resolution recommending that Catholic institutions in South Carolina disengage themselves as rapidly as possible from forms of wagering, including bingo, as a major source of income.

Many pastors and parish councils will say that it would be wonderful if they could maintain their churches, schools and programs from Sunday collections and regular giving. Yet they would also say it just will not work. These parish leaders would like to be without all the work bingos and festivals require, but would insist bingos and festivals are not immoral and succeed where other means of fund-raising do not. One could argue that the parish bingo or festival no more encourages addiction to gambling than the family restaurant serving wine or beer encourages alcoholism.

Should alcohol be permitted at church festivals and social affairs?

The moderate use of alcoholic beverages is not wrong. It is the abuse of alcohol that is wrong and sinful.

But, because of the dangers of alcohol abuse and the impression that others might have of a permissive alcohol policy, many bishops are encouraging their dioceses and parishes to eliminate alcohol from their functions.

What is the church's position on capital punishment?

The Fifth Commandment has always been understood as forbidding the taking of innocent human life. The right of legitimate self-defense is not outlawed by the commandment, and the Sinai Code prescribed the death penalty in certain cases. It is often quoted by those advocating frequent use of the death penalty.

These advocates, though, seem to ignore God's action toward Cain, the murderer of Abel (Genesis 4:14–15). God marks Cain, "So that no one who came upon him would kill him." God says, "Whoever kills Cain will suffer a sevenfold vengeance." Nor do promoters of the death penalty give much attention to the action of Jesus toward the woman taken in adultery and her accusers. He refuses to sanction her stoning or to condemn her to death.

When Pope John Paul II and the bishops today talk about the death penalty they do so in the context of modern society and the new millennium. They are not talking about crime and punishment to a nomadic people in a primitive society without prisons or places of detention.

The pope and bishops make their case in regard to crime and punishment today and the way society actually administers capital punishment now. They consider the effectiveness of the death penalty as a deterrent compared to other punishments and the justice—or lack of justice—with which the penalty is imposed in view of wealth and ethnic status.

So it is, then, that Pope John Paul II says in one of his encyclicals, *Evangelium Vitae* (*The Gospel of Life*, 1995),

The primary purpose of punishment which society inflicts is to "redress the disorder caused by the offense." Public authority must redress the violation of personal and social rights by imposing on the offender an adequate punishment for the crime as a condition for the offender to regain the exercise of his or her freedom. In this way authority also fulfills the purpose of defending public order and ensuring people's safety, while at the same time offering the offender an incentive and help to change his or her behavior and be rehabilitated.

It is clear that for these purposes to be achieved, the nature and extent of the punishment must be carefully evaluated and decided upon and ought not to go to the extreme of executing the offender except in cases of absolute necessity. In other words, when it would not be possible otherwise to defend society. Today, however, as a result of steady improvements in the organization of the penal system, such cases are very rare if not practically nonexistent.

The pope repeats the new *Catechism:* "If bloodless means are sufficient to defend human lives...to protect public order... public authority must limit itself to such means..." (2267).

Is it sinful to resist extraordinary means of resuscitation?

In 1976 the National Conference of Catholic Bishops published *To Live in Christ Jesus: A Pastoral Reflection on the Moral Life.* In the course of that reflection, they addressed the question of euthanasia, stating, "It is a grave moral evil to deliberately kill persons who are terminally ill or deeply impaired. Such killing is incompatible with respect for human dignity and reverence for the sacredness of life."

But they went on to say:

Something different is involved, however, when the question is whether hopelessly ill and painfully afflicted people must be kept alive at all costs and with the use of every available medical technique. Some seem to make no distinction between respecting the dying process and engaging in direct killing of the innocent. Morally, there is all the difference in the world. While euthanasia or direct killing is gravely wrong, it does not follow that there is an obligation to prolong the life of a dying person by extraordinary means. At times the effort to do so is of no help to the dying and may even be contrary to the compassion due them. People have a right to refuse treatment which offers no reasonable hope of recovery and imposes excessive burdens on them and perhaps also their families. At times it may even be morally imperative to discontinue particular medical treatments in order to give the dying the personal care and attention they really need as life ebbs. Since death is part and parcel of human life, indeed the gateway to eternal life and the return to the Father, it, too, we treat with awesome respect.

In 1980 the Congregation for the Doctrine of the Faith issued a declaration on euthanasia. That declaration addressed the question of whether it is necessary in all circumstances to have recourse to all possible remedies. The congregation answered,

In the past, moralists replied that one is never obliged to use "extraordinary" means. This reply, which as a principle still holds good, is perhaps less clear today, by reason of the imprecision of the term and the rapid progress made in the treatment of sickness. Thus some people prefer to speak of "proportionate" and "disproportionate" means. In any case, it will be possible to make a correct judgment as to the means by studying the type of treatment to be used, its degree of complexity or risk, its cost and the possibilities of using it, and comparing these elements with the result that can be expected, taking into account the state of the sick person and his or her physical and moral resources.

Later on, the declaration states,

It is also permissible to make do with the normal means that medicine can offer. Therefore, one cannot impose on anyone the obligation to have recourse to a technique which is already in use but which carries a risk or is burdensome. Such a refusal is not the equivalent of suicide;

on the contrary, it should be considered as an acceptance of the human condition, or a wish to avoid the application of a medical procedure disproportionate to the results that can be expected, or a desire not to impose excessive expense on the family or the community.

The U.S. bishops and the Congregation for the Doctrine of the Faith have thus stated the principles to be followed. (The *Catechism of the Catholic Church* speaks to these principles in 2278–2279.) We cannot do something that will actually cause death. In circumstances when death seems inevitable, as is the case with terminal illness, we do not have to use extraordinary means to prolong the dying process—especially when this entails great pain and hardship.

The difficulty and differences of opinion come in applying the principles. What exactly are extraordinary means? What is especially burdensome or a grave hardship? What are ordinary means of sustaining life? What is a medical procedure as opposed to a life-sustaining or maintenance procedure? When is a medical procedure to be classified as an extraordinary means of prolonging life?

Doctors, courts and medical ethicists and moralists do not always agree about what is ordinary and extraordinary. At this time there is disagreement among moral theologians about the moral necessity of providing nutrition and hydration by way of nasogastric tubes (feeding through a nose tube) or a tube surgically inserted into the stomach. It would be fair to say that advice given in specific cases by bishops or groups of bishops does not always seem to agree.

One group of moralists strongly insists that providing nourishment and hydration is always a matter of providing ordinary care. Food and water are basic to life; taking them away causes death by starvation or dehydration. Thus, they say, the individual or health-care giver may never refuse nourishment or fluids even by tubal feeding or stop tubal feeding once begun.

Others argue that there is a considerable difference between taking food by mouth and artificial feeding. They say tubal feeding can be classified as an invasive medical procedure that can at times, at least, be called extraordinary means. They argue that some procedures, which might be called ordinary from the medical or nursing perspective, may be extraordinary from a patient's perspective and impose considerable burdens on a patient. Tubal feeding may not be burdensome or painful for a comatose patient, but to the elderly patient in declining health, it may well be so. They argue that a nasogastric tube can produce a constant source of pressure and irritation to the throat and nasal passages. Nurses may have to use restraints on the patient's hands to keep the patient from removing the tube. Complications such as diarrhea and aspiration pneumonia can occur.

In the matter of providing artificial hydration and nutrition for those in irreversible comas, Father Kevin O'Rourke, O.P., makes this observation, in an issue of *The Medical-Moral Newsletter:*

> In hospices and in infirmaries of religious sisters, the latter institutions being the embodiment of compassionate care for the dying, artificial hydration and nutrition are not utilized when a dying patient lapses into coma. In sum, evidence is lacking that removing or withholding tube feeding for the reasons listed above [in his article] induces a new cause of death.

Addressing the question of prolonging life in the case of a terminal disease or a person with a fatal pathology in general, O'Rourke also said,

> If the person with a fatal pathology is competent, then he or she should be allowed to make the decision whether or not to prolong life, the decision taking into account personal, familial and social circumstances because one has responsibility to self, family and society insofar as fulfilling the purpose of life is concerned. For example, a father whose life is threatened with cancer may decide that his purpose in life would be better fulfilled if he rejected chemotherapy and surgery in order to devote time to his family during his remaining days, and to devote his savings toward the education of his children. Realizing that he must die sometime, he

determines that it is spiritually more beneficial for him to die in the immediate future, rather than to prolong his life and as a result sacrifice other important values, such as meaningful time with loved ones or the education of his children.

In all cases like this it is difficult to state obligations from afar or to make sweeping statements of what is right and wrong. Each case and person is somewhat unique. Anyone advising must know the person and the particular circumstances before making judgments.

Is it permissible to torture criminals or prisoners of war?

The *New Catholic Encyclopedia* begins talking about torture by briefly tracing the use and acceptance of judicial torture. It then notes that it was not until the sixteenth century and the harshening of penal law under absolutist governments and the extravagances of the witch-hunts and trials that thoughtful people began to take a fresh look at the barbarous practice of torture.

D. Hoffleit, the author of the entry, states,

The use of torture as a means of uncovering the truth appears so futile, so unjust and so revolting that it is difficult for the modern mind to understand how it could have been tolerated by a civilized people. The barbarity cannot be objectively justified, and it is only when it is seen against the background of the times that it is possible to understand why people did in fact accept it.

Against the argument that the right to immunity from violence must yield before the greater right of the state to discover guilty secrets that menace its welfare or existence, he responds that this defense is insufficient to the modern mind. He maintains that not only are individuals hurt by the use of torture but the common good also suffers.

Hoffleit writes,

The use of torture has always been attended by the gravest abuses, against which protest and other forms of legal and moral counteraction have invariably proven ineffective. It lessens the majesty of law and weakens the security of all men who must see themselves as potential victims of similar mistreatment.

Hoffleit further argues that use of torture is really futile because any evidence gained by it is useless unless verified by other means. It is an unnecessary and degrading practice that does more harm than good. And the dignity of the human person requires that a person not be used as a mere means to the common good. The human person has rights even against the state.

Since its founding, the United Nations has continually spoken out against the use of torture as being opposed to human rights. In the supplement to the Charter of the United Nations adopted December 10, 1948, the United Nations stated no one shall be subject to torture or other acts of degrading treatment or punishment. In 1955 the first U.N. Congress on Prevention of Crime and the Treatment of Offenders adopted standard minimum rules for the treatment of prisoners. Those rules completely prohibit as disciplinary measures for offenses the following: corporal punishment, punishment by placing in a dark cell and all cruel, inhuman and degrading punishment. The 1957 International Covenant on Civil and Political Rights and Optional Protocol adopted by the U.N. General Assembly incorporated these rules.

In his great encyclical *Pacem in Terris,* dated April 11, 1962, Pope John XXIII spoke approvingly of the United Nations and its Declaration of Human Rights. He called for the recognition and complete observance of all the rights and freedoms outlined in the declaration as an ideal to be pursued by all peoples and all nations.

On February 14, 1974, the Administrative Board of the U.S. Catholic Conference issued a *Statement of Solidarity on Human Rights: Chile and Brazil.* The board members associated themselves with Brazilian bishops in their call for greater respect for human rights, as illustrated by a statement of the bishops of the southern region of Brazil.

Those Brazilian bishops publicly chastised their government saying:

> It is not lawful for you to arrest people the way you do, without identification of agents, without communication to judges, without sentencing. Many of the arrests are kidnappings. It is not lawful for you to submit people to physical, psychological or moral torture in order to obtain confessions, even more so when this leads to permanent damage to health, psychological breakdowns, mutilations and even death.

Catholic thought today rejects all torture, including that of prisoners of war, as immoral and opposed to human rights. The *Catechism of the Catholic Church* speaks to this in 2297–2298.

One final remark on torture and prisoners of war: The Geneva Convention of 1929, revised in 1949 and subscribed to by most nations, requires the humane treatment of prisoners of war and provides that the only information a prisoner must give is name and rank. Surely a nation that has subscribed to this convention is morally obligated to abide by it.

Is it a sin to mistreat animals?

The *Catechism of the Catholic Church* cites the creation account and God's words to Noah and his sons in Genesis as the scriptural background for its teaching about animals. God says to Noah and his sons,

> The fear and dread of you shall rest on every animal of the earth, and on every bird of the air, on everything that creeps on the ground, and on all the fish of the sea; into your hand they are delivered. Every moving thing that lives shall be food for you.... (Genesis 9:2–3)

Against that background the *Catechism* states that it is legitimate to use animals for food and clothing, to domesticate them to help in human work and leisure. It is morally acceptable to use animals within reasonable limits for medical and scientific research or experimentation, it says. At the same time humans owe animals kindness. It is contrary to human dignity to cause animals to suffer or die needlessly. While animals, along with mineral and vegetable resources, are entrusted to the stewardship of human beings, our dominion over them is not absolute and requires religious respect for the integrity of creation. The *Catechism* also says we human beings owe animals the kindness and gentleness shown them by saints such as Francis of Assisi and Philip Neri (2415–2418).

Dominican Father Philip Boyle has addressed the question of animal rights. He argued that there is a qualitative difference between humans and animals:

> If qualitative considerations are not allowed to distinguish among species, the unqualified reverence for life might require us to go to the absurd lengths of protecting bacteria against penicillin. Limiting legal rights to human beings is not unreasonable, because laws are made by humans for humans.

Father Boyle wrote further,

> Framing the issue in the language of "rights" for animals creates an ethical quagmire. Responsibilities toward animals in research should be based not on the rights of animals, but rather on the responsibilities that humans have toward other beings.... Ethical theory acknowledges the legitimate use of animals while also accounting for the deeply held concerns that animals not be abused or mistreated.

What is a just war?

To briefly condense *The Challenge of Peace: God's Promise and Our Response,* the U. S. Bishops' historic 1983 pastoral on war and peace, the moral theory of the "just-war" or "limited-war" doctrine begins with the presumption which binds all Christians: We should do no harm to our neighbors. Just-war teaching has evolved as an effort to prevent war. Only if war cannot be rationally avoided does the teaching then seek to restrict and reduce its horrors. It does this by establishing a set of rigorous conditions that must be met if the decision to go to war is to be morally permissible. Such a decision, especially today, requires extraordinarily strong reasons for overriding the presumption in favor of peace and against war. The conditions for a just war are as follows:

- *Just cause.* War is permissible only to confront "a real and certain danger," i.e., to protect innocent life, to preserve conditions necessary for decent human existence and to secure basic human rights.

- *Competent authority.* War must be declared by those with responsibility for public order, not by private groups or individuals.

- *Comparative justice.* In essence: Which side is sufficiently "right" in a dispute, and are the values at stake critical enough to override the presumption against war? Do the rights and values involved justify killing? Given techniques of propaganda and the ease with which nations and individuals either assume or delude themselves into believing that God or right is clearly on their side, the test of comparative justice may be extremely difficult to apply.

- *Right intention.* War can be legitimately intended only for the reasons set forth above as a just cause.

- *Last resort.* For resort to war to be justified, all peaceful alternatives must have been exhausted.

- *Probability of success.* This is a difficult criterion to apply, but its purpose is to prevent irrational resort to force or hopeless resistance when the outcome of either will clearly be disproportionate or futile.

- *Proportionality.* This means that the damage to be inflicted and the costs incurred by war must be proportionate to the good expected by taking up arms.

Because of the destructive capability of modern technological warfare, the principle of proportionality (and that of discrimination) takes on special significance. Today it becomes increasingly difficult to make a decision to use any kind of armed force, however limited initially in intention and in the destructive power of the weapons employed, without facing at least the possibility of escalation to broader, or even total, war and to the use of weapons of horrendous destructive potential.

> Indeed, if the kind of weapons now stocked in the arsenals of the great powers were to be employed to the fullest, the result would be the almost complete reciprocal slaughter of one side by the other, not to speak of the widespread devastation that would follow in the world and the deadly after-effects resulting from the use of such weapons. (*Pastoral Constitution*, #80).

To destroy civilization as we know it by waging such a "total war" as today it could be waged would be a monstrously disproportionate response to aggression on the part of any nation.

Just response to aggression must also be discriminate; it must be directed against unjust aggressors, not against innocent people caught up in a war not of their making. The Council therefore issued its memorable declaration: "Any act of war aimed indiscriminately at the destruction of entire cities or of extensive areas along with their population is a crime against God and man himself. It merits unequivocal and unhesitating condemnation."

If taxes are used for an immoral purpose (such as abortion), should we stop paying?

Since there are so many taxes and taxing bodies these days, it is difficult to say exactly what taxes are used for what purpose. But after talking about taxes and the obligation of citizens to pay them, moral theologian Father Bernard Häring writes, in volume three of *Free and Faithful In Christ*:

> No responsible citizen can be indifferent to how legislators and administrators use the taxes collected. The burning question today seems to be: What can be done in the rich industrialized countries and in developing countries to prevent the rulers from spending more for armament

347

than for education, medicare, rehabilitation of the hand-icapped and so many other humane purposes?

In a democratic welfare state where the rules of the tax game are fairly well observed, the very affirmation of democracy recognizes that tax laws must generally be observed in conscience. Of course, this does not exclude a critical mind and efforts to amend legislation and un-cover frauds by legislators and the administration. There can arise extreme situations when, for instance, tax mon-eys are used for nationalistic military goals, where the defense budget grows because of an unjust power poli-tics, or where tax money is used to finance abortions which have no serious therapeutic purpose. In such cir-cumstances, public protest and eventually even tax strike cannot be categorically excluded.

The ordinary citizen's obligation is not to refuse payment of taxes but to support and join in the efforts of our bishops and others to prevent and oppose the use of tax monies for abortion—and other immoral purposes.

In their recent pastoral on civic responsibility, *Faithful Citizenship*, the U.S. bishops write that

Catholics are called to be a community of conscience within the larger society and to test public life by the moral wisdom anchored in Scripture and consistent with the best of our nation's founding ideals.... Our responsi-bility is to measure every party and platform by how its agenda touches human life and dignity.

If a baptized Catholic has an abortion, is she excommunicated from the church?

Canon 1398 of the present *Code of Canon Law* says, "A person who actually procures an abortion incurs a *latae sententiae* ex-communication."

That means a Catholic woman who has an abortion—and accomplices without whose assistance the offense would not have been committed (Canon 1329.2)—is excommunicated automatically by the law itself if all the other requirements of the code are present. Those conditions are as follows: (1) the abortion was directly intended and was successful. It was not a case of miscarriage or accidental loss of the child; (2) the woman involved knew a penalty was attached to the law forbidding abortion; (3) she was at least eighteen years old at the time of the abortion; (4) she had the full use of reason (she was not mentally retarded or psychologically disturbed); (5) she did not act out of serious fear.

If a woman (or accomplice, such as the abortionist) has incurred the penalty of excommunication, canon law (1355.2) gives the local ordinary (the bishop) power to remit it. Many bishops delegate all confessors to absolve from this excommunication without recourse to themselves—at least in the case of a first abortion.

Is organ donation permissible?

Doctors, philosophers and theologians, too, have struggled with questions that arise because of transplanting organs from living persons to living persons and from corpses to living persons. Perhaps a good place to start with your question is the Ethical and Religious Directives for Catholic Health Facilities, issued by the United States Conference of Catholic Bishops. Those directives state:

> The transplantation of organs from living donors is morally permissible when the anticipated benefit to the recipient is proportionate to the harm done to the donor, provided that the loss of such organ(s) does not deprive the donor of life itself nor of the functional integrity of the body.
>
> Postmortem examinations must not be begun until death is morally certain. Vital organs, that is organs necessary to sustain life, may not be removed until death has taken place. The determination of the time of death must be made in accordance with responsible and commonly accepted scientific criteria. In accordance with current medical practice, to prevent any conflict of interest, the dying patient's doctor or doctors should ordinarily be distinct from the transplant's team. (30–31)

Theologians justify a living person's gift of an organ as an act of love. If a person may lay down his life for a friend, one may do the lesser act of charity of donating an organ. On the question of organ transplants from a cadaver to a living person, Thomas O'Donnell, S.J., in *Medicine and Christian Morality*, writes,

> There is nothing morally objectionable in the concept of transplantation of anatomic structures or tissue from a cadaver to a living human being. This is evident from the nature of the graft itself, and is clear from the already mentioned address of Pius XII to the Italian Association of Donors of the Cornea. Here the Roman Pontiff enthusiastically approved this type of homograft, explicitly with regard to cornea transplants, and implicitly in the case of other structures.

Medical moralists, in discussing the transplant of an organ from a cadaver to a living person, note that, if the person who has died has objected to such a transplant, it should not be done. And if the deceased made no indication of his or her wishes before death, the wishes of the heirs should be respected.

But there is also the problem of determining when death has actually occurred. There is a clinical advantage, says O'Donnell, of removing a vital organ for transplant from an already deeply moribund and terminally unconscious patient with an absolutely negative prognosis, and it is tempting to do so. That is why, where states have enacted legislation in regard to transplants from cadavers, they stipulate that transplant teams can in no way be involved in the terminal care of the patient-donor.

The traditional signs of death have been taken to be the irreversible cessation of spontaneous functions of heart and lungs, or breathing and circulation. But with modern medicine and the use of heart-lung machines and other mechanical resuscitators, says O'Donnell,

> [T]he question arises of the merely mechanical stimulation of the heart-lung system far beyond the point of the actual death of the patient. This makes pertinent such

questions as "What is death and when can it be said to have occurred?"

After discussing what Judeo-Christian theology says about death, O'Donnell notes that "Modern popes have pointed out that the moment of death is a clinical rather than a theological problem" and Pope Pius XII said it remains for the doctor and especially the anesthesiologist to give a clear and precise definition of *death* and the moment of death of a patient who passes away in a state of unconsciousness.

In 1985 the Pontifical Academy of Scientists, an advisory group to the Vatican, recognized the irreversible cessation of all brain function as clinical death. In 1990 Pope John Paul II urged a meeting of experts to try to determine as precisely as possible "the exact moment and indisputable sign of death" for the purpose of removing organs for transplants, recognizing the moment of death is a scientific and clinical question rather than a theological question. O'Donnell states the current clinical approach tends to identify clinical death of the entire brain (including the brain stem) and nervous system as the death of the patient even though other functions are still being artificially maintained.

How do you discern death when the traditional signs cannot be discerned because a respirator is being used? In 1968 the Harvard Medical School offered these widely accepted guidelines: (1) There must be total unawareness to externally applied stimuli—even the most painful stimuli. (2) Observation covering a period of at least an hour by doctors is adequate to satisfy the criteria of no spontaneous muscular movements or spontaneous respiration or response to any stimuli. If a person is on a mechanical respirator, the total absence of spontaneous breathing may be established by turning off the respirator for three minutes and observing whether there is any effort to breathe spontaneously. (3) Irreversible coma with abolition of central nervous system activity is evidenced in part by the absence of elictable reflexes. (4) Of great confirmatory value is a flat electroencephalogram.

As Kevin O'Rourke, O.P, and Dennis Brodeur observe in *Medical Ethics*, published by the Catholic Health Association of the United States, "The declaration of human death from the signs of brain death implies, however, that the more traditional signs of human death would soon appear if the respirator were removed."

Are Catholics exempt from jury duty?

Jesus' words about judging others is also in the context of the Sermon on the Mount. He is telling us we have no right to judge others without knowing motives and reasons for their actions. So Benedict T. Viviano, O.P., in the *New Jerome Biblical Commentary*, observes,

> This verse liberates us from the need to be everyone's conscience or censor but it does not free us from all need for judgment. Every simple sentence such as "this cow is brown" is a judgment and in adult life we cannot escape the obligation to make some judgment even on the moral character of others. Parents, friends, employers, civil judges, church administrators, etc. all have this duty.
>
> Jesus' teaching warns against the definitive judgment of God who alone sees the heart. By contrast our judging must be tentative, partial and inadequate (see Samuel 16:76; Jeremiah 17:10). But wherever possible we should try to mind our own business and not meddle in others'.

Imagine the effects on society or the church itself if no one had the power of interpreting or enforcing law. The result would be chaos and lawlessness.

When a question about order in the church and Paul's practices among the Gentiles arises (Acts 15), he goes to Jerusalem for a judgment from the church and apostles there.

Appeals and cases today are brought to the Apostolic Signatura and the Roman Rota in Rome for church judgment. Each diocese has a tribunal with judges to judge claims that certain marriages were invalid.

In the civil realm what would it be like if no Christians were able to act as judges in any of the courts from a municipal court to the U.S. Supreme Court? We can ask the same of Christians acting as jurors. Therefore, various books and other resources in the area of moral theology speak to us of the moral obligations of judges and juries.

The first obligation is to do jury service if there are no reasons to excuse the person called.

Are Catholics obligated to support pro-life candidates?

Back in 1996 John Carr, Secretary of the U.S. Catholic Conference Department of Social Justice and World Peace, told a workshop on political responsibility that voting on the basis of a single issue is not new and it is a legitimate option for Catholics—but not the only option. He remarked that abortion is a fundamental human rights issue but not the only issue.

In 1992 the California Catholic Conference published *Guidelines for Pastor and Parishes Lobbying and Electioneering*. In those guidelines we find the bishops saying,

> [W]e urge citizens to avoid choosing candidates simply on the basis of narrow self-interest. We hope that voters will examine the positions of candidates on the full range of issues, as well as their personal integrity, philosophy and performances.

The bishops emphasized the importance of the right to life and stated that when this right is in jeopardy all other rights are in danger. They wrote,

> But abortion is not the only issue facing the people of California. The consistent ethic of life demands a concern for all the weak and vulnerable members of society: not just the unborn, but all the frail elderly, the disabled and helpless. People in the Church are involved in many issues, such as abortion, agricultural workers' rights, capital punishment, criminal justice, housing, parochial schools, pornography and sex education.

Cardinal Roger M. Mahony of Los Angeles said much the same thing May 21, 1998, giving advice to voters in California primary elections. He said a candidate's stand on abortion is "one significant test of commitment to the protection of human life." Mahony listed other issues connected with a consistent ethic of life as well: euthanasia, military force that does not respect the rights of innocent noncombatants, violence, capital punishment, inadequate healthcare for children, the needy and elderly.

There are still other issues today with great moral implications. What are the implications of unregulated cloning, legalized suicide and assisted suicide, promoting the use of tobacco among teenagers, legalizing casino gambling, housing development that displaces the poor, legalizing the use of marijuana, laws controlling the use or possession of handguns, welfare laws that leave children hungry and without medical attention?

What is the voter to do when a candidate is right on some issues and wrong on others? What is the voter to do when both or all candidates are right or wrong in the voter's judgment on different issues? The voter has to decide what are the most fundamental issues, learn where the candidate stands on the greater number of those issues and then vote accordingly.

As the U.S. bishops make clear in their pastoral letter on civic responsibility, *Faithful Citizens*, "responsible citizenship is a virtue; participation in the political process is a moral obligation. Every believer is called to faithful citizenship, to become an informed, active and responsible participant in the political process."

What is the sin of contumely?

A manual of moral theology defines *contumely* as unjustly dishonoring another person in his presence and thus showing contempt for that person. The author adds that the person dishonored might be actually present or only by proxy or picture. The gravity of this sin depends on how insulting the words and actions used are and the dignity of the person dishonored. Thus, to show contempt for a Supreme Court justice or the bishop of the diocese is more serious than to offend an ordinary citizen or pastor because of all its implications.

Examples of contumely? To show how little he regards another head of state, a ruler keeps the other's ambassador waiting hours or days to see him. Or when another head of state comes for an official visit, the ruler refuses the usual signs of courtesy and respect. Or a cafe owner who doesn't like poor people or Asians coming into his place of business simply lets them sit endlessly without anyone offering to take their orders. Or the serving person snarls, "We don't want your kind in here." Someone who dislikes a political candidate throws eggs at her, scrawls obscenities over her picture on a poster or spits on her as she goes by.

As is the case with all grave sins, there must be awareness and realization of the gravity of what a person is doing at the time of the act. It is possible that something is said or done as a reaction or with such spontaneity that malice is not involved. In such a case there would be no grave guilt or serious sin.

CHAPTER EIGHT

✝

SACRAMENTS

Finding out where a word comes from often can tell us a lot about its meaning. Sacrament *comes from the Latin* sacramentum, *which means "oath" or "pledge." In the Roman army, before men officially became soldiers, they had to take a* sacramentum. *The oath was followed by a branding, much like today when soldiers get tattoos telling of which service branch they belong to. The pledge indicated which general the Romans were to serve. Given the word's rich symbolism the Christian church eventually adopted it to describe the process whereby one became a "soldier for Christ."*

The sacraments are at the heart of the Catholic tradition. In and through the Incarnation, the invisible God becomes visible. Many people today, therefore, before considering the seven sacraments, like to speak of Jesus as the foundational sacrament of God. The simple fact is that if there is no Jesus there are no sacraments. As the catechisms of old stated, if there is any "outward sign instituted...to give grace," it is Jesus. Through the church and through the seven sacraments, Jesus continues to become present and active and make the love of the Father real and effective.

Introducing the sacraments of the church, the Catechism of the Catholic Church *says,*

> *Christ instituted the sacraments of the new law. There are seven: baptism, Confirmation (or Chrismation), the Eucharist, Penance, the Anointing of the Sick, Holy Orders and Matrimony. The seven sacraments touch all the stages and all the important moments of Christian life: they give birth and increase, healing and mission to the Christian's life of faith. There is thus a certain resemblance between the stages of natural life and the stages of the spiritual life. (1210)*

•

What is required in a baptism?

The *General Introduction to the Rites of Christian Initiation* states:

1. The baptismal font, or the vessel in which on occasion the water is prepared for the celebration of the sacrament [baptism] should be very clean and attractive.

2. The water used in baptism should be true water and it should be clean.

3. Either the rite of immersion, which is more suitable as a symbol of participation in the death and Resurrection of Christ, or the rite of infusion [pouring] may lawfully be used in the celebration of baptism.

4. The words for baptism in the Latin Church are: "I baptize you in the name of the Father and of the Son, and of the Holy Spirit."

5. It is a very ancient custom of the Church that an adult is not admitted to baptism without a godparent.

6. In the baptism of children too the godparent should be present.

7. In the case of baptism by immersion decency and decorum are to be kept present.

The sacramentary indicates that for the Easter Vigil the priest wears white Mass vestments. Otherwise (outside the imminent danger of death), when baptism is conferred, the ritual indicates the priest is to be vested in an alb or surplice and a stole. He may also wear the chasuble.

In the case of baptism by immersion, the person is immersed three times while the celebrant recites the Trinitarian formula.

According to sacramental theologians, in administering the sacraments there must be a union of matter and form—in the case of baptism union of the act of immersion or pouring of water and the words of baptism. Together they constitute the sacramental sign.

If no words are spoken there is not a valid baptism. And while liturgists greatly favor baptism by immersion, they also expect celebrants to have respect for the sensibilities of people and the other symbols and ceremonies of baptism, as well as to administer the sacrament validly.

How soon should a baby be baptized?

Canon 867 states that if an infant is in danger of death, he or she is to be baptized without any delay. Under ordinary circumstances, states Canon 867, parents are to see to the baptisms of their infants within the first few weeks: "As soon as possible after birth, even before it, they are to approach the parish priest to ask for the sacrament for their child and to be themselves prepared for it."

The first consideration in determining the time is the welfare of the child, says Father John Huels, O.S.M., in *The Pastoral Companion*. Also to be taken into account is the health of the mother so that if possible she may be present for the baptism. There may also be necessary some time to prepare the parents for the sacrament and planning the ceremony. Huels notes that the phrase "within the first weeks after birth" may be interpreted broadly to allow for special family considerations, for example, to await the return of a family member who lives out of town.

Is baptism a license to sin?

Baptism is not a license to sin. Nor is it a guarantee a person will never be guilty of personal sin—again or for the first time. A person is "born again" at baptism because it is the beginning of or initiation into the life of grace. Baptism incorporates the baptized into the church of Christ. Baptism renders the baptized capable of receiving other sacraments.

Sadly, however, baptism does not render a person incapable of sinning. There is no conversion experience, by any name, that guarantees the sinner will persevere or continue in grace.

Salvation is a lifelong struggle and process. Jesus told his disciples to watch and pray lest they fall into temptation. And Saint Paul, even after his conversion, spoke of his struggle to remain faithful to the gospel and bring his body into subjection lest having preached to others he himself might become a castaway.

Conversion, for most of us, is a many-times thing. We sin and fall but with grace rise again. The sacrament of penance and reconciliation is always a kind of conversion. If it is not a conversion from grave sin to grace, it is at least a conversion to greater holiness.

No religious group or sect is without its "backsliders." We all need to pray for perseverance and faithfulness.

How should godparents be chosen?

Baptism is much different from christening a battleship, dedicating a building or cutting the tape to open a new highway. It marks the beginning of a new life in Christ.

A person can certainly feel honored in being asked to be a godparent. But the church did not institute this office so parents could make relatives or friends feel good. Being a godparent means more than showing up for the baptism and performing a few ceremonial acts. It means more than giving the child birthday or Christmas presents. It is the beginning of a spiritual relationship. Indeed, to agree to be a godparent means to accept certain religious and spiritual responsibilities to the godchild.

Look through the baptismal ceremony and see how the priest repeatedly addresses the godparents. He speaks of the continuing role each godparent is to play in the life of the child. The godparent is to give the child an example of faith and religious practice to hold up the light of faith to the child in his or her own life. The child is to learn the meaning of faith by looking at the godparent as well as his or her own parents.

In the ceremony the godparent professes to be a person of faith and makes promises. It mocks faith if the godparents' professions and promises are not genuine! Parents should ask prospective godparents if they can honestly make a profession of faith and feel they can and want to fulfill all the obligations and promises godparents make.

There are many good reasons for having godparents and why, in ordinary circumstances, the baptism of a child should take place in the parish of the parents. Good order favors that. And twenty-five years from now, when it may be necessary to obtain a baptismal record, will anyone know where to go?

Attending instructions may be inconvenient. But accepting that inconvenience may also tell you how serious your prospective godparents are about being real godparents and taking on the continuing duties of godparents.

So serious does the church take this commitment that a bishop, for good reason, may designate a substitute sponsor whose name can be entered onto the baptismal record if the first one does not take the responsibility and obligation seriously. If a person is not a Christian, does not practice or have any enthusiasm about his or her faith and does not fulfill the most basic religious duties, why would one think he or she will do anything to foster the faith of your child?

Is confirmation required?

Unlike the other sacraments, the history, meaning and ritual of confirmation has shown great change over the years. In 1971, Pope Paul VI, in his apostolic constitution on the sacrament of confirmation *(Divinae Consortium Naturae)*, revised the sacrament's celebration rite and changed the form of the sacrament in the Latin Rite. He adopted much the same words used in the Eastern rite. Pope Paul wrote that he felt the Eastern formula more clearly expressed the outpouring of the Spirit than our previous Latin formula. At that time the pope also clearly established the essential sign or actions connected with the words.

Obviously, Paul VI thought this an important sacrament. He stressed the responsibility of pastors to see to it that *all* the baptized come to the fullness of Christ and be prepared for confirmation.

He established that when adult converts are baptized they should be immediately confirmed by the baptizing priest. In other circumstances, such as danger of death, when the bishop and others authorized to confirm are unavailable, "any priest who is not subject to censure" can confirm. In danger of death even children who have not attained the use of reason should be confirmed so that they are not deprived of the benefit of this sacrament.

These provisions were incorporated in the present (1983) *Code of Canon Law*. Canon 883 provides that in danger of death a parish priest or any priest may confirm. Other canons provide that the bishop is bound to ensure that the sacrament is conferred upon those who "reasonably request it." A priest who has the faculty to confirm must use it for those in whose favor it is granted. And, significant to this discussion, Canon 890 states that the faithful are bound to receive this sacrament at the proper time.

Those who are ministers of the sacrament have a serious obligation to provide for its reception. But what of the obligation of a Catholic to receive it? Our earlier *Code of Canon Law* (1917) said that although the sacrament "is not an absolutely necessary means of salvation, none may neglect to receive it when occasion offers." The present (1983) code says that the faithful are obliged to receive this sacrament at the appropriate time. That seems to leave it to the moral theologians to deal with the strength or seriousness of an individual's obligation to receive the sacrament.

In his manual *Moral Theology*, published by the Newman Press in 1962, Heribert Jone, O.F.M. CAP., wrote that it could not be proved with certainty that there was a grave obligation to be confirmed (because it is not a necessary means for salvation). He did state, however, that if refusal to receive the sacrament came from contempt, it would be a grave sin.

Bernard Häring, C.SS.R., in *The Law of Christ*, stated his opinion that there is an objectively grave obligation to receive the sacrament. At the same time, he acknowledged that theologians "are not agreed that the obligation to receive confirmation is serious," though "in certain instances special circumstances may give rise to a grave obligation.... Surely the sacrament may not be disdained."

Granting that there is an obligation to receive and administer the sacrament, we might ask further questions about *when* the sacrament is to be received.

Pope Paul VI, in his apostolic constitution, spoke of the sequence of the sacraments of initiation as baptism, confirmation and Eucharist. Confirmation was certainly regarded as a sacrament of initiation in the early church. It also appears that in the early church confirmation immediately followed baptism as part of the baptismal rite. The Eastern church still maintains that practice. The disturbance of the baptism-confirmation-Eucharist order of reception in the Latin Rite seems to have been largely occasioned by Pope Pius X's (1903–1914) emphasis on early reception of the Eucharist (receiving First Communion near the coming to the age of reason).

Today there are differences of opinion about the proper time for receiving the sacrament of confirmation. Some theologians and liturgists emphasize that the closer to baptism, the better for confirmation.

Others see confirmation as a kind of "coming of age" sacrament associated with maturity in faith or more active discipleship. Some would advocate confirming around the age of reason and others during early adolescence or on the brink of adulthood.

It has been said that confirmation is a sacrament in search of a theology. Just what effects and purposes should be accentuated or stressed? There was evidence of disagreement about that at the 1984 meeting of our U.S. national bishops' conference when the bishops discussed setting a national norm for the age of confirmation.

Some simply would have followed the age given by the 1983 *Code of Canon Law* as the usual age—about the age of reason. Others thought the right time would be near the seventh or eighth grade of elementary school, before many Catholic schoolchildren would go to a public high school, which makes preparation for the sacrament extremely difficult. Others wanted to confirm well into or near the end of the high school years as an incentive to keep adolescents coming to religious instruction.

At that 1984 meeting the bishops agreed to disagree and thought they could fulfill the requirements of canon law by having the conference determine as a national norm whatever age the local bishop established for his diocese.

Through some administrative error that action was never submitted for approval to the Vatican Congregation for Bishops. This was realized in 1991, and when Vatican approval was sought, the Vatican responded that the conference would have to either agree on one age for the entire country or follow the present code, which uses the age of reason. As it stands now, with the approval of the Vatican, depending on the policy and practice of the particular diocese, there is some flexibility as to when the sacrament is conferred. Some dioceses confirm at the age of discretion (before or with First Communion). Others confirm during the early to mid-teenage years.

At what moment does our Lord become present at Mass?

Over the centuries East and West have argued when, precisely, the body and blood of Christ become present in the Eucharist. According to Johannes Emminghaus in *The Eucharist*, a practical question was at the base of the discussion:

What is to be done if, for some reason (for example, the sudden death of the celebrant), the Canon is broken off? When could the bread and wine simply be removed? From what point on is it consecrated?

The Western church asserted the body and blood are present at the completion of the words of consecration. The Eastern church supported the view that the real presence takes place through the epiclesis (the prayer for the sending or coming of the Spirit to sanctify the gifts of bread and wine).

According to Richard McBrien, in his *Encyclopedia of Catholicism*, present-day ecumenical theologians avoid attempts to locate a moment of consecration at either the epiclesis or words of institution. They prefer, he says, to consider the entire prayer over the gifts, and not one of its isolated moments, as the consecratory prayer.

Emminghaus observes that the church has never made a dogmatic pronouncement on the point (cf. *Catechism of the Catholic Church* for the church's most recent position, 1377).

Ludwig Ott, however, in his *Fundamentals of Catholic Dogma*, states it as certain that the form of the Eucharist consists in Christ's words of institution uttered at consecration. And Ott cites the Council of Trent as teaching, according to the standing belief of the church, "'immediately after the consecration,' that is, after the uttering of the words of institution, the true body and the true blood...are present."

As Emminghaus notes, the practice of the celebrant genuflecting immediately after the consecration of the wine indicates belief that the real presence takes place at the consecration through the words of institution.

Is the Eucharist a symbol?

The teaching of the church is clear—with the words of consecration, Christ becomes really and truly present among us. The substance of the bread and wine is changed into Christ's body and blood. The accidents and appearances of bread and wine remain, however. "There is no change in the *perceptible* [italics added] reality of the bread, for example, the reality which we see and touch, and which is the subject of study in physics and chemistry." (For more on this, see the supplement to *A New Catechism.*) The consecrated bread and wine become signs of the supernatural (cf. *Catechism of the Catholic Church* 1356–1381).

Eating and drinking the consecrated bread and wine (the body and blood of Christ) symbolize or sign our unity with Christ. Sharing in the one bread and cup further signs our unity with each other in Christ. God's gift of the Eucharist is a sign of his care and providence just like the manna in the desert.

So the church can pray on the Solemnity of Corpus Christi, "You give us your body and blood in the Eucharist as a sign that even now we share your life."

Or on the Solemnity of the Epiphany, we can pray at the prayer over the gifts,

> Lord accept the offerings of your Church [the bread and wine], not gold, frankincense and myrrh, but the sacrifice and food they symbolize, Jesus Christ, who is Lord for ever and ever.

The bread and wine, offered at the offertory, are signs of Christ who will become present in the gifts and of his sacrifice being recalled and represented to the Father in the eucharistic celebration.

Does the Mass contradict the Bible?

It is important to start by understanding what the church is saying and believes when it proclaims the Mass is a sacrifice. Edouard Dhanis, s.j., and Jan Visser, c.ss.r., writing on behalf of the commission of cardinals appointed to examine *A New Catechism*, say in the supplement, "Some words in the Eucharistic Prayer indicate that a sacrifice is being offered." What does this mean?

During the Last Supper, Jesus himself already made present the sacrifice of the cross, in a symbolic action, an "anticipatory memorial." It was a memorial which already made the death on the cross present in the symbol. The broken bread became Jesus' body, the wine in the chalice his blood shed for us. Thus Jesus "instituted the eucharistic sacrifice of his body and blood. He did this in order to perpetuate the sacrifice of the cross throughout the centuries until he should come again" (Vatican II, *Constitution on the Liturgy, Sacrosanctum Concilium*, 47). And each time the church does this and so proclaims the death of the Lord, the one sacrifice is present in it.

Note that they tell us the *one* sacrifice is present. The church does not say a new sacrifice or a different sacrifice is being offered in the Eucharist. Rather, Jesus makes it possible to *re-present* his sacrifice—offered once for all. In this way he makes himself present, offering this sacrifice and gathering us into himself as we in turn offer his sacrifice and the sacrifice of ourselves with him to the Father.

We do not say that Jesus dies again. The Mass is the *renewal* of Christ's sacrifice. As Anthony Wilhelm put it,

> At each Mass Christ becomes present; he prolongs and renews his sacrifice so we can be a part of it, so we can pass with him through this world to eternity, and with him continually renew our own covenant.
>
> Christ is present among us at Mass with the same intention or desire to give himself for us, but now he shows this by the separate signs of bread and wine. Instead of showing it by a bloody death, he now expresses his giving of himself by this ceremony with bread and wine.... Christ becomes present among us at Mass with the same inner intention, the same desire to be sacrificed for us that he had on Calvary 2,000 years ago....
>
> At Mass Christ does not suffer or die again. Rather he represents, prolongs, continues, renews his great moment of sacrifice down through the centuries so that we can be a part of it. There are millions of Masses but only one sacrifice of Christ.

The *Catechism of the Catholic Church* echoes these same thoughts in 356–1381.

When does Christ cease to be present
after consecration?

On the subject of the real presence of Jesus in the Blessed Sacrament, Ludwig Ott states in *Fundamentals of Catholic Dogma*, "According to the general teaching of theologians, the real presence continues as long as the species, which constitute the sacramental signs ordained by Christ, remain." Ott does not elaborate on that very much. But it is commonly explained that Christ remains present in the consecrated bread and wine as long as they (or their parts), or better the accidents of bread and wine, are recognizable (they have not been corrupted).

R. Kevin Seasoltz, in *New Liturgy, New Laws*, refers to a declaration of the Sacred Congregation for the Doctrine of the Faith, issued on May 2, 1972, which commented on the fragments of hosts and the respect due them. This instruction, he notes, insisted that the particles should be either consumed or reserved in the tabernacle.

Seasoltz says that reverence should certainly be observed in this regard,

> ...but scrupulosity is to be avoided. The Eucharist has been left to the Church under the signs of bread and wine, both substances that are to be taken of as food. Minuscule particles, even though chemically constituted from the same substances that make up bread, do not look like bread nor taste like bread, neither can they be eaten like bread.
>
> Likewise, droplets and stains, even though chemically constituted from the same substance that makes up wine, do not look like wine nor taste like wine; neither can they be drunk like wine. Hence, excessive purification rites, derived from the Middle Ages and concentrating on the physical presence of Christ under the eucharistic signs rather than on his personal presence, are more a distraction to the community and a caricature of dignified ritual behavior than a manifestation of true reverence and devotion.

As long as the species of bread and wine are recognizable as such, the real presence perdures. When they can no longer be distinguished from dust or any other liquid, we can conclude the presence of Christ has ceased (cf. *Catechism of the Catholic Church* 1377).

Who consecrates the Eucharist?

The Liturgical Press's book *The Mass*, by Lucien Deiss, C.S.SP., asks the question, "Who consecrates?" after speaking of traditions in the East and West concerning the epiclesis or invocation of the Holy Spirit during Mass.

Father Deiss answers his own question:

> The epiclesis underlines with superb precision the humility of the priestly ministry. Sometimes it is said that the priest consecrates. Strictly speaking, the affirmation does not hold up. In any case the epiclesis reveals exactly what the priest does: He says the prayer through which the celebrating community asks the Father to send his Holy Spirit over the bread and wine so that they may become the body and blood of Jesus.
>
> Eucharistic Prayer III says explicitly: "...Father, we bring you these gifts. We ask you to make them holy by the power of your Spirit, that they may become the body and blood of your Son, our Lord, Jesus Christ...." Therefore it is the Father who consecrates through his Spirit. The priest merely says the prayer, in the name of the community.

The consecration is not a kind of magic. It is God who works the change, though only an ordained priest may validly lead the congregation.

Who is the minister of the Eucharist?

When legislating about the celebration of the Eucharist, canon law states some of the theology involved and speaks of the minister of the sacrament in a twofold sense.

Canon 900 of the *Code of Canon Law* says, "The only minister who, in the person of Christ, can bring into being the sacrament of the Eucharist, is a validly ordained priest." It is here speaking of consecrating bread and wine.

Canon 910 states, "The ordinary minister of Holy Communion is a bishop, priest or deacon.... The extraordinary minister of Holy Communion is an acolyte, or another of Christ's faithful...."

We can speak of whoever distributes Holy Communion as a minister of the sacrament.

May women lead Communion services?

The present *Code of Canon Law* (918) states that it is highly recommended that the faithful receive Holy Communion during the celebration of the Eucharist itself. But it should be administered outside Mass to those who request it for just cause, the liturgical rites being observed.

Among the examples of a just cause given by John M. Huels, O.S.M., who wrote the commentary on the Eucharistic canons in *The Code of Canon Law: A Text and Commentary,* is the absence of a priest who can preside at the celebration of the Eucharist.

The rite to be observed for Communion outside of Mass is given in the Roman ritual. That includes (a) an introductory rite; (b) a celebration of the Word; (c) distribution of Communion.

The rite ends with a blessing. But if the minister is not a priest, instead of praying God bless *you,* he or she prays, "May the Lord bless *us,* protect *us* from all evil and bring *us* to everlasting life." Or, "May the almighty and merciful God bless and protect *us,* the Father and the Son and the Holy Spirit" (emphasis added).

None of the canons indicates that only men may act as extraordinary ministers. The canons use the term "layperson(s)" or "other member of the Christian faithful."

When the Eucharist is distributed outside of Mass, there should be no recitation of the Eucharistic Prayer (which we sometimes call the Canon of Mass). Also, if the minister presiding at the distribution of Communion outside of Mass is not a priest or deacon, the minister is not to preach a homily. But the directory indicates it would be proper to read an explanation of the Word (Scriptures) or a homily written by a priest.

May vegetarians receive the Eucharist?

The reception of the Eucharist does not violate a vegetarian diet. Catholic belief says that in the Eucharist the *substance* of bread and wine are changed into Christ's body and blood. The *accidents* of bread and wine remain. That is, the taste, color, appearance and weight of the consecrated elements remain the same. So, too, the nutritional effects or properties are unchanged.

That is what the church tries to express in the doctrine of transubstantiation. The effects of the Eucharist, in receiving the body and blood of Christ, are spiritual. They are in the order of grace rather than physical or nutritional order.

Should water be added to the wine before consecration?

According to the rubrics of the sacramentary, the priest (or deacon) in preparing the chalice at the offertory is to pour wine and "a little water" into the chalice. That is not optional and it is not left to the discretion of the celebrating priest. It is a binding rubric.

Mixing water with the wine can certainly be traced back as far as Saint Justin the Martyr who died in A.D. 163. In describing the Eucharist in the *First Apology*, he stated, "There is then brought to the president of the brethren bread and a cup of wine mixed with water; and he taking them gives praise and glory...."

Most Scripture scholars and historians would hold that Jesus mixed water with the wine he consecrated at the Last Supper since it was the usual practice to water the wine. Adding a bit of water, then, becomes part of doing what he did.

The church over the centuries has seen a symbolic meaning in the mixing of the water and wine, which is reflected in the prayer that accompanies the act of mixing. Wine is symbolic of divinity and water symbolic of humanity. The act of mixing recalls the Incarnation of Christ, the Son of God who took on our human nature. The mixing further recalls our own call to participate in the divine life of Christ.

Should both bread and wine be taken during Communion?

The greatest value of receiving both the host and the consecrated wine is symbolic. Together the consecrated bread and wine are fuller signs of eating and drinking and fuller signs of body and blood.

Anyone, however, who receives Jesus under either of the signs, bread or wine, receives Jesus wholly and entirely, body and blood, soul and divinity. The church makes partaking of the chalice optional. Liturgists encourage us to drink from the cup as well as receive the host. It is hoped that the fuller sign will help us to greater devotion and help us to enter more fully into the spirit of the sacrament.

Is it possible to offer Communion to non-Catholics?

By direction of the U.S. Conference of Catholic Bishops, there appears a statement of guidelines for the reception of Communion in every missalette.

In the case of Christians who are not Catholics, the guidelines say:

> We welcome to this celebration of the Eucharist those Christians who are not fully united with us. It is a consequence of the sad divisions in Christianity that we cannot extend to them a general invitation to receive Communion. Catholics believe that the Eucharist is an action of the celebrating community signifying a oneness of faith, life and worship of the community. Reception of the Eucharist by Christians not fully united with us

would imply a oneness which does not yet exist, and for which we all must pray.

In the case of those who are not Christians, the guidelines say:

> We also welcome to this celebration those who do not share our faith in Jesus. While we cannot extend to them an invitation to receive Communion, we do invite them to be united with us in prayer.

In other words, according to the guidelines established by the Holy See, those who are not Catholic are not to be invited to Communion. There are some circumstances and situations when the Eucharist may be given to Christians who share our belief in the real presence of Jesus in the Eucharist. In the case of Eastern (Orthodox) Catholics not in union with Rome, they must spontaneously ask for the sacrament and be properly disposed.

Non-Catholics may be given the Eucharist if they are in danger of death or if there is some other serious need, in the judgment of the local bishop or episcopal conference. But in such cases the Christian non-Catholics must be unable to go to a minister of their own community and they must spontaneously ask for the sacrament. They must manifest Catholic faith in the sacrament and be properly disposed.

May the mentally disabled receive the sacraments?

First we must ask what kind of intention is needed for the reception of the different sacraments. That gets a bit more complicated in the case of an adult with a mental disability.

In regard to the Eucharist, in some of the Eastern rites, Communion is given to babies at the time of baptism (with some drops of consecrated wine). That is not the practice in the Latin (Roman) rite. Our *Code of Canon Law* requires that a child have the use of reason and be properly instructed before receiving Communion for the first time. The code says children should have "sufficient knowledge." But it further says Communion may be given to children in danger of death if they are able to distinguish the Eucharist from ordinary food and receive Communion reverently.

We are required to make judgments and draw conclusions. It may not be easy to judge just how much a child or "childlike" person really knows and understands. The code does not speak directly of mentally disabled people. But the commentary produced by the Canon Law Society of America does consider the question of giving the Eucharist to them.

It notes that the use of reason is usually taken to mean the acquisition of "abstract cognitive skills." But it says the code does not exclude a broader definition that places primacy on symbolic and intuitive ways of knowing. The commentary suggests that some mentally handicapped people may not be able to conceptualize or articulate the difference between the Body of Christ and ordinary food but may be able to appreciate the sacredness of the eucharistic food from observing reverence shown the sacrament by their families.

Significantly, the commentary states,

> Some dioceses and conferences of bishops have policies which permit the distribution of Communion to such persons. In the absence of a local policy, pastors should not arbitrarily deny the sacraments to mentally handicapped people who are suitably prepared and disposed "according to their capacity" (913.1) and who are supported by the faith of family and community.

Confirmation also presents problems. The theology of confirmation even yet demands clarification. Bishops and theologians approach the sacrament from different points of view, sometimes putting different emphasis on the purposes of confirmation.

The Eastern rites confirm infants at the time of baptism because they emphasize confirmation as one of the sacraments of initiation. Our own Roman rite emphasizes that in the case of adult converts confirmation is given immediately after baptism. The original practice in the church, which changed over time in the West, was to baptize and confirm at the same time.

Some theologians now see confirmation more as a rite of passage, a sacrament that marks the passage from youth to adulthood or mature faith. If confirmation is a sacrament of initiation given to infants, the use of reason as an intention to receive it is not necessary. If it is a sacrament in which the confirmed affirms his or her belief and commitment to Christ, considerably more would seem to be required.

The *Code of Canon Law* does not really go into the theological questions surrounding confirmation. It states:

> Outside the danger of death, to be licitly confirmed it is required, if the person has the use of reason, that one be suitably instructed, properly disposed and able to renew one's baptismal promises (889.2).

And the code says that the sacrament is to be conferred on the faithful at about the age of discretion, "unless the conference of bishops determines another age or there is danger of death or in the judgment of the minister a grave cause urges otherwise" (891).

There has been a wide difference in practice among bishops in the United States concerning the proper age for the sacrament.

So, in the case of confirmation, we come down to about the same questions we face in giving Communion to the mentally disabled. How much ability to reason, how much ability to understand is necessary? The age-old formula *sacramenta sunt propter hominess*, "Sacraments are for people," seems to apply here.

The United States Conference of Catholic Bishops offer some materials in this area that may be helpful. They include "Welcome and Justice for Persons with Disabilities," "Guidelines for the Celebration of the Sacraments with Persons with Disabilities" and "Pastoral Statement of the U.S. Catholic Bishops on Persons with Disabilities."

Why must we go to confession?

Christians have been confessing their sins and forgiving one another since the days of the New Testament. Already in the second century, certain sins were considered so inconsistent with Christian behavior that a more disciplined program of penance and reconciliation was established in all the churches under the direction of the bishops. The discipline was modeled after the catechumenate, or program of preparation for baptism.

Only in the Middle Ages were Christians permitted to receive this sacrament more than once in a lifetime or for less serious or venial sins. Although it is true that the church did not demand individual confession annually before 1215, Christians continued the practice of confessing their sins to one another outside of the sacrament.

It is next to impossible to write a complete history of the sacrament of reconciliation here. But obviously there has been a development in the rites and sacrament of penance over the centuries.

If people have the idea that penance and reconciliation were "easier" in the early church, they are somewhat mistaken. Some in the early church even questioned whether certain sinners (adulterers, murderers, apostates) could ever receive forgiveness and reconciliation. For seven centuries public forgiveness for sins like these could be received only once in a lifetime. (Of course, sinners can repent by God's grace right up to the moment of death, however great their sins may be.)

And for those guilty of such grave sins, it was not simply a matter of going quietly and privately to a priest to confess and receive absolution. At least in the case of public sinners, reconciliation meant entering the ranks of public penitents, doing rigorous penance for all to see and in some cases only after *years* of such penance being absolved and reconciled. As humbling as it may be now to come before a priest confessor and confess all our grave sins as we know them, it is a much milder discipline.

Exactly how the Council of Trent (1545–1563) was using the expression "by divine law" when it said it is necessary for all who have fallen after baptism to confess all mortal sins is not clear to some historians.

The case for private confession is well made by Father Jared Wicks, S.J. Writing in *Chicago Studies*, he said:

When a person has made a decisive shift of personal direction away from God (mortal sin), then conversion back to God is not brought about lightly. A sharp change of course is needed to bring one's heart back under the gentle sway of God's presence and grace. Here the Sacrament of Penance has a primary role, by setting us in dialogue with another person, by engaging the church on our behalf and by articulating our submission to God in submission to a forgiving person representing the Lord.

Therefore, even if one has moved from serious sin to a wholehearted and loving sorrow outside the sacrament, there remains an obligation to submit one's serious sins to a confessor. This saves us from self-deception and leads us to articulate the fact that the forgiveness attained was not from ourselves but from God who touched our heart. We must come out of our anonymity to seek reconciliation with the priestly people whose mission our sin has damaged.

For more on the sacrament of reconciliation consult the *Catechism of the Catholic Church* (1422–1498).

Are communal penance services and general absolution allowed?

In the Roman ritual, the *Catechism of the Catholic Church* and the *Code of Canon Law* there are three rites or ways in which the sacrament of reconciliation may be celebrated:

1. A rite for reconciliation of individual penitents. One person prepares individually for the sacrament, confesses to the priest and receives absolution from him.

2. A rite for reconciliation of several penitents with individual confession and absolution. This is often called a communal celebration of the sacrament. A group of people prepares for the sacrament together with prayers, songs, readings, a homily and acts of contrition. Each then confesses individually and is individually absolved.

3. A rite for reconciliation of several penitents with general

confession and absolution. A group of people in danger of death or in circumstances in which they will be deprived of the sacrament for a long time because of a lack of priests accuses themselves of a sin in a general way, makes an act of sorrow together and receives absolution together in one act. They are instructed that later, when the opportunity presents, they must individually confess all their grave sins.

Many people confuse communal penance services with general absolution services. In April 1986 Pope John Paul II reminded the conferences of bishops they should make it clear to their people that general absolution without individual confession of sins is reserved for cases of necessity. He said,

> The exceptional use of the third form of celebration must never lead to a lesser regard for, still less an abandonment of, the ordinary forms nor must it lead to this form being considered an alternative to the other two forms.

As to whether the conditions for general absolution exist or not (grave necessity), the *Catechism of the Catholic Church* defers to the judgment of the diocesan bishop. It adds that "a large gathering of the faithful on the occasion of major feasts or pilgrimages does not constitute a case of grave necessity" (1483).

Has confession become outmoded?

It is no secret that the number of people regularly or frequently receiving the sacrament of reconciliation has declined tremendously in the last several decades.

It seems that many people have chosen to receive the sacrament two or three times a year. They do so participating in communal penance services during Advent and Lent. At the instruction of their pastors, their confession is kept as brief as possible, and the priest merely gives a penance and absolution.

Many people find this attractive because it entails a minimum of embarrassment or feelings of shame. It also allows no opportunity for the confessor to ask questions about the occasions of sin and discuss with the penitent what must be done to escape a continuing pattern of serious sin.

One reason for drawing these conclusions is that, until the Holy See insisted that the conditions for general absolution were being misinterpreted or incorrectly applied, large numbers of people were coming to services where they anticipated general absolution would be given. Seeing that people were enthusiastic about absolution without confession, some pastors appeared to create deliberately the situations in which they believed they could give general absolution.

Bishops, under the direction of the Holy See, have now spelled out in detail when and under what conditions general absolution may be given. They have reminded pastors to instruct penitents receiving general absolution that they must, in a later confession, confess any and all grave sins as yet unconfessed.

Nearly everyone would agree that the renewal of the sacrament of penance after Vatican II has been one of the least successful renewals in the liturgy. There will likely be a further effort to revise the rite(s) more successfully.

In the meantime the most basic legislation concerning the sacrament of penance (or reconciliation) has not changed. We are all still required to confess our grave sins at least once a year according to number and kind. Further, canon law (916) states:

> Anyone who is conscious of grave sin may not celebrate Mass or receive the Body of the Lord without previously having been to sacramental Confession, unless there is a grave reason and there is no opportunity to confess; in this case the person is to remember the obligation to make an act of perfect contrition, which includes the resolve to go to Confession as soon as possible.

The penitential rite of the Mass has not replaced the sacrament of penance. It could well be that, entered into with real sincerity, an act of perfect contrition would be present and our sins would be forgiven during this rite. But it does not satisfy the canonical requirement of confession of grave sins before one receives Communion.

We must not attempt to judge other people going to Communion or conclude that many of them are consciously or unconsciously doing so without having confessed grave sins.

In our society there is a very diminished sense of sin and guilt. That is probably true of Catholics as well as the general population. Catholics are influenced by what they see and hear on TV and in the movies. They are influenced by magazines and newspapers. Many are being educated in schools where it is not permitted to speak of religion and religious values—much less sin.

At best we might find many people speaking of appropriate or inappropriate conduct, or of socially harmful acts. Morality becomes a matter of opinion. And it is often presumed that people are unable to control biological appetites or resist certain temptations.

At the same time, though, there have also been some healthy developments. It is not too common anymore for confessors to hear people who have been in hospital intensive care for five weeks confessing that they missed Mass on Sunday. We rarely hear people confessing as sin what were really acts of virtue—they were tempted but struggled against the temptation and successfully resisted! And most people realize it is unlikely that we fall in and out of mortal sin like flicking a light switch on and off.

Any further renewal of the sacrament of penance, to be really successful, will have to accomplish a change in attitudes also. People must be convinced—not just in their heads, but in their hearts—that the sacrament truly has blessings to offer them. They must be helped to deal with the feelings of shame that hold them back from confessing to another human being their serious failures. They must be convinced they will be received with compassion and understanding, with sympathy and kindness rather than with condemnation and harshness. There are, after all, people around us who have had negative experiences while receiving the sacrament.

Certainly the sacrament of reconciliation is intended to be a source of peace and joy. The penitent should experience the same sense of reconciliation and acceptance as the prodigal son in the parable, and the joy of the father whose lost son has returned.

Furthermore, people will have to be willing to invest at least a little time in receiving the sacrament if it is to be grace filled. It will be helpful if they can rise above the embarrassment of face-to-face confession. It is hard for a confessor to administer this sacrament in a truly reconciling and loving way when he faces an assembly line of penitents all interested in getting this over as quickly as possible. The confessor knows he does not have the attention of someone he hears hobble into the confessional on a cane and then painfully shift from knee to knee on the kneeler.

What should we confess?

The reminder of the *Catechism of the Catholic Church* that we must confess all mortal sins of which we are aware following a diligent examination of conscience is taken for granted here. Also to the point is the *Catechism*'s advice that, while it is not necessary, it is good to confess our everyday faults (venial sins).

The ritual for the sacrament of penance gives us a five-page examination of conscience in Appendix III. The examination follows the Ten Commandments under three general headings that look at our relations with God and each other and our efforts to grow in the likeness to God.

Any spiritual director would suggest that in using any examination of conscience we look for what is called the "predominant fault." What drives us in our daily lives? What motivates our actions? What determines the decisions we make in family life, in social life, in our business dealings? And we must look not just at the wrong we may have done but the good we have left undone.

Is personal comfort the great determinant of our lives? Is pleasure and sensual satisfaction our main consideration or motive for our actions? Or are our lives characterized by pride, vanity or ambition? What would a confession following such an examination of conscience sound like? It might go something like this:

> I find that I am very self-centered in my life. I spend more on my own pleasure and amusement than on anyone else in the family. I control the TV all the time. I determine with whom we are going to socialize and visit. I overspend on clothing for myself. I took credit for another employee's idea to get ahead on the job.

Or,

> I discover I am proud and overly ambitious. I can never admit I was wrong, that a mistake was mine. I brag and take credit for all that goes right and blame others in the family or at work for what goes wrong. I'm so busy trying to make a buck I have no time to spend with my spouse and children. I have to have the newest in everything and put my family in debt unnecessarily to have it. I jeopardize the security of my spouse and family because of my extravagance and failure to provide for sickness and our old age.

How can we go to confession and be forgiven when we know we will go out and do the same thing again?

Every sincere Catholic has wrestled with this question, realizing how often we fall into the same sins despite repeated Acts of Contrition and receiving the sacrament of reconciliation. We seem to have attachments to certain faults, and whatever our good resolutions, some habits of sin seem so deeply rooted in us that even as we confess our faults we fear we will sin again. How then can we say we have a firm purpose of amendment?

After speaking of the necessity of a firm purpose not to sin again and the determination to take the steps necessary to carry that resolution through when we go to confession, the authors of the *Dutch Catechism* say:

> Our struggle against sin may seem to remain in vain. But this does not prove that our sorrow has not been gen-

uine. There may be a long process of growth before us, growth towards the hour of grace, growth also towards other virtues than those we asked for. In all our lapses we must remember that our Lord does not break the bruised reed or quench the dimly burning wick.

The entry on the purpose of amendment in the *New Catholic Encyclopedia* tells us that it must be remembered that purpose of amendment is an act of the will, not of the mind. The writer here also says we must not confuse this act of the will with certainty on the part of the mind that a person will succeed in carrying out this resolution to reform. He says,

> It is indeed compatible with strong doubt of the mind. What is required for the purpose of amendment is but a present act of the will to turn away from sin. Failure to keep the resolution does not necessarily mean that a person was insincere when he made it.

Finally, speaking in the same vein in his small book *Moral Theology*, Father Heribert Jone says that even if a person is fearful or even convinced that he or she will sin again, that individual may have a firm purpose of amendment.

In other words, while we are here and now resolved to avoid this sin and to do what we must to avoid it, we cannot have prophetical knowledge that we will never fall again or be certain we will never repeat it. What matters is what is in our heart and will here and now.

How can we know the confessor is right?

Priests and confessors have various degrees of intelligence, education, experience and competence. Maturity and good judgment can vary from priest to priest, confessor to confessor.

Further, the problems encountered in moral theology are (like those in civil law and medicine) different in kind from those in mathematics. When dealing with constraints such as two plus two we know the answer is and will always have to be four.

The priest in confession must consider many factors and variants. He must first of all know the laws of God and church and principles of moral conduct. He must be able to take into consideration the obligation of the penitent to other people in his or her life. He must make some kind of judgment about a person's freedom from ignorance and emotional disturbance or some psychological disorder and physical compulsion. Some priests will be more skilled and able to put all those things together to make accurate judgments about guilt and innocence. Some will be better in giving advice and counsel. These are facts.

It is also fact that priests can give wrong answers—wrong because of their own ignorance or because they have not been given all the relevant facts, wrong because of personal pride in putting their own judgment ahead of that of the church and its magisterium.

So, we can never have absolute certainty that any priest is giving the "right" advice or answer.

Before he is ordained, however, every priest must go through at least a basic education in Scripture, dogmatic theology, canon law, spiritual direction, moral theology and many other subjects. He is constantly being tested as he takes these courses. When he has finished his training and education, he goes through examinations in all the basic fields he has studied before the bishop ordains him and gives him faculties to hear confessions.

Bishops and superiors are carefully satisfying themselves that, before a priest is permitted to enter the confessional, he is able and competent to exercise this ministry and responsibility. As penitents, we ordinarily have the right to presume this competency and are justified in acting upon the advice and judgment of the confessor. And we commit no sin in doing so.

However, it is possible that we might recognize what the priest says is in conflict with the teaching of the church, or obviously contrary to moral principles accepted by everyone. To act on advice that we recognize as obviously wrong would be a sin.

Can a person go to confession too much?

Very frequent confession *may* be a sign of scrupulosity. In such a situation it reveals an obsession with sin. A person's judgment has become confused, and he or she is no longer able to distinguish right from wrong, sin from an honest act. The scrupulous person may run in and out of the confessional confessing and reconfessing the same sins. The scrupulous one may wonder if she or he told it right the first time, had real sorrow or had the intention to change. Scrupulous persons should put themselves in the hands of the confessor and follow his advice.

In some cases frequent confession can become just a routine affair done with little devotion. How spiritually helpful that is is questionable. But if the sacrament is received with devotion and the proper sentiments to obtain the graces of the sacrament and as a condition for indulgences, that does not indicate a spiritual sickness.

The Roman ritual says,

> Confession of everyday faults [venial sins] is nevertheless strongly recommended by the Church. Indeed the regular confession of our venial sins helps us form our conscience, fight against evil tendencies, let ourselves be healed by Christ and progress in the life of the Spirit. By receiving more frequently through this sacrament the gift of the Father's mercy, we are spurred to be merciful as he is merciful.

Can one confess without any major sins?

It is always appropriate to make what theologians call a confession of devotion. That means the penitent has no unconfessed, unforgiven mortal sins to confess but wishes to receive the grace of the sacrament to grow in his or her spiritual life.

As quoted previously, the *Catechism of the Catholic Church* states:

> Without being strictly necessary, confession of everyday faults [venial sins] is nevertheless strongly

recommended by the Church. Indeed the regular confession of our venial sins helps us form our conscience, fight against evil tendencies, let ourselves be healed by Christ and progress in the life of the Spirit. By receiving more frequently through the sacrament the gift of the Father's mercy, we are spurred to be merciful as he is merciful. (1458)

If a person has no serious sins to confess, he or she may simply confess one or more venial sins. And if someone has been so fortunate as not to have committed any sin since his or her last confession, the person may confess a sin from his or her past life.

A confession of devotion might sound something like this:

Bless me, Father, for I have sinned. It has been a month since my last confession. I am not aware of any grave sin since then. But I accuse myself of being unkind and impatient with my wife (husband) and children, neglectful of my parents who are lonely and ill. And I want to acknowledge again my sorrow for any and all serious sins I have ever committed, particularly the sin of....

When did marriage become a sacrament?

The sacraments of the church, their definition and number, were not high in the order of things to be discussed and debated by the fathers of the church and early theologians. The first few centuries were given to argument over the person and nature of Christ and the relationship of the divine Persons in the Trinity. Those subjects consumed most of the time and energy of the early Christian writers and thinkers.

As in the case of other dogmas, teachings and beliefs about the sacraments were refined and became more explicit as traditional teaching was challenged and people sought a deeper understanding of them.

From early on the church believed that there were certain signs or rites in or through which Christians personally encountered Christ and were given grace. A clear definition of a sacrament was lacking in the early church, however. There was not always agreement about which or how many such signs were sacraments.

Some, for example, thought of the Sign of the Cross as a sacrament. Saint Augustine spoke of the Lord's Prayer as a sacrament. Peter Damian in the eleventh century identified twelve sacraments. Among them he listed the anointing of kings, canons, monks and hermits, the consecration of virgins and the dedication of a church. Saint Bernard regarded the washing of feet as a sacrament. Liturgical books used the term *sacrament* rather loosely. And some sacramentaries referred to Lent as a "venerable sacrament." In the twelfth century Hugh of Saint Victor spoke of holy water and blessed ashes as being receptacles of grace (sacraments). Others limited the number of sacraments to two or three—baptism, the Eucharist and perhaps penance.

It was not until the middle of the twelfth century that a well-developed concept of a sacrament emerged and sacraments began to be clearly defined. It was about this time that marriage began to be clearly identified as one of the seven sacraments in the sense that we now understand them.

When the Protestant reformers of the sixteenth century argued there were only two sacraments instituted by Christ, the Council of Trent defined that Christ instituted seven sacraments, no more, no less. Among the seven was the sacrament of matrimony.

Since the council was responding to specific questions raised by the Protestants, it did not develop a systematic treatment or theology of the sacraments. And while the council defined that Christ instituted seven sacraments, it did not define how he instituted them. Theologians went on to debate whether he instituted them all immediately and if Christ himself determined the matter and form of each.

Many theologians took and argued for that position. Others maintained that Christ instituted some of the sacraments directly and instituted other sacraments and their specifics by empowering the church to do so.

On this subject the adult catechism issued by the German Bishops' Conference in 1985 says,

She [the Church] cannot institute sacraments on her own authority. The *institution of the sacraments* can have its origin only in Jesus Christ, the one mediator between God and men (Timothy 2:5). For that reason, it is the binding teaching of the Church that all sacraments of the New Covenant have been instituted by Christ (DS 160; NR 506). This does not mean that Jesus explicitly established every sacrament during his earthly life. An explicit institution can also take place through the Risen Lord, as in the case of baptism, for instance. Neither must we think in every case of an explicit word or act of institution by Jesus. We cannot at all expect that Jesus Christ himself laid down all the details of the rites. It is enough if the general nature of the sacraments is founded in Jesus' whole saving work.

This catechism goes on to say that what Christ founded needed to be interpreted in apostolic tradition, kept alive and made present in the church. And the catechism further explains,

It is not an embarrassment—indeed, it is appropriate—if the Church performed the individual sacraments from the beginning, but recognized them explicitly and clearly distinguished them from other rites only over the course of time.

The *Catechism of the Catholic Church* says something similar as it echoes the words of Trent:

"Adhering to the teaching of the Holy Scriptures, to the apostolic traditions, and to the consensus...of the Fathers," we profess that "the sacraments of the new law were...all instituted by Jesus Christ our Lord." (1114)

The sacrament of marriage has its own history among the others. It does seem that it came to be recognized as a sacrament rather well after the others—at least recognized as such by most of the church. And it took some centuries for church authority to take over the regulations of marriage and insist that marriages be celebrated with religious rites.

The point involved in internal forum solution cases is this: What does a person do when the facts are in conflict with what on the surface appears true? What does a person do when he or she is certain in conscience that by divine and human (church) law a marriage is actually invalid but cannot prove it in a public ecclesiastical court?

That is illustrated by Bernard Siegle's example in *Marriage According to the New Code of Canon Law*. A woman knows that in truth her marriage was/is invalid by divine law. Her partner never intended to enter a genuine permanent union with her and be faithful to her to death. But she cannot prove that in a church tribunal. The husband is gone. He would not be willing to give testimony in a church tribunal. There are no letters written before the marriage in which he tells someone what he is doing. There are no people in whom he confided who are willing to testify.

If he were to come back for a day or week in these circumstances and she had marital relations with him, she would in fact and in conscience be guilty of fornication! They are not actually married.

But without evidence and proof of the real facts, a church tribunal cannot pronounce the marriage invalid. The common good demands that courts (church or civil) decide cases on the basis of available evidence, proof of the facts. The church in the public or external forum says we cannot pronounce this marriage invalid. We must consider her and her partner husband and wife with the corresponding obligations of spouses.

What a dilemma! It seems whatever way she turns is wrong. She knows she cannot morally live with this man as her husband, but the church law says she is bound to.

She asks her pastor or a priest in confession what she must do. To assist her to live faithful to her conscience and the real truth, he explains her situation to her, gives her the facts and information on which she can judge whether she is truly married or not. And he explains the options she has in such a situation. In the end *she* must make the final judgment about the validity or invalidity of her marriage. In either instance this is called an internal forum solution to her marriage dilemma. It is *internal* as opposed to the *external* forum with its judges, advocates and official judgments entered in the public records of the church.

This is not an attempt to contravene divine law. It is rather an effort to help the person in such a situation live with what is actually the divine law—despite contrary appearances.

When questioned about a letter to the U.S. bishops that dealt with the use of the internal forum or pastoral solution, Archbishop J. Jerome Hamer, then of the Congregation for the Doctrine of the Faith, in effect recognized the legitimacy of the internal forum solution. He was explaining that a phrase *"probate praxis Ecclesiae"* used in the letter was to be understood in the context of traditional moral theology—which teaches the internal forum as a way of handling such cases.

It is possible that some people, unaware of all the facts and that the internal forum solution is being legitimately used, would be scandalized to see such a person receiving Communion. In that case the person could be instructed to receive Communion where he or she is not known.

But how can a person in this situation enter a new marriage if no priest can witness it in the external forum because there is no church pronouncement of invalidity? Canon law itself provides that when a priest is unavailable for a length of time a couple can marry by exchanging consent before witnesses alone.

Pastors and canonists who have recourse to this pastoral solution or the internal forum are not sneaky, crafty, corner-cutting priests trying to "get around" the law or avoiding its consequences. They are priests trying to help people in very difficult and trying circumstances to live in the love of God and in accord with his law and the truth.

Does an annulment make children illegitimate?

Legitimacy is really a legal term and can be important because of the legal ramifications, for example, the rights of inheritance or qualification for certain positions. In most civil codes legitimacy is sometimes an important factor.

The present *Code of Canon Law* (1983) continues to define and explain legitimacy and illegitimacy. The canons continue to provide means for gaining legitimacy for illegitimate children. But, this is important only to the extent that it would influence considerations in civil law.

The fact is that in today's *Code of Canon Law* there are no disqualifications for office, admission to the priesthood or to religious communities, because of illegitimate birth. And the fact of illegitimacy has no moral or spiritual implications in itself for the person born illegitimate.

The *Code of Canon Law,* now as before, says that "children born in a valid or putative marriage are legitimate." A putative marriage is one that—even though subsequently proved invalid—was presumed by at least one of the parties to be valid.

So a subsequent annulment or declaration of invalidity does not make the children of such a marriage illegitimate. In short an annulment does not affect the legal status of the children in church law.

Can a transsexual marry in the church?

Where governments have dealt with this problem, they have not recognized a change in sex when transsexual surgery has been done. The Italian Constitutional Court in 1985 declared such changes were not legally effective for entering into marriage.

In Great Britain a transsexual was refused permission to marry a man after surgery to change from male to female. The European Court of Human Rights refused her appeal to change her birth certificate. According to notes supplied by the tribunal official, the European court based its decision on biological principles. It in effect declared that *sex change* is a misnomer for the operations. In these operations there is a mutilation of the body, but it is impossible to change the gender determined by sex chromosomes.

A New York court also refused to alter the sex designation on a transsexual's birth certificate, calling the surgery done simply a mutilation.

Any Catholic pastor would have to refuse to witness a ceremony uniting a male to a female transsexual. If such a ceremony took place, a Catholic tribunal asked to judge the case would most likely declare the marriage null and void.

Is marriage in the church possible for Siamese twins?

A moral theologian who taught theology in a major seminary and is also an author responded,

> I see no possibility of marriage in any sense that the Catholic Church would recognize. The simple fact is that marriage is a covenant of love between one man and one woman, which is obviously impossible here so long as the twins are enjoined.
>
> Also, since "marriage" in the Church presumes one that is *"ratum"* *"consummatum"* (sacramentally valid and consummated—see Canon 1141) I don't see how this would be possible in this case. Who (of the twins) would be spouse to whom, and whose "marriage" is being consummated?

Is a man forever a priest once ordained?

The *Catechism of the Catholic Church* states that the sacrament of holy orders, like baptism and confirmation, confers an indelible spiritual character. This sacrament can neither be repeated nor conferred temporarily.

The *Catechism* then says:

> It is true that someone validly ordained can, for a just reason, be discharged from the obligations and functions linked to ordination, or can be forbidden to exercise them; but he cannot become a layman again in the strict sense, because the character imprinted by ordination is forever. The vocation and mission received on the day of his ordination mark him permanently. (1583)

It would be more accurate to speak of a priest who is inactive by choice and personal request as being *dispensed from the obligations* of the priesthood. In some less typical cases it would be correct to say a man is an excommunicated or a suspended priest.

There are practical and important consequences of all this. Canon law gives any priest—whether inactive, suspended or excommunicated—jurisdiction to absolve a person in danger of death from any sins and censures.

Who can administer and receive the anointing of the sick?

One commentary, *The Canon Law: Letter and Spirit*, prepared by the Canon Law Society of Great Britain and Ireland in association with the Canadian Canon Law Society, notes that the doctrinal question of whether someone not validly ordained a priest could validly confer the sacrament of anointing of the sick has not been settled.

Canon 1003 states, "Every priest, but only a priest, can validly administer the Anointing of the Sick."

Those who argue that priesthood must be necessary cite the text of James 5:14, "Is anyone among you sick? He should summon the *presbyters* [italics added] of the church and they should pray over him and anoint [him] with oil in the name of the Lord." So, at least in the present discipline of the church, deacons cannot confer the sacrament of the anointing of the sick.

People, including priests, can certainly pray for someone who is sick and not baptized. However, a person who has not been baptized cannot receive the sacrament of the anointing of the sick or any other sacrament. It is baptism that initiates a person into the life of grace and the liturgical life of the church. It is through baptism that a person acquires the capacity to grow in grace.

Canon 842 therefore states the constant teaching of the church, "A person who has not received baptism cannot validly be admitted to the other sacraments."

In order for a nonbaptized person to receive last rites (including anointing of the sick), the following conditions must be met: be seriously ill and in danger of death, be convinced of the teaching of the church, wish to be incorporated into the church and desire the last rites. That person would first be baptized and confirmed, then anointed and lastly given the Eucharist as viaticum.

Ordinarily only Catholics may lawfully receive the sacraments from Catholic ministers. Canon 844 states,

> Catholic ministers may lawfully administer the sacraments only to Catholic members of Christ's faithful, who equally may lawfully receive them only from Catholic members, except as provided in numbers 2, 3, and 4 of this Canon and in Canon 861.2.

These numbers in canon 844 regulate the *exceptional* circumstances in which the sacraments of reconciliation, Eucharist and anointing of the sick may be received by Catholics from non-Catholic ministers in whose churches these sacraments are valid. They also regulate Catholic ministers administering these sacraments in exceptional circumstances to members of the Eastern churches or other churches in the same position so far as the sacraments are concerned.

Canon 844.4 specifically legislates,

> If there is danger of death or if, in the judgment of the diocesan bishop or of the bishops' conference, there is some other grave and pressing need, Catholic ministers may lawfully administer these same sacraments to other Christians not in full communion with the Catholic Church who cannot approach a minister of their own community and who spontaneously ask for them, provided that they demonstrate the Catholic faith in respect of these sacraments and are properly disposed.

For more details you can consult the various commentaries on canon law and the Vatican's *Directory for the Application of Principles and Norms of Ecumenism.*

When should a priest be called
in the event of a death?

It is never out of place to call a priest in the event of death. But it is even better for a priest to be present *before* someone dies. Every effort should be made to provide last sacraments for such a person—confession, the anointing of the sick and communion as viaticum. The priest can then administer the apostolic blessing at the time of death, which conveys a plenary indulgence.

We would hope that relatives or the hospital or nursing home personnel would have alerted the chaplain or pastor when death first seems possible. When a person has already died, the priest can only console relatives and join them in prayer for the dead person. Once dead, a person can no longer receive the sacraments.

Sacraments at the end of life are meant to help a person prepare for departing this life:

> ...[I]t can be said that Penance, the Anointing of the Sick and the Eucharist as viaticum constitute at the end of Christian life "the sacraments that prepare for our heavenly homeland..." (*Catechism of the Catholic Church* 1525)

Obviously it is not always possible for a priest to be present at the time of death. In such a case friends, relatives and caretakers should spiritually assist the dying. They can pray with and for the dying person. They can strengthen the faith of the dying by their own show of faith and trust in God's goodness and mercy.

Those assisting the dying should encourage them to make acts of contrition, faith, hope and love. They should encourage the dying to put themselves in the hands of God.

How many times may a person
receive the anointing of the sick?

There is a Latin adage *"in medio stat virtus,"* which means "virtue stands in the middle."

Is there a time when repeating rituals again and again betrays a lack of faith and trust, like Moses striking the rock twice? Or is it a matter of persevering in prayer, of persisting in knocking and waiting and asking as Jesus urged us to do?

In any event we do know the mind of the church is that sacraments should not simply be routine actions. Each time we receive a sacrament, it should be marked by faith and devotion. Some sacraments are to be onetime events (for example, baptism, confirmation or holy orders). Even in the case of the Eucharist we are not supposed to simply multiply Communions.

Anointing of the sick was once called extreme unction. People thought of the sacrament as a kind of extreme action— a sacrament to be given when a sick person practically was gasping the last breath. Friends and relatives did not want to request the sacrament for someone ill because it might frighten the sick person and suggest death would shortly follow.

Against that attitude the Second Vatican Council said,

> Extreme Unction, which may also and more fittingly be called anointing of the sick, is not a sacrament for those only who are at the point of death. Hence as soon as anyone of the faithful begins to be in danger of death from sickness or old age, the appropriate time for him to receive this sacrament has certainly already arrived.

The revised rite for this sacrament is called the *Rite of Anointing and Pastoral Care of the Sick*. In publishing the rite December 7, 1972, the Congregation of Divine Worship gave guidelines for administering the sacrament. It noted that, faithful to the letter of James, there should be special care and concern that those who are dangerously ill due to sickness or old age receive the sacrament.

The congregation said a prudent and probable judgment about the seriousness of the sickness is sufficient and in such a case "there is no reason for scruples."

The sacrament, said the congregation, may be repeated "if the sick person recovers after anointing or if, during the same illness, the danger becomes more serious."

"Old people may be anointed if they are in weak condition although no dangerous illness is present," the congregation said.

Those are the rules or principles involved. Applying them is a matter of pastoral sense and good judgment.

What is the purpose of having the body at the funeral Mass?

Whether a body is present for a funeral Mass or not, we believe that a deceased person can be helped by offering a Mass on his or her behalf. In fact, prayer for the dead is included in every Mass.

The church encourages—if not presumes—that the body of a deceased person will be brought to the church for the celebration of a funeral Mass. But there may be times when that is impossible. Perhaps the person died at sea and was buried by shipmates or the person's body was destroyed in a fire. In such a case a memorial Mass may be celebrated as an occasion to pray for the eternal welfare of the deceased.

The efficacy of our prayer and the Mass offered for a person who has died does not depend on the presence of that person's body. There are, however, compelling reasons for celebrating a burial Mass in the presence of the body. It is an occasion for honoring the body that has been the temple of God. It gives us the opportunity as Christians to witness to our belief in the Resurrection: In the words of the Preface to the Eucharistic Prayer, life is not ended but changed.

Mass in the presence of the deceased gives expression to our belief in the communion of the saints, and our belief that all who die in grace are linked in the Lord with the living.

Even on a purely human level, psychologists would say it is helpful to the survivors. The rituals surrounding death give survivors the opportunity to express their love for the deceased and find comfort in the prayer and support of fellow mourners.

$$\boxed{+}$$

PRAYER

Before he placed his hands on the keys to play the organ or put ink to paper to compose a melody, Johann Sebastian Bach (1685–1750) first called upon the Lord. At the top of each manuscript, he wrote the Latin words Iesu, iuva! ("Jesus, help!). For this great German composer it was a powerful recognition that all was gift.

There are those of us who remember doing something like this on our own papers in school. There we placed the initials "JMJ," which stood for "Jesus, Mary, Joseph." It was a subtle but memorable reminder that all we did, wherever we did it, was an act of prayer.

At its simplest and most basic, prayer is communicating with God, a "raising of one's mind and heart to God." It is expressed in a variety of forms and ways. The purposes of prayer are well summarized in the acronym PACT—petition, adoration, contrition and thanksgiving.

The Catechism of the Catholic Church begins its section on prayer (2558–2865) with these words:

"Great is the mystery of the faith!" The church professes this mystery in the Apostles' Creed...and celebrates it in the sacramental liturgy..., so that the life of the faithful may be conformed to Christ in the Holy Spirit to the glory of God the Father.... This mystery, then, requires that the faithful believe in it, that they celebrate it, and that they live from it in a vital and personal relationship with the living and true God. This relationship is prayer.

•

How should we pray?

Reading through, in one or two sittings, one of the Gospels will put this question in perspective. It might be best to start with the Gospel of Luke—sometimes called the Gospel of Prayer.

Jesus prays to prepare himself for his mission. He prays to give thanks and glory to the Father. He prays to unite himself with the Father and to do the Father's will.

But Jesus also makes prayers of petition and teaches his disciples to ask, to petition, the Father. In the parable of the widow and the unjust judge (Luke 18:1–8), Jesus urges us to be persistent, to keep asking. He assures us that the Father hears and responds to our prayers. That, of course, is only part of what Jesus teaches about prayer.

But, how can prayer change the mind or will of God if God knows and wills in advance? Who is changed by prayer—God or the person praying?

Certainly prayer should change one who prays. The very act of praying reminds us of our dependency on God. It reminds us of our need for God. It should help us begin to see things through the eyes of God as far as that is possible. It should lift us to gratitude for the gift of being, the gift of salvation, the many gifts and graces we have already received from the goodness of God.

Prayers of petition should lead us to prayers of love, contrition, adoration.

At the same time, if we have learned Jesus' lessons about prayer, our prayer of petition should recognize there must be order and priorities in what we ask. Jesus sets out those priorities in the Lord's Prayer, the Our Father. Everything we ask must be subjected to those priorities.

That is true of Jesus' own prayer. Jesus does ask the Father. He prays for his disciples (John 17:9). He prays for all who will believe through their words (John 17:20). He prays for those who put him to death, asking God's forgiveness for them (Luke 23:34).

In the garden he prays that the cup of suffering be taken away from him, but subject to the Father's will (Luke 22:42). The prayer is answered—but not in the way Jesus asked. The Father sends an angel to strengthen him, and Jesus conforms himself to the will of the Father.

Suffering, pain and sorrow may come from doing things God's way. Is the Father sadistic? Does he enjoy seeing Jesus suffer? No. But the mission of the Son is to save by being faithful to the will of the Father. And pain can come from being faithful in the face of others whom God allows to be free to do his will or reject it. It is the faithfulness of Jesus that gives the Father glory and teaches us who we are to be and become.

Yet there is still that lurking question, "Can prayer change God's mind or will?" Theologians deal with that question by speaking of the attributes of God, divine providence and God's immutability. Ludwig Ott, in his *Fundamentals of Catholic Dogma*, observes,

> ...it is impossible for any event to happen which is not foreseen and desired, or at least permitted in the Divine world-plan. For God, therefore, there can be neither an accident, nor any fate existing above him or conjointly with him. To him all world events are necessarily and inevitably subject.... By reason of God's absolute unchangeability, the Eternal Plan of Providence is immutable. But this does not make prayer of petition purposeless, nor does it interfere with the Eternal Plan of Divine Providence. On the contrary, prayer is from all eternity foreseen and included as *causa secunda* (secondary cause), in the Divine Providence.

Karl Rahner and Herbert Vorgrimler deal with the question in much the same way in their *Dictionary of Theology:*

> Prayer of petition raises the theological question whether and how God can be "moved" from without. Closer analysis shows this question to be wrongly put, as it confuses God's eternity, in which all [human] activity and thought, and therefore also prayer, is absolutely present with [human] temporality.

Should we ask God for small things? There is nothing wrong with that as long as we keep the right priorities in our prayer. We can ask for our daily bread but subject ourselves to the will of God in greater things.

Is God more generous to those who pray, who do God's will, who strive to honor and serve God? While God does not preserve them from an untroubled life or spare them discomfort and pain, they are blessed most certainly in the things of ultimate value.

Generous Christians pray not only for those whom they know by name but also for all who need God's help. All God's people are remembered every time the Eucharist is offered. We remember all in the Eucharistic Prayer and pray for many people in need in the General Intercessions. Many people pray for "the most abandoned," "all who are in pain," "the souls in purgatory most abandoned," "all who are in need of God's help this day" or "those who have no one to pray for them." Praying in this way is to be encouraged.

Is it unrealistic to believe in physical healings?

God does work miracles—among them miracles of healing. But by definition they are rare. They are worked for God's good purpose and glory, to further his purposes. Obviously they are not everyday events.

God is present in our lives and in the lives of those who are sick, and responds to their prayers for healing—usually through human instruments, such as doctors, nurses and medical technology.

Pray with faith but in the spirit of Jesus in the garden,

"Nevertheless, not my will but yours be done." The ultimate gift is the strength and courage to "come after Jesus" and take up our crosses and follow him offering our pain and suffering for the redemption of God's people.

What does it mean to make reparation to the hearts of Jesus and Mary?

In general, reparation means repairing or making up for damages done. For example, after World War I, Germany was made to pay reparations for damages done to France and Great Britain in the war. In the sacrament of reconciliation a person who has done an injustice to another will be required to make reparation, if that is possible. One who has slandered or libeled another is required to repair the damage done to that person's reputation. A thief is required to make reparation by restitution—paying back or returning the money or property stolen.

In a spiritual sense we sinners make reparation for our sins and the sins of others through voluntary acts of penance or works of piety and devotion done in the spirit of reparation.

To make reparation for acts of blasphemy and profanity, Catholics recite the divine praises ("Blessed be God, Blessed be his holy name...") especially after Benediction of the Blessed Sacrament.

Devotion to the Sacred Heart of Jesus, as promoted by Saint Margaret Mary Alacoque, calls for prayers and acts of reparation as well as Communions (especially on First Fridays) received in the spirit of reparation and atonement.

The old Roman *Raccolta* contained prayers of reparation to the Sacred Heart of Jesus and the Immaculate Heart of Mary. So do some prayer manuals and books of prayers and devotions in honor of the Sacred Heart of Jesus.

The present *Enchiridion of Indulgences* (which superseded the *Raccolta*) contains an Act of Reparation, "Most Sweet Jesus," which carried with its recitation a partial indulgence, whenever it is prayed, and a plenary indulgence, if it is publicly recited on the Feast of the Sacred Heart of Jesus.

And the Roman *Ordo* (a calendar and daily guide with directives for the celebration of the liturgy) reminds pastors that Pope Pius XI required special prayers on the Solemnity of the Sacred Heart. In all churches there is to take place a renewal of consecration to the Sacred Heart, and a prayer of consecration and reparation is to be recited. Also, the Litany of the Sacred Heart is to be prayed during exposition of the Blessed Sacrament.

What is the origin of healing Masses?

Certainly the tradition or practice of prayer for healing is rooted in the Gospel and is as old as the church. The Gospels contain numerous stories of Jesus responding to the prayers of the sick or petitions offered on their behalf. And Mark tells us how the disciples, "cast out many demons, and anointed with oil many who were sick and cured them" (Mark 6:13).

Further, the letter of James bids us,

> Are any among you sick? They should call for the elders of the church and have them pray over them, anointing them with oil in the name of the Lord. The prayer of faith will save the sick, and the Lord will raise them up; and anyone who has committed sins will be forgiven. (5:14–15).

Through the centuries Christians have prayed for the sick. Ministers of the church have visited and prayed for and with the sick.

Does God answer prayers for healing? A tour of shrines (such as Lourdes) around the world will discover testimonials of healing in answer to prayers.

In the wake of Vatican II, emphasis was again placed on the healing aspects of the sacrament of the sick. Instead of calling the sacrament extreme unction, viewing it as a prayer for those on the verge of death, the ritual speaks of the anointing of the sick and the pastoral care of the sick.

But let us note that even those who receive or received miraculous healings eventually succumb to sickness and death—even those who were healed by Jesus. There is a provisional aspect for every cure.

The charismatic movement in these later years has also emphasized prayers for healing and healing services among many Christians, among them many Catholics. It is in this context we can locate healing Masses—Masses dedicated to prayers and petitions for the sick. In some cases the sacrament of the anointing of the sick is conferred during these Masses.

Not all those who attend such Masses or pray for healing are physically cured or made whole. Not everyone who goes on pilgrimage to Lourdes is miraculously cured. Miracle cures are by nature exceptional. But those who fail to obtain physical cures at Lourdes often speak of a kind of spiritual healing, a new peace and acceptance. Surely there is grace in the prayers and support of those who gather to pray with and for the sick.

The seventeenth volume (supplement) of the *New Catholic Encyclopedia,* in speaking of Christian healing, comments,

> Ministers and theologians of Christian healing continue to debate the reasons some persons are healed, some are only improved and some do not respond at all to prayers for healing.

We do know that in the Gospels Christ responded to, and often demanded, the faith of the people asking for healing.

We also know that we cannot view prayer as granting us an entitlement of some kind. Any properly ordered prayer contains, at least implicitly, the petition of the Lord's Prayer—"*thy* will be done on earth as it is in heaven." Prayers are not magical formulas.

Perhaps a person's eternal welfare is better being served by enduring sickness. Sickness has its own graces, after all. It teaches us to become truly dependent on God. It helps to detach us from material things, prepares us to find our hope in God. It is in sickness that we learn humility and in the goodness of those who serve us that we begin to appreciate the love and compassion of Christ.

Sickness also can make us stop and rethink our goals. It

is in the experience of sickness that many have found God and set their feet on the way to holiness.

What is the prayer of self-dedication?

This prayer uses hyperbole, or excessive and exaggerated speech, and figurative language. It simply voices one's desire to give oneself completely over to God, to dedicate all that the person is and every act of the person to God. It is an act of total commitment. It is a surrender of the use of freedom, a prayer to use the gifts of memory, understanding and senses for the glory of God.

One who prays this gives up freedom in the sense that one gives self over to doing the will of God no matter how difficult that might be or how much, humanly speaking, he or she is pulled in a different direction.

There are other prayers in which those praying give their eyes, their ears or whatever to God. They are expressions of the same thing—an offering to God of all that we have and are. They are a prayer that we may prefer God's will to anything and everything else.

What is a Pardon Crucifix?

When the Pious Union of the Pardon Crucifix was founded, it was attached to the old Church of the Annunciation of Lyons. This church was destroyed by a bomb during World War II in 1944. The priests who served the church were killed in the bombing. A new Church of the Annunciation was built on another site in 1953.

However, the indulgences attached to membership in the Pious Union and the old Church of the Annunciation were not attached to the new church.

So the Pious Union came to an end with the destruction of the Church of the Annunciation in Lyons. And because enrollment in the Pious Union at the Church of the Annunciation was one of the conditions for obtaining the plenary indulgence for kissing a blessed crucifix at the time of death, the indulgence came to an end with the destruction of the church and end of the Pious Union.

More important, however, Pope Paul VI revised the whole matter of indulgences in 1968 with the publication of the new *Enchiridion of Indulgences*. In the new *Enchiridion*, Pope Paul granted a plenary indulgence to all the faithful in danger of death who cannot be assisted by a priest to give them the sacraments and apostolic blessing for the dying. All that is required to gain this indulgence is the desire and intention to receive it, as long as the dying person is properly disposed and has been in the habit of reciting some prayers during his or her lifetime. It is not necessary to belong to any pious union or even kiss a crucifix to receive this indulgence.

Does God hear our prayers?

Catholics believe that God is omniscient, that is, all-knowing. God knows everything. God is also omnipresent—everywhere. For more on the attributes of God, you can read the *Catechism of the Catholic Church*.

How God knows and how he is present differs from the way in which we humans know and are present to someone or someplace. Whenever we speak of God we can say only, "It is something like." There is a vast difference between the divine and the human. The human attributes we assign to God are by analogy only. Theologians call this "the analogy of being." God is spirit; he does not have eyes, ears or tongue. How God knows and communicates with human beings is a subject for theologians to explain and ponder.

Yet Scripture and our experience make it evident that God is aware of what is happening to his creatures and can act upon our senses to communicate with us.

In the book of Exodus (2:23–24) we read, "Their cry for help rose up to God. God heard their [the Hebrews'] groaning and God remembered his covenant with Abraham, Isaac and Jacob."

Exodus will go on to tell of Moses' encounters with God in the burning bush and at Mt. Sinai. When Elijah restores the widow's son to life, 1 Kings (17:22) tells us, "The Lord heard the prayer of Elijah."

The New Testament, too, is full of instances where God sees, hears, knows and responds to the pleas of humans. Luke tells us both Zechariah and Elizabeth were righteous in the eyes of God (Luke 1:6) and the angel tells Zechariah, "your prayer has been heard" (Luke 1:13).

Jesus' words on prayer "Ask and you will receive" (Luke 11:9) presuppose God hears and is aware of our prayers.

The parable of Lazarus and the rich man takes as fact that the dead have some awareness of what is happening on earth (Luke 16:19–31). The rich man fears his brothers will share his fate and asks to be allowed to have Lazarus warn them.

The church plainly believes the holy ones are aware of our prayers of intercession and that God responds to their prayers on our behalf. This is evident, for example, when the church accepts as genuine a miracle following prayers to someone proposed for beatification or canonization.

The extent of how much the saints and angels know of earthly affairs, and how they know, is again a question of discussion for theologians.

In speaking of the beatific vision (knowledge of God after death), Adolphe Tanquerey calls it *intuitive* knowledge (not sensory). He goes on to speak of other knowledge, secondary to the knowledge of God, that belongs to the just after death. He says the blessed see many other things, especially those that pertain to their own proper state—past, present and future.

The blessed will know the mysteries they have believed on earth, and they will know the other saints. Scientists will have greater knowledge of the things they studied on earth. They will know more about the things that pertained to them in their former state of life. And, says Tanquerey, the blessed will look upon their parents and friends who are still living on earth and hear the prayers that are directed to them.

In the end, remember, we are talking about mysteries. We have no firsthand knowledge of these things. Therefore, outside of faith, we can only speculate and theorize.

Who wrote the peace prayer of Saint Francis?

According to *St. Anthony Messenger* columnist Albert Haase, O.F.M., Saint Francis had nothing to do with writing the prayer. The earliest version has been found in the breviary of England's William the Conqueror, king from 1066 to 1087. That is nearly two hundred years before Francis of Assisi.

According to Haase, Cardinal Francis Spellman of New York attached the name of Saint Francis, his patron saint, to the prayer. In visiting Assisi to celebrate his appointment to the College of Cardinals, he found the prayer under the title of A Simple Prayer with a picture of Saint Francis.

After the cardinal returned to the United States he passed out copies under the title of The Peace Prayer of Saint Francis.

Another Franciscan, Father Patrick McCloskey, O.F.M., reports that he heard from an expert on Franciscan and medieval writing, Father Ignatius Brady, that Cardinal Spellman's contribution was that he printed the prayer on his First Mass holy cards. Spellman said he got the prayer in Rome but did not have an author to cite.

Whatever the case, and while Francis did not write the prayer, it is very much in keeping with his spirit.

Who are the dead we pray for at Mass?

The prayer for the dead is never worded quite the same in the four usual Eucharistic Prayers or in the Masses of Reconciliation or with Children. Sometimes we pray simply "for those who have died"; at others, for "those who have died and gone before us marked with the sign of faith especially..." and that "these and all who sleep in Christ find in your presence light, happiness and peace." At still other times we remember "our brothers and sisters who have gone to their rest in the hope of rising again" and ask, "Bring them and all the departed into the light of your presence," or for our "departed brothers and sisters and all who left this world in your friendship" or "all the dead whose faith is known to you alone."

In speaking of the communion of the saints, Pope Leo XIII wrote that the Eucharist (the august sacrifice) can be offered for us "and also, according to apostolic tradition, to wash away the strains of those brethren *who died in the Lord* but without yet being wholly purified."

To die in the friendship of God or to die in the Lord means to die in the state of grace. Those who lived before Christ have died in the friendship of God even though not baptized. Those who die after Christ unaware of the necessity of baptism but in the love of God (baptism of desire) can die in the state of grace or in the Lord.

The prayer of the dead, however it is phrased, cannot be taken to say the church believes "all persons will be saved." Yet the church surely takes an optimistic view of God's grace, love and mercy. It sees no one beyond the power of God's saving grace. And even though the church surely teaches as a matter of faith that damnation is possible, it is not the same to say that the church teaches as a matter of faith that anyone has in fact actually been damned.

Johannes Emminghaus says in regard to the fourth Eucharistic Prayer:

> The Spirit is the one who effects the communion of pope and bishops, priests and deacons, the givers of the gifts and the whole congregation, the entire people and all who seek God with a pure heart, those who have died in the peace of Christ and all the deceased, whose faith only God knows.

These final lines have a new ring: They embody the optimism about salvation that has been familiar to us since Pope John XXIII.

What is necessary to pray the Way of the Cross?

There is a long and changing story behind the Stations of the Cross, conditions for erecting them and obtaining the indulgences of the Way of the Cross. A number of popes have issued guidelines throughout history. In the past erecting the stations was reserved to Franciscans or the bishop or one with special delegation. Today, the *Book of Blessings* (drawn from the official Roman ritual) says it is preferable that the blessing and erection of stations be carried out by the rector of the church or a priest appointed by him.

If the stations have already been installed in a new church being dedicated, they do not require a distinct celebration of their erection. There may be images (pictures, sculptures) to accompany crosses. But fourteen crosses are the essential elements of the Way of the Cross.

For one to receive the indulgences of the stations, once they are erected, he or she must meditate on the passion of Christ while moving from cross to cross or meditate on the passion while the leader walks the crosses.

To obtain a plenary indulgence the devotee must also fulfill the usual conditions of Communion, sacramental confessions and prayers for the intention of the Holy Father.

When is Benediction appropriate?

Benediction presupposes a period of prayer and exposition before it takes place.

The Roman ritual (*The Rites of the Catholic Church*, published by authority of Pope Paul VI) says in the section on Exposition of the Holy Eucharist: "Exposition which is held exclusively for the giving of benediction is prohibited" (89).

The *Instruction on Certain Norms Concerning the Worship of the Eucharistic Mystery* (from the Sacred Congregation for the Sacraments and Divine Worship, April 3, 1980) states it must not be forgotten that "before the blessing with the Sacrament an appropriate time should be devoted to readings of the Word of God, to songs and prayers and to some silent prayer."

In other words Benediction should not be given as something like an afterthought to other devotions or occasions of worship. The Blessed Sacrament is not to be taken out of the tabernacle for a few brief moments just to give benediction with it. Whenever Benediction takes place it should be preceded by some period of prayer, readings, homilies and/or silent worship with due attention given to the Blessed Sacrament itself.

Finally, it may be that the chancery officials think of putting the Way of the Cross together with Benediction something like celebrating Christmas and Easter on the same day. Each mystery deserves some special reflection and attention.

What is the Jesus Prayer?

The Jesus Prayer commonly takes the form, "Lord Jesus Christ, son of God, have mercy on me." There are variations of this, but all of them are brief calls for Jesus' love and mercy. According to Per-Olof Sjogren in his author's preface to *The Jesus Prayer*, the Jesus Prayer should be seen as a prayer with biblical roots. It has been used in the form we know it since the sixth century. It was used then in the monastery of Saint Catherine on Mount Sinai. From there Gregory of Sinai took the prayer to Mount Athos in Macedonia. There he taught the prayer to "holy men who knew a good deal about prayer" but who were unaware of this prayer.

Those who adopted this form of prayer began to write about it. Their writings were gathered together in the eighteenth century and published in a collection titled the *Philokalia*.

These writings were then translated into Russian and circulated broadly where Russian was spoken, and the prayer made its way into the Russian Orthodox church.

This prayer seems to have been discovered by Western Christians within the last fifty to sixty years.

The prayer is noted for its simplicity. It is rather like the kind of aspirational prayer or the ejaculations many of us were taught by sisters when we were children in grade school, for example, "Jesus, Mary, Joseph," "My God and my all," "Sweet heart of Mary be my love, sweet heart of Jesus my salvation."

The prayer is meant to foster a consciousness of Christ as we go about our daily work. It is, indicates Sjogren, a prayer for everyone—not just the specially devout. He writes,

> With its remarkable combination of brevity and fullness
> it is singularly suited for busy people of our workday
> world...who have "no time to pray."

...People who have come to know and understand the Jesus Prayer find that it springs to their lips before they are even aware of it, before they even have time to think about it.... The prayer simply becomes part of their life.

The Jesus Prayer helps persons to be conscious of God even in the busiest of times in the midst of the most worldly environments.

What is a charismatic?

According to René Laurentin, in *Catholic Pentecostalism*, the Catholic charismatic movement got its start when some lay professors at Duquense University (Pittsburgh) were searching for something that would fully activate the power of faith in them and call forth total generosity. At a Cursillo congress they met Steve Clark and Ralph Martin, who became leaders of the charismatic community in Ann Arbor, Michigan.

A book by David Wilkerson, *The Cross and the Switchblade*, awakened in Clark and Martin an awareness of the importance of the Bible, the Holy Spirit and the charisms of the Spirit. This book became the basis of prayer and discussion and the attempt to apply what they learned to their daily lives.

They were further influenced by John Sherrill's book *They Speak with Other Tongues*. Now it was prayer, in which the Catholic hymn "Come, Holy Spirit" played an important part, that led them to investigate the Protestant Pentecostals. An Episcopalian priest put them in touch with a member of a charismatic group, and they were invited to a prayer meeting. According to Laurentin, Martin was impressed by the shared and "living theology" he found but "offended" by the naive approach to Scripture and the idea of direct communication with God.

Of the four Catholics who attended that first meeting, only Martin returned. But he brought with him another theology professor. They asked to receive the "baptism in the Holy Spirit." Martin felt a kind of peace and says he found himself speaking in tongues.

A week later Martin laid hands on two other Duquense

colleagues. They had the same experience as he. Perhaps three or four weeks later, thirty students and professors gathered for a birthday celebration. Some of them went apart to pray. Some spoke in tongues. According to Laurentin a similar event took place at the University of Notre Dame two or three weeks later. Then it happened in other places. Between 1967 and 1974 attendance at the annual charismatic meetings at Notre Dame grew from ninety to thirty thousand.

According to the *New Dictionary of Theology*, the movement is found in Europe, North America, Latin America and Asia. And by Vatican estimate, within twenty years, there were well over thirty million Catholic charismatics.

In 1987 leaders from one hundred countries met in Rome, where Pope John Paul II encouraged them and praised the movement.

Over the years bishops have made statements urging charismatics to guard against any spirit of elitism or a false biblical fundamentalism, as well as cautioning against neglect of the intellectual and doctrinal content of the faith or reduction of faith to a "felt" religious experience.

It can be said that the charismatic renewal movement, in general, has been attentive to what the bishops have said. Local groups have obtained approval of the bishop, usually have a diocesan moderator and are integrated in the diocesan parish context.

Laurentin describes a prayer meeting in Paris:

> Chairs are set up in concentric circles. There is a greeting and the meeting begins without a preconceived plan or imposed direction. It will take its course from the members of the group.
>
> Scripture readings, brief exhortations or teachings, and witnessings alternate with singing and spontaneous prayer. All express themselves freely, whether individually or in groups, in words or in song, and yet no one interrupts anyone else.... At times all speak or sing at once, each with his own rhythm and in his own tongue, but this happens by common consent.

What is written here is hardly adequate to fully describe the

Catholic charismatic movement. There is not enough space here, either, to talk about the theological implications and the meaning and reality of the various charisms (for example, tongues and healing).

What is the Morning Offering?

Practically any prayer book intended for general use should contain the words of this general prayer you remember. It is called the Morning Offering. The words are as follows:

> O Jesus, through the immaculate Heart of Mary, I offer
> You my prayers, works, joys and sufferings of this day,
> for all the intentions of Your Sacred Heart, in union with
> the Holy Sacrifice of the Mass throughout the world, in
> reparation for my sins, for the intentions of all of our
> associates, and for the general intention recommended
> this month.

In many parishes leaflets published by the Apostleship of Prayer containing the Morning Offering and the general and mission intentions specified by the pope are made available each month.

The Apostleship of Prayer was begun in 1844 by Father Francis X. Gaultrelet, s.j., in response to the revelations of the Sacred Heart to Saint Margaret Mary Alacoque. It promotes the daily offering of all our prayers, works, joys and sufferings to the Sacred Heart of Jesus, and through him to the Father, uniting our offering with the sacrifice of Christ renewed in the Mass. The Apostleship of Prayer also urges receiving Holy Communion at least once a month in reparation for sins and praying the rosary—or at least one decade of it—daily.

Is the Divine Office liturgy?

The *New Dictionary of Theology* defines liturgy as the official public worship of the church. Official means that it is authorized by the church. Public suggests that it is an act of an assembly of believers.

The *General Instruction on the Liturgy of the Hours* speaks of the Hours as the prayer of the church. While the word *liturgy* implies it takes part as a group or community action, certain members of the church, such as bishops, priests, deacons and religious, have a special mandate and obligation to pray the Hours alone if they do not pray them with others. No one in such a case would say they are not liturgy.

Pastors and those obliged by law to celebrate the Hours are also urged to celebrate them with the laity when possible. All engaged in such prayer are engaged in liturgy—the public worship of the church.

The General Instruction also says:

> Lay groups gathering for prayer, apostolic work, or any other reason are encouraged to fulfill the church's duty by celebrating part of the Liturgy of the Hours.
>
> The laity must learn above all how in the liturgy they are adoring God the Father in Spirit and in truth: they should bear in mind that through public worship and prayer they reach all humanity and can contribute significantly to the salvation of the whole world.

We are still using the language of the instruction talking about liturgy and the prayer of the church even though there is no priest or religious leader or presider. The instruction also urges families as domestic church to pray the Liturgy of the Hours together.

What is *The Cloud of the Unknowing*?

An anonymous English mystic and contemplative wrote *The Cloud of the Unknowing* in the second half of the fourteenth century.

In the work the mystic explains that we cannot know God in his absolute reality through the human intellect: "The movement of the contemplative must be a movement of the whole man, he must precipitate himself, free and unfettered into the bosom of Reality."

God, says the mystic, in his absolute reality is unknowable—is dark—to the human intellect: "When I say darkness I mean thereby a lack of knowing...and for this reason it is not called a cloud of air, but a cloud of unknowing, that is between thee and thy God."

We pass through darkness and the cloud of unknowing and reach God through the heart and love, says the mystic.

What is necessary for a novena?

Some people find novenas reminiscent of the nine days the disciples spent with Mary in prayer between Christ's ascension into heaven and Pentecost. The *New Catholic Encyclopedia*, however, finds the prototype for modern novenas in the burial customs of the ancient Greeks and Romans. For nine days after death they observed a period of mourning culminating with a special feast on the ninth day.

Christians adopted a similar period of mourning but changed it to seven days. There were seven days in the Christian week, and they wanted to avoid a pagan connection. There is a remnant of this practice in the pope's novena after a pope's death.

The *New Catholic Encyclopedia* goes on to say the kind of devotional novenas we know did not appear until the early Middle Ages. They began in France and Spain as days of preparation for the feast of Christmas. Nine days of prayer were observed in honor of the nine months Jesus spent in the womb of Mary.

In time, such periods of preparatory prayer were associated with other feasts and the observance of novenas was indulgenced by the church. The old *Raccolta*, or *Prayers and Devotions Enriched with Indulgences*, published in 1938, listed more than thirty-five novenas in preparation for various feasts, for the faithful departed and in honor of many saints.

The present *Enchiridion of Indulgences*, published in 1968 with the revision of the indulgences, contains indulgenced novenas for the feasts of Christmas, Pentecost and the Immaculate Conception of the Blessed Virgin Mary alone.

While the word *novena* in itself suggests a series of prayers over nine days or nine weeks, the term has come to be applied to other definite periods of prayer, for example, thirteen Tuesdays in honor of Saint Anthony. There is no set pattern of nine times a day or nine days for novenas.

Should Masses be said for the dead?

Scripture (2 Maccabees 12:43–46) does say that it is a holy and wholesome thought to pray for the dead. And the councils of the church have taught this in one way or another many times. The belief that our prayers and intercession can be of help to the dead who have not yet entered the eternal happiness of heaven is part of our belief in the communion of the saints that we proclaim every Sunday in the Nicene Creed.

It is also the constant teaching and belief of the church that the Mass is the highest form of prayer we can offer to God— it is the representation to the Father of Jesus' offering of himself and his sacrifice, an offering in which we join and associate ourselves.

And it is absolutely true that no one can buy his or her way into heaven, or buy it for others. To say that, however, is not to discourage offering Masses for the dead or for other intentions. It is simply to acknowledge that we cannot bind or obligate God to do something by giving alms. We cannot, as it were, put God in debt to us. The value of the Mass is infinite because it is the offering of Christ, but God can apply the merits of Christ as he deems good and just.

Perhaps it would help in thinking about this to keep in mind the Gospel story of the widow's mite (Luke 21:1–4). Jesus noticed she gave to the temple treasury all that she had while the offering of others who were better off than she cost them comparatively little. Jesus' point was that the widow's offering was more pleasing to God, of greater value in his eyes, because she gave so much of herself. So we should not think that the rich have an advantage because they can have more Masses said than a poor person. God has his own "value" system. And what he values is the love, the sacrifice, the generosity behind an offering.

Pope Paul VI in an apostolic letter concerning Mass stipends *(Firma in Traditione)* dated June 15, 1974, said,

> It is a firm tradition in the Church that the faithful, desiring to participate more intimately in the Eucharist sacrifice, add to it a form of sacrifice of their own by which they contribute to the needs of the Church and especially to the sustenance of all its ministers.... This practice by which the faithful unite themselves more intimately with Christ offering himself as a victim, thus deriving more abundant fruit from the sacrifice, has been...positively encouraged by the Church. It is regarded as a sign of the union of the baptized person with Christ and of the faithful with the priest who exercises his ministry for their good....

The person who offers the stipend can unite himself or herself with the sacrifice of Christ without being present for the particular Mass. But Father Edward Kilmartin, S.J., advises pastors to encourage those who offer stipends to be present for the Masses they request. He suggests that it becomes more an expression of their faith and the depth of their union with the sacrificial Christ if they are present and participate in the celebration of these Masses.

In suggesting that people enroll their dead in a Mass league or in encouraging them to have Masses offered for the dead, a religious society is reminding us of our responsibility to pray for the dead, especially those with whom we had a special bond in life. At the same time the society is asking our support and help in doing its work. If we enroll a loved one in a parish Mass league or request the offering of a Mass for our intention, we are making an offering for the support of the priests who will say the Masses or for the support of our parishes—according to the provisions of the diocese. At the same time we are joining ourselves to the offering of Christ in an intimate and personal way by giving something of our labor and sustenance in the form of the money we contribute.

Why do we ask God not to lead us into temptation in the Our Father?

Actually, almost all the English translators of Matthew 6:9–13 (from which we take this prayer rather than the shorter version in Luke) do not use the word *temptation*. In one way or other they translate the next to last petition in the sense of the *New American Bible* version's, "And do not subject us to the final test," followed by, "but deliver us from the evil one."

Father Raymond Brown (in *New Testament Essays*) and Father Eugene LaVerdiere, s.s.s. (in *When We Pray...Meditation on the Lord's Prayer*) explain why. In Greek the word used here, *peirasmos*, can have several meanings. It can be translated as *temptation*, *trial* or *test*. Most translators believe Jesus is urging the disciples to pray that they be spared the testing or trial that comes at the end of time. They believe this because of theological reasons (which some of the early fathers of the church also noted) and Jesus' use of this word in other passages (as with his apostles in the Gethsemane passage, Mark 14:38). Christ is telling us to pray that we be preserved from the final onslaught of the devil. Father Brown notes that Jesus said, if God had not shortened the days of this tribulation, no human being would be saved!

Biblical translators also believe, on the basis of Greek usage, the last plea is better translated "deliver us from the evil one" rather than "from evil." Father Brown notes that the Greek fathers of the church long ago supported the translation "evil one."

Father LaVerdiere argues repeatedly that the whole Lord's Prayer should be taken as an eschatological prayer—a prayer that looks forward to the last days of time and the final realization of God's kingdom. He grounds his view in the words of Jesus at the Last Supper and in the garden:

> In praying not to be brought to the test, but according to the Father's will (as Jesus prayed in the Garden), we recognize our creaturely limitations and the Father's dominion. We respond to the original temptation and react to our sinful tendency to exalt our lives and to exercise God's dominion as though it were our own. We stand

before the Father as children who hallow his name and welcome his kingdom.

The Garden of Gethsemane is our answer to the Garden of Eden. The Lord's table with its bread of life is our answer to Eden's table with its fruit of death. The test of the Cross is our answer to the test of serpent. Not seeking the test, but accepting it if it be our Father's will, we find life, not by grasping for it, but by giving it.

Why are devotions of the scapular, First Friday and First Saturday not now taught and practiced as they once were?

A number of trends and movements have converged to draw attention and emphasis from popular devotions. Among them was the accent the Second Vatican Council placed on the liturgy in the spiritual and prayer lives of Catholics. With the prominence given the liturgy, there also came insistence on the importance of the Scriptures in our prayer and worship.

With the change from Latin to English as the language of our liturgy, popular devotions became less important as ways of expressing our religious feelings and sentiments.

As long as our liturgical rites were in Latin, English-language popular devotions, such as the Way of the Cross, the rosary, Forty Hours devotion, May crowning and novenas, provided occasions when people could express their deepest faith, hopes and feelings in their own language. Latin sometimes got in the way of that. The symbols used in popular devotions were more moving than those in the liturgy.

With English as the language of the liturgy, priests and people—faithful to the urging of the council—turned more and more completely to liturgical prayer and devotions to nourish and celebrate their lives in God. They felt less need for other kinds of devotions. And as the law of the church changed to admit the celebration of the Eucharist in the afternoon or evening hours, the Mass often replaced other exercises of piety or devotion in the parish's common prayer and worship.

In other instances, taking the cue from Vatican II, more

traditional devotions or services were replaced by Evening Prayer from the Liturgy of the Hours or services incorporating greater use of the Scriptures and modeled on the liturgy.

Some of these devotions stem from private revelations and people's personal piety. They fit the needs, piety, culture and character of the times in which they originated. Why did the rosary become such an important prayer form in Western Christianity and not Eastern? Why did devotion to the Holy Name become so important in the Middle Ages? Why did God choose to reveal himself to Saint Margaret Mary in apparitions of the Sacred Heart and call for Communions of reparation in the eighteenth century? Why, in the nineteenth and twentieth centuries, do Saint Bernadette and the children of Fatima receive calls for penance, conversion and praying of the rosary through apparitions of the Blessed Virgin?

The message and devotion are suited to the needs and demands of the church and people of the time. Just as religious orders or pious movements are born to meet the needs of God's people at particular moments in history, so, too, forms of devotion and piety. When God wants us to appreciate the love poured out for us in Christ, along comes a Francis of Assisi to give us the devotion of the crib and devotion to the poor and suffering Christ. When God wants us to appreciate the Eucharist as a means to grow in love and intimacy with him, he inspires Margaret Mary Alacoque to call for more frequent Communion and gives us the image of his heart burning with love for us.

Why do some of these devotions become less popular with the passage of time? Perhaps because times and needs have changed. Perhaps because, in some instances, the real spirit of the devotion gets lost—what was a call to burning love, driving faith, total conversion of life is reduced to formulas or numbers of prayers.

If the numbers become more important than what the acts of devotion are to express, the heart has gone out of the devotion. If the accidentals are emphasized over the substance of the devotion, it will fall into disuse.

Numbers are only important to the extent they express

what must be in the heart. When a devotion loses its impact, God will in God's own good time act anew in a way most fitting and opportune to rekindle flames of love, faith and hope in hearts grown cold. Nothing should gainsay your desire to practice some favorite devotion. Indeed, the rosary and Way of the Cross, among others, are still quite popular.

What is mysticism?

Father John Hardon, S.J., defines mysticism in his *Pocket Catholic Dictionary* in this way:

> The supernatural state of soul in which God is known in a way that no human effort or exertion could ever succeed in producing. There is an immediate personal experience of God that is truly extraordinary, not only in intensity and degree, but also in kind. It is always the result of a special, totally unmerited grace of God.... In Christian mysticism all union between the soul and God is a moral union of love, in doing his will even at great sacrifice to self; there is no hint of losing one's being in God or absorption of one's personality into the divine.

Hardon's definition or description includes elements stressed in the writings of Saint Bonaventure, Saint Theresa of Avila, Saint John of the Cross and the contemporary writers on mysticism such as William Johnston, S.J., who says mysticism is "wisdom or knowledge that is found through love; it is loving knowledge."

To see what mystic experience is like in the concrete, lives of the saints and descriptions of them at prayer can be helpful. For instance, in what is called the *Major Life of Saint Francis*, Saint Bonaventure described an experience of Saint Francis of Assisi while he was at prayer:

> One day as he prayed in one of his usual haunts, he became completely absorbed in God in the excess of his fervor. Then Jesus Christ appeared to him, hanging on his cross. His soul melted at the sight and the memory of Christ's Passion was impressed on the depths of his heart so vividly that, whenever he thought about it, he could

scarcely restrain his sighs and tears, as he afterwards confessed towards the end of life. He realized immediately that the words of the Gospel were addressed to him, "If you have a mind to come my way, renounce yourself, and take up your cross and follow me (Matthew 16:24)."

Harvey Egan, S.J., in *Christian Mysticism: The Future of a Tradition*, looks at Johnston's definition and writing and says saints have the advantage of being open to a variety of different lifestyles. Johnston maintains that all are called to mysticism, that there is a universal call. Father Egan points out that Johnston thus removes mysticism from the realm of esoteric experiences reserved only for an elite:

> Not only a monastic atmosphere of asceticism and formal prayer can nurture mystical loving knowledge, but also the self-surrender required for authentic love in hectic, secular activity.

It should not surprise us, then, that there is a steady stream of books on mysticism and contemplative prayer coming from writers and publishers. To mention just a few: *The Mysticism of Everyday*, by Edward Carter, S.J., *Contemplative Prayer* by Thomas Merton; *Reaching Out*, by Henri Nouwen; and *The Cloud of Unknowing* and *The Book of Privy Counseling*, edited by William Johnston, S.J. An older classic is Saint Bonaventure's *The Mind's Journey to God*, translated by Lawrence S. Cunningham.

Are months and days still dedicated?

According to the *Catholic Source Book,* the months of the year are dedicated as follows:

January—The Holy Childhood;

February—The Holy Family;

March—Saint Joseph;

April—The Holy Spirit (also the Eucharist);

May—Mary;

June—The Sacred Heart;

July—The Precious Blood;

August—The Blessed Sacrament;

September—The Seven Sorrows;

October—The Holy Rosary;

November—The Souls in Purgatory;

December—The Immaculate Conception.

Days of the week are dedicated as follows:

Sunday—The Holy Trinity;

Monday—The Souls in Purgatory (also The Holy Spirit);

Tuesday—Guardian Angel;

Wednesday—Saint Joseph;

Thursday—The Blessed Sacrament;

Friday—His Precious Blood;

Saturday—Mary.

It is hard to say when or how this custom took effect. According to the *Dictionary for Catholic Devotions*, the first month of the Sacred Heart was observed in 1833. Incidentally, *Catholic Source Book* also notes the connection between the First Fridays and the Sacred Heart.

Pope Leo XIII extended the custom of October devotions to all parish churches who were to pray for the normalization of relations between the Holy See and the Kingdom of Italy after the desegregation of the Papal States. The linking of Mary with May goes back to Spain as far as the thirteenth century. A Jesuit author had produced a small book, *The Month of Mary, or the Month of May*, describing customs around the world.

CHAPTER TEN

CHURCH HISTORY

John Tracy Ellis (1905–1992) has been described as the "dean of American Catholic historians." He spent the majority of his academic life at the Catholic University of America teaching generations of priests and seminarians. One day a bishop friend of his visited him in his study at the school. The walls of Monsignor Ellis's study were lined with books. At one point in the conversation, the bishop could not help but smile and say, "John, it must be wonderful to have a hobby like history."

As we enter into the third millennium, with the pace of life seeming to get only faster, the study and knowledge of history can no longer be seen as a hobby but must be diligently pursued as a necessity. For if we do not remember our roots—where we came from, why we do what we do and the like—the experience of faith will eventually become shallow and lifeless. Ignorance is not bliss but loss, not of knowledge so much as a faith relationship with God.

Speaking to this new condition and the need to challenge and confront it, the fathers of the Second Vatican Council, in their Pastoral Constitution on the Church in the Modern World, had this to say:

History itself speeds along on so rapid a course that an individual person can scarcely keep abreast of it. The destiny of the human community has become all of a piece, where once the various groups of men had a kind of private history of their own. Thus, the human race has passed from a rather static concept of reality to a more dynamic, evolutionary one. In consequence, there has arisen a new series of problems, a series as important as can be, calling for new efforts of analysis and synthesis. (5)

In an age of historical amnesia, in fields ranging from culture to politics, the follower of Jesus is reminded that one sure way to proclaim the gospel is to know one's faith roots. This endeavor, with the passage of time, becomes only more important rather than less.

•

When did the Christian church officially begin to be called the Catholic church?

Catholic comes from the Greek word *catholicos,* which means "universal." Even now we speak of the New Testament letters addressed to the church at large as the Catholic epistles.

Early in the New Testament we find the apostles and early followers of Christ coming to realize that the church is to be truly *universal* or *catholic.* In early church writings such as those of Saint Polycarp and the Didache we find universality spoken of as one of the marks or characteristics of Christianity.

However, it is in the letter of Saint Ignatius of Antioch to the Smyrneans that we first find the expression "Catholic church." Saint Ignatius lived between A.D. 35 and 107. The name goes back a long way.

The *Catechism of the Catholic Church* also speaks to the church as *Catholic* in 830–835.

There is a legend that before the apostles separated to proclaim the gospel to all peoples they met and determined what they would preach and teach. As the story goes, each of the twelve contributed one idea or article of faith for the preaching that was to take place. These articles of faith—articulated with the inspiration of the Holy Spirit—were compiled or put together in a kind of creed or symbol. The result was declared to be the standard for their teaching and evangelization.

It is true that some passages in the Acts of Apostles 8:36–38 and 16:14–15, Romans 10:9 and Ephesians 1:13 suggest some kind of declaration of belief was required before baptism. Some of the early fathers speak about the rule of faith handed down by the apostles.

Yet one of the difficulties with the legend that the text or form of the Apostles' Creed goes back directly to the apostles is that there is no written record of the creed in the form that we know it or one nearly like it until at least the third century. Furthermore, the Apostles' Creed appears to be used only by the Western church. If the creed went back to the apostles we would probably find it in the church of the West and the church of the East.

We do know that by the middle of the third century some kind of formula of faith with minor variations was to be found in all the main churches. Usually it was in a question-and-answer form and appeared in the ceremony of baptism— much like the questions and answers for the celebrant and parents or godparents in today's administration of the sacrament. There does not appear to be any evidence of a declaratory creed in the early rituals, but there did develop around this same time different declaratory formulas of faith that were used and commented on in the catechetical instruction of converts.

There was a Roman Creed in use that may have first been formulated in Greek before the end of the second century while Greek was still being used in Rome. It was handed over orally by the bishop to the catechumens as part of their instruction. It was part of the so-called discipline of the secret so that the candidates for baptism memorized it to profess before baptism.

According to F. X. Murphy, in the *New Catholic Encyclopedia*, the *textus receptus* (the "received text"), the text of the Apostles' Creed as we know it now, seems to be found first in liturgical and instruction books of the seventh and eighth centuries and probably had its origin in southern Gaul.

How old are the requirements for the Easter duty?

According to John M. Huels, O.S.M., in *The Code of Canon Law: A Text and Commentary,*

> As a result of widespread neglect of the sacrament [Eucharist] in the Middle Ages, various Church councils from the sixth century onward enacted disciplinary laws obligating the faithful to receive the Eucharist, especially on feasts. Lateran IV in 1215 established a general law for the Latin Church requiring the reception of Communion at least once a year at Easter by those who had attained the age of discretion, unless for some reasonable cause one's priest has advised against it for a time.

Huels says this law was confirmed by the Council of Trent and is basically the same law found in the 1917 *Code of Canon Law*. The 1983 code retains the annual precept but allows for its fulfillment outside of Easter season for a just cause. And it specified that it applies to all the faithful after they have been initiated into the Eucharist (made their First Communion) rather than giving the age of discretion for the beginning of the obligation.

Concerning the precept for the sacrament of reconciliation, Frederick R. McManus, in the same commentary, writes that canon 989 is rephrased from canon 906 of the 1917 code. Those laws were based on the norm produced by the Fourth Lateran Council. McManus says that the present law makes it clear that the obligation of annual confession is applicable only in the case of grave sins. That was not specifically stated in the old law. At the same time, it may be good to note that the present law recommends that venial sins be confessed as well as grave sins. And the church would surely recommend frequent confession, not just once a year.

Who changed the Sabbath observance from Saturday to Sunday?

In *The Liturgical Year: Celebrating the Mystery of Christ and His Saints*, the secretariat of the Bishops' Committee on the Liturgy asserts:

> One cannot write that the early Jewish Christians observed the Sabbath until year "X" when the influence of Gentile converts pressed them to change to Sunday.... Even while the earliest Christians revered the Sabbath, the first day of the week became the day to celebrate the paschal mystery. All the evangelists agree that this was the day of the Lord's resurrection. Many of the postresurrection appearances of Jesus were on the first day of the week. It was the day on which the gift of the Holy Spirit was bestowed. As Acts 20:7 tells us, early Christians gathered that day "for the breaking of bread."

The *New Catholic Encyclopedia* states, "It was made clear to early Christians that they were not bound by Jewish practices as such, but only to the extent that they embodied the natural law (Acts 15:28–29)." The Christians believed among the practices abrogated was the keeping of the Sabbath.

It is possible, says this same source, that Christians in Jerusalem and some other Judeo-Christians "continued to observe the Sabbath but Saint Paul did not impose the obligation on the communities he established outside Palestine (Colossians 2:16; Galatians 4:10; Romans 14:5)."

The *New Catholic Encyclopedia* says that "under the Jewish [Sabbath] observance there was a certain kernel of obligation attributable to the natural law" demanding that God be worshipped and honored. This obligation would "be fulfilled with sufficient regularity only if certain times are set aside" for it. So there came into use among Christians the observance of Sunday (the Lord's Day) as a day of worship and prayer.

431

In one of the earliest Christian writings, dating back to about A.D. 90, the *Didache*, there appears the instruction, "Every Sunday of the Lord, being assembled break the bread and give thanks."

In Volume 113 of the *Twentieth Century Catholic Encyclopedia*, Noelle M. Denis-Boulet says that Saint Ignatius of Antioch, in his *Epistle to the Magnesians*, wrote,

> Having passed that which is old to the newness of hope, no longer observing the Sabbath but living according to the Lord's Day (secundam dominicam), in which our life began through him and through his death....

It is clear from this excerpt that Christians were observing Sunday rather than the Sabbath.

John Koenig in Volume 64 of the same work, *God's Word at Mass*, quotes from Saint Justin the Martyr's description of the Sunday observance in his *First Apology* (about A.D. 150). He says, "On the day which is called Sunday we have a common assembly of all who live in the cities or in the outlying districts...."

Nearly everyone would say the apostles found authority for transferring the day of worship from the Sabbath to Sunday in Jesus' words to the disciples in Matthew 18:18, "I assure you, whatever you declare bound on earth shall be bound in heaven, and whatever you declare loosed on earth shall be loosed in heaven."

Is it true Martin Luther gave the world the question-answer catechism?

According to Father Alfred McBride, O. PRAEM., writing in the February 21, 1993 issue of *Our Sunday Visitor*, the first catechism in question-and-answer form was done by Martin Luther in 1529.

After the Council of Trent had off and on talked about a catechism and the Holy Roman Emperor Ferdinand I and other Catholic kings urged the fathers of the Council of Trent to issue a catechism, Pope Saint Pius V brought the *Roman*

Catechism to completion in 1566. It was not a question-and-answer catechism. Rather it was done as a collection of essays directed to parish priests and divided into four sections: the Creed, the Sacraments, the Commandments and the Our Father. The new *Catechism of the Catholic Church* follows this same order.

The first Catholic catechism, according to McBride, was written by Saint Peter Canisius for Germany in 1566 and was used very successfully for teaching the faith to children. A year later Saint Robert Bellarmine produced a question-and-answer book for Italy.

In response to the Council of Baltimore in 1884, Father Vincent de Consilio and Bishop John Lancaster Spalding authored our well-known *Baltimore Catechism*. They relied much on a catechism by George Hay of Edinburgh (1778) and an Irish catechism published in 1775 by Archbishop James Butler (revised by the synod of Maynooth in 1885).

Why are today's descendants of Abraham, Isaac and Jacob called Jews rather than Israelites?

Our English word *Jew* is derived from the Latin word *Judaeus* and the Hebrew word *Yehudi*, "belonging to Judah."

Israel was a name given to Jacob because he wrestled or contended with God (Genesis 32:29). One of Jacob's (Israel's) twelve sons was Judah. After Jacob's son Joseph was sold into slavery by his brothers, Joseph was taken to Egypt. Later, in the time of the famine, he was reconciled with his brothers. In Egypt he was joined by his brothers and his father, Jacob (Israel).

This was basically the people of Israel whom Moses led to the promised land. They became the Kingdom of Israel.

After the death of Solomon the northern inhabitants rebelled. The people and land became divided into a northern kingdom (Israel) and southern kingdom (Judah).

In 721 B.C. the northern kingdom (Israel) was conquered by Assyria. Its people were dispersed into captivity. The kingdom was ended.

In 587 B.C. Jerusalem fell and the southern kingdom (Judah) was overcome by Nebuchadnezzar. Many of its inhabitants were taken into Babylonian captivity.

In 538 B.C. Cyrus and the Persians permitted those in exile to return to their land. The returnees were predominantly from the tribe of Judah. They settled in the land formerly occupied by the Judeans. All came to be called Yehudi, Judeans or Jews.

Why does the priest dress the way he does at Mass?

For the first three centuries there were no special clothes for the presider or celebrant of the Eucharist. The celebrant wore ordinary street clothes.

Late in the third century or early in the fourth century, writers began to mention special garb for liturgical actions. Saints Athanasius, Jerome and John Chrysostom all mentioned liturgical garb for clerics. They particularly referred to the orarion, a primitive stole. The Council of Laodicea (343–381) often referred to vestments for sacred functions.

Today's vestments have their origins in the ordinary clothes of the later Greco-Roman world. The alb, a long loose-fitting garment, was worn around the house. The more decorative chasuble was worn over it in public.

As Father Thomas Richstatter, O.F.M. points out, in a *Catholic Update* article entitled "A Tour of a Catholic Church":

> If you attended Mass in fourth century Rome, the leader of the liturgical assembly would be dressed in much the same way as the priest vests for Sunday Mass. But at that time, everyone in the church would be wearing an alb and chasuble.

How did we get the names of the wise men?

The names Caspar (Gaspar), Melchior and Baltassar do not come from the Scriptures. And, as a matter of fact, Matthew's account of the coming of the magi does not even say how many wise men came seeking the newborn king.

Early paintings or icons picture any number from two to eight magi coming to worship Jesus. Among Eastern Christians there were said to be twelve wise men.

In the West devotion and tradition after a while settled on the number three. Probably because the Gospel of Saint Matthew speaks of three gifts—gold, incense and myrrh. The magi came to be regarded as kings because of passages in the Psalms and Isaiah.

The *New Catholic Encyclopedia* and other reference books state that no earlier than the eighth century were the wise men given the names Gaspar, Melchior and Baltassar. Yet, the *New Catholic Encyclopedia* illustrates the entry about the magi with a photo of a mosaic dating from the sixth century in which the names Gaspar, Melchior and Baltassar clearly appear over three figures in the mosaic.

It may also be interesting to note that in Syrian tradition the names Larvandad, Harmisdas and Gushnasaph are given for the wise men. Some names found in Armenian legends or traditions are Kagba and Badalima.

The Cathedral in Cologne, Germany, holds what are reputed to be the relics of the three wise men. They were brought there from Milan in the twelfth century. Little is known of the history of these relics before that time. So there is certainly a question about their authenticity.

How did the tradition of ashes on Ash Wednesday get started?

The use of ashes and dust, with religious, magical or medical meanings was common among the ancients, says the *New Catholic Encyclopedia*. They were often symbolic of mortality, mourning or penance. In the Hebrew Scriptures, after Jonah has announced the destruction of Nineveh and the news reaches the king, he rises from the throne, lays aside his robe, puts on sackcloth and sits in ashes. The king then proclaims a fast. Nineveh mourns its sins and does penance (Jonah 3:1–6). In foreseeing the destruction to come upon Israel, Jeremiah says, "O my poor people...roll in ashes. Make mourning as for an only child, most bitter lamentation, for suddenly the destroyer will come upon us" (6:26). Jeremiah calls Israel to conversion.

In the Gospel of Matthew, Jesus reproaches Chorazin and Bethsaida, saying, "For if the deeds of power done in you had been done in Tyre and Sidon, they would have repented long ago in sackcloth and ashes" (11:21).

Christians, then, seem to have taken the use of ashes as a sign of penance from Jewish tradition. According to the *New Catholic Encyclopedia*, ashes were originally signs of private penance. But early on they became part of the ritual for public penance.

Adolf Adam, in *The Liturgical Year*, points to Tertullian and Cyprian, in the third century, as evidence early Christians were familiar with ashes as a sign and part of the ritual for public penance.

As early as the fourth century, local churches had a ritual for the beginning of public penance at the start of Lent. Those who had been guilty of public serious sins, such as murder, apostasy, heresy or adultery, were clothed in penitential garment and sprinkled with ashes.

The sinner was then expelled and led from the church as Adam had been cast out of paradise. Later those ending their penance (which could go for years) were received back into the church on Maundy Thursday. They were led back into the church in procession as part of a rite of reconciliation.

According to Herman Wegman, in *Christian Worship in East and West*, texts and ceremonies were added to the rite for the reception of penitents in the ninth century and carried over into the *Pontificale Romanum* of the Council of Trent.

Adolf Adam says public ecclesiastical penance disappeared around the end of the first millennium. Wegman suggests that the severity of the practice was at least partially the reason for its disappearance. But there was also a growing conviction that every person is a sinner and must do penance.

Pope Urban II (1088–1099) recommended to all the churches the custom of all receiving ashes. Ashes were put on the heads of men and the Sign of the Cross traced with ashes on the foreheads of women, presumably because their heads were covered. In the eleventh century there appeared a special prayer for the blessing of ashes. And the twelfth century gave rise to the rule that the ashes be made from the palm branches of the previous year.

Who established the liturgical season of Advent and when?

Thomas J. Talley, in *The Origins of the Liturgical Year*, sees the beginning of an Advent season in the fourth canon of a Council of Saragossa in 380. In 567 a synod at Tours established a December fast. And in 581 the Council of Macon ordered an Advent fast for the laity from the feast of Saint Martin (November 11) to Christmas. This took the name of Saint Martin's Lent.

In the seventh and eighth centuries, lectionaries (books containing the scriptural readings for the Liturgy of the Word) provided for six Sundays in Advent.

According to the *HarperCollins Encyclopedia of Catholicism*, Gregory the Great, who died in 604, was the real architect of the Roman Advent. Gregory fixed the season for four weeks and composed seasonal prayers and antiphons. Gaul (France) enriched the season with eschatological elements. The fusion of the Roman and Gallican observances returned to Rome by the twelfth century.

How long has the Feast of the Assumption been a holy day?

The feast of the Assumption has been a holy day of obligation for the entire Latin rite church since early in the ninth century. Since it has only been since 1950 that the dogma of the Assumption was proclaimed by Pope Pius XII, we can see the feast day obligation goes back centuries before the definition of this truth.

By tradition there has been an August 15 feast honoring Mary since before 529. At this early date it was celebrated as the feast of the Dormition of Mary (the falling asleep of Mary). In the seventh and eighth centuries, the title became the Assumption of Mary. And in 813 the Council of Mainz legislated the feast as a holy day for the whole empire of the West. Shortly after that the pope extended to the entire Latin rite church the obligation to observe this feast.

What is the papal tiara?

In its simplest form the papal tiara seems to have appeared about the third century. Over the years it became much more ornate and took on a kind of beehive shape.

The tiara came to consist of three crowns. According to James Charles Noonan Jr., in *The Church Visible*, the bottom crown became ornamentation at the base of the miter in the ninth century. When the popes assumed temporal power the base crown became decorated with jewels to resemble the crown of princes. A second crown was added by Boniface VIII in 1298 to symbolize spiritual dominion. Very soon after, a third crown and lappets (cloth strips) were added.

According to Noonan the triple tiara represents the pope's universal episcopate, his supreme jurisdiction and his temporal power. It is also said to represent his role as priest, pastor and teacher. In our century the tiara came to be regarded as inappropriate because of its ornateness and rich character. Pope Paul VI stopped wearing the tiara and sold his, using the funds for the poor.

Where did the rosary come from?

The following very short history of the rosary appeared in the preface of Joanne Turpin's book *The Healing Mysteries: A Rosary for the Sick:*

> Pious tradition has it that the mother of Jesus, Mary herself, gave the rosary to Saint Dominic Guzman and told him to preach this prayer. More likely, the rosary developed out of the 12th century chaplets of Pater's or Ave's recited by the Catholics of that time.

These chaplets were a kind of poor person's Breviary made up of 150 Our Fathers (Pater Noster's) or Hail Marys (Ave's) corresponding to the 150 psalms of the Psalter, they were sometimes divided into sets of three 50's and counted on strings of beads called "paternosters." Each of the prayers was associated with a mystery in the lives of Jesus and Mary pronounced and meditated on at each bead or prayer of the chaplet.

In time the "psalters" of Our Fathers and Hail Marys came to be joined and merged. The Our Fathers and Hail Marys were prayed alternately, each Our Father followed by a Hail Mary. The 50 mysteries came to be reduced to five—one for each decade. Finally the rosary took its present form.

The *Enchiridion of Indulgences* tells us,

> The rosary is a certain formula of prayer, which is made up of 15 decades of "Hail Marys" with an "Our Father" before each decade, and in which the recitation of each decade is accompanied by pious meditation on a particular mystery of our redemption.

Commonly these are the traditional joyful, sorrowful and glorious mysteries listed in the appendix of the *Enchiridion* and our prayer books. The *Enchiridion* does not say, however, that we must meditate on these particular mysteries in Jesus' and Mary's lives.

When were kneelers introduced into worship?

Liturgist Thomas Richstatter, O.F.M., answers,

> I would refer you to *The Postures of the Assembly during the Eucharistic Prayer*, by John K. Leonard and Nathan D. Mitchell, regarding the practice of kneeling at prayer.
>
> Regarding kneelers as furniture, I would presume they were relatively late. Originally there were no pieces of furniture for the 'circumstantes' (those standing about), simply a chair for the president. As a concession to the infirm, stone seats began to be attached to pillars, or to walls. By the end of the thirteenth century many

churches in England appear to have some wooden benches—often called pews.

When kneelers began to be attached to pews, I do not know. Pews became common as printing becomes more common and we pass from a manuscript culture [where books were rare and more often heard than read] to a print culture [with wide distribution of books]. People line up in pews in churches as words line up on a page in books.

As public worship expresses who we are as a community in the presence of God, I find it interesting that Leonard and Mitchell say, "It is not for no reason that the Orthodox have been characterized as 'the Church standing,' the Roman Catholics as 'the Church kneeling,' and the Protestants as 'the Church sitting.'

"These basic bodily postures communicate a great deal about the self-identity of these Christian communions. Though none of these postures is exclusive to the Church that it characterizes, each one tells us something about basic attitudes: standing as praising God with upright bodies, kneeling as an act either of adoration or of penitence, and sitting as an act of receptivity, listening and participating in a common meal. Each posture certainly has its advantages, and each makes a great deal of difference in the self-understanding of the Church."

Why does Texas have a city named for Saint Anthony?

In 1691 a Spanish expedition camped at a little-known village in present-day Texas. The *New Catholic Encyclopedia* explains the Franciscan chaplain of the expedition named the site for Saint Anthony of Padua, whose feast was being celebrated that day.

In 1691 this area was still Spanish territory. So, rather than speaking of Texas naming the city, we would have to say that Spain named it. It was not until 1718 that a mission was established at San Antonio. In 1731 the inhabitants formed the first city government in Texas.

When the Republic of Texas and later the state of Texas

took over the territory, there was already existing the Spanish-named city of San Antonio. A look at a map will show that the Spanish often named cities for a saint. Cities grew up around a Catholic mission named for a saint and took the name of the mission.

Why did the Jews not accept Jesus?

Not all Jews rejected Jesus or were involved in his condemnation. All his apostles and first followers were, after all, Jews. Also, it must never be forgotten that Jesus himself was a Jew! In the case of those who rejected Jesus, the *Catechism of the Catholic Church* suggests a number of reasons for their actions, based on the Gospels themselves. Those in power saw Jesus as a threat to their leadership. They viewed him as rocking the political boat and inviting more intervention in Jewish affairs by their Roman occupiers. Jesus was also a personal reproach to them, an accuser of their way of life and their personal sins and failings.

Some Pharisees saw Jesus making an attack on the law of Moses and Jewish institutions. Some were scandalized because Jesus mixed and ate with sinners. And some could not accept Jesus' claims to power and authority, especially the power to forgive sins. In many cases Jesus just did not fit their preconceived ideas of who or what the messiah should be.

Where did the brown scapular come from?

Saint Simon Stock was a general of the Carmelite Order in the thirteenth century. He died in Bordeaux on May 16, 1265. A number of stories have been handed down about him. One legend has it that Simon was a vegetarian and that once when a cooked fish was put before him he told those who served it to throw it back into the river and it swam away restored to life. Another story has it that, as a boy, he adopted the life of a hermit and lived in the hollow trunk of a tree.

There is also a tradition that once when Simon was praying for his Carmelite Order the Blessed Virgin appeared to him holding in her hand the scapular of his Order. According to this story the Blessed Virgin told Simon that anyone who died in the scapular would be preserved from hell and on the first Saturday after dying would be taken by her to heaven. This has been called the Sabbatine privilege.

Whether the vision was indeed a fact or a mere story, as well as what the promise means, has been debated for centuries. As for the reality of the vision, there is no contemporary or near-contemporary document that attests to it or refers to it.

In the *New Catholic Encyclopedia* article on scapulars, P. N. Zammit wrote that it is disputed whether the vision or even the scapular was known to Carmelite friars of the mid–thirteenth century. And whatever the fact of the vision, Zammit says, the promises cannot be reasonably represented as requiring the mere fact of wearing the scapular without respect to interior dispositions with which it is worn. "To do so," he says, "would be to attribute a magical efficacy to the scapular and make it out to be a more potent channel of grace than the sacraments." He says the wearing of the scapular must therefore be understood to include the right and salutary interior dispositions with which it is worn.

The *New Catholic Encyclopedia* entry on Saint Simon Stock by D. Nicholl states, "The obvious sense [of the promise] is that whoever lives and dies as a Carmelite will not be lost."

Anthony Buono, in Catholic Book Publishing's *Dictionary of Mary*, reminds us,

> The symbol of the scapular or any other symbol adopted knowingly and spiritually vivified becomes an aid to faith and in some way renders what it signifies. Hence, the scapular is not a talisman or good-luck charm. Rather, it is a stimulus to faith and all that follows from it. That is why today without any difficulty many replace the scapular with a similar medal. It is the commitment that matters.

What is the difference between a Jew and a Gentile?

Originally the word *Jews* applied to those of the tribe of Judah. It was already used in the time of Jeremiah (born about 650 B.C.) to designate the inhabitants of the Kingdom of Judah. After the Babylonian Exile (587–538 B.C.) all those from the twelve tribes returning from the captivity who settled in Judea were called Jews.

Ultimately the word *Jews* came to designate all Israelites throughout the world. At the time of Jesus any member of the Israelite race was, in ordinary usage, called a Jew.

The Catholic Biblical Encyclopedia (Volume II, *The New Testament*), however, notes that the word *Jews* has three senses in the Gospel of John: (a) an ethnic sense—any persons belonging to the Jewish race and following the Jewish feasts and custom (John 2:6, 13; 5:1; 19:40); (b) a political sense—people belonging to the nation of Judea (John 1:19; 11:19; 12:11); (c) a leadership sense—those religiously representing the people, for example the Sanhedrin, high priests and Pharisees (John 18:14).

A somewhat different element is present when Paul speaks of the Jews. He stresses the mental attitude of people who reject Christ as the Messiah (1 Corinthians 1:22–24) or insist on the complete observance of the Mosaic Law (Romans 2:17, 28; Galatians 2:13). Paul also uses the word *Jews* to distinguish people from Greeks or Gentiles (Romans 9:24), not on the basis of race or nationality but as recipients of God's revelation.

Jews used the word *Gentiles* to designate all who were not of the Hebrew race. Biblical writers at times also called such people heathens and considered them beyond God's concern as noted in the *Concise Bible Dictionary*, by Donald McFarland. They could be of many beliefs and religions.

Have there been any bad or married popes?

Even now it is theoretically possible to elect a man who is not a priest or bishop to be pope. Patrick Granfield points this out in *The Papacy in Transition*, saying,

Any baptized male Catholic who is capable of accepting the election and of exercising authority may be elected. There is no provision in the law governing the candidate's age, nationality or status in the church.

The present *Code of Canon Law* and the requirements established by Pope Paul VI for the election of a pope say that the one elected obtains full and supreme power in the church by means of legitimate election accepted by him, together with episcopal consecration. If the one elected is not already a bishop, he is to be ordained a bishop immediately.

Details concerning the early popes are sparse. We simply do not know a great deal about them and the circumstances of their lives before election to the papacy.

It seems to have been a pattern for many centuries, however, to elect a pope from the clergy of Rome—a presbyter or deacon. In fact, Joseph Brusher, commenting on the election of Pope Marinus (882), says those electors went against custom to elect a man already bishop. Marinus was, at the time, bishop of Caere.

There is no example of anyone marrying after he became pope. But Saint Hormisdas (514–523), a deacon at the time of his election, was married before his ordination, and his son Silverius later also became pope. There is some reason to believe that Saint Agatho (678–681) was married and had a daughter at the time of his election. He had been married before being ordained a priest.

Leo VIII (963–965) and John XIX (1024–1032) were both laymen when elected bishop of Rome and pope. They had to be ordained immediately.

One of the reasons we had "bad" popes was that so much political and economic power became attached to the papacy. Especially during the years of the fifteenth and sixteenth centuries, the church offered, perhaps, the only road to power and wealth for those who were not born of nobility or, if nobles, were far down the line in rights to succession. Powerful noble families pushed their sons into the clergy and strongly promoted their careers and advancement. A son, an uncle, a cousin elected pope could bestow wealth and power on other family members. Kings and princes used raw power to put their own subjects or men friendly to them on the papal throne to protect and promote national interests.

Very often it was not the pious or most holy men who were the most adept at playing the political game and winning the way to power. And those promoting candidates for the papacy weren't all that interested in their piety. They were looking for men who would play the game their way and serve their interests. Lamentable as it is that inadequate and unworthy men became popes during this period, it is also remarkable how many disappointed their worldly sponsors and sought reform for the church and turned out to be genuinely concerned with the life of the spirit. And the fact that the church survived incompetent or sinful popes may be a sign of the Spirit's presence.

Some recent books on popes are *Lives of the Popes*, by Richard McBrien; *Vicars of Christ*, by Michael Riccards; and *Saints and Sinners*, by Eamon Duffy.

How many nails were used at the crucifixion?

The Gospels tell us very little about how Jesus was crucified. Each of the evangelists simply says something like, "They crucified him." There are few if any physical details about how this was done, what the cross was like or how the body was positioned.

It is from the account of the appearance of Jesus to the apostles after the Resurrection that we know Jesus was nailed to the cross. After the other apostles tell Thomas they have seen the Lord, he refused to believe, "Unless I see the mark of the nails in his hands and put my fingers into the nailmarks..." (John 20:25).

Further, it is not until the fifth century that we find any works of art depicting the crucifixion. For any details beyond the Scriptures, then, artists are pretty much dependent upon their own imaginations. Over the centuries the crucifixion has been painted or sculpted in many ways. The body is twisted in all different shapes. The cross assumes different forms.

Sometimes it is shaped like the uppercase letter *T*; at other times more like a plus sign.

When we discuss points such as how the feet were nailed, we can only speculate. We can make educated guesses from our knowledge of anatomy and from what history tells concerning the Roman method of crucifixion at the time of Jesus.

The ancient Romans, in crucifying, sometimes tied the body to the cross with ropes and at other times nailed it to the cross. Sometimes the cross beam was at the very top, at other times part way down the trunk. Usually, it seems, there was some kind of support, a kind of saddle or seat to partially support the weight of the body.

In describing crucifixion, Father John L. McKenzie writes, in the *Dictionary of the Bible:*

> The arms of the criminal were first attached to the cross beam while he was stretched flat on the ground; he was then, together with the cross beam attached to the upright beam. The fastening was done either by ropes or by nails; if nails were used, *four* [italics added] were employed. The criminal was always attached by ropes bound around arms, legs and belly; the nails would not support the weight of the body and the ropes prevented the victim from wriggling loose. Most of the weight was supported by a peg (Latin *sedile*, "seat") projecting from the upright beam on which the victim sat astride.... The support for the feet (Latin *suppedaneum*) so common in Christian art was unknown in antiquity. The victim was elevated scarcely more than a foot or two above the ground, low enough for a bystander to reach his mouth by putting a sponge upon a reed.

McKenzie goes on to say the victim was usually stripped entirely naked. His clothing went to the soldiers as a kind of gratuity. A placard with the criminal's name and crime was first worn around the neck and then affixed to the top of the cross.

According to those who write on the crucifixion, the wrists were viewed as part of the hands. And the nails were probably driven through the wrists because the palm of the hand would simply be torn apart by the weight of the body hanging on the nail.

We can be pretty sure that the feet were individually nailed to the cross, side by side, rather than one foot on top of the other with one nail driven through both. It would be most difficult to nail the feet to the cross with one nail.

Where did we get the Sign of Peace?

The Sign or Kiss of Peace goes far back into history. In fact, the exchange of the kiss (sign) of peace was probably taken over from the secular and court practices of the Semitic or Arab world.

We know from the *First Apology of Saint Justin* that already by the middle of the second century in the celebration of the Eucharist a Sign or Kiss of Peace was given following the prayer of general intercessions and before the blessing of the gifts of bread and wine. The writings of Tertullian and Saint Cyprian also placed the Sign of Peace at that point in association with the Lord's Prayer.

We also know from the *Apostolic Tradition* of Hippolytus that a Kiss or Sign of Peace was given to the newly baptized at the Easter Vigil baptismal and eucharistic celebration.

In the early fifth century Pope Innocent I spoke of the Kiss of Peace being given in the Roman liturgy before Communion. By this time, incidentally, recitation of the Lord's Prayer had also been moved to this place in the liturgy.

Even in the Tridentine liturgy we celebrated before the liturgical renewal following Vatican II, the clergy exchanged the Sign of Peace before Communion in a solemn high Mass.

Whether the Sign of Peace is placed after the prayer of intercessions or almost immediately before Communion, and whether it is given by brushing cheeks or shaking hands, it is an expression of our desire to fulfill Christ's command in the Gospel of Saint Matthew:

> So when you are offering your gift at the altar, if you remember that your brother or sister has something against you, leave your gift there before the altar and go,

447

first be reconciled to your brother or sister, and then come and offer your gift. (5:23–24)

It is an expression of our desire to live out what we say in the Lord's Prayer when we ask God to forgive us as we forgive each other.

It is also worth noting that the Kiss or Sign of Peace has been a part of other liturgical ceremonies such as the reception of candidates into a religious community or the profession of vows in religious orders.

Is the candy cane a religious symbol?

According to one legend the choirmaster of the Cologne Cathedral gave his young singers sugar sticks in 1670 to keep them quiet during a long crèche ceremony. He bent them in the shape of shepherds' crooks. In 1847 a German-Swedish immigrant named August Imgard decorated a small tree in Wooster, Ohio, with candy canes.

Another source says that an Indiana candy maker wanted to make a Christmas witness. He began with a stick of pure white hard candy to symbolize the virgin birth and sinless character of Jesus. Hard candy symbolized the church's rock foundation. Upright the staff-like shape represented Jesus the Good Shepherd. Upside down the cane became the letter J for "Jesus." The candy maker added one broad red stripe and three narrow ones. The broad stripe calls to mind the blood of Jesus shed on the cross. The narrow ones represent the stripes of his scourging. Peppermint, like hyssop, belongs to the mint family. It reminds us of the hyssop used in the Old Testament for purification and sacrifice.

When did Latin become the official language of the church?

In *The Story of the Mass*, Pierre Loret traces the history of the Eucharist. Exactly when Greek replaced Aramaic is not clear. But it was probably quite early in the New Testament era. The New Testament writings were in Greek, and early Christians reading from them in the celebration of the Eucharist read them in Greek.

In Rome itself Latin replaced Greek as the language of the eucharistic celebration early in the third century. Hippolytus of Rome separated from the church in 222 and became the first antipope after clashing with Popes Zephyrinus and Callistus. One of his reasons for schism was his "bristling opposition" to the introduction of Latin in the liturgy in place of Greek. His opposition may have been influenced by the fact he was probably born in Alexandria and his cultural background was Greek. At that time Greek was still the language of the "cultured." Callistus, however, had been born a slave and felt very close to the ordinary people in Rome who spoke Latin. He decided that in Rome, at least, the language of the people should be the language of the liturgy. The aristocrats and intellectuals opposed Latin in the liturgy, as did Hippolytus.

Just to complete the story, Hippolytus was reconciled to the church by Pope Pontianus when they were both exiled to Sardinia. And Hippolytus was martyred in 235.

In Rome, Latin and Greek existed side by side for over a century. There was a kind of pluralism in which each could pray in his or her own language. The liturgy was not completely Latinized until the second half of the fourth century— 150 years after Hippolytus. Latin gained ascendancy because of the greater number of those who spoke Latin.

It is also interesting to note that in the seventh century, when Greek Christians became rather numerous in Rome, a kind of bilingual liturgy evolved again mingling prayers in both Latin and Greek. Even today, as a holdover from those days, when the pope celebrates Mass in St. Peter's Basilica the Epistle and Gospel are read in both Latin and Greek.

Things took a different course in the East. And today, as in the past, the Eucharist is celebrated in many different ways and languages. At this time there are ten different liturgies in ten different languages.

For centuries the church of the West, or Roman rite, has struggled over the issue of which is more important: that the people understand what they are praying and saying in the

449

liturgy or that the liturgy be celebrated everywhere in the same way and language.

Why has the *filioque* been omitted from the creed?

As we read the history of the *filioque* debate, it increasingly appears that the quarrel began more as a matter of words to be used than of real theological substance. But it progressed to a matter of rights, authority and wounded feelings. From early on bishops and doctors in the East and the West had their own particular theological and spiritual perspectives.

The earliest councils settled debates over the divinity and humanity of Jesus and the relationship of the Son to the Father. They condemned the great heresies that denied Jesus was divine or that made him a kind of lesser god. Attention then shifted to the relationship of the Holy Spirit to the Father and Son and whether the Holy Spirit was truly God.

The great doctors and bishops of the West used the word *Godhead* in two senses. Sometimes they spoke of the Father or First Person alone as the Godhead. At other times they spoke of the Trinity as the Godhead. The Eastern church was not accustomed to speaking of the Trinity as the Godhead but used that word to speak only of the Father from whom the Son proceeds.

The Western fathers and doctors were very much concerned with preserving the truth of the oneness and unity in God. They used the language of theology and spoke of the inner life of the Trinity in terms of the Son being begotten by the Father and of the Holy Spirit proceeding from the Father *and* the Son.

The Eastern father and doctors were more concerned with preserving the truth that in God there are three distinct persons. They adhered closely to the words used in the Scriptures and spoke of the Father begetting the Son and of the Spirit proceeding from the Father *through* the Son.

The Eastern church felt that to speak of the Spirit proceeding from the Father and the Son as well was to assert two processions and therefore two separate Godheads.

In the context of their writings, the Western fathers and bishops were speaking of the Spirit proceeding from the Father and Son as from one (not two) principles. He is spirated, or breathed forth, by the Father and Son. He is the breath of life, the Spirit, of both the Father and the Son as from a single source.

The Nicene-Constantinopolitan Creed (which we call the Nicene Creed) that emerged from the Ecumenical Council of Constantinople spoke simply of the Holy Spirit "who proceeds from the Father."

The Third Council of Toledo (a local Spanish Council) in 589 added to "proceeds from the Father" the word "*filioque*," meaning, "and the Son." From Spain the practice spread. It was finally inserted in the recitation of the creed in Rome in the eleventh century.

The Eastern church reacted strongly to adding anything to the creed outside of an ecumenical council. They regarded it as arbitrary and insulting. The quarrel moved from a question of rights and etiquette to charges of heresy.

At the reunion Council of Florence in 1438, the legitimacy of adding *filioque* to the creed was argued and debated for over two months in thirteen sessions. The council members finally agreed that the quarrel was over words rather than basic doctrine.

The final decree signed by both Latins and Greeks defined that the Holy Spirit proceeds from the Father and the Son as from one principle and one spiration, *from* and *through* being equivalent and causal.

Even so, the council did not demand the Greeks add the *filioque* in reciting the creed. In 1742 Benedict XIV ruled the Eastern rites in union with Rome were not obliged to include it in the Oriental Creed.

It is true, of course, that the union achieved at Florence was only temporary. The agreement of Florence was renounced by some of the Eastern participants. And to this day the *filioque* remains a bone of contention.

Yet, as Ladislas Orsy pointed out, in an article in *America*, the Council of Florence offers us a model of ecumenism. It urges us to look behind the words we use and to talk *to* each other rather than *at* each other and respect differences in insights and expressions of the same mysteries in different words.

The gift of Florence, wrote Orsy,

> consisted in drawing both sides away from rigid stances, misunderstandings and futile accusations, and giving them a new intelligence that went beyond the differences in vocabulary and perceived something of the core of the one mystery. They reached "the same intelligence... under different expressions."

Finally, to answer more directly the question, Roman Catholics have not changed their belief in the Trinity or the procession of the Spirit from the Father and from the Son (as from one principle).

The dispute is not entirely resolved. What has been resolved is simply whether the *filioque* is to be added to the Nicene-Constantinopolitan Creed when Orthodox and Roman Catholics worship together.

This is a reasonable decision that respects the consciences and feelings of both the Orthodox and Catholics. If Eastern rite Catholics in union with Rome are not required to add the *filioque*, why should the Orthodox be asked to do so in common worship?

What were the religions of Arabia before Mohammed?

According to *Eerdman's Handbook to the World's Religions*, the dominant religion in Arabia at the time of Mohammed (A.D. 570–632) was a form "of the old Semitic religion." Its adherents worshipped a number of gods and goddesses with a high or supreme god with whom others could be asked to intercede. The supreme god was identified as Allah.

Followers of this religion had different shrines to the various gods and goddesses and were believers in fate *(Kismet)*. At the same time, says this handbook, there were some Christian tribes and a Jewish community in Medina.

The *New Catholic Encyclopedia* states that Mohammed

began as a follower of pagan practices and beliefs of his Hashim family and Quraysh tribe. His experience with this religion, says this encyclopedia, influenced the ritual and practices of Islam, even though he was convinced the religion had to be overthrown as a system.

In this regard, the encyclopedia says, "Mohammed must gradually have been appalled at the absurdities of pagan worship and the low level of pagan morals around him—for instance, the live burial of female infants." It seems likely that Mohammed, as a young man, came into contact with Judaism and Christianity and had forty years to learn about these religions before his prophethood began.

According to the *New Catholic Encyclopedia,* Mohammed was also associated with a small group who thought of themselves as "the pure ones" *(hunafa)* and were monotheists (believers in one God) who tended neither to Judaism or Christianity—although some of the hunafa later became Christian.

Many new books on the history and development of the Islamic faith are available in the aftermath of the September 11, 2001, attacks on the World Trade Center and the Pentagon. It is important to real well-balanced accounts to become informed about this important religious tradition.

Is it wrong to eat blood sausage?

It may help us understand why the apostles and presbyters in Acts told Gentile converts "to avoid pollution from...the meat of strangled animals, and blood" if we reflect on many of the things going on in our post–Vatican II church. We have had heated debates about whether women or girls should be allowed to serve at the altar, about whether people should be allowed to receive Communion in the hand, about using inclusive language, about kneeling and standing.

We struggle with questions about adapting liturgical rites to reflect the customs and ways of particular nations or ethnic groups. Just before the recent African Synod in Rome, the Congregation for Divine Worship issued a statement on inculturation—how a people or peoples can be permitted to express their faith and worship in their own way, according to their own customs and ways of life. Perhaps some people wondered about African dances and music in St. Peter's Basilica that opened the African Synod.

In Acts 15, when Paul and Barnabas came from Antioch to Jerusalem, they found themselves in the midst of a quarrel over demands of the Mosaic Law. The church was still in its infancy. Most of its members did not think of themselves as church, as an entity apart from the Jewish people. They thought of themselves as Jews who followed Christ. They were still to be found worshipping and praying in the Temple and synagogues and observing the Mosaic Law. But as followers of Christ, they also gathered to celebrate the Eucharist and reflect on his word and teaching.

Now Peter has had a vision that the word and faith are not just for Jews but for Gentiles as well. And Paul and Barnabas have successfully carried the gospel, "the good news," to Gentile peoples and baptized them as followers of Christ. But the Gentiles are not circumcised; they did not follow the Mosaic Law or think of themselves as Jews. The Christian Pharisees and Judaizers in Jerusalem argue that to be accepted as followers of Jesus, as members of this new community of believers, the Gentile must accept the Mosaic Law! They must be circumcised and follow Jewish religious practices. These Jewish Christians find the idea of sitting down at table and celebrating Eucharist with people who eat nonkosher food, meat with blood in it, abhorrent! Jewish tradition forbids that. It thinks of blood as life itself, which is sacred and belongs only to God.

At a meeting of presbyters and apostles, Peter recounts his experience and argues that the Law is not to be imposed on the Gentiles. Then Paul and Barnabas describe the working of grace among the Gentiles.

It is resolved that the Gentile converts do not have to be circumcised and the obligations of the Mosaic Law are not to be imposed upon them. But the Gentiles are called upon to respect the sensibilities of their Jewish brothers and sisters.

454

If you invited Jewish guests to a meal today, you would try to serve kosher food. Or if you entered a home in Japan, you would take off your shoes out of respect for your hosts and their customs. So the Gentiles were instructed to respect the Jewish dietary laws so that Jewish and Gentile Christians could share the same table and Eucharist.

It was kind of a modus vivendi agreed to by Jewish and Gentile Christians. The prohibition of blood meats seems to have lasted until the time of Tertullian at the end of the second century.

As the followers of Christ separated completely from the Jewish community and their practices, you can see why observing Jewish dietary laws was no longer an issue of importance. In short, it was a disciplinary law that lost its purpose and meaning. It is no longer a part of church discipline. Today, the only thing to keep you back from a rare steak or blood sausage is the question of how healthy or hygienic they are.

Why haven't the creeds been revised to include our belief in the eucharistic real presence?

The creeds are historical documents and, besides being statements of faith, are also reactions to questions being raised at the times of their formations. The creeds are in some instances responses to heresies of their times.

The Nicene Creed that we recite on Sunday in the Eucharist is the product of the Council of Nicaea (A.D. 325) and Constantinople (A.D. 381). In a sense talking about amending this creed is like talking about rewriting the Declaration of Independence.

As a matter of fact, as other theological questions and disputes arose, later councils and synods as well as popes responded to them. So, for instance, the much longer creed incorrectly attributed to Saint Athanasius was produced in the fifth century.

The real presence of Jesus in the Eucharist was not seriously challenged or questioned until the time of the Protestant

Reformation. At that time the fact of the real presence or the way it takes place came under heavy debate. So the Council of Trent (1545–1563) responded to these as well as other questions. The council gave us statements, which, if not in a neat, concise credal form, are as much statements of faith as the creeds.

Pope Paul VI on June 30, 1968—after Vatican II—gave us the Credo of the People of God. While we do not use it in the liturgy (it is about ten pages long), that creed devotes three paragraphs to our belief in the Mass and Eucharist. You can find the text of this creed in *Vatican II: More Postconciliar Documents*, Volume II, edited by Austin Flannery, O.P.

Have there ever been married priests?

As a matter of fact, there are still some married priests (legitimately married) in the Eastern rites of the Catholic church in union with Rome. The canon law of many of these rites permits men to marry before, but not after, they are ordained.

This option is not granted to men of these rites ordained in the United States. The apparent reason for this exclusion is the confusion Rome believes it would cause in view of the Latin rite discipline in the United States.

While priests and clergy in both East and West often remained celibate out of choice, in the first three centuries there was no law against married clergy. J. R. Rehage, however, in the *New Catholic Encyclopedia*, asserts that by the fourth century, custom or unwritten law prohibited married clerics in major orders from using their marriage rights and excluded unmarried men from marrying after ordination.

The first law demanding celibacy in the Latin church came from the Council of Elvira (A.D. 306) which forbade bishops, priests, deacons and other ministers of the altar to have wives. Not much later the Council of Carthage explicitly included subdeacons in these rules.

However, these were regional statutes and not universal law even for the Latin church.

In 1123 the First Lateran Council extended the law of celibacy to all major clerics of the Latin rite and declared null the marriages of major clerics who attempted marriage. Trent confirmed this practice.

A book that might interest you on this subject is *Celibacy: Gift or Law?* by Heinz J. Vogels.

Have there ever been women deacons or priests?

It has not been definitively settled whether, historically, women have been or can be ordained deacons. The text in Romans 16:1–2 does use the word *diakonos* in Greek. The *New Oxford Annotated Bible: Revised Standard Version* reads, "I recommend to you our sister Phoebe, a Deaconess of the church at Cenchreae." Yet the footnote tells the reader that *deaconess* may mean simply "helper."

The Good News Bible: The Bible in Today's English Version speaks of Phoebe "who serves the church at Cenchreae." It does not translate *diakonos* as *deaconess*. The *New American Bible* translates the verse to read, "I commend to you Phoebe, our sister, who is (also) a minister of the Church at Cenchreae." Nelson's *A New Catholic Commentary on Holy Scripture*, edited by Reginald Fuller, tells us the exact meaning of this title is disputed although the corresponding masculine noun indicates an official title.

John McKenzie, in his *Dictionary of the Bible*, also notes that the title does not indicate a hierarchical office and can refer to services rendered by Phoebe to the community of Cenchreae. The *New Jerome Biblical Commentary* states that *diakonos* may designate a member of a special group in the church of Cenchreae or may be only a generic designation—for example, servant or assistant. The commentary states there is no way of being sure that the term already designated a special order of ministers.

Father Norbert Brockman, S.M., author of *Ordained to Service*, a book on the theology of the permanent diaconate, is reported to have said in 1978 that the appeal to tradition for admitting women to the ordained diaconate is on shaky grounds—evidence is lacking that a female deaconess was a female deacon. And, said Brockman, ordaining women to orders was not even considered in the writings of the fathers of the church.

Monsignor Donald Hamilton, writing in the *Long Island Catholic*, noted that at least one Eastern Orthodox church continues to have a few deaconesses but the ordination by which they are set apart is not viewed as a conferral of the sacrament of holy orders.

When it speaks of the sacrament of holy orders and who may receive the sacrament, the *Catechism of the Catholic Church* does not distinguish between the order of diaconate and priesthood. It says simply, "Only a baptized man (*vir*) validly receives sacred ordination" (1577). It goes on to say that the "Lord Jesus chose men (*viri*) to form the college of twelve apostles, and the apostles did the same when they chose collaborators to succeed them.... The church recognizes herself to be bound by this choice made by the Lord himself. For this reason the ordination of women is not possible."

Some theologians argue that, cultically, only a male can adequately represent Christ in the eucharistic liturgy. Elden F. Curtiss, now archbishop of Omaha, Nebraska, compared the central figure in the celebration of the Eucharist to an actor playing Shakespeare's Hamlet. Curtiss wrote that only a male actor can properly be cast to represent Hamlet—a male. He writes, "The Eucharistic sacrifice makes present to us the reality of the crucifixion of Jesus as it touches our lives. It is precisely in this representation of the suffering and death of Jesus as a man that the ordained priest must be able to portray him in his total human dimension." Curtiss later says, "Because Jesus is a male in his human existence, his life and death are represented by a male priest."

The strongest argument against the ordination of women to Holy Orders is tradition and the appeal to authority. I think the 1994 apostolic letter of John Paul II to all bishops in the Catholic church, *Priestly Ordination Reserved to Men Alone (Ordinatio Sacerdotalis)*, is basically an appeal to tradition and the consistent understanding of the church. In that apostolic letter Pope John Paul II appealed to the response of Pope Paul VI to the debate among Anglicans concerning the ordination of women. Paul VI said that it was inadmissible to ordain women because of the example of Christ in the Scriptures— he chose apostles from among men only. Paul VI appealed to the constant practice of the church and said the teaching authority of the church has consistently held the exclusion of women from the priesthood to be in accordance with God's plan for his church.

Pope John Paul II concluded his apostolic letter by writing, "In virtue of my ministry of confirming the brethren (see Luke 22:32) I declare that the Church has no authority whatsoever to confer priestly ordination on women and that this judgment is to be definitively held by all the Church's faithful."

In other words Pope John Paul II believes that it was determined by Christ himself that only males be ordained to the priesthood and that he, John Paul, has no power to deviate from what Jesus has determined.

Who presided at the Eucharist in early times?

Father Richard McBrien, in his book *Catholicism*, wrote about the sacrament of holy orders, "This is perhaps the most difficult sacrament of all to treat. It is exceedingly complicated in its origin and in the development of terminology."

McBrien, like other writers and reference books, points out that the New Testament does give out a blueprint for the early church. However, there is no nice list of job descriptions or any organizational flowchart giving a picture of the chain of command and horizontal and vertical relationships in the church.

The writings of Paul, the Acts of the Apostles and the first letter of Peter do indicate there was some organization in the different churches of the New Testament. But the indications are that whatever offices or positions were recognized existed for some kind of service to the Christian community or church.

Again, historians are in agreement that the early church

did not speak in terms of priesthood or priests when talking of those who served the early churches or communities. Priest and priesthood had implications of the Temple and Temple worship for the early Jewish followers of Jesus. It was only after some time and a developed self-understanding that the first Christians saw Christianity as the new Israel—that the Temple and sacrifices had passed away and been replaced by the church and the sacrifice of Christ's people, the Eucharist.

We do know that the New Testament writings speak of *presbyteroi* (elders), *diakonoi* (deacons) and *episkopoi* (overseers) among others exercising duties or responsibilities in the early Christian communities. And Tertullian (ca. 200) uses the word *ordo* to apply to the clergy as a whole. He speaks of bishops or *episkopoi*, presbyters or priests, and deacons (ministers or servants).

An American Catholic Catechism, edited by George Dyer, reminds us that several New Testament passages refer to the act of appointing persons to ministry within the church by laying on hands with prayer. The writer says this was the traditional biblical sign of blessing and consecration by which the early church conferred the gifts of the Holy Spirit.

It may be something of an oversimplification, but, in general, it seems that the churches founded by the apostles were put in the care of groups of elders or presbyters. Gradually, one of the elders or presbyters emerged as *the* leader of a community, the spokesman or governor. It also appears this leader who came to be called an episkopos (bishop) was assisted by a group or "college" of presbyters (priests). Usually the episkopos presided at the Eucharist. But in his absence and in places distant from the community's center, a presbyter would preside. *Diakonoi* (deacons) were chosen to minister to the needs of the community.

Looking at the Scriptures, McBrien says,

> There is no explicit mention that any of the apostles presided over the Eucharist. Indeed, there is no compelling evidence that they presided when they were present or that a chain of ordination from apostle to bishop to priest was required for presiding. Someone

must have presided, of course, and those who did so presided with the approval of the community.

But, as one Scripture scholar has observed, we would surely expect that if an apostle was present he would have presided. McBrien goes on to say,

> We simply do not know how a certain individual came to preside and whether it came to be a permanent or regular function for that person. As we have already seen, there was a remarkable diversity of structure and form in the New Testament churches. The most that can be said is that those who presided did so with the consent of the local church and that this consent was tantamount but not always equal to ordination.

We do know from Hippolytus's *Apostolic Tradition* that in the third century a bishop or *sacerdos* was elected by the people and received an imposition of hands from another bishop. A presbyter or priest was ordained by the bishop with other priests joining in, and a deacon was ordained to the service of the bishop.

You can find much more about these subjects in *The Churches the Apostles Left Behind,* by Raymond Brown, S.S., and *This Is Our Church,* by William Herr.

What is necessary for a saint to be declared doctor of the church?

According to *A Concise Guide to the Catholic Church,* by Felician Foy, O.F.M., and Rose M. Avato,

> Doctors of the Church were ecclesiastical writers of eminent learning and sanctity who have been given this title because of the great advantage the Church has derived from their work. Their writings, however, were not necessarily free from error in all respects.

Three things are necessary that a person be considered a doctor of the church: (1) great sanctity on the part of the person, (2) eminent learning, (3) proclamation by a pope or ecumenical council that the person is a doctor of the church.

Pope Boniface VIII in 1298 declared four Western saints doctors of the church. They were saints Ambrose, Augustine, Jerome and Gregory the Great. In 1568 Pope Pius V recognized four Eastern saints as doctors—John Chrysostom, Basil the Great, Gregory Nazianzus and Athanasius.

All the other doctors have been proclaimed such since the Reformation. To name just a few, Saint Thomas Aquinas, Saint Bonaventure, Saint John of the Cross, Saint Alphonsus Liguori, Saint Anthony of Padua and Saint Francis de Sales. In all, thirty men and three women have been named doctors of the church. The first woman, Saint Teresa of Avila, was proclaimed a doctor on September 27, 1970. Just days later, on October 4, 1970, Saint Catherine of Siena was also proclaimed a doctor. Most recently, Pope John Paul II added the name of Therese of Lisieux.

In the future there may well be other women and men who will be given the title of doctor, women such as Saint Hildegaard, Saint Mechtilda, Saint Bridget of Sweden, Saint Catherine of Genoa and Blessed Angela of Foligno, as well as men such as John Henry Newman and Saint Louis de Montfort. A book you may be interested in is *The Doctors of the Church*, by Bernard McGinn.

Are there any dogmas about "the church militant"?

In most encyclopedias of the faith, there are no more than passing references to the church militant as part of the communion of saints—identifying it as the church on earth, those still working toward salvation. Even then, not all of the reference books employed the term at all. There are no references to dogmatic pronouncements or definitions concerning the church militant.

In *A History of Christian Spirituality*, by Louis Bouyer, Dom Jean Leclerq and Dom Francois Vandenbroucke, on the spirituality of the New Testament and the Fathers, it is mentioned that Origen, one of the early fathers of the church who lived in the third century, had written and preached about the ascetical life as a spiritual combat. He pictured the spiritual life as a struggle against demons. And Origen saw this struggle against the forces of the devil to be of concern to the whole body of Christ as well as to the ascetic. In his writing on this spiritual kind of warfare, Origen draws much on Saint Paul and the letter to the Colossians.

According to Gerard Austin, O.P., in his entry on the sacrament of confirmation in the *New Dictionary of Theology,* in the fifth century Bishop Faustus of Riez delivered a famous and much quoted Pentecost homily. It was a doctrinal explanation of the confirmation ceremony. He spoke of confirmation bringing an increase of grace that enables one to take part in the struggle of human life. This homily influenced the understanding of confirmation in the church of the West right down to our times. The concept of militancy, if not the word itself, became evident in other writings and even in the administration of the sacrament itself. Confirmation was conceived of as strengthening the disciple for battle. The follower of Jesus would be given fortitude to contend with the enemies of the faith.

Those of us on the way to becoming senior citizens remember the tap—sometimes slap—on the cheek the bishop gave us at confirmation. It was explained to us as a reminder we must be willing to suffer for Jesus, that we were called to be soldiers for Christ. That tap on the cheek has disappeared from the present ritual of confirmation.

At the time of the Crusades, the soldier of Christ was involved in more than an ascetical war against the world, the flesh and the devil. The crusader literally took up arms to promote the cause of Christ and war against those then perceived to be enemies of God and his church.

You can find some three and a half pages on that subject in Volume Two of *A History of Christian Spirituality.* This work informs us the Crusades were thought of as wars to end all wars, a way to unify the churches of the West and East and to protect the rights of Christians in the Holy Land. They were thought of as a pilgrimage in arms. The crusaders were called upon to fast, pray and give alms before entering battle.

This is not to romanticize the Crusades or to deny that

those "ideals" did become perverted, that they were often more politically than spiritually motivated or that at least some of the crusaders were guilty of great cruelty. It is only to say that in their original conception they were seen as religious and spiritual warfare.

There are also some two and a half pages in the same book on the military orders such as the Knights Templar, Knights of the Holy Sepulchre and Knights of Malta. Saint Bernard justified the activities of these monk-soldiers on the grounds that they were fighting for Christ's cause and to protect members of the church.

But the Crusades and the military orders were a long way from the gospel and the ideals preached by Jesus. After all, Jesus called upon his disciples to be people of peace, to turn the other cheek, to walk the extra mile with an exploiter. It was Jesus who commanded Peter to put up the sword and warned that those who live by the sword will perish by the sword.

Saint Paul did speak of spiritual warfare or battle. He wrote of contending with evil spirits and the powers of darkness in chapter six of the letter to the Ephesians. But it is the armor of God, the helmet of salvation, the shield of faith, the breastplate of righteousness and the sword of the spirit with which Christians are to arm themselves—all *spiritual* weapons.

In short, Vatican II's "Dogmatic Constitution on the Church" did not use the image of the church militant because the council fathers did not think it corresponds well with how the church thinks of itself today or best expresses the mission of the church in an age of nuclear weapons and religious and ethnic wars. They preferred to speak of the church as the people of God, a pilgrim people making its way to the kingdom, or as the Mystical Body of Christ. They would think of the church more in terms of a peacemaker than war maker.

Was St. Patrick's Cathedral Archbishop Hughes's folly?

Facts concerning the present St. Patrick's Cathedral and the administration of Archbishop John Joseph Hughes run throughout *A Popular History of the Archdiocese of New York,* written by Msgr. Florence D. Cohalan.

Apparently the present site was first purchased for a cemetery in 1829. But when it was discovered unsuitable for such a use, the trustees of the then-cathedral bought out the share held by the trustees of St. Peter's Parish in 1852.

Archbishop John Joseph Hughes declared the new St. Patrick's Cathedral should be built at this location. After some years of planning, a contract to build the cathedral was signed in 1859. It envisioned the completion of the church in eight years but allowed the archbishop to halt building at any time.

The cornerstone was laid in August of 1859, but building was suspended in 1861 because of the Civil War.

Cohalan writes that at the time some people did call the project "Hughes's Folly" because the place chosen was "too far out" in the country.

Work on the building was resumed after the Civil War. In 1879 it was dedicated by Cardinal John McCloskey. The spires of the cathedral were started in 1885 and the Lady Chapel addition begun in 1891.

St. Patrick's Cathedral was finally consecrated on October 5, 1910, after a great drive to pay off the remaining debt of $850,000.

How did Saint Paul become a Roman citizen?

Paul became a Roman citizen simply by being born in the city of Tarsus of parents who were already citizens.

Tarsus was the leading city in Cilicia, a province of Rome, in what would be modern-day Turkey. Mark Anthony awarded the residents of Tarsus citizenship for their loyalty to him in the military and political struggles of the day. That grant of citizenship was confirmed by Augustus Caesar. Earlier, Julius Caesar had given citizenship to many communities that had supported him in civil war.

Citizenship brought certain rights. A Roman citizen could not be sentenced for any crime without due process of Roman law. A citizen could not be scourged, given other degrading punishments or questioned under torture, says Father John McKenzie, in his *Dictionary of the Bible*. And a Roman citizen had the right to appeal his case to the imperial tribunal in Rome.

To the advantage of the government, Roman citizens became subject to military service—though Jews may have been exempt.

While citizenship was granted to provincials for service or goodwill to Rome, it could also be bought for a considerable amount of money.

Have there ever been any Franciscan popes?

There were at least three Franciscan popes and a Franciscan antipope. The antipope was Nicholas V (Pietro Rainalducci) who claimed to be pope between 1328 and 1330 and died in 1333. The genuine pope, John XXII, had chosen to support Frederick of Austria against Louis IV of Bavaria when they were engaged in a struggle for power in Italy. Unfortunately for John XXII, Louis defeated Frederick and took possession of Rome. John declared Louis excommunicated and Louis "deposed" John.

In place of John XXII, Louis had Pietro Rainalducci elected pope by a committee of thirteen from the clergy of Rome. Rainalducci had aligned himself with the Franciscan dissidents known as Spirituals, who were at odds with John XXII over the question of poverty and other papal policies.

In 1471 Cardinal Francesco Della Rovere was elected pope and took the name of Sixtus IV. Della Rovere had been minister general of the Franciscan Order and was known as a reformer of the Order. He was a theologian and author who had lectured at universities. He promoted not very successful crusades. At the request of Catholic kings, he established the Spanish Inquisition but later tried to temper its abuses.

Sixtus established the feast of the Immaculate Conception of the Blessed Virgin and was a patron of the arts. Unfortunately, his zeal for reform did not carry over into his rule as pope. He practiced a rule of nepotism and, according to *The*

Oxford Dictionary of Popes, enriched a swarm of relatives. He died in 1484.

A century later another Franciscan was chosen, Pope Sixtus V. Felici Peretti, also known as Cardinal Montalto because of his birthplace, was a doctor of theology and a striking preacher. Peretti was an advocate of church reform and like Sixtus IV had been minister general of the Franciscans. Pope Paul IV appointed him inquisitor of Venice. Paul IV recalled Peretti because of his severity but later reappointed him as inquisitor. Peretti fell out of favor with Paul IV's successor, Gregory XXIII. They had clashed on a mission to Spain.

After years of obscurity under Gregory, the cardinal knew little about that pope. In a conclave rather free from the influence of the great political powers, Peretti emerged as a kind of compromise candidate and was elected Sixtus V. *The Oxford Dictionary of Popes* describes Sixtus "a man born to rule, energetic, violent and inflexible." Sixtus put order into the Papal States. He harshly punished criminals and those who sheltered them. Among other things he established economic and financial reforms, initiated public works and regulated food prices.

Sixtus reorganized the central administration of the church and enforced the decrees of the Council of Trent. He attacked simony and required bishops to visit and report to the Holy See. He undertook a building program and revamped the layout of Rome. Sixtus has been called the Iron Pope. Effective as he was, he was so disliked by the people of Rome they tore down his statue after his death.

The last of the Franciscan popes was Lorenzo Gangenelli (baptized Giovanni Vincenzo Antonio), who took the name Clement XIV. He emerged as pope from a stormy conclave after the death of Clement XIII in 1769. Gangenelli was a doctor of theology and teacher in the Franciscan order. He had been appointed Cardinal by Clement XIII and was an author and consultant to the Holy Office. He is perhaps best known for yielding to pressure from the demands of France and Spain to suppress the Society of Jesus. Clement XIV died in 1774.

Where did we get the law of the fast?

The word *fast* comes from the Old English (Anglo-Saxon) word *faestan,* which meant "to abstain from certain foods." Fasting can be either religious or political in nature. It goes back centuries and has been practiced by many peoples. Christians and Jews, Muslims, Confucianists, Hindus, Taoists, Jainists (an Indian sect), some Buddhists and Native Americans fast or have fasted.

Fasting is sometimes a way of making atonement. It is a way of doing penance and is a form of spiritual discipline. In the past some people saw fasting as a way of giving extra force or power to their prayers of supplication. Fasts were a part of some fertility rites. In other instances they were observed to ward off catastrophes.

In Jonah 3:6–8, after Jonah announced the destruction of Nineveh, the king declared neither man nor beast should taste anything, or eat or drink. It was an act of penitence and a prayer for deliverance.

In recent times Mahatma Gandhi fasted to call his followers to nonviolence. Prisoners in Northern Ireland turned to fasting to gain world attention. Cesar Chavez, one time leader of farmworkers in the United States, went on a hunger strike to demand better working conditions and win public sympathy and support.

Not much is known about the origin of fasting in Israel. The custom, according to one reference source, was ancient before it entered law. Among Jews it was a sign of mourning and a way of giving force to prayers for deliverance.

In the original Mosaic law the day of atonement was a day of fasting. Other days were added later.

In 2 Samuel 12:16 David fasted in repentance after arranging the death of Uriah.

Jesus himself fasted when he went into the desert and faced temptation. In his time the Pharisees fasted twice a week and wanted to know why the disciples of Jesus did not fast. Jesus' response was that the guests don't fast while the bridegroom is present.

The early Christians tended to observe the practices of

their Jewish heritage. But as they separated from the synagogue and their past, new practices developed. In the early centuries, Friday, the day of Jesus' death, was kept as a day of abstinence. In some places it was carried over into Saturday in memory of the time Jesus was in the tomb.

Customs of fasting and abstinence developed differently in different places and took different forms in the West and East.

In the Middle Ages abstinence became abstinence from meat. The original Lenten fast was associated with preparing for baptism. The faithful fasted in solidarity with the catechumens. Lent became a time of retreat and penance. Later, other days of fast and/or abstinence were added.

Well into our own century the laws and customs of fasting and abstinence were very demanding. For the sake of laboring men and women, the Holy See granted a "working man's indult," relaxing the demands of fasting and abstinence for working people.

Then in 1966 Pope Paul VI reformed the church's whole practice of penance. He insisted on the constant need for penance. But he granted greater freedom in the choice of penitential acts.

Fridays throughout the year and Lent remain days of penance. In the general legislation Fridays are days of abstinence from meat. Ash Wednesday and Good Friday are days of fast and abstinence.

However, in the United States only the Fridays in Lent are days of abstinence from meat. (Eggs, milk, cheese and condiments made from animal fat are not considered meat.) Ash Wednesday and Good Friday remain days of fast and abstinence.

Fasting demands that we eat only one full meal a day. But two smaller meals that together do not equal another full meal may be taken. All who are fourteen years old are bound to abstain. Fasting binds all from the age of eighteen to the beginning of their sixtieth year.

The law of fast and abstinence binds substantively. That means continual nonobservance would be a grave sin. To miss one or the other, say, would not be regarded as a serious sin.

While our U.S. bishops have dispensed from abstinence on the Fridays outside of Lent, they recommend that we voluntarily abstain from meat on these days as a sign of solidarity with the poor of the world. And they urge that we perform other acts of penance throughout Lent and the rest of the year, for example, attending Lenten devotions, participating in daily Mass, helping the poor and sick, giving alms.

Fast and abstinence, together with other acts of penance, remain ways of showing our sorrow from sin, expressing our solidarity with Jesus in his suffering and with all who suffer, and strengthening ourselves to say no to temptation and sin.

What is the reason for no meat on Fridays during Lent?

Reference books usually treat the topics of fast and abstinence under the same heading. And in practice they frequently go hand in hand. Fasting refers to doing without food or limiting the amount of food we eat. Abstinence refers to doing without a kind of food or drink or something else—meat, alcohol, cigarettes.

Apparently, fasting as a religious practice goes back before written history. But already in the book of Exodus (34:28), we find Moses fasting forty days to placate the Lord for the guilt of his unfaithful people.

In the New Testament Jesus fasts forty days and forty nights before the beginning of his public ministry (Matthew 4:2 and Luke 4:1–2).

According to Adolf Adam in *The Liturgical Year*, writings from the second century refer to a complete fast in which no food or drink at all were taken. At Easter Christians were obliged to spend forty hours or two full days without eating or drinking.

The New Catholic Encyclopedia tells us abstinence from certain foods, especially flesh meats, was established early in the church. The observance of Friday abstinence in commemoration of the passion and death of Jesus was common both in East and West.

Days and customs regarding fast and/or abstinence varied and changed from place to place and from one time to another. For details over the centuries you can consult *The New Catholic Encyclopedia*. But it seems evident abstinence from flesh meat was chosen because for most people it was a real sacrifice.

The latest revision of the laws of fast and abstinence was made by Pope Paul VI in 1966 in an apostolic constitution called *Poenitemeni*. In that constitution he left certain things to the judgment of the national conferences of bishops. The U.S. bishops determined that Catholics in the United States should fast and abstain on Ash Wednesday and Good Friday and abstain from meat on all Fridays during Lent. They also recommended voluntary fasting throughout Lent and voluntary abstinence on all Fridays during Lent. In *Poenitemeni*, Paul VI reminded us of the need we all have to do penance. And penance can take many forms: acts of charity, such as visiting the sick or people in jail; tutoring slow learners; almsgiving; doing without candy, liquor, TV or other luxuries.

Our Sunday Visitor's Catholic Encyclopedia briefly gives the purpose of fast and abstinence: "to unite the believer through a discipline of self-sacrifice to the sacrificial love of Christ and to free the person from self-centeredness, in order to facilitate deeper prayer and more generous charity."

Those fasting and abstaining seek to die to self with Christ in order to share his victory over sin. Those doing penance offer it in reparation for their sins and the sins of the world. Through their self-denial they hope to detach themselves from the pursuit of material things and pleasure and seek first the kingdom of God.

BIBLIOGRAPHY

BOOKS

Abata, Russell M. *Helps for the Scrupulous*. Liguori, Mo.: Liguori Publications, 1976.

Abbott, Walter M., ed., Joseph Gallagher, trans. *The Documents of Vatican II*. New York: The America Press, 1976.

Ashley, Benedict M. *Theologies of the Body: Humanist and Christian*. St. Louis: The Pope John Center, 1985.

Ashley, Benedict M., and Kevin D. O'Rourke. *Health Care Ethics: A Theological Analysis*. St. Louis: The Catholic Hospital Association, 1978.

Barclay, William. *The Gospel of John*. 2 vols. Philadelphia: The Westminster Press, 1975.

————. *The Gospel of Luke*. Philadelphia: The Westminster Press, 1975.

————. *The Gospel of Matthew*. 2 vols. Philadelphia: The Westminster Press, 1975.

————. *The Gospel of Mark*. Philadelphia: The Westminster Press, 1975.

Benedictine Monks of St. Augustine's Abby, Ramsgate. *The Book of Saints: A Dictionary of Servants of God Canonized by the Catholic Church: Extracted from the Roman and Other Martyrologies*. New York: MacMillan Company, 1947.

Bergant, Dianne, and Robert J. Karris, eds. *The Collegeville Bible Commentary*. Collegeville, Minn.: The Liturgical Press, 1989.

Boadt, Lawrence. *Introduction to Wisdom Literature, Proverbs.* Collegeville, Minn.: The Liturgical Press, 1986.

————. *Reading the Old Testament: An Introduction.* Mahwah, N.J.: Paulist Press, 1984.

Bonaventure, Saint. *The Mind's Journey to God.* Lawrence S. Cunningham, trans. and ed. Chicago: Franciscan Herald Press, 1979.

Bouyer, Louis, Charles Underhill Quinn, trans. *Dictionary of Theology.* New York: Desclee, 1965.

Brown, Raphael, ed. *The Life of Mary as Seen by the Mystics.* Rockford, Ill.: TAN Books and Publishers, 1991.

Brown, Raymond. *The Birth of the Messiah.* New York: Doubleday, 1993.

————. *The Death of the Messiah.* 2 vols. New York: Doubleday, 1994.

————. *The Gospel and Epistles of John.* Collegeville, Minn.: The Liturgical Press, 1988.

————. *New Testament Essays.* New York: Doubleday, 1982.

————, Joseph A. Fitzmyer, and Roland Murphy, eds. *The New Jerome Biblical Commentary.* Englewood Cliffs, N.J.: Prentice Hall, 1990.

Bunson, Matthew, et al. *Our Sunday Visitor's Encyclopedia of Saints.* Huntington, Ind.: Our Sunday Visitor, 1998.

Cahill, Thomas. *How the Irish Saved Civilization.* New York: Doubleday, 1996.

Carter, Edward. *The Mysticism of Everyday.* Sheed and Ward, 1991.

Catoir, John. *Catholics and Broken Marriage: Pastoral Possibilities of Annulment, Dissolution: The Internal Forum.* Notre Dame, Ind.: Ave Maria Press, 1979.

————. *World Religions: Beliefs behind Today's Headlines.* New York: The Christophers, 1992.

Coleman, Gerald D. *Divorce and Remarriage in the Catholic Church.* Mahwah, N.J.: Paulist Press, 1988.

Conway, J. D. *What They Ask about Morals*. Notre Dame, Ind.: Fides, 1960.

Coriden, James A., Thomas J. Green, and Donald E. Heintschel. *The Code of Canon Law: A Text and Commentary*. Mahwah, N.J.: Paulist Press, 1985.

Cruz, Joan Carroll. *Secular Saints: 250 Canonized and Beatified Lay Men, Women and Children*. Huntington, Ind.: Our Sunday Visitor, 1989.

Dahmus, John. *The Puzzling Gospels: Suggested Explanations of Puzzling Passages in Matthew, Mark, Luke and John*. Chicago: The Thomas More Press, 1985.

Dallen, James. *The Reconciling Community: The Rite of Penance*. Collegeville: Minn.: The Liturgical Press, 1992.

D'Angelo, Lousie. *The Catholic Answer to Jehovah's Witnesses: A Challenge Accepted*. Meriden, Conn.: Maryheart Catholic Information Center, 1981.

Deedy, John. *The Catholic Fact Book*. Chicago: The Thomas More Press, 1986.

Deiss, Lucien, Michael S. Driscoll, trans. *The Mass*. Collegeville, Minn.: The Liturgical Press, 1992.

Delaney, John J., ed. *Dictionary of Saints*. New York: Doubleday and Co., 1980.

———. *A Woman Clothed with the Sun*. New York: Image Books, 1990.

Dietzen, John J. *New Question Box: Catholic Life for the Nineties*. Peoria, Ill.: Guildhall Publishers, 1992.

Dyer, George J. *An American Catholic Catechism*. New York: The Seabury Press, 1975.

Egan, Harvey D. *An Anthology of Christian Mysticism*. Collegeville, Minn.: The Liturgical Press, 1991.

———. *Christian Mysticism: The Future of a Tradition*. New York: Pueblo Publishing Co., 1984.

Elliott, Peter J. *Ceremonies of the Modern Roman Rite*. San Francisco: Ignatius Press, 1995.

———. *Liturgical Question Box: Answers to Common Questions*

about the Modern Liturgy. San Francisco: Ignatius Press, 1998.

Ellis, Peter F. *The Genius of John: A Compositional-Critical Commentary on the Fourth Gospel*. Collegeville, Minn.: The Liturgical Press, 1980.

Emminghaus, Johannes, Matthew J. O'Connell, trans. *The Eucharist: Essence, Form, Celebration*. Collegeville: Minn.: The Liturgical Press, 1978.

Fairlie, Henry. *The Seven Deadly Sins Today*. Notre Dame, Ind.: The University of Notre Dame Press, 1978.

Farmer, David Hugh. *The Oxford Dictionary of Saints*. Oxford: Oxford University Press, 1992.

Farrell, Melvin L. *Getting to Know the Bible: An Introduction to Sacred Scripture for Catholics*. Milwaukee: HI-TIME Publications, 1984.

Ferguson, George. *Signs and Symbols in Christian Art*. Oxford: Oxford University Press, 1961.

Filas, Francis. *Joseph: The Man Closest to Jesus*. Boston: St. Paul Editions, 1962.

Fischer, Balthasar. *Signs, Symbols and Gestures*. New York: Pueblo Publishing Co., 1981.

Flanagan, Neal. *The Gospel According to John and the Johannine Epistles*. Collegeville: Minn.: The Liturgical Press, 1985.

Foley, Leonard. *Believing in Jesus*. Cincinnati: St. Anthony Messenger Press, 2000.

————, and Pat McCloskey, ed. *Saint of the Day*. Cincinnati: St. Anthony Messenger Press, 2001.

Foy, Felician, O.F.M., and Rose M. Avato. *A Concise Guide to the Catholic Church*. Huntington, Ind.: Our Sunday Visitor, 1986.

Freze, Michael. *Patron Saints*. Huntington, Ind. Our Sunday Visitor, 1992.

————. *They Bore the Wounds of Christ*. Huntington, Ind.: Our Sunday Visitor, 1995.

———. *Voices, Visions and Apparitions*. Huntington, Ind.: Our Sunday Visitor, 1993.

Fuller, Rev. Reginald, ed. *A New Catholic Commentary on Holy Scripture*. London: Thomas Nelson, 1969.

Gallen, Joseph. *Canon Law for Religious*. New York: Alba House, 1983.

German Bishops' Conference. *A Catholic Adult Catechism: The Church's Confession of Faith*. San Francisco: Ignatius Press, 1987.

Gilles, Anthony E. *Fundamentalism: What Every Catholic Should Know*. Cincinnati: St. Anthony Messenger Press, 1984.

Granfield, Patrick. *The Limits of the Papacy*. New York: Crossroad, 1987.

Hardon, John A. *Pocket Catholic Dictionary*. New York: Image Books, 1985.

Häring, Bernard. *Free and Faithful in Christ*. 2 vols. New York: Seabury, 1978–1979.

———, Edwin G. Kaiser, trans. *The Law of Christ*. 3 vols. Westminster, Md.: The Newman Press, 1961–1966.

Hartman, Louis F. *Encyclopedic Dictionary of the Bible*. New York: McGraw-Hill, 1963.

Hellwig, Monika. *The Role of the Theologian in Today's Church*. Kansas City: Sheed and Ward, 1987.

———. *Sign of Reconciliation and Conversion: The Sacrament of Penance for Our Times*. Rev. ed. Collegeville, Minn.: The Liturgical Press, 1991.

Herr, William A. *This Our Church: The People and Events that Shaped It*. Chicago: The Thomas More Press, 1986.

Hoppe, Leslie. *A Guide to the Lands of the Bible*. Collegeville, Minn.: The Liturgical Press, 1999.

———. *The Synagogues and Churches of Ancient Palestine*. Collegeville, Minn.: The Liturgical Press, 1994.

Huels, John M. *Disputed Questions in the Liturgy Today*. Chicago: Liturgy Training Publications, 1988.

————. *More Disputed Questions in the Liturgy*. Chicago: Liturgy Training Publications, 1996.

————. *The Pastoral Companion: A Canon Law Handbook for Catholic Ministry*. Quincy, Ill.: Franciscan Press, 1995.

Johnston, William. *The Cloud of Unknowing* and *The Book of Privy Counseling*. New York: Doubleday, 1973.

Jone, Heribert. *Moral Theology*. Westminster, Md.: The Newman Press, 1962.

Jones, Alexander. *The Gospel According to St. Mark*. New York: Sheed and Ward, 1963.

————. *The Gospel According to St. Matthew*. New York: Sheed and Ward, 1965.

Jungmann, Joseph A., Mary Ellen Evans, ed., Julian Fernandes, trans. *The Mass: A Historical, Theological, and Pastoral Survey*. Collegeville, Minn.: The Liturgical Press, 1976.

Kelly, J.N.D. *The Oxford Dictionary of Popes*. New York: Oxford University Press, 1986.

Kelly, Joseph F. *Why Is There a New Testament?* Wilmington, Del.: Michael Glazier, 1986.

Kelly, Sean, and Rosemary Rogers. *Saints Preserve Us! Everything You Need to Know about Every Saint You'll Ever Need*. New York: Random House, 1993.

Kern, Walter. *New Liturgy and Old Devotions*. Canfield, Ohio: Alba Books, 1979.

Kohmescher, Matthew F. *Catholicism Today: A Survey of Catholic Belief and Practice*. Mahwah, N.J.: Paulist Press, 1999.

Komonchak, Joseph A., Mary Collins, and Dermot A. Lane, eds. *New Dictionary of Theology*. Collegeville, Minn.: The Liturgical Press, 1987.

Lang, Jovian P. *Dictionary of the Liturgy*. New York: Catholic Book Publishing, 1989.

Larentin, René, Matthew J. O'Connell, trans. *Catholic Pentecostalism*. Garden City, N.Y.: Image Books, 1978.

LaVerdiere, Eugene. *Fundamentalism: A Pastoral Concern.* Collegeville: The Liturgical Press, 2000.

———. *Luke.* Wilmington, Del.: Michael Glazier, 1980.

Lawler, Ronald, Donald W. Wuerl, and Thomas Lawler, eds. *The Teaching of Christ: A Catholic Catechism for Adults.* Huntington, Ind.: Our Sunday Visitor, 1976.

Leary, James F. *Hear, O Israel: A Guide to the Old Testament.* Waldwick, N.J.: Arena Lettres, 1980.

———. *A Light to the Nations: A Guide to the New Testament.* Waldwick, N.J.: Arena Lettres, 1983.

Leclerq, Jean. *A History of Christian Spirituality.* 2 vols. New York: Seabury, 1982.

Leonard, John K., and Nathan D. Mitchell, eds. *The Postures of the Assembly during the Eucharistic Prayer.* Chicago: Liturgy Training Publications, 1994.

Lohfink, Gerhard, Daniel Coogan, trans. *The Bible: Now I Get It: An Entertaining Look at the Bible for People Who Think They Know It Already.* New York: Doubleday, 1979.

Loret, Pierre, Dorothy Marie Zimmerman, trans. *The Story of the Mass: From the Last Supper to the Present Day.* Liguori, Mo.: Liguori Publications, 1983.

Lovasik, Lawrence G. *Our Lady in Catholic Life.* New York: The MacMillan Co., 1957.

MacMath, Fiona. *Saints' Names for Your Baby.* Collegeville, Minn.: The Liturgical Press, 1997.

Marthaler, Berard M. *The Creed.* Mystic, Conn.: Twenty-Third Publications, 1987.

McBrien, Richard, ed. *Catholicism.* San Francisco: Harper-SanFrancisco, 1994.

———. *The HarperCollins Encyclopedia of Catholicism.* San Francisco: HarperSanFrancisco, 1995.

McCarthy, Donald G., and Edward J. Bayer, eds. *Handbook on Critical Sexual Issues.* St. Louis: The Pope John Center, 1983.

McFarlan, Donald M. *Concise Bible Dictionary.* Mystic, Conn.: Twenty-Third Publications, 1986.

McGinn, Bernard. *Doctors of the Church: Thirty-Three Men and Women Who Have Shaped Christianity.* New York: Crossroad, 1999.

McKenzie, John L. *Dictionary of the Bible.* Milwaukee: The Bruce Publishing Co., 1965.

———. *Light on the Gospels.* Notre Dame, Ind.: Fides, 1978.

———. *New Testament without Illusion.* Chicago: The Thomas More Press, 1980.

Merton, Thomas. *Contemplative Prayer.* New York: Doubleday, 1972.

Noonan, James Charles, Jr. *The Church Visible: The Ceremonial Life and Protocol of the Catholic Church.* New York: Viking, 1996.

Nouwen, Henri. *Reaching Out.* New York: Doubleday, 1976.

O'Collins, Gerald, and Edward Farragia. *A Concise Dictionary of Theology.* Mahwah, N.J.: Paulist Press, 1991.

O'Donnell, Thomas J. *Medicine and Christian Morality.* New York: Alba House, 1996.

O'Rourke, Kevin D. *Medical Ethics: Sources of Catholic Teaching.* Washington, D.C.: Georgetown University Press, 1999.

Ott, Ludwig, Patrick Lynch, trans. *Fundamentals of Catholic Dogma.* St. Louis: Herder, 1955.

Pelletier, Joseph A. *The Sun Danced at Fatima.* New York: Image Books, 1983.

Pilch, John J. *The Cultural World of Jesus.* Collegeville, Minn.: The Liturgical Press, 1997.

Prat, Ferdinand, John J. Heenan, trans. *Jesus Christ: His Life, His Teachings and His Work.* 2 vols. Milwaukee: Bruce, 1950.

Prümmer, Dominic M. *Handbook of Moral Theology.* Ft. Collins, Colo.: Roman Catholic Books, 1957.

Rahner, Karl, and Herbert Vorgrimler, Richard Strachnan, et al., trans. *Dictionary of Theology.* New York: Crossroad, 1985.

Ratzinger, Joseph, J. R. Foster, trans. *An Introduction to Christianity*. San Francisco: Ignatius Press, 1990.

Richter, Klemens, Linda M. Maloney, trans. *The Meaning of the Sacramental Symbols: Answers to Today's Questions*. Collegeville, Minn.: The Liturgical Press, 1990.

Robinson, Geoffrey. *Marriage, Divorce and Nullity*. Collegeville, Minn.: The Liturgical Press, 2000.

Schreck, Alan. *Basics of the Faith: A Catholic Catechism*. Ann Arbor, Mich.: Servant Books, 1987.

Seasoltz, R. Kevin. *New Liturgy, New Laws*. Collegeville, Minn.: The Liturgical Press, 1980.

Siegle, Bernard A. *Marriage According to the New Code of Canon Law*. New York: Alba House, 1986.

Sjogren, Per-Olof, Sydney Linton, trans. *The Jesus Prayer*. Philadelphia: Fortress Press, 1975.

Stravinskas, Peter, ed. *Our Sunday Visitor's Catholic Encyclopedia*. Huntington, Ind.: Our Sunday Visitor, 1991.

Tanquerey, Adolphe, John J. Byrnes, trans. *A Manual of Dogmatic Theology*. 2 vols. New York: Desclee, 1959.

——, Herman Branderis, trans. *The Spiritual Life*. Rockford, Ill.: TAN Books and Publishers, 2001.

Taylor, Michael J. *Purgatory*. Huntington, Ind.: Our Sunday Visitor, 1998.

——. *John, the Different Gospel*. New York: Alba House, 1983.

Turpin, Joanne. *The Healing Mysteries: A Rosary for the Sick*. Cincinnati: St. Anthony Messenger Press, 1983.

U.S. Catholic Conference, *Catechism of the Catholic Church*. Vatican City: Libreria Editrice Vaticana, 2000.

Vawter, Bruce. *On Genesis: A New Reading*. New York: Doubleday, 1977.

Vogels, Heinz-Jürgen. *Celibacy: Gift or Law?* Kansas City: Sheed and Ward, 1993.

Walsh, Michael. *Dictionary of Catholic Devotions*. New York: HarperSanFrancisco, 1993.

———. *Opus Dei: An Investigation into the Secret Society Struggling for Power within the Roman Catholic Church*. New York: HarperCollins, 1992.

———, ed. *Butler's Lives of the Saints*. Concise ed. Foreword by Basil Cardinal Hume, O.S.B., San Francisco: Harper and Row, 1985.

Ward, Kaari, ed. *Jesus and His Times*. Pleasantville, N.Y.: Reader's Digest, 1987.

Weber, Gerard P. *The Capital Sins: Seven Obstacles to Life and Love*. Cincinnati: St. Anthony Messenger Press, 1997.

Wegman, Herman, Gordon W. Lathrop, trans. *Christian Worship in East and West: A Study Guide to Liturgical History*. New York: Pueblo Publishing Co., 1976.

Weiser, Francis X. *Handbook of Christian Feasts and Customs*. New York: Harcourt, Bruce and Co., 1958.

Wenig, Laurin J. *The Spring of Your Life: Your Introduction to Sacred Scripture*. Milwaukee: HI-TIME Publications, 1981.

Whalen, William. *Separated Brethren: A Survey of Protestant, Anglican, Eastern Orthodox and other Denominations in the United States*. Huntington, Ind.: Our Sunday Visitor, 1979.

Wilson, Ian. *Stigmata: An Investigation into the Mysterious Appearance of Christ's Wounds in Hundreds of People from Medieval Italy to Modern America*. San Francisco: Harper and Row, 1989.

Woodward, Kenneth L. *Making Saints: How the Catholic Church Determines Who Becomes a Saint, Who Doesn't, and Why*. New York: Simon and Schuster, 1990.

Zimdars-Swartz, Sandra L. *Encountering Mary: Visions of Mary from LaSalette to Medjugorje*. New York: Avon Books, 1991.

Zwack, Joseph P. *Annulment: Your Chance to Remarry within the Catholic Church*. San Francisco: Harper and Row, 1983.

•

For many of the topics addressed, St. Anthony Messenger Press has several newsletters, specifically *Catholic Update*,

Youth Update, and *Scripture from Scratch.* Here you will find many of the same issues dealt with in the book, responded to in clear, concise and Catholic ways. Each monthly newsletter carries with it the *imprimatur* (ecclesial approval), of the Archdiocese of Cincinnati. Contact St. Anthony Messenger Press, 28 W. Liberty Street, Cincinnati, OH 45210; 1-800-488-0488.

For the encyclicals of Popes John Paul II, Paul VI and John XXIII, as well as the pastoral statements of the U.S. Catholic Bishops, write or fax: Libreria Editrice Vaticana V-00120 Vatican City, 011-3906-6988-4716. Or, search online at www.Vatican.va.

If you wish to obtain any of the books listed above, call or visit St. Francis Bookshop, 1618 Vine Street, Cincinnati, OH 45210; 513-241-7304. The staff will be happy to lend assistance or suggest other books on that subject.

INTERNET RESOURCES

The substance of the faith is one thing, the way in which it is transmitted is another. —POPE JOHN XXIII

If anything bears this saying out, it is the ongoing development and place of technology in our lives. So many of the things taken for granted today would have been unheard of decades ago—personal computers, fax machines, pagers, E-mail—the list goes on. As it has been for society in general, so, too, has it been for the church. Advances in technology have allowed the church the possibility to communicate in ways never before available. It is both an opportunity and a challenge.

An unavoidable means of communication is the Internet. What once would have taken hours of time researching, wading through countless books, magazines and journals, can be referenced in seconds. Though perhaps slow in embracing this information revolution, the church has been quickly catching up. Many Catholic publishing companies, universities, hospitals, and other church-related institutions now have their own

Web pages. The Internet is one, some would say indispensable, way of spreading the Good News. To give you a sense of what is out there, consult *Catholics on the Internet: 2000–2001*, by Brother John Raymond (Prima Publishing, 800-632-8676). Another resource that might be helpful is *Your Family and Cyberspace.* Published by the U. S. bishops, this booklet provides a brief summary of the popular areas of the Internet and outlines both concerns and opportunities with respect to use. Additionally, the Vatican is also preparing a document that addresses issues related to the Internet.

The Internet truly makes real the saying, "It's a jungle out there." One is encouraged when using the Internet to use good judgment. Many sites do offer what are authentic representations of the Catholic faith. The same cannot be said for all however. Given its size and constantly changing character, there is simply no way to keep track of all the sites on the Internet. Warning: Just because it says it is a Catholic Web site does not mean it is. As a result, Internet users are encouraged to be responsible in the way they surf the Internet and the resources they use. When in doubt it always makes sense to refer to another Web site or go to a print source. The *Catechism of the Catholic Church* will provide you with *the* official Roman Catholic position on any number of, though not all, subjects. With that said the Internet is a treasure trove of information for Catholics and even for those just searching about the truths of the faith.

What follows is a brief offering of places to go for those who are computer literate. Many of the sites that you will go to have links to other Web addresses as well.

www.vatican.va
> The "mother" of all Catholic Web sites. Includes most everything having to do with the "official" church: papal and curial texts and addresses and links with other Vatican services.

www.nccbuscc.org

Home of the United States National Conference of Catholic Bishops. Offers a wide range of services and links with the dioceses in the United States.

www.catholicnews.org

Site of Catholic News Service. Reports news that affects Catholics in their everyday lives.

www.AmericanCatholic.org

Web site of St. Anthony Messenger Press, publisher of St. Anthony Messenger magazine and a host of other Catholic and catechetical material.

www.christophers.org

Site of nonprofit organization founded in 1945 by Father James Keller. Uses print and electronic means to spread a message of hope and understanding.

www.claretianpubs.org

Home to *U.S. Catholic* and other publications related to church, family life, social justice, etc. Associated with the Claretian missionaries.

www.litpress.org

The Liturgical Press's site, connected with the Benedictine Abbey of St. John's in Collegeville, Minnesota, specializes in providing products to facilitate Catholic worship though it is not limited to this area.

www.ltp.org

Web site of Liturgy Training Publications. Mission statement: "Provides materials that assist parishes, institutions and households in preparation, celebration and expression of liturgy in Christian life."

www.avemariapress.com

Concentrates its publishing efforts in five areas: prayer and spirituality, adolescent catechesis, pastoral care and guidance, parish and ministry resources, and elementary catechetical resources.

www.paulistpress.com

Offers a wide range of materials for both the beginner and the serious scholar.

www.orbisbooks.com

Ministry of Maryknoll, the U.S.-based Catholic mission movement. Has material on theology, spirituality and mission. Links to the popular *Maryknoll* magazine.

www.liguori.org

Web ministry of the Redemptorists. Offers daily reflections, prayer requests and a wide range of print material. Links to *Liguorian* magazine.

www.osv.com

Home to Our Sunday Visitor. Publishes books related to catechetical, theological, reference, devotional and historical matters. Links to *Our Sunday Visitor* newspaper.

www.ewtn.org

Home of Eternal Word Television Network, founded by Mother Angelica and located in Irondale, Alabama. Provides a range of information regarding the network and its activities.

www.Pauline.org

Contact site for the Daughters of St. Paul and their media apostolate.

www.ignatius.com

Web site of Ignatius Press. Offers a wide range of material, including books, tapes and periodicals on theology, Scripture, saints and spirituality.

INDEX

A

abortion, 145, 348–349, 353–354

Abraham the Patriarch, 30, 197–198

absolution, 377–378, 379

abstinence, 114–116, 290, 469

abuse, physical/sexual, 18, 151–152

acolytes, 274–275

actors, patron saint of, 7

Adam and Eve, 55, 193–197

adultery, 52, 222, 333

Advent, 437

African Synod, 453–454

afterlife
  faith in existence of, 93–94
  final resurrection, 92–93, 168–169
  hell, 95, 101–102, 249–250
  and loss of earthly pleasures, 171–172
  nature of, 152–153
  purgatory, 100–103
  for those outside church, 80–81, 134–135

Agnus Dei, 110

AIDS, 311–312

Alacoque, Saint Margaret Mary, 57, 403

Albigensian heresy, 5

alcohol at church functions, 337

Aldazabal, Bishop Beita, 48

Alexander VI, Pope, 62

Allah, 452–453

angels
  archangels as saints, 7–8
  definition, 3–4
  development of, 11–13
  gender issue, 9–10
  hearing of prayers, 408
  seraphim, 24

animals, status of, 157–158, 344–345

annulment, 389–391

anointing of the sick, 393–397, 404, 407

Antichrist, 254

antipopes, 449, 466

Apocalypse, book of, 55, 68, 251–252, 253–255, 272

Apocrypha, 187

apostles, 432, 460–461

Apostles Creed, 249–250, 288–289, 429–430

Apostleship of Prayer, 415

apparitions of Mary, 42–43, 47–49, 57, 441–442

Arabia, pre-Muslim religions of, 452–453

archangels as saints, 7–8

archeology and Biblical scholarship, 190

Ark of the Covenant, 51

Armaggedon, 167–169, 239–240, 248–249, 252–253

artists, patron saints of, 7

asceticism and saints, 34–35

Ash Wednesday, 290, 435–437

Assumption of Mary, 54, 62, 437–438

attendance at church, reasons for, 258–261

authority of church
  and bishops, 110, 296, 362
  to establish parishes, 112

authority of church (*continued*)

and infallibility question, 83–85

liturgical practices, 264–265

pastoral role, 116

for preaching, 273–274

for teaching, 85

and theologians, 106–107

See also tradition, church

auxiliary bishops, 113–114

B

Bach, Johann Sebastian, 399

Bakhita, Saint Josephine, 16–17

baptism

of children with inactive Catholic parents, 161–162

and creed origins, 429–430

finding appropriate names, 6–7

godparents, 360–361

and Lent, 295

and original sin, 86–87

requirements for, 358–359

and Sign of Peace, 447

timing of, 359

basilica, requirements for, 110–111

Basilica of Saint Mary Major, 61, 111

Basilica of the Annunciation, 61

beatification, 38

beatific vision, 408

beatitudes, 227–229

belief, resolving disagreements on matters of, 155–156

See also faith

Bellarmine, Saint Robert, 433

beloved disciple, 230–232

Benediction, 288, 411–412

Benedict XIII, Pope, 176, 293

Benedict XIV, Pope, 451

Bernard of Montjoux, 6

bishops

authority of, 109–110, 124, 296, 362

and charismatic movement, 414

and infallibility question, 85

liturgical role of, 273

origins of, 460

and parish councils, 116–117

and right to name churches, 111–112

selection of, 113–114

vestments of, 295–296

Black Madonna, 44

Blessed Sacrament, Forty Hours devotion for, 17

Blessed Virgin. *See* Mary, Mother of Jesus

blessings

Ash Wednesday, 290

of homes, 282–283

ministers' role in, 262–263

blood banks, patron saint of, 27–28

blood sausage, 453–455

bodily resurrection, 92–93, 152–153, 168–169, 215

Boniface VIII, Pope, 22, 438, 461

born again concept, 234

bowing of heads for name of Jesus, 275–277

bread and wine in Communion, 372

brown scapular, 441–442

Butler, Archbishop James, 433

C

Cain's wife, 196–197

Caleb, 205–206

Callistus, Pope, 449

Canaanite woman, 229–230

candy canes as religious
symbols, 448

Canisius, Saint Peter, 433

canonization, process of, 37–39
See also saints

canon law, violations and sin,
325–327

capital punishment, 337–338

carbuncles, invoking Saint Cloud
for, 6

cardinals, 110, 295

Carmelite Order, 441–442

Carroll, Bishop John, 118

Cassian, John, 320

cassock, 108

catechism, origins of, 432–433

Catholic Church, origins of
name, 428–430
See also tradition, church

celibacy, priestly, 124–125,
330–331, 456–457

chair, celebrant's, 284–285

chalices, 284–285

charismatic movement, 404–405,
413–415

charity, 116, 137, 162–163

Chartres Cathedral, 62

chasubles, 284–285

Chesterton, G. K., 303

children
as angels, 11–12
and Eucharist, 373–374
of Mary, Mother of Jesus, 47
Mary's experience of
childbirth, 64

Masses for, 273–274
as models of innocence, 238
saints' names for, 117
See also baptism

Christ. See Jesus Christ

Christmas, 119–120, 121, 437, 448

churches
filming of movies in, 131
naming of, 111–112

church militant, 462–464

Cistercian Order, 5

Clark, Steve, 413

cleanliness, ritual, 44–45

Clement XIII, Pope, 467

Clement XIV, Pope, 467

clerical hierarchy
deacons, 273–274, 288,
457–459, 460
overview, 122–125
See also bishops; priests

clothing, clerical, 107–110,
295–296, 358–359, 434

Cloud of the Unknowing, The,
416–417

cohabitation outside marriage,
169–170, 332

comas, treatment of persons in,
341

commandments and free will,
305–306

communal penance, 377–378
See also public penance

Communion
apostolic celebration of, 49–50
Biblical basis for, 366–368
bread and wine in, 371–372
Christ's presence in, 364–366,
368–369, 371, 455–456

Communion (*continued*)
    clerical roles, 369–370
    consecration of host, 365–366,
        368–369
    distribution of, 278–279
    and Imelda Lambertini, 23
    and mental disability, 373–375
    and non-Catholics, 372–373
    number of times to receive,
        284
    obligations, 127, 430
    outside of church, 180,
        291–292
    preparation for, 281–282, 289
    symbolism of, 365–366
    and tabernacle location,
        286–287
    women's role, 370–371
communion of saints, 409–410
community, importance of, and
    church attendance, 258–260
compassion, as central to Jesus'
    nature, 307
confession
    confessor role, 383–384
    contemporary issues with,
        378–381
    and excommunication, 89
    origins of, 430–431
    overdoing, 385
    reasons for, 375–377, 381–382
    and sinfulness of human
        nature, 382–383
    See also penance
confession of devotion, 385–386
confirmation, 361–364, 374–375,
    463
Congregation for the Causes of
    Saints, 38

conscience, examination of, 305,
    328, 381–382
consecration of Eucharist,
    365–366, 368–369
content vs. process of church
    tradition, 75–76
Contractus, Herman, 58
contrition, perfect, 308
controversy in church, reasons
    for, 76–78
conversion, 13–14, 81, 360
Co-Redemptrix, Mary as, 65–66
corporal acts of mercy, 129
Council of Elvira, 456
Council of Florence, 451
Council of Laodicea, 434
Council of Mainz, 438
Council of Nicea, 455
Council of Saragossa, 437
Council of Trent, 187, 455
Cousin, Saint Germaine, 18
creation
    and God's plan, 148–149
    and human views of God,
        173–174
creeds
    Apostles, 249–250, 288–289,
        429–430
    filioque issue, 450–451
    Nicene, 268–270, 451, 455
    and transubstantiation,
        455–456
cremation, 298–299
crime and punishment, 337–338,
    342–344, 352–353
Crimthaann, (Saint Columba), 25
crowns, 67–68, 438
crucifixion, 445–447
Crusades, 201, 463–464

cultic recital form of story, 201

cursing of fig tree, 223–224

Cyprian, 436

D

dairy workers, patron saint of, 34

Damian, Peter, 387

dark night of the soul, 149–150

Daughters of Charity of Canossa, 16–17

David, King of Israel, 30

days and months, dedication of, 424–425

deacons, 273–274, 288, 457–459, 460

dead, Masses for the, 176–178, 297–300, 397, 409–410, 418–419

Dead Sea Scrolls, 190

death

and being asleep in Christ, 217–218

dead children as angels, 11–12

euthanasia, 164–165, 338–342

funerals, 176–178, 297–300, 397, 409–410, 418–419

and judgment, 153, 173

of Mary, Mother of Jesus, 54

organ donation, 349–352

and original sin, 64

priest's role, 395

See also afterlife

death penalty, 337–338

De Consilio, Father Vincent, 433

De Lellis, Saint Camillus, 26, 27

Della Rovere, Cardinal Francesco, 466

De Montfort, Saint Louis Marie, 310

dependence upon God, reminders of, 138, 228–229, 258–260, 400

devil, origins of, 11, 138

Diego, Juan, 57, 62

dietary traditions, 114–116, 289, 290, 454–455, 468–470

diocesan bishops, 113–114

Diocletian, Emperor of Rome, 7

disciples

as successors to Jesus in works of love, 235

women as, 236

discipleship and message of Luke, 82–83

discipline of the church vs. dogma, 82–83

dissent, criteria for convincing, 83–85

distractions during Mass, 165–166

Divine Office, 415–416

divorce, 52–53, 160–161, 222–223

doctor of the church, saint as, 461–462

doctors, patron saints of, 27

dogma, definition, 81–82

Dominican Order, 21, 26

dormition of Mary, 47

Dubois, Bishop John (Saint John Neumann), 17–18

Duns Scotus, 62

Duquesne University, 413

Durandus, Bishop William, 291

E

Easter, 119–120, 299–300

Eastern Orthodox Church

and assumption of Mary, 54

Eastern Orthodox Church
(*continued*)
Catholic study of, 97
   receiving Communion at,
   291–292
   rites vs. Roman church,
   265–267, 362, 374, 450–451
ecumenism, 96, 97–99, 451–452
emergency medical workers, patron saint for, 27
Emmerich, Catherine, 54
emotionally disturbed people,
   intercessory saint for, 18
Enchiridion of Indulgences, 78–79
end of the world, 167–169,
   239–240, 248–249, 251–252
epiclesis, 369
eschatological test, 252–253
Escriva, Josemaria, 105
essential vs. nonessential church
   tradition, 76
Eucharist. *See* Communion
eucharistic minister, role of,
   262–263
Eucharistic Prayer, 280–281
Eugenius, Pope, 5
eulogies, 297–298
euthanasia, 164–165, 338–342
evangelism, 80–81, 128
evil
   and Antichrist, 254
   problem of existence of, 11,
   138
   See also sin
evil spirits, intercessory saints
   for fighting, 10
evolution, biological, 175
excommunication, 88–89, 103,
   348–349
Exodus, 183, 200–203

exploitative sexuality, 317
extraordinary magisterium, 81, 85
extraterrestrials, 178–179
Ezekiel, book of, 210

F
faith
   crises of, 149–150
   importance of, 134
   and *sola fide*, 95–97
faith healing, 402–403, 404–405
fasting, 115–116, 289, 290,
   468–470
Father, refering to priests as,
   242–243
Fatima, Mary's appearances at,
   57, 72–74
Faustus of Riez, Bishop, 463
feast days, 117–119
feminism, Catholic, 125–126
Fernandez of Santander, Bishop
   Doroteo, 47–48
fertility goddess, queen of
   heaven as, 49
filioque, 450–451
filming of movies in churches,
   131
First Lateran Council, 456
fish on Friday tradition, 114–115
flags in churches, 301
forgetting vs. forgiving wrongs,
   151–152
Forgione, Francesco (Padre Pio),
   21, 32–33
forgiveness
   absolution, 377–378, 379
   and baptism, 86, 360
   vs. forgetting wrongs,
   151–152

God as master of, 145

See also confession; penance

Forty Hours devotion, 17

Fourth Lateran Council, 430

Franciscan Order, 8, 21, 32, 266, 466–467

free will, 11, 135, 148–149, 305–306

friendship and Jesus, 233–234

fundamentalist Christians, relating to, 150–151

fundamental option in moral theology, 327

fundraising methods, 335–336

funerals, 176–178, 297–300, 397, 409–410, 418–419

G

Gabriel, Archangel, 7–8

gambling, 26, 335–336

Gangenelli, Cardinal Lorenzo, 467

Garabandal visions, 47–49

Garden of Eden, 194–196

genealogy of Jesus, 218–219

general absolution, 377–378, 379

Genesis creation story, 193–197

Gentiles vs. Jews, 442–443, 454–455

genuflection, 276, 277

godparents, 360–361

gold chalices, 284–285

good faith, acting in, and salvation, 80

Good Friday, 290, 469

good works and salvation, 80, 95–96, 308

Goretti, Saint Maria, 18

Gospels

ash symbolism in, 436

differences in, 211

and discipleship, 82–83

heretical, 191–192

issues about Jesus, 218–251

and Jewish revolt against Rome, 209–210

kissing of book, 279–280

lack of biographical information, 66–67, 69

and prayer, 400–401

reading during Mass, 263–264, 270–272

synoptic nature of three, 211

grace, 96–97, 217, 305, 410

gratitude, 162–163, 400

Greek as official church language, 448–449

Greek Orthodox Church, 28, 50

green martyrs, 25

Gregorian Masses, 175–178, 293

Gregory XXIII, Pope, 467

guilt, 142, 310, 380

See also penance

H

habits, religious, 108–109

Hail Mary prayer, 51, 62, 64, 439

healing

miraculous (faith), 402–403, 404–405

and rosary, 71

and Saint Bridget, 34

and Saint Cloud, 6

health care professions, patron saints for, 27

heaven, 80–81, 154, 168–169, 171–172

hell, 95, 100–102, 249–250

Henry VIII, King of England, 34

heretical Gospels, 191–192

hermits, 25, 29

Heroic Act, 310–311

Hippolytus of Rome, 449

holiness, 35–36, 50

   See also saints

Hollis, Bishop Crispian, 154

holy days of obligation, 117–119, 260–261, 437–438

   See also specific days

Holy Family, 67

   See also Mary, Mother of Jesus; Saint Joseph

holy orders, 392–393, 458, 459–461

Holy Spirit

   and charismatic movement, 413

   and consecration of Eucharist, 369

   and history of popes, 445

   Jesus' comments on, 248

   nature of, 450–451

   and Pentecost, 253–254

Holy Thursday, 294–295

Holy Week

   Easter, 119–120, 299

   Good Friday, 290, 469

   Holy Thursday, 294–295

   prohibition on funeral Masses during, 299

homes, religious celebration in, 282–283, 285–286

homilies, proper uses of, 371

homosexuality, 311, 312–313, 331–332

host, Eucharistic, handling of, 283, 285–286

Hughes, Archbishop John Joseph, 464–465

humanity vs. divinity of Jesus. *See* Jesus Christ

human rights issues, 343–344, 353

human sacrifice, Old Testament rejection of, 197–198

humans as made in image of God, 173–174

humility, 35–36, 238

   See also dependence upon God, reminders of

humor as necessary to balanced human experience, 141

I

ICEL (International Commission on English in the Liturgy), 268–269

idols, sacred images as, 315–316

illegitimacy, 390–391

illnesses

   AIDS, 311–312

   and Communion at home, 282, 283

   and euthanasia, 338–342

   leprosy in Bible, 208–209

   as punishment for sin, 311–312

   and suffering, 137

images, sacred

   Black Madonna, 44

   chalices, 284–285

   changes in church tradition, 300–301

   as idols, 315–316

images (*continued*)

    Infant of Prague statue, 127

    as signs of reverence, 315–316

    statues of Mary, 64–65

    veiling for Lent, 290–291

Immaculate Conception, feast of, 62, 466

Immaculate Heart of Mary, 403

immortality. *See* afterlife

imperfect world vs. perfect God, 148–149

Incarnation of Jesus, 92, 145–146

incense, 272–273

incest, 18, 222, 223

indulgences, 71, 78–79, 406–407, 411, 417

inerrant nature of Bible, 183–184

infallible teachings, 81–82, 84–85, 156

Infant of Prague, 127

Inquisition, 201, 466

INRI, meaning of, 246

intercessory prayer, 402

internal forum solution to marriage, 389

interpretation, Biblical, 183–186

intuitive knowledge, 408

Ireland, uniqueness of Christian evangelism in, 25

Isaac, sacrifice of, 197–198

Islam, 16–17, 80, 452–453

Israelites, 203–205, 433–434

    See also Jewish people

J

Jehovah's Witnesses, 158–159

Jesuits, 467

Jesus Christ

    and attitude of child, 238

on being born again, 234–235

and beloved disciple, 230–233

as bringing division, 225–227

and Canaanite woman, 229–230

commandment of love, 306–307

crucifixion of, 147–148, 246, 445–447

cursing of fig tree, 223–224

and discipleship, 82–83, 234–235

dual nature of, 59–60, 142–143, 145–146, 232–233

existence prior to Incarnation, 92

fasting of, 468

as final judge, 172–173

finding in Temple, 45–46

and friendship, 233–234

genealogy of, 218–219

on hating father and mother, 237–238

healing response to prayer, 404

Jewish rejection as Messiah, 441

and John the Baptist, 220–221

Last Supper, 244–245

on marriage, 222–223

and Mary and Martha, 236–237

and Mass as sacrifice, 366–367

miracles of, 99–100

Nazirite vow, 229

pacifism of, 205

and poor in spirit concept, 227–229

prayers of, 400–401, 420–421

Jesus Christ (*continued*)

presence in Eucharist, 364–366, 368–369, 371, 455–456

and refering to priests as "Father," 243–244

relationship to Trinity, 450–451

Resurrection of, 49–50, 247–248, 250–251, 431

and sacraments, 357–358, 387–388

scourging of, 58–59

signs of reverence for, 275–277

on sins against Holy Spirit, 248

as Son of Man, 238–239

as source of salvation, 66, 86

stumbling stone reference, 241–242

on suffering, 136

temptations of, 219–220

on timing of end of world, 240

visit to hell, 249–250

Jesus Prayer, 412–413

Jewish people and traditions

ash symbolism, 435–436

Christian changes in, 431–432

dietary rules, 114, 454–455

and fasting, 468

vs. Gentiles, 442–443

and incense in Old Testament, 272

Israelites vs. Jews as label, 433–434

marriage and divorce, 52–53, 222–223

and origins of Scripture, 186–187

and purification of Mary, 44–45

rejection of Jesus, 441

revolt against Rome, 209–210

John, Gospel of, 211, 220–221

John Paul II, Pope

angels, 9

canonization process, 38

charismatics, 414

cohabitation, 169–170

death penalty, 337–338

ecumenism, 97–99

evolution, 90–91

Fatima secret, 73–74

general absolution, 378

married saints, 15, 16

Opus Dei, 105–106

ordination of women, 458–459

organ donation, 351

priestly celibacy, 124

problem of evil, 138

Saint Joseph, 67

suffering, 135

work on Sunday, 324

John the Baptist, 170–171, 220–221

John XIX, Pope, 444

John XXII, Pope, 466

John XXIII, Pope, 73, 98, 343

Joshua, book of, 205–206

Judas Iscariot, fate of, 139

judgment

at death, 153, 173

and fate of sinners, 139

as God's job, 330

Jesus as spiritual judge, 239–240

judgment (*continued*)

    Jesus vs. God the Father, 172–173

    and jury duty, 352–353

    of self, 140–142, 328

jury duty, 352–353

just war, 345–347

K

karma, 91–92

Kempis, Thomas á, 62

killing, commandment against, 203–205, 338–342

kingdom of God, timing and nature of, 238–240–241

kissing of altar and Gospel book, 279–280

Kiss of Peace, 447–448

kneeling, 277–278, 280–281, 439–440

Knights of Columbus, 104

Kowalska, Saint Faustina, 26–27

L

Laboure, Saint Catherine, 55

Lachiondo, Bishop Jose Cirarda, 48–49

The Lactation of Saint Bernard (painting), 5

languages

    of Bible, 189

    of Mass, 292–293, 448–449

lapsed Catholics, treatment of, 153, 161–162

Last Supper, 244–245

Latin, 265, 292–293, 448–449

Latin Vulgate, 187

lawyers, patron saint for, 34

lay ministers

    and Benediction, 288

    Eucharistic role, 370–371

    and funeral Masses, 297–298

    hierarchy of, 121–122

    and Liturgy of the Hours, 416

    ministerial role, 262–263

lay people as saints, 15–16

Lazarus, 218, 230

Lefebvre, Archbishop Marcel, 89–90

legends and saints' credibility, 30–31

Legion of Mary, 62

Lent

    abstinence and penance in, 115–116, 469–471

    Ash Wednesday, 435–436

    dates of, 120

    funerals during, 299

    Holy Thursday, 294–295

    liturgical practice, 290–291

    Palm Sunday, 294

    sacraments during, 295

Leo VIII, Pope, 444

Leo XIII, Pope, 409–410, 425

lepers in Bible, 208–209

levirate marriages, 218

libelous behavior, 354–355

life after death. *See* afterlife

life on other planets, 178–179

Limbo of the Fathers, 95

Litany of Loreto, 50

Litany of the Blessed Virgin, 50–51, 62

Litany of the Saints, 50

literal interpretation of Bible, dangers of, 174–175

Liturgy of the Hours, 415–416

Lord's Prayer, 52

lost books of Bible, 191–192

Louis IV, King of Bavaria, 466

Lucia, Sister, 73

Luke, Gospel of, 82–83, 210, 212, 239–240, 400–401

Luther, Martin, 62, 432–433

M

Mark, Gospel of, 210, 211, 212, 248–249

marriage

    children and annulment, 390–391

    clerical, 124–125, 443–445, 456–457

    cohabitation outside of, 169–170, 332

    and divorce, 52–53, 160–161, 221–222

    incest taboo, 222–223

    internal forum solution, 389

    Jesus' views on, 222–223

    levirate, 218

    and meeting spouses in heaven, 154

    outside Catholic faith, 165

    as sacrament, 386–388

    and sainthood, 15–16

    sexuality in, 334

    and Siamese twins, 392

    suitable music for weddings, 296–297

    and transsexuals, 391–392

    unfaithfulness in, 333

Martha and Mary, Jesus' followers, 236–237

Martin, Ralph, 413–414

martyrs, 24, 31, 38

Mary, Mother of Jesus, 5, 42–58, 61–66, 67–74, 135–136, 171, 310, 438–439, 441–442

Mary Magdalene, 247–248

Mary of Agreda, 54

masochism and saints, 34–37

Masons, the, 103–104

Mass

    changing words for, 264–265, 267–270

    clerical roles, 273–275

    creed recitation, 288–289

    for the dead, 176–178, 297–300, 397, 409–410, 418–419

    distractions during, 165–166

    Eastern vs. Roman rites, 265–267

    Gregorian, 175–178, 293

    for healing, 404–405

    history of leadership in, 459–461

    incense in, 272–273

    languages of, 292–293, 448–449

    obligations, 127

    physical symbology, 284–285

    readings for, 263–264, 267–268, 270–271

    rosary recitation during, 261–262

    as sacrifice, 366–367

    Sign of Peace, 447–448

    signs of reverence in, 271–272, 275–277, 279–281

    Sunday obligation, 258–261, 321–323

    vestments for, 434

Mass (*continued*)

    and working on Sunday, 323–324

    See also Communion

masturbation, 334–335

material possessions, praying for, 335

mates, seeking, patron saint for, 24

Matthew, Gospel of, 210, 211, 212, 219–220, 436

McCloskey, Cardinal John, 465

meat abstinence on Fridays, 470–471

medical professions, patron saints for, 27

meekness, 227–229

memorized recitation of Gospel reading, 270–271

memory of God, 143–144

mental disability and sacraments, 373–374

mercy

    God's, 27, 134–135, 139, 145, 163–164

    works of, 129

mercy killing, 164–165

Messiah, Jewish rejection of Jesus as, 441

Michael, Archangel, 7–8, 10, 28

militancy of church, 462–464

miracles

    church tradition on, 99–100

    faith healing, 402–403, 404–405

    and Mary, Mother of Jesus, 43

    and sainthood, 4, 8, 14, 19, 20, 23

Miraculous Medal, 55

missionary work, church's call to, 80–81

miters, 295–296

Mohammed, 452–453

monastic orders

    Carmelite, 441–442

    Cascia convent, 13

    Cistercian, 5

    Daughters of Charity of Canossa, 17

    Dominican, 21

    Franciscan, 8, 21, 32, 266, 466–467

    and hermits, 25, 29

    in Ireland, 25

    Maronite, 20

    military, 464

    and mysticism, 424

    Redemptorist, 17

    and Saint Bridget, 34

    and saints lives, 30

    Theatine, 310

money, praying for, 335

Montalto, Cardinal, 467

months and days, dedication of, 424–425

Monti, Bishop Puchol, 48

Morning Offering prayer, 415

Morning Star, Mary as, 51

mortal sins, 318–319, 320–321, 327–330, 377, 381

mortification by saints, 35–37, 305

movies and morality, 318–319

Murillo, Bartolome Esteban, 5

music for weddings, 296–297

musicians, patron saint of, 7

Muslims, 16, 80, 452–453

Mystical Rose, Mary as, 51

mysticism, 416–417, 423–424

N

nail makers, patron saint of, 6
names
    baptismal, 6–7, 117
    of Biblical books, 188
    of churches, 111–112
    for God, 198–199
natural disasters and evil in human experience, 138
Nazirite vow, 229
Neumann, Saint John (Bishop John Dubois), 17–18
Newman, John Henry, 303
Nicene Creed, 268–270, 451, 455
Nicholas V, antipope, 466
nirvana, 91
nonessential vs. essential church tradition, 76
Norway, patron saint of, 15
Notre Dame of Paris, Cathedral of, 62
novenas, 417–418
nudity and pornography, 317–318
nuns, 13, 17, 34
nursing homes, Communion in, 180
nursing profession, patron saints of, 27

O

obscenity, 316–318
offering, Masses of, 175–178, 293, 418–419
Olaf II, King of Norway (Saint Olaf), 14
Old Testament, 30, 435–436
    See also Jewish people and traditions

Opus Dei, 105–106
oral vs. written church tradition, 76
ordinary magisterium, 81, 85
ordination, 392–393, 458, 459–461
organ donation, 349–352
Origen, 462–463
original sin, 64, 86–88, 170–171, 195–196, 305
Orthodox churches. See Eastern Orthodox Church
Ottaviani, Cardinal, 48, 73
Our Father prayer, 52, 420–421, 439
Our Lady of Grace statues, 55

P

Padre Pio, 21, 32–33
paganism, 49, 121, 417, 452–453
painters, patron saint of, 7
Palestinian Canon, 187
Palm Sunday, 294
pantheism, 103
papacy, historical controversy over, 77
    See also popes
Pardon Crucifix, 406–407
parish councils, responsibilities of, 116–117
parishes, authority to establish, 112
parochial schools, founding of American, 17
pastor, as ultimate authority in parish, 117
Patron of the Universal Church, Saint Joseph as, 42
Paul IV, Pope, 467

Paul VI, Pope
confirmation, 361–362
Credo of the People of God, 456
indulgences, 78–79, 406–407
ordination of women, 458–459
papal tiara, 438
and penance, 115, 469, 471
restriction of liturgical participation to men, 275
and Saint Joseph, 67
stipends, 419
peace, Jesus as bringer of, 225–227
peace prayer of Saint Francis, 409
penance
church tradition, 115–116
and fasting, 468–470
and Lent, 290–291
and perfect contrition, 308
and prayer, 403–404, 415
public, 115, 376, 436
of saints, 35–37
See also confession
Penitential Rite, 260, 379–380
Pentateuch, origins of, 186
Pentecost, 253–254
Pentecostals, 413
Peretti, Cardinal Felici, 467
perfection of God vs. imperfect world, 148–149
petition, prayers of, 335, 400, 401–402, 418
pets, memorial services for, 157–158
Pharisees, Jesus' criticism of, 241–242

pharmacists, patron saints of, 27
pietistic Gospels, 191
Pious Union of the Pardon Crucifix, 406–407
Pius IX, Pope, 42
Pius V, Pope, 461–462
Pius X, Pope, 363
Pius XI, Pope, 97
Pius XII, Pope
ecumenism, 97–98
evolution, 90
and Fatima secret, 73
Mary, Mother of Jesus, 54, 58, 64, 437
plagues of Egypt, 200, 202
plenary indulgences, 406–407
poets, patron saint of, 7
political power and papacy, 444–445, 463–464
Pontius Pilate, 28
poor in spirit concept, 227–229
popes
Franciscan, 466–467
humanity of, 443–445
infallibility positions, 83–84
papal tiara, 438
power of indulgences, 79
and selection of bishops, 113
See also individual popes
pornography, 316–317
potters, patron saint of, 14
pride and vanity, 333
priests
anointing of the sick, 393–396
and authority to confirm, 362
authority to preach, 273–274
Benediction, 288
celibacy of, 124–125, 330–331, 456–457

priests (*continued*)

    confessor role, 383–384

    Eucharistic role, 264–265, 288, 369–370, 459–461

    Father title, 243–244

    funeral role, 297, 300

    ordination of, 392–393, 458, 459–461

    role of, 123–125

    and sacred images, 411

    vestments for, 358–359, 434

    washing of feet, 295

prisoners of war, treatment of, 344

private revelation, determining authenticity of, 63, 74

process vs. content of church tradition, 75–76

procreation as primary purpose of sexuality, 334

promiscuity, pornography as encouraging, 317

promises of God, 146–147

Protestants

    Bible differences with Catholics, 186–187

    vs. Catholics on salvation, 95–97

    and Communion, 372–373

    as disciples of Jesus, 83

    and Mary, Mother of Jesus, 41, 47, 54, 57

    Pentecostal movement, 413

    relating to fundamentalists, 150–151

    and sacraments, 387

    and transubstantiation, 455–456

psychics, 319–320

public penance, 115, 376, 436

public vs. private prayer, 421–423

punishment as imperfect motivation for contrition, 308

purgatorial societies, 102–103

purgatory, 100–103, 175–176

purification, 44–45, 101

Q

quality of life and euthanasia, 339–342

Quattrochi, Luigi and Maria Beltrame, 16

queen of heaven, Mary as, 49

Queenship of Mary, 58

R

radiologists, patron saint of, 28

Rainalducci, Pietro, 466

rape, intercessory saint for victims of, 18

Raphael, Archangel, 7–8, 24

Rapture, the, 168–169

RCIA (Rite of Christian Initiation of Adults), 81

readings for Mass, 263–264, 267–268

reconciliation, sacrament of. *See* confession

redemption, suffering as leading to, 136–137

Redemptorist Order, 17

Red Mass (Lawyer's Mass), 34

Reformation and Bible changes, 187

reincarnation, 91–92, 104

relatives, marriage rules concerning, 222–223

reparation prayers, 403–404, 415

resurrection, bodily, 92–93, 152–153, 168–169, 215

Resurrection of Jesus, 49–50, 247, 249–251, 431

resuscitation, extraordinary means of, 338–342

retirement of priests, 122–123

revelation
discernment in, 63
multiple forms of divine, 57
private, 74, 83
and visions of Mary, 42–43
See also visions

Revelation, book of, 55, 67, 68, 252–253, 254–256, 272

reverence, signs of
bowing of head at Jesus' name, 275–276
and Communion, 278–280
genuflection, 276, 277
kneeling, 277–278, 280–281, 439–440
and sacred images, 315–316

rings, episcopal, 109–110

Rite of Christian Initiation of Adults (RCIA), 81

Rite of Election, 295

Roman citizenship of Saint Paul, 465–466

Roman collar, 108

Roman Martyrology, 30

Roman Missal, 269, 292

Roman vs. Eastern rites. *See* Eastern Orthodox Church

rosary, 62, 64, 70–72, 261–262, 438–439

roses and Mary, Mother of Jesus, 51

Rosicrucians, 103–104

Russian Orthodox Church, 412

Rusticus, Bishop of Trier, 14

S

Sabbath observance, changes in, 431

Sabbatine privilege, 442

sacraments
anointing of the sick, 393–397, 404, 407
confirmation, 361–364, 374–375, 463
and excommunication, 88–89
holy orders, 392–393, 458, 459–461
liturgical practice, 265
marriage, 386–392
origins of, 430–431
role in church, 357–358
See also baptism; Communion; confession

sacrarium, 285

Sacred Congregations of Indulgences, 293

Sacred Heart of Jesus, 57, 403, 415

sacred images. *See* images, sacred

sacrifice, Mass as, 366–367

saints
as doctors of the church, 461–462
hearing of prayers, 408
and miracles, 100
and mysticism, 424
questions on, 3–10, 13–39
as source of children's names, 117
as worthy of reverence, 315–316

Saint Agatho, 444

Saint Albert the Great, 27

Saint Alodia, 18

Saint Ambrose, 61,113

Saint Anne, 15, 69

Saint Anthony of Egypt, 29

Saint Anthony of Padua, 24,
440–441

Saint Athanasius, 61, 434

Saint Augustine, 3–4, 387

Saint Bernadette Soubirous, 57

Saint Bernard, 387, 464

Saint Bernardine of Siena, 26

Saint Bernard of Clairvaux, 5–6,
62

Saint Bernard of Montjoux, 28

Saint Blaise, 28

Saint Bridget of Ireland, 34

Saint Bridget of Sweden, 54

Saint Camillus de Lellis, 26, 27

Saint Catherine Laboure, 55, 62

Saint Catherine of Bologna, 7

Saint Catherine of Siena, 27

Saint Cecilia, 7

Saint Charbel Makhlouf, 20

Saint Christopher, 31–32

Saint Clare, 7

Saint Cloud (Clodoald), 6

Saint Columba
(Columcille/Crimthaann), 25

Saint Cosmas, 27

Saint Damian, 27

Saint Diana (also Cynthia), 25–26

Saint Dympha, 18

Saint Elizabeth of Hungary, 27

Saint Elizabeth of Schonau, 54

Saint Fabiola, 18

Saint Faustina Kowalska, 26–27

Saint Francis of Assisi
and charity, 163
mortification, 35, 36–37
peace prayer of, 409
and stigmata, 21, 24
and suffering, 137
and temptation, 304
vision of Jesus speaking, 57,
423–424

Saint Gabriel, 7

Saint Genesius, bishop of
Clermont, 7

Saint Genesius, bishop of Lyons,
7

Saint Genesius of Arles, 7

Saint Genesius the Comedian, 7

Saint George, 31

Saint Germaine Cousin, 18

Saint Germanus of
Constantinople, 54

Saint Goar, 14

Saint Godelieve, 18

Saint Gregory the Great,
175–176, 293, 437

Saint Hormisdas, 444

Saint Ignatius of Antioch, 428

Saint Ignatius of Loyola, 137

Saint Imelda Lambertini, 23

Saint Isidore the Farmer, 16

Saint Januarius, 27

Saint Jerome, 434

Saint Joachim (Mary's father), 15,
69

Saint John Chrysostum, 434

Saint John Neumann (Bishop
John Dubois), 17–18

Saint John of God, 27

Saint John of the Cross, 140

Saint John the Baptist Vianney, 10, 19, 134–135

Saint John the Evangelist, 33

Saint Joseph, 41–47, 59–60, 66–67, 218–219

Saint Josephine Bakhita, 16–17

Saint Leo the Great, 304

Saint Louis Marie de Montfort, 310

Saint Lucy, 7

Saint Luke, 27

Saint Margaret Mary Alacoque, 57, 403

Saint Maria Francesca of Naples, 8

Saint Maria Goretti, 18

Saint Matthias, 26

Saint Mungo (Kentigern), 29

Saint Nicholas of Myra, 4

Saint Olaf, 14–15

Saint Patrick of Ireland, 26, 31

Saint Patrick's Cathedral, New York, 464–465

Saint Paul of Tarsus, 14

    "asleep in Christ" phrase, 217–218

    Jewish dietary law vision, 454

    letters authored by, 212–214

    on original sin, 86

    on rapture, 214–215

    Roman citizenship of, 465–466

    self-perceived weakness of, 216

    as spiritual father to Christian community, 243

    on spiritual warfare, 464

    thorn in the flesh statement, 216

Saint Peter Canisius, 433

Saint Peter's Basilica, 61

Saint Philomena, 18–20

Saint Pius V, Pope, 432–433

Saint Pius X Society, 89–90

Saint Priscilla, 61

Saint Rita, 13–14

Saint Robert Bellarmine, 433

Saint Serf, 29

Saint Simon Stock, 62, 441–442

Saint Solangia, 18

Saint Stephen, 14

Saint Synesius (Cynthia), 25

Saint Teresa of Avila, 27, 140

Saint Thenaw, 29

Saint Thomas More, 34

Saint Veronica, 22

salvation

    as dependent solely upon Christ, 66

    and extraterrestrials, 179

    and good works, 80, 95–97, 308

    knowledge of, 217

    and Masses for the dead, 410

    and mercy of God, 139

    and non-Christians, 80–81, 95, 134–135

    and *sola fide*, 95–97

Samson, 208

San Giovanni Rotondo, Friary of, 33

Santa Maria de la Cabeza, 16

scapular, brown, 441–442

schisms, papal, 449

scientific methods for Biblical scholarship, 189

scourging of Jesus, 58–59

scrupulosity, dangers of, 140–142, 385

Seat of Wisdom, Mary as, 50–51

Second Lateran Council, 5

Second Vatican Council
  on church militant, 464
  and controversy within
    church, 76
  Easter date, 120
  and ecumenism, 98
  emphasis on liturgy, 421–422
  and Latin Mass, 292
  on Mary as Co-Redemptrix,
    65
  on meeting new millenium,
    427–428
  and physical changes in
    churches, 300–301
  and Saint Pius X Society,
    89–90
  on selection of bishops, 113

self-dedication, prayer of, 406

self-delusion vs. revelation, 63

self-denial, 35–37, 305
  See also penance

seminaries and formation of
  priests, 123

seraphic saint, 24

serpent in Genesis, 55

servile work on Sunday, 323–324

seven capital sins, 320–321

seven sorrows of Mary, 63–64

sex-change operations, 313–314

sexual abuse, intercessory saint
  for victims of, 18

sexuality
  cohabitation outside mar-
    riage, 169–170, 332
  homosexuality, 311, 312–313,
    331–332
  in marriage, 334
  masturbation, 334–335

and obscenity, 316–318
  See also marriage

shalom, 225–226

Sheol, 95, 249

shrine, requirements for, 111

Shrine of Our Lady of Loreto, 50

Siamese twins, 392

Sigebert I, King of Austrasia, 14

Sign of Peace, 447–448

Simon of Cyrene, 245–246

sin
  adultery, 52, 221–222, 333
  and Ash Wednesday, 436
  and baptism, 360
  contumely, 354–355
  and excommunication, 88–89
  and God's forgiveness, 145
  and Masons, 103
  mortal, 318–319, 320–321,
    327–330, 377, 381
  original, 64, 86–88, 170–171,
    195–196, 305
  origins in Genesis, 55
  and penitential life, 35–37
  reparation through prayer,
    403–404
  as spanning generations,
    308–310
  suicide as, 164–165
  See also confession; morality;
    temptation

sinners and salvation, 134–135

sins of the fathers, 308–310

Sirach, book of, 206–207

Sixtus III, Pope, 61

Sixtus IV, Pope, 466

Sixtus V, Pope, 50, 108, 467

skullcaps, 109

slander, 354–355

snakes, 33, 55

social justice, patron saint of, 67

Society for the Propagation of the Faith, 19

Society of Jesus, 467

Sodano, Cardinal Angelo, 73

sodomy, 311, 312–313

sola fide, 95–97

Solemnity of the Sacred Heart, 403–404

Son of Man, interpretation of, 238–239

sorrowful mysteries, scourging of Jesus, 58

Sorrows of Mary, 62, 63–64

souls, 90–91, 94, 152–153
    See also afterlife

Spalding, Bishop John Lancaster, 433

Spanish Inquisition, 466

speaking in tongues, 413–414

Spellman, Cardinal Francis, 409

spiritual aridity, 139–140

Spirituals, 466

spiritual vs. bodily creatures, 10, 11–12

spouses, patron saint of, 24

standing during Mass, 270–271

Stations of the Cross, 410–411

sterility, intercessory saint for, 8

stigmata, 8, 21–22

stipends, Mass, 419

stumbling stone reference by Jesus, 240–242

suffering, 35–36, 135–137, 140, 164, 401

suicide, 163–165, 208, 339–340

Sunday as Sabbath day, 431

Sunday obligation, 260–261, 321–324

T

tabernacle, location of, 286–287

Tarsus, city of, 465

taxes, morality of paying, 347–348

teaching authority of the church, 84–85

television workers, patron saint of, 7

Temple in Jerusalem, 45–46, 50

temptation
    of Christ, 219–220
    and confession, 382–383
    and human nature, 304–305
    inevitability of, 217
    and Our Father, 420–421
    and Saint Paul, 215–216

terminal illnesses, treatment of, 338–342

Tertullian, 436

Theatine Order, 310

theologians, 106–107, 155–156

theology
    and creation story, 174–175
    and dogma, 82
    and infallibility question, 83–84

thieves crucified with Jesus, 247

Third Council of Toledo, 451

Thomas, doubting, 247–248

tiara, papal, 438

time, divine vs. human, 143–144

tithing, 129–130

tomb, Mary's, 54

torture, morality of, 342–344

Tower of David, 51

Tower of Ivory, Mary as, 51

tradition, church
    Agnus Dei, 110

tradition, church (*continued*)

and Biblical interpretation, 86–88, 192–193

bodily resurrection, 92–93

childrens' names, 117

Christmas and Easter, 119–121

and church buildings, 111–112

clergy, 107–110, 113–114, 122–125

controversy in, 76–78

definitional issues, 75–76

ecumenism, 97–99

evangelism, 128

evolution, 90–91

excommunication, 88–89

and feminism, 125–127

and filming movies in churches, 131

fish on Fridays, 114–115

holy days of obligation, 118–119

immortality, 93–95

indulgences, 78–79

infallibility question, 81–85

Infant of Prague, 127

Jesus' eternal existence, 92

karma and reincarnation, 91–92

Knights of Columbus, 104–105

lay ministries, 121–122

marriage rules, 223

Masons, 103–104

on miracles, 99–100

Opus Dei, 105–106

parish councils, 116–117

penance and abstinence, 115–116

purgatory, 100–103

and reasons for controversy, 76–78

Saint Pius X Society, 89–90

salvation, 80–81, 95–97

Saturday Masses, 127

theologians, 106–107

tithing, 129–130

vestments, 107–110, 295–296, 358–359, 434

works of mercy, 129

transplantation of organs, 349–352

transsexuals, 313–314, 391–392

transubstantiation, 364–366, 368–369, 371, 455–456

travelers, patron saint of, 32

trial by ordeal, 52, 53

Tridentine Mass, 292–293, 447

Trinity, 87, 92, 450–451

trusting in God, 27, 134, 138

truth and responsibility of church, 84–85

twelve-starred crown of Mary, 67–68

U

uncleanness, ritual, 44–45

unfaithfulness in marriage, 333

United Nations, 343

unity of church and ecumenism, 97–99

universal salvation, 80–81, 95

Unterkoefler, Bishop Ernest, 336

Urban II, Pope, 436

V

vanity, 333

Vatican Congregation for Bishops, 113–114

Vatican Congregation for Catholic Education, 123

Vatican II. *See* Second Vatican Council

vegetarianism and Eucharist, 371

veil, Saint Veronica's, 22

venial sins, confession of, 385–386

vestments, clerical, 107–110, 295–296, 358–359, 434

victim souls, 310–311

violence and pornography, 317

violence in Old Testament, 203–205

virginity of Mary, 47, 56, 61

visions

apparitions of Mary, 42–43, 47–49, 57, 441–442

Saint Francis of Assisi, 57, 423–424

Saint Paul of Tarsus, 454

W

war

just, 345–347

treatment of prisoners of war, 344

washing of feet, 294–295

Way of the Cross, 410–411

weddings, suitable music for, 296–297

wine, 33, 371–372

wisdom as feminine, 206–207

wise men at Bethlehem, 31, 434–435

women

and Catholic feminism, 125–126

as clerics, 457–459

as Communion leaders, 370–371

Gospel treatment of, 236–237

liturgical participation restrictions, 275

as priests, 124–125

and stigmata, 21

wood-carvers, patron saint of, 15

workers, patron saint of, 67

working on Sunday, 323–324

works of mercy, 129

worship. *See* liturgical practices

wounds of Christ. *See* stigmata

writers, patron saint of, 7

written vs. oral Church tradition, 76

Y

Yahweh, 199

Z

Zephyrinus, Pope, 449